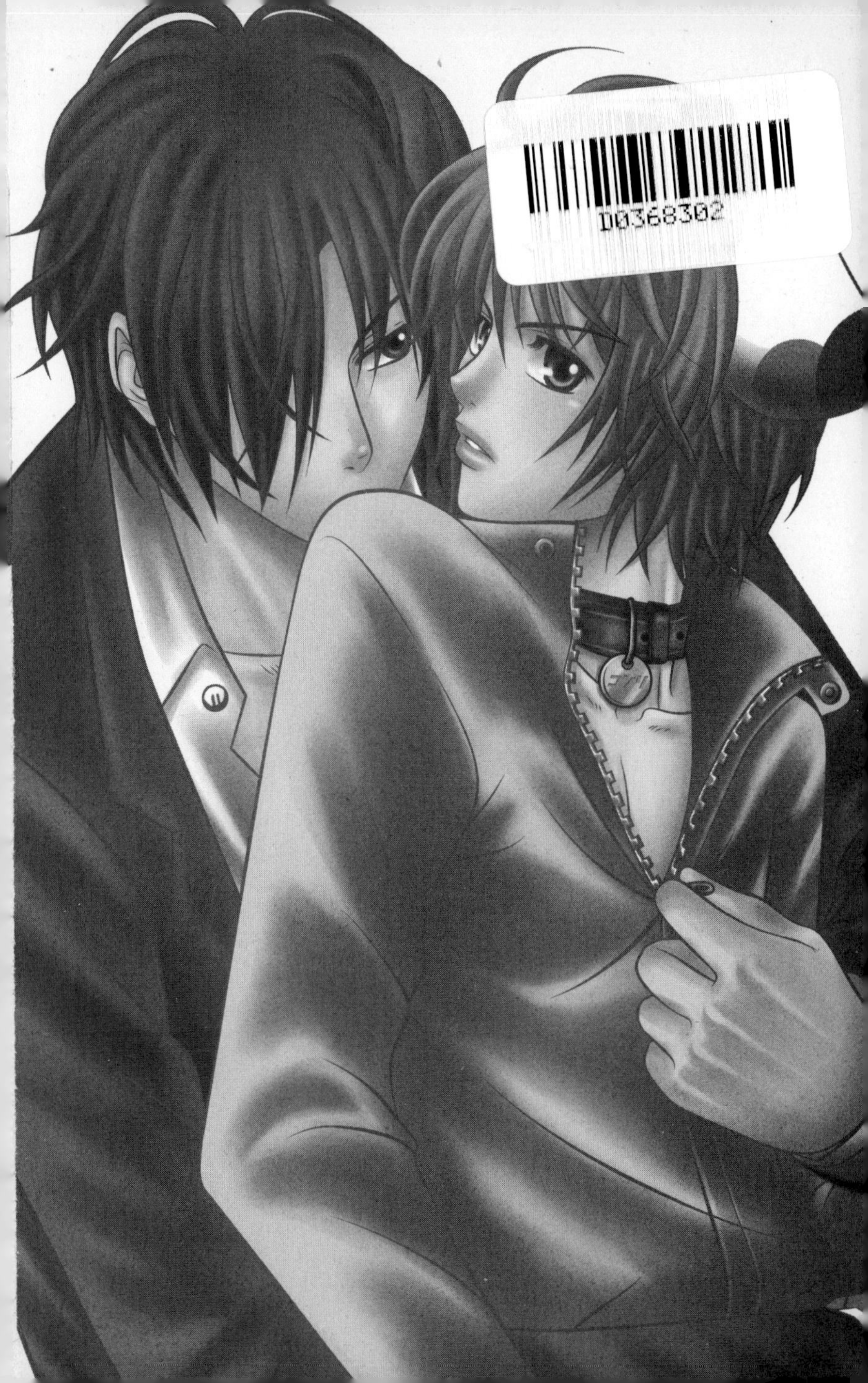

the 9LIVES ™

Vol. 1

Created by Bayou

Script by Rachel Manija Brown

TOKYOPOP®

HAMBURG // LONDON // LOS ANGELES // TOKYO

The 9 Lives Vol. 1
created by Bayou
script by Rachel Manija Brown

Retouch and Lettering - Michael Paolilli
Graphic Designer - Jose Macasocol, Jr.

Editor - Alexis Kirsch
Pre-Production Supervisor - Vicente Rivera, Jr.
Print-Production Specialist - Lucas Rivera
Managing Editor - Vy Nguyen
Senior Designer - Louis Csontos
Senior Designer - James Lee
Senior Editor - Bryce P. Coleman
Senior Editor - Jenna Winterberg
Associate Publisher - Marco F. Pavia
President and C.O.O. - John Parker
C.E.O. and Chief Creative Officer - Stu Levy

A **TOKYOPOP** Manga

TOKYOPOP and 🌐 are trademarks or registered trademarks of TOKYOPOP Inc.

TOKYOPOP Inc.
5900 Wilshire Blvd. Suite 2000
Los Angeles, CA 90036

E-mail: info@TOKYOPOP.com
Come visit us online at www.TOKYOPOP.com

ISBN: 978-1-4278-0615-4

First TOKYOPOP printing: October 2008
10 9 8 7 6 5 4 3 2 1
Printed in the USA

the 9LIVES ™

Contents

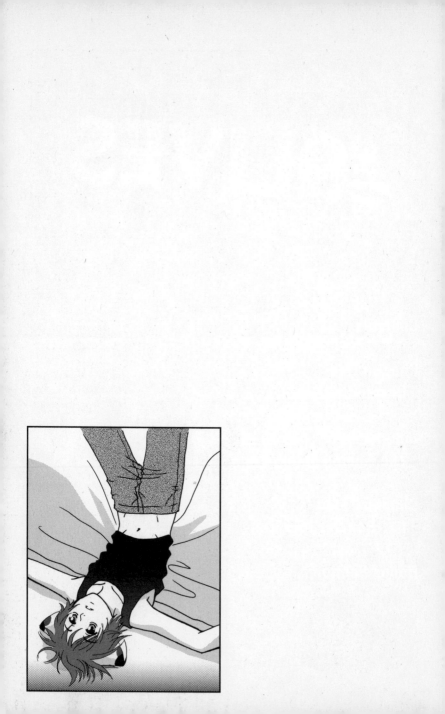

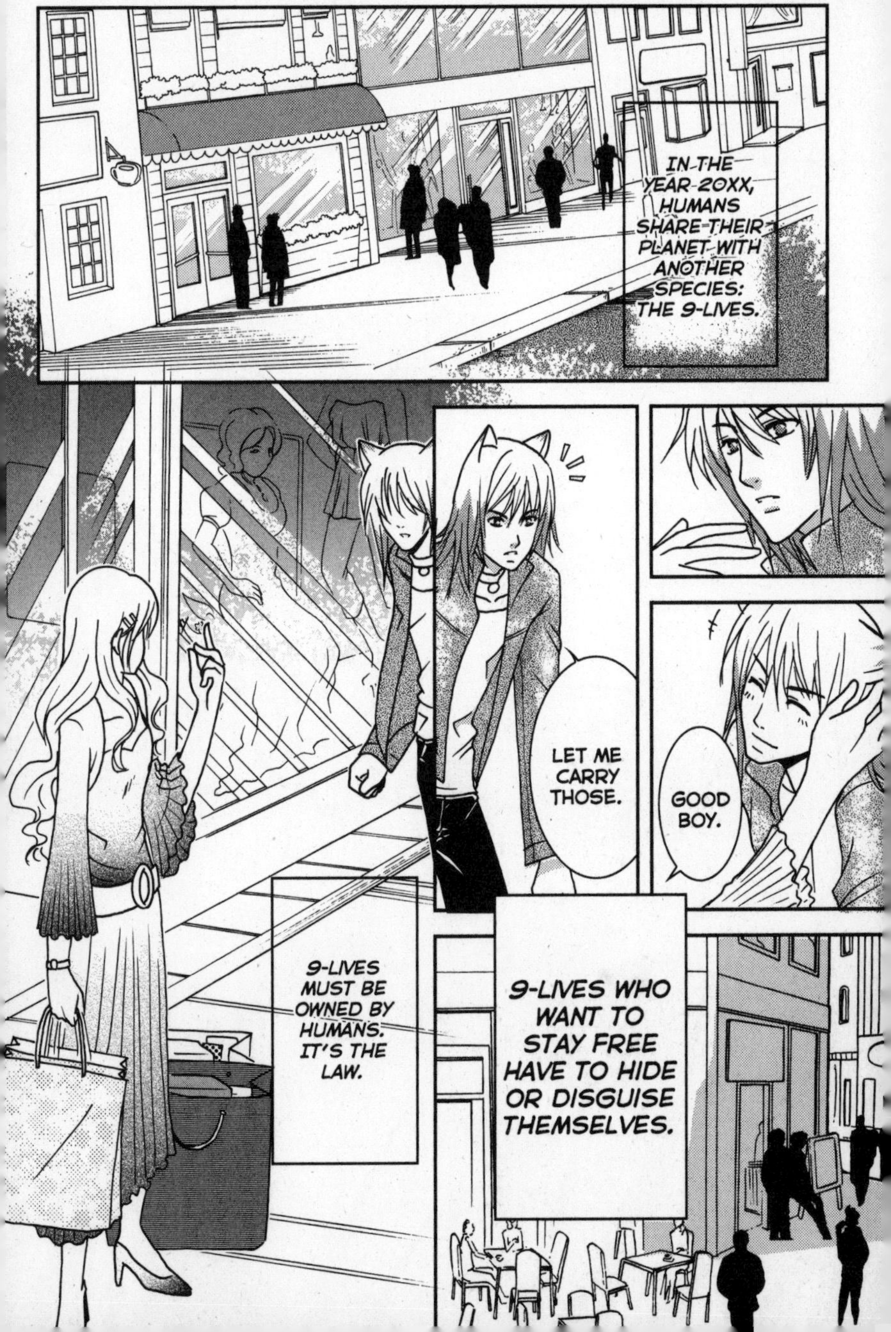
IN THE YEAR 20XX, HUMANS SHARE THEIR PLANET WITH ANOTHER SPECIES: THE 9-LIVES.
LET ME CARRY THOSE.
GOOD BOY.
9-LIVES MUST BE OWNED BY HUMANS. IT'S THE LAW.
9-LIVES WHO WANT TO STAY FREE HAVE TO HIDE OR DISGUISE THEMSELVES.

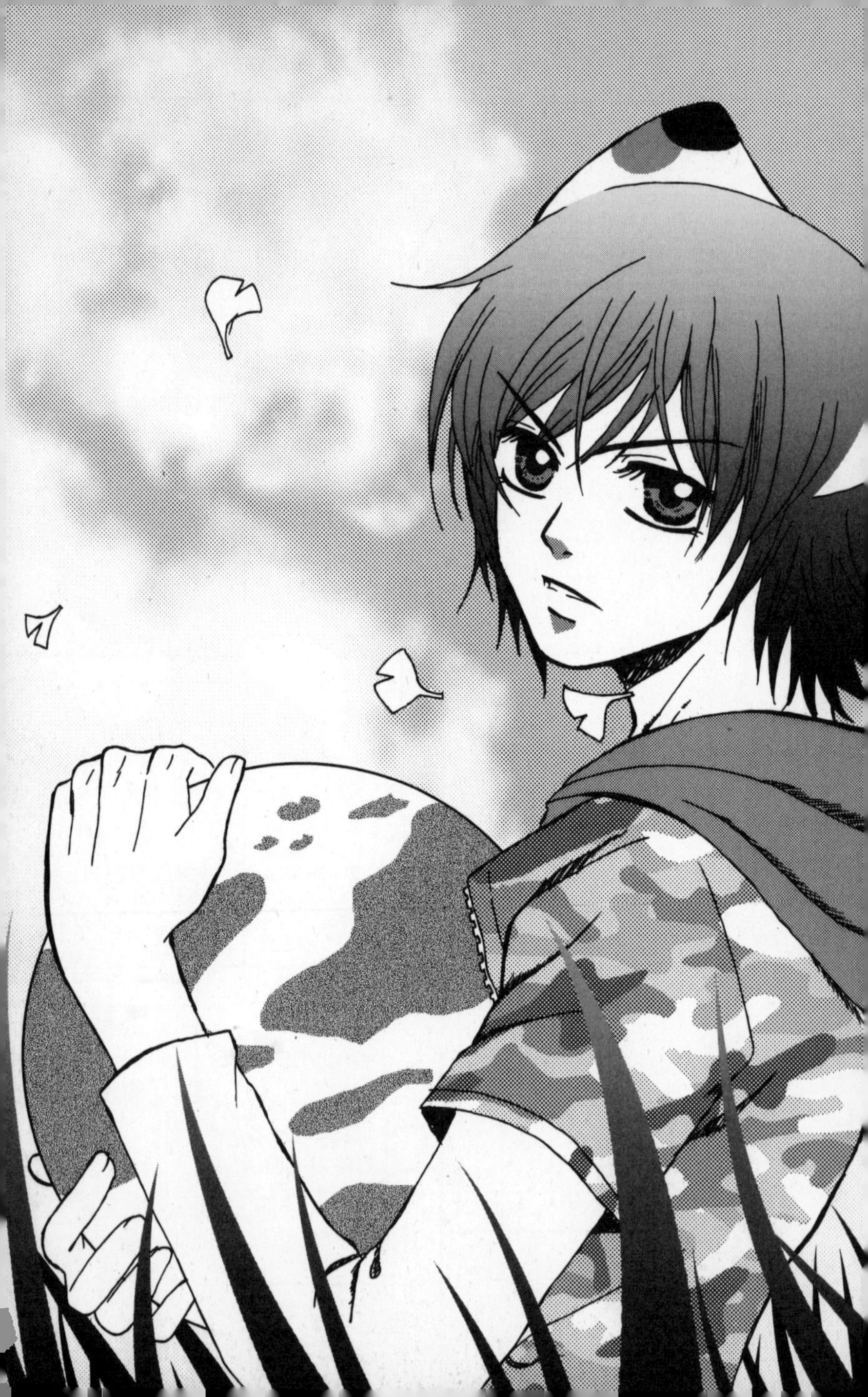

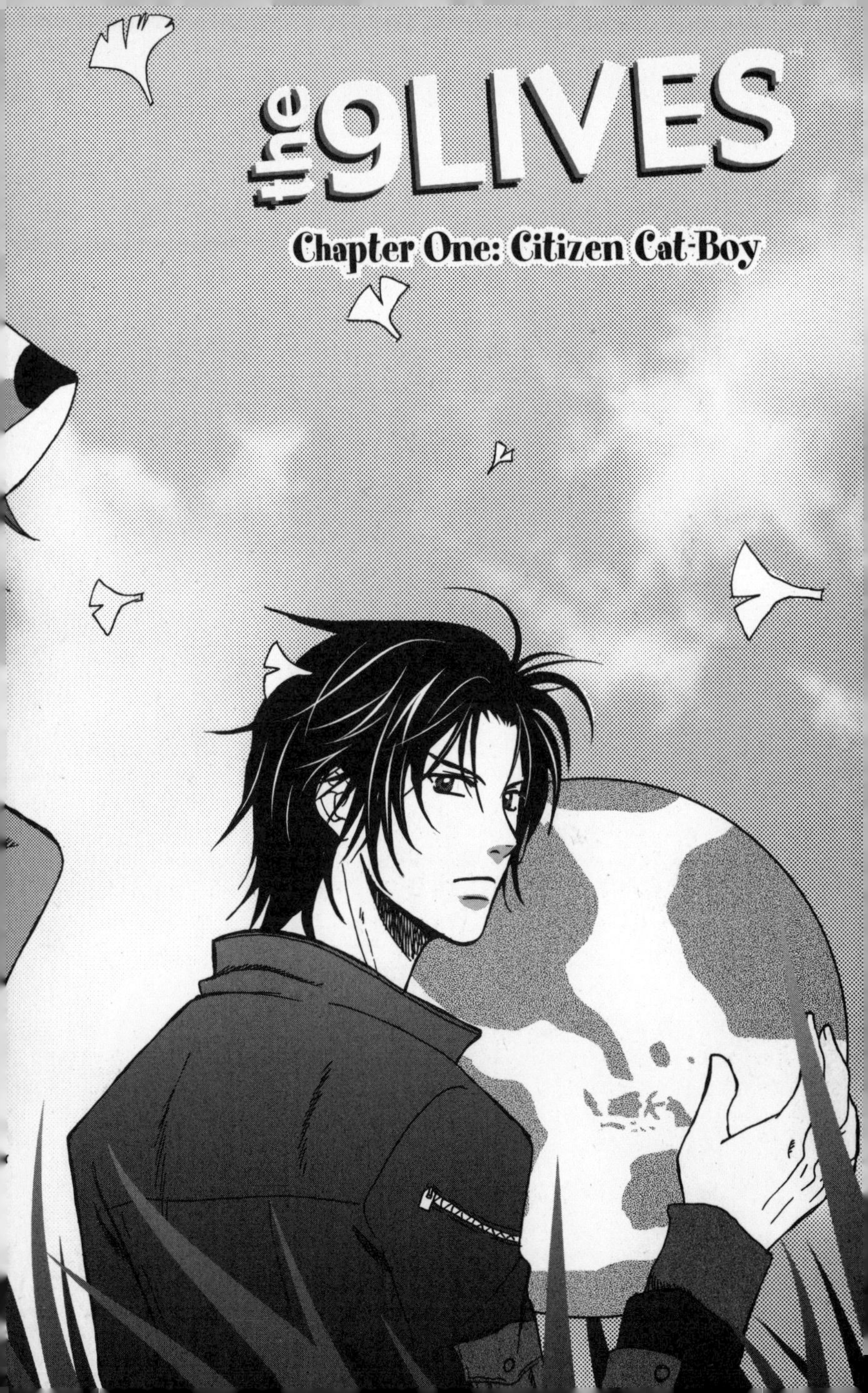
the 9LIVES
Chapter One: Citizen Cat-Boy

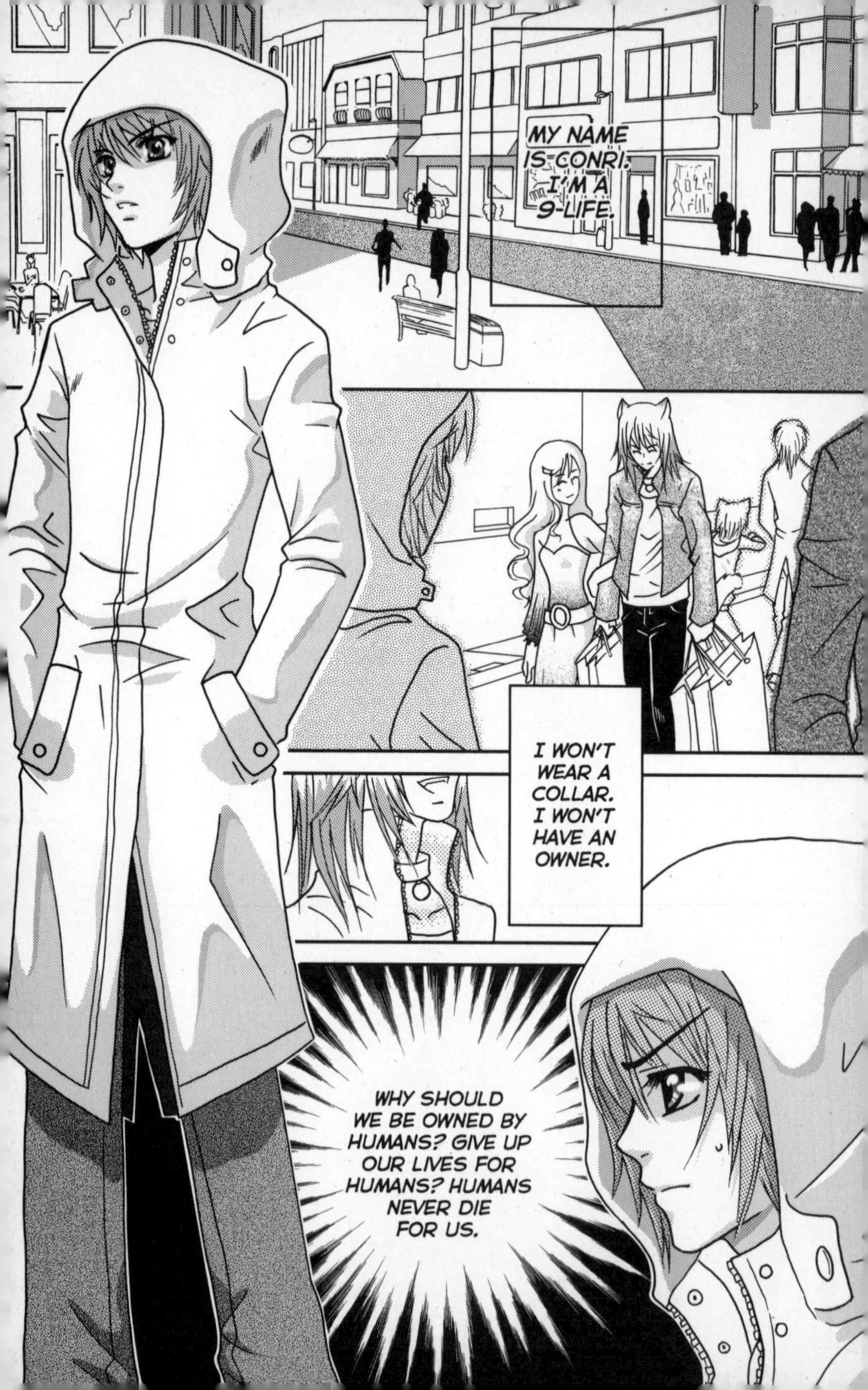
MY NAME IS CONRI. I'M A 9-LIFE.
I WON'T WEAR A COLLAR. I WON'T HAVE AN OWNER.
WHY SHOULD WE BE OWNED BY HUMANS? GIVE UP OUR LIVES FOR HUMANS? HUMANS NEVER DIE FOR US.

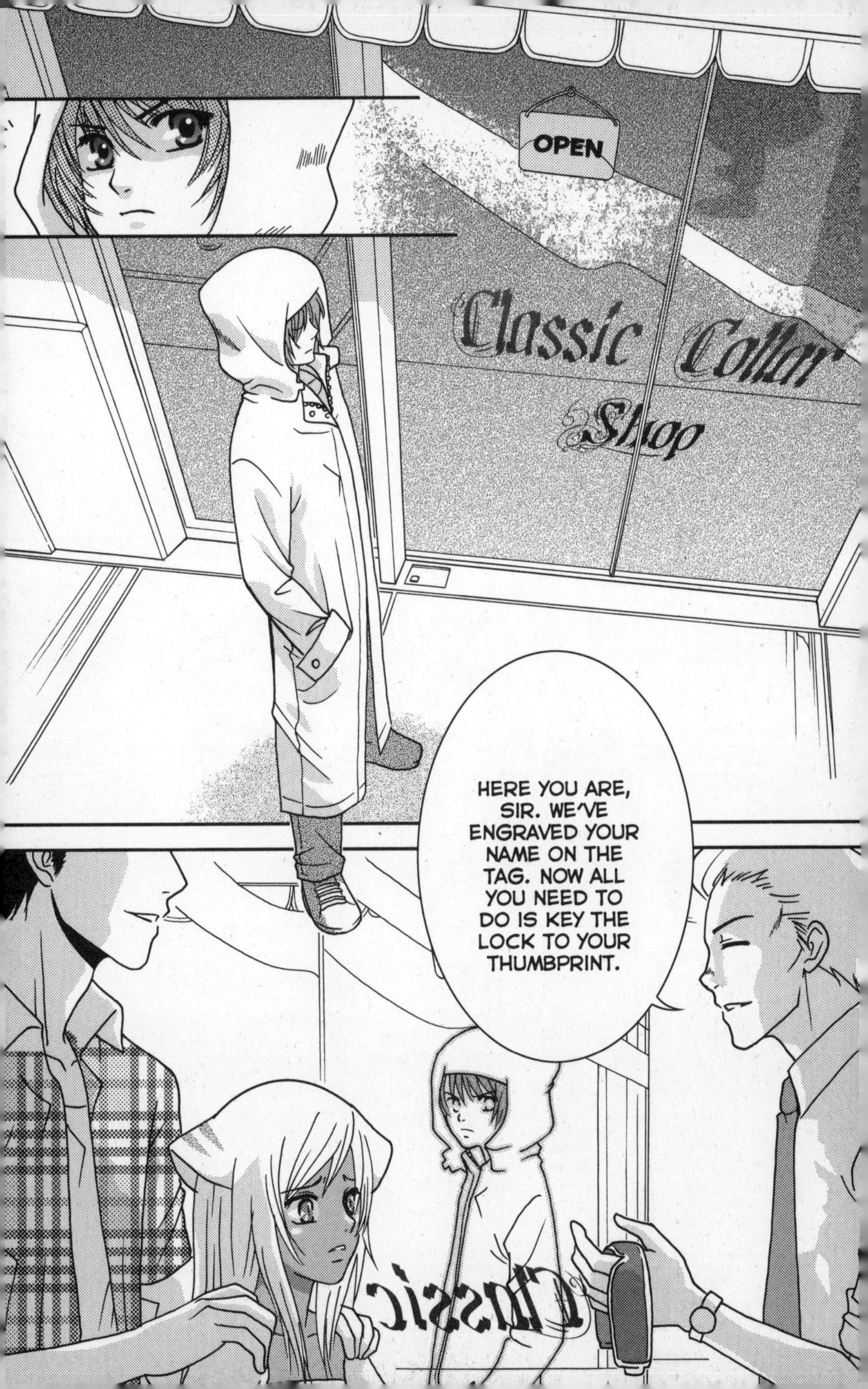
OPEN
Classic Collar Shop
HERE YOU ARE, SIR. WE'VE ENGRAVED YOUR NAME ON THE TAG. NOW ALL YOU NEED TO DO IS KEY THE LOCK TO YOUR THUMBPRINT.

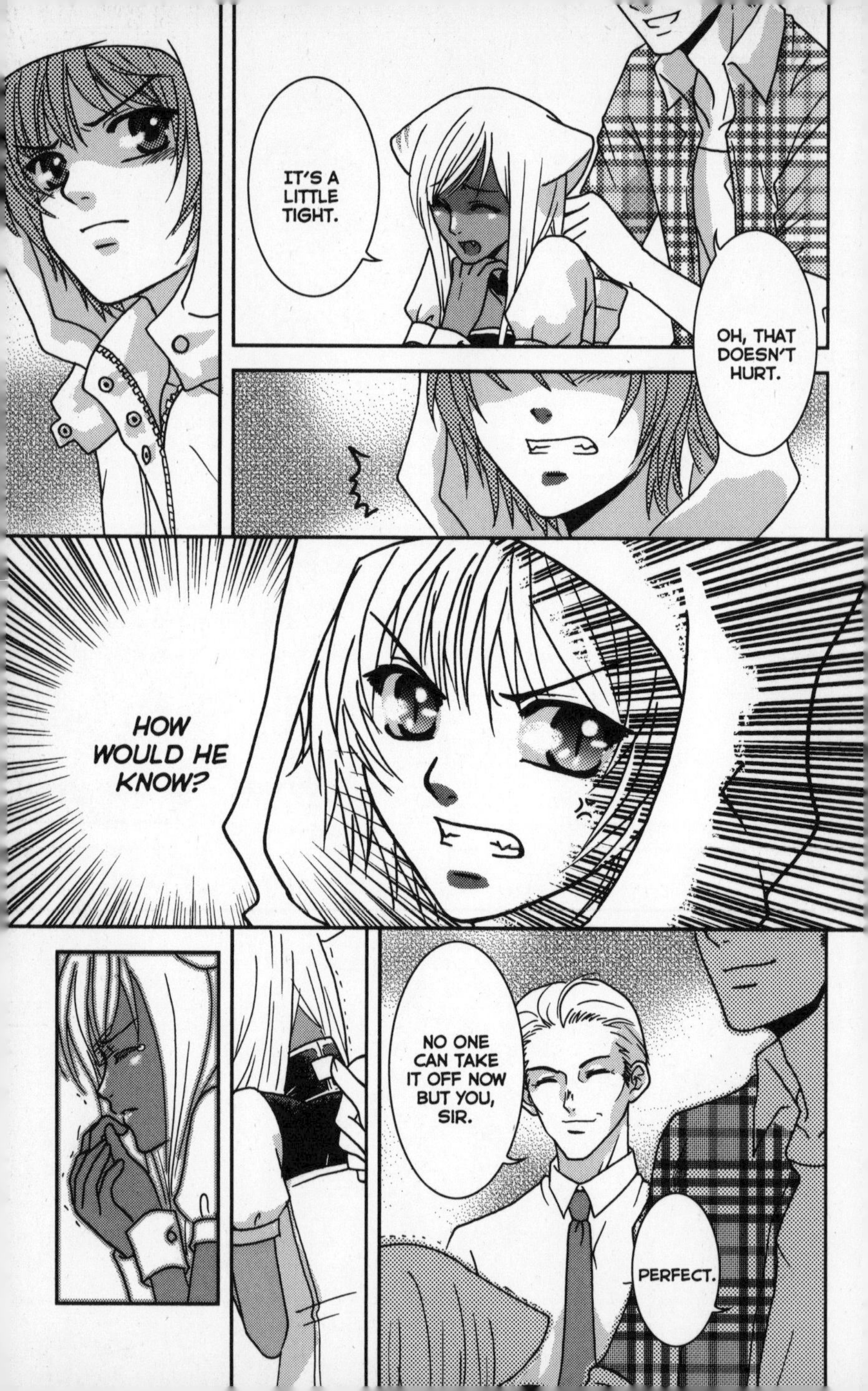
IT'S A LITTLE TIGHT.
OH, THAT DOESN'T HURT.
HOW WOULD HE KNOW?
NO ONE CAN TAKE IT OFF NOW BUT YOU, SIR.
PERFECT.

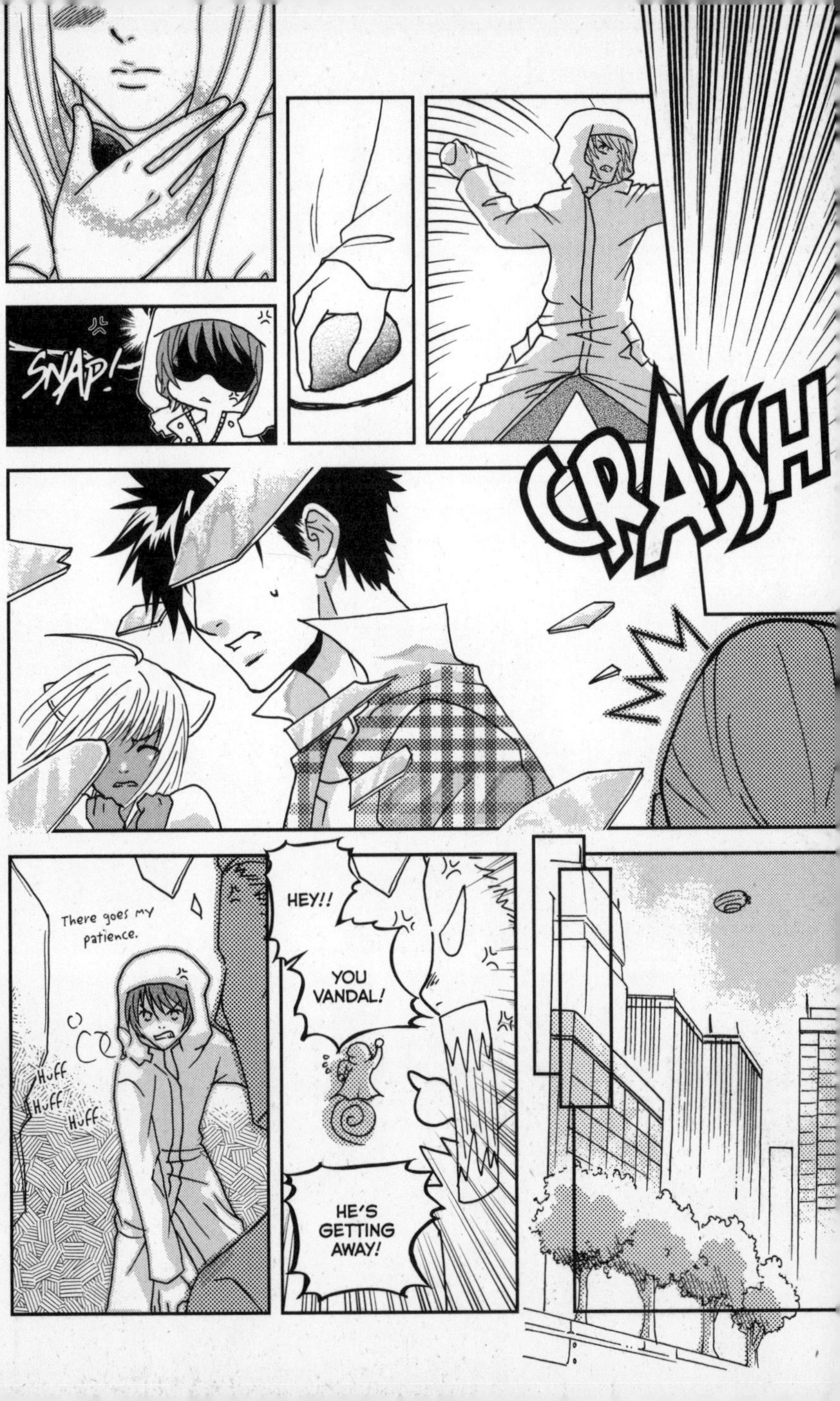
SNAP!
CRASH
There goes my patience.
Huff
Huff
Huff
HEY!!
YOU VANDAL!
HE'S GETTING AWAY!

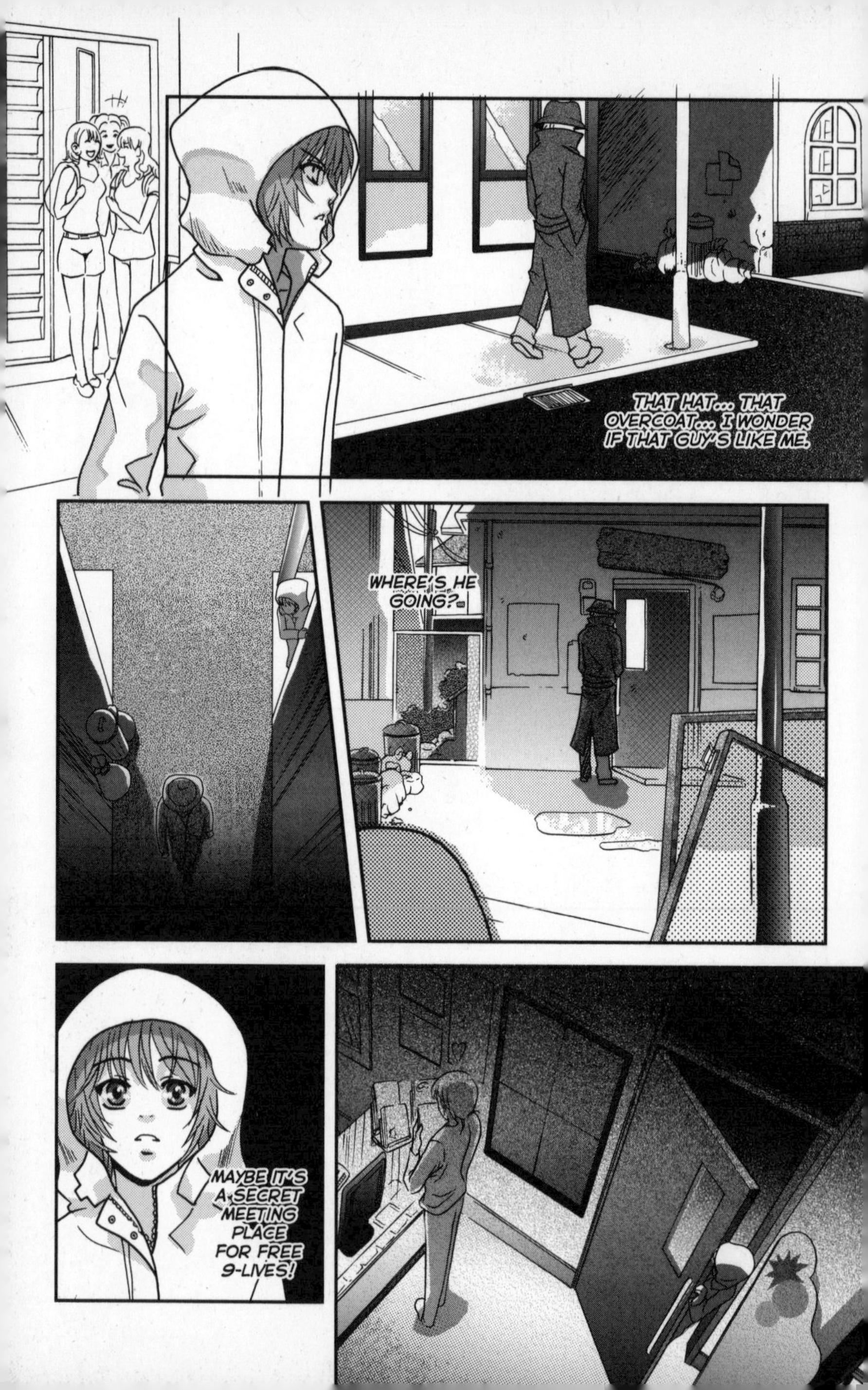
THAT HAT... THAT OVERCOAT... I WONDER IF THAT GUY'S LIKE ME.
WHERE'S HE GOING?...
MAYBE IT'S A SECRET MEETING PLACE FOR FREE 9-LIVES!

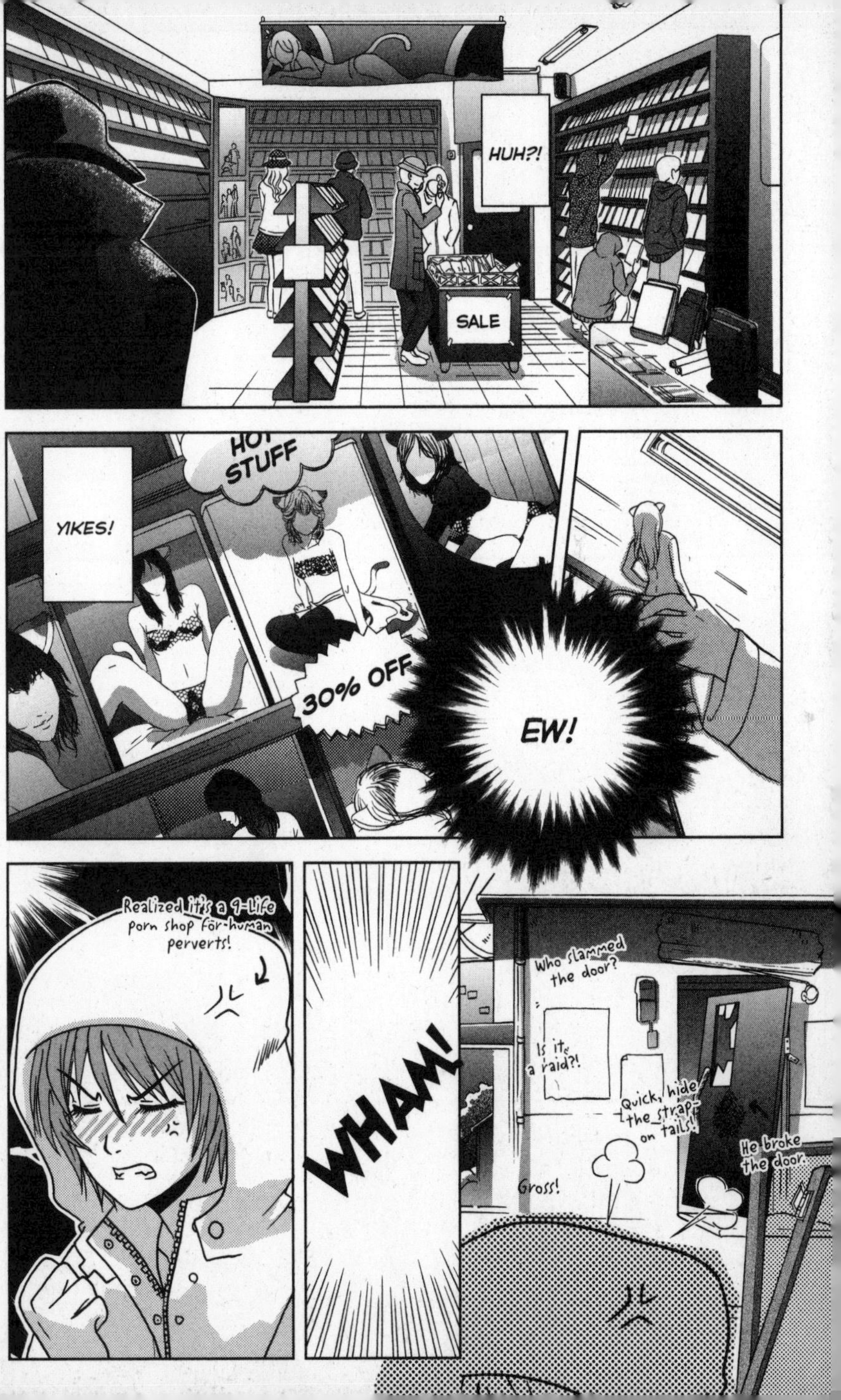
HUH?!
SALE
YIKES!
HOT STUFF
30% OFF
EW!
Realized it's a 9-Life porn shop for human perverts!
WHAM!
Who slammed the door?
Is it a raid?!
Quick, hide the strap-on tails!
He broke the door.
Gross!

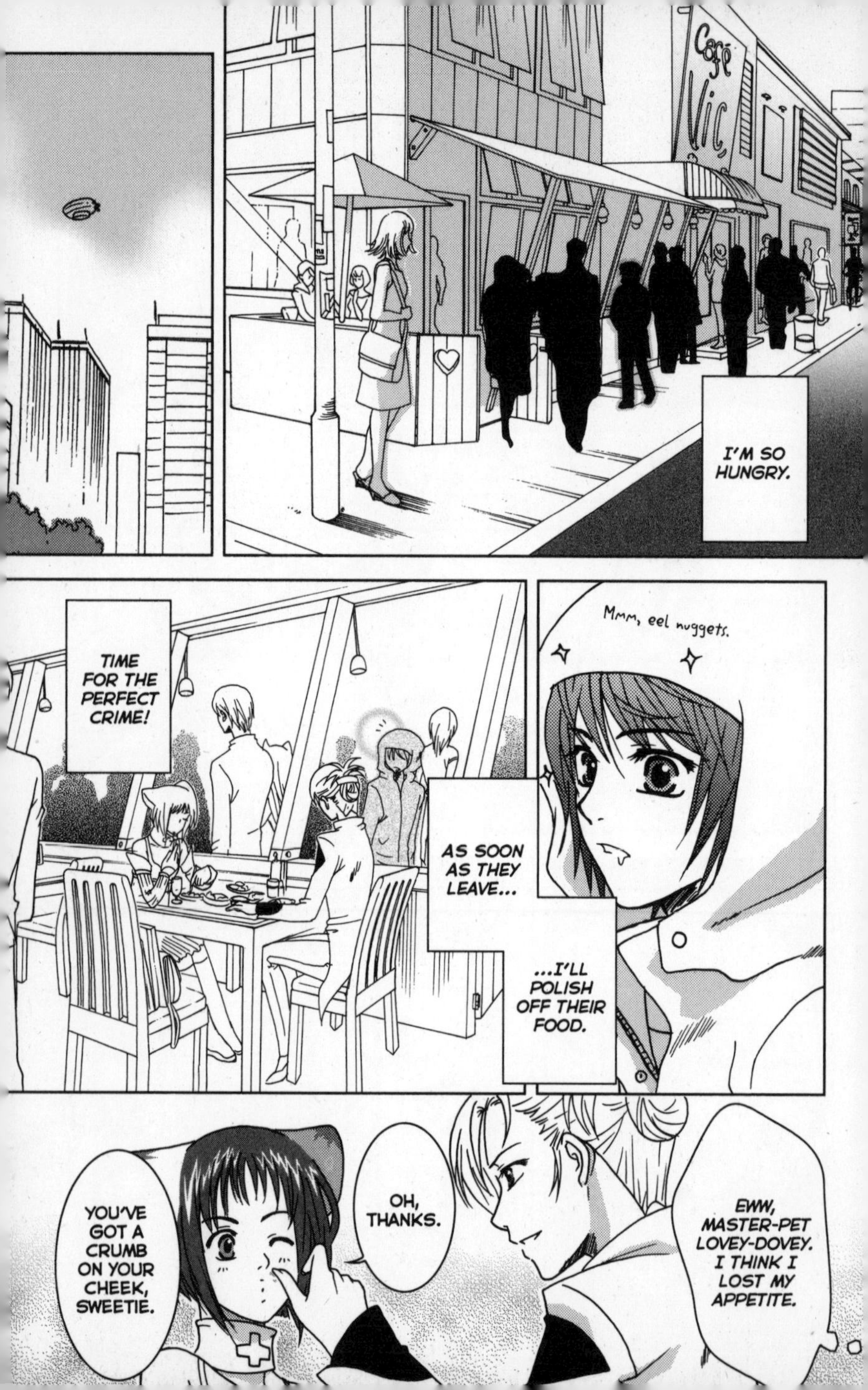
Café Vic
I'M SO HUNGRY.
TIME FOR THE PERFECT CRIME!
AS SOON AS THEY LEAVE...
...I'LL POLISH OFF THEIR FOOD.
Mmm, eel nuggets.
YOU'VE GOT A CRUMB ON YOUR CHEEK, SWEETIE.
OH, THANKS.
EWW, MASTER-PET LOVEY-DOVEY. I THINK I LOST MY APPETITE.

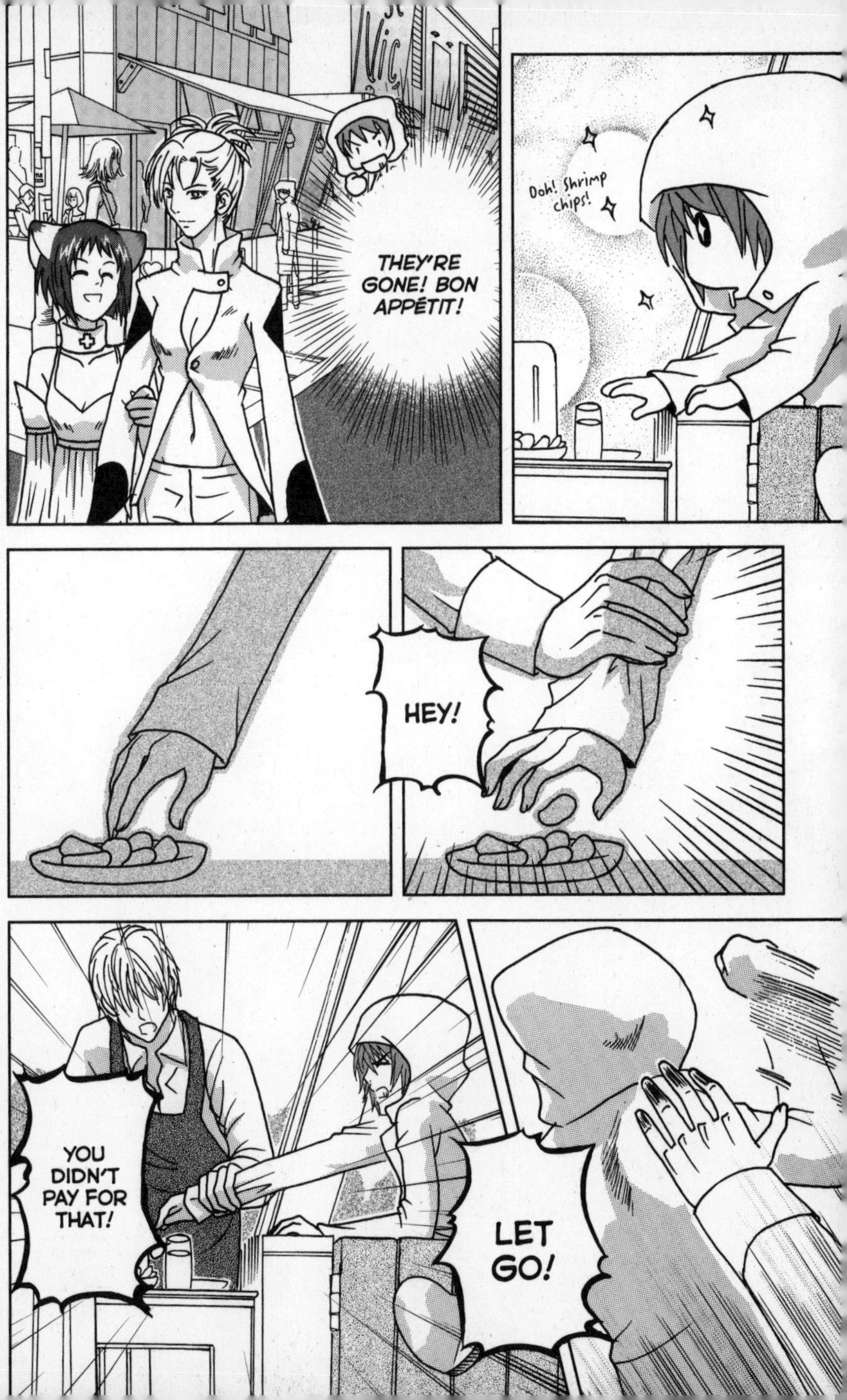
THEY'RE GONE! BON APPÉTIT!
Ooh! Shrimp chips!
HEY!
YOU DIDN'T PAY FOR THAT!
LET GO!

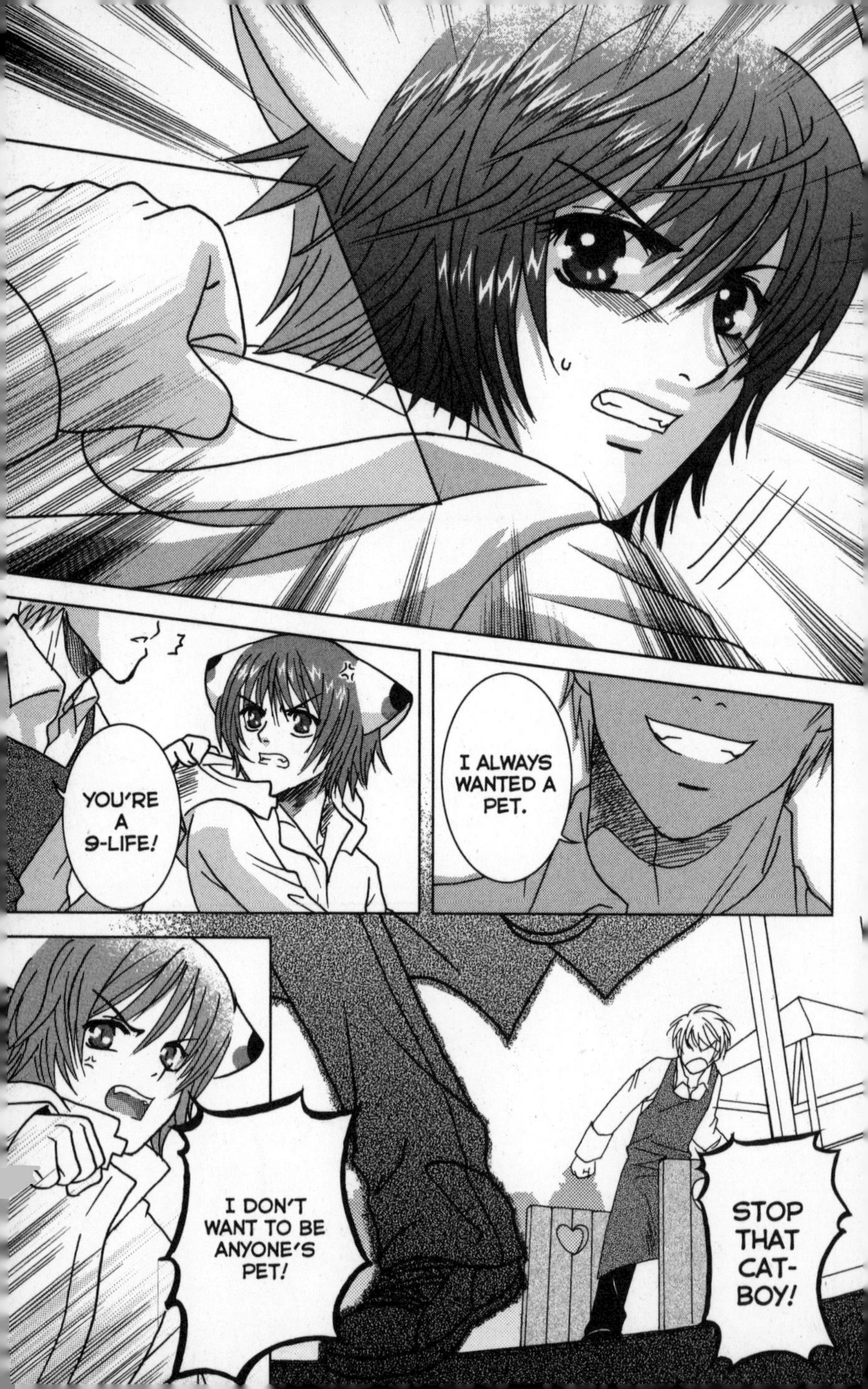
YOU'RE A 9-LIFE!
I ALWAYS WANTED A PET.
I DON'T WANT TO BE ANYONE'S PET!
STOP THAT CAT-BOY!

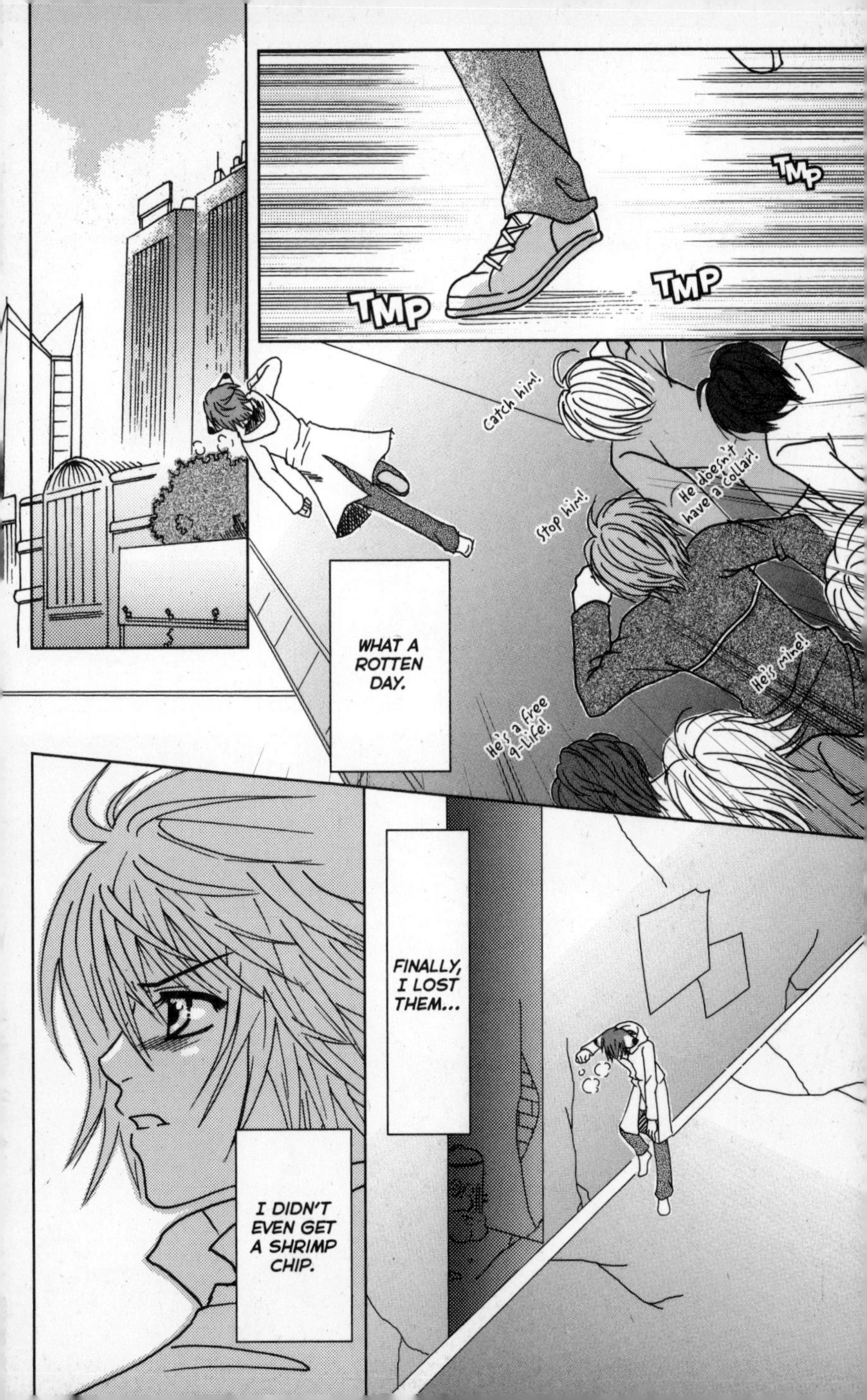
TMP
TMP
TMP
Catch him!
He doesn't have a collar!
Stop him!
WHAT A ROTTEN DAY.
He's mine!
He's a free 9-Life!
FINALLY, I LOST THEM...
I DIDN'T EVEN GET A SHRIMP CHIP.

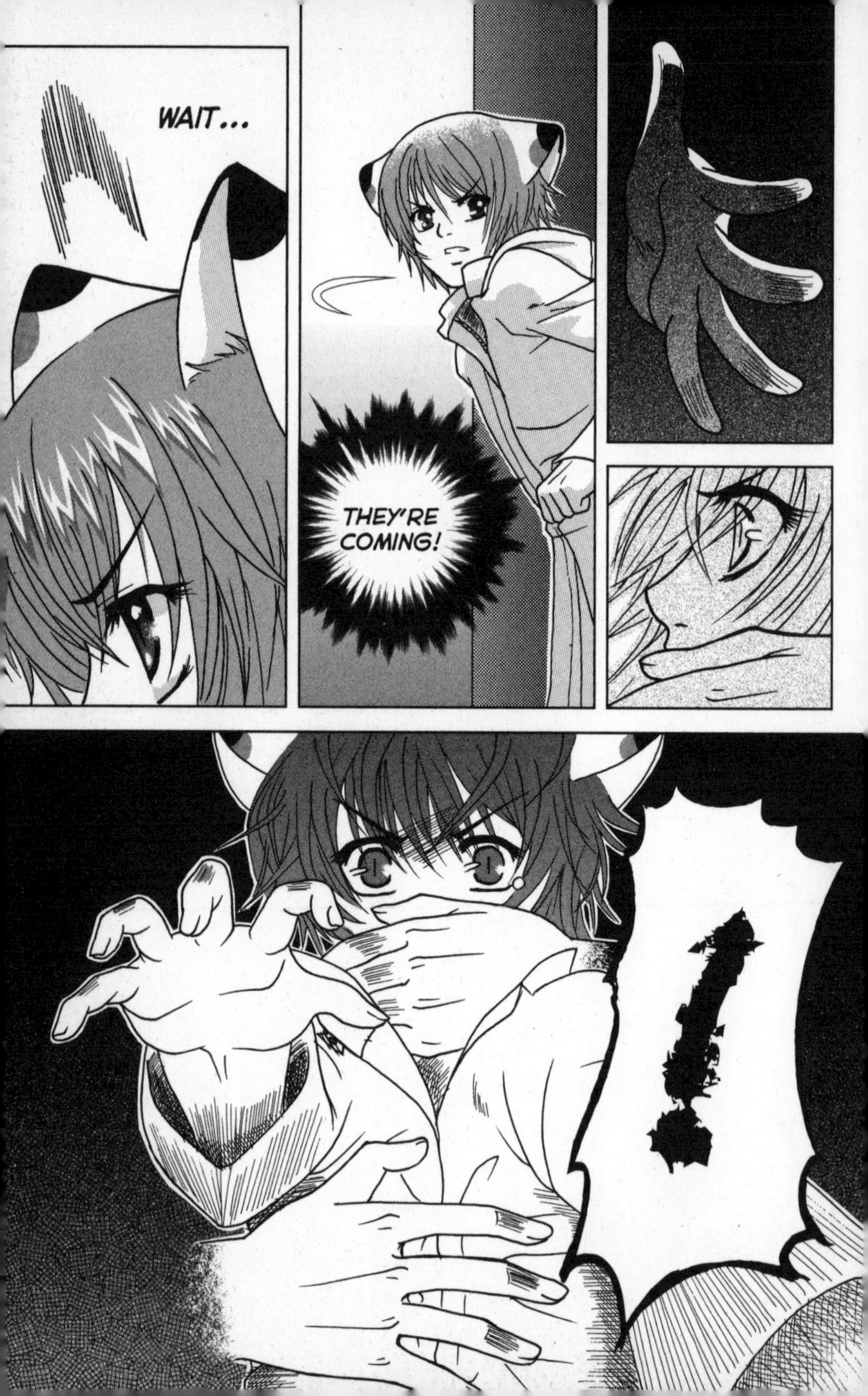
WAIT...
THEY'RE COMING!
!

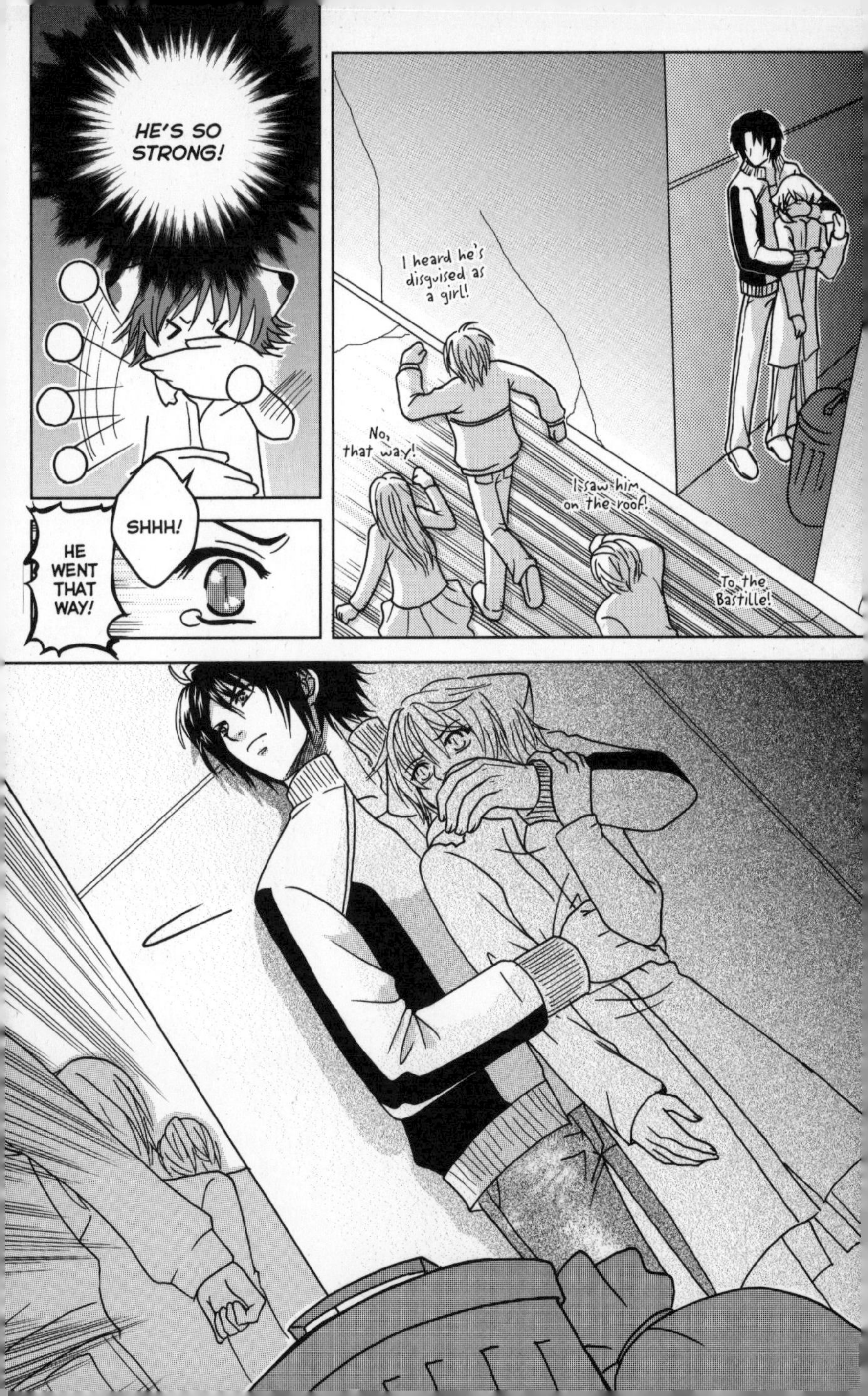
HE'S SO STRONG!
HE WENT THAT WAY!
SHHH!
I heard he's disguised as a girl!
No, that way!
I saw him on the roof!
To the Bastille!

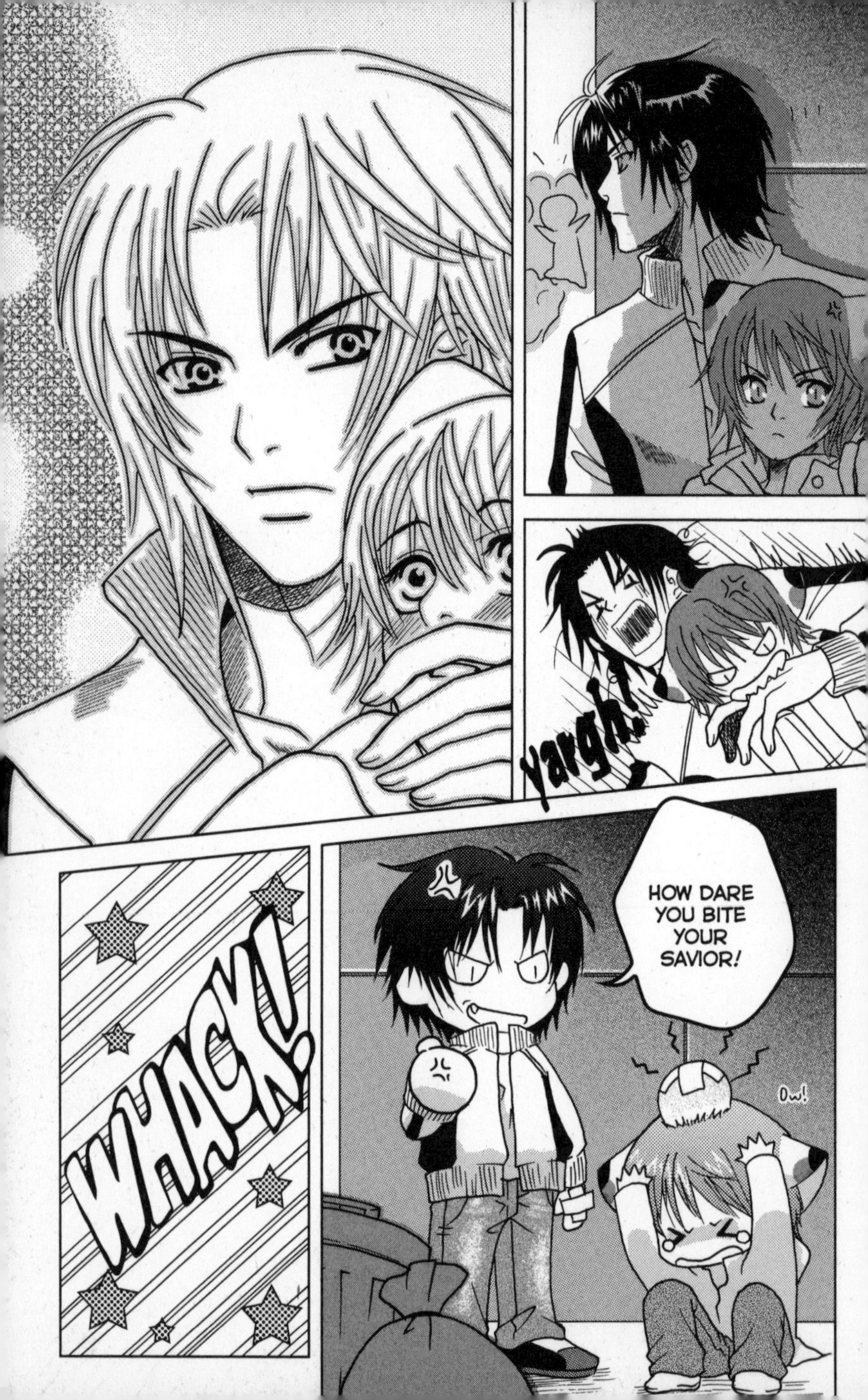
Yargh!
WHACK!
HOW DARE YOU BITE YOUR SAVIOR!
Ow!

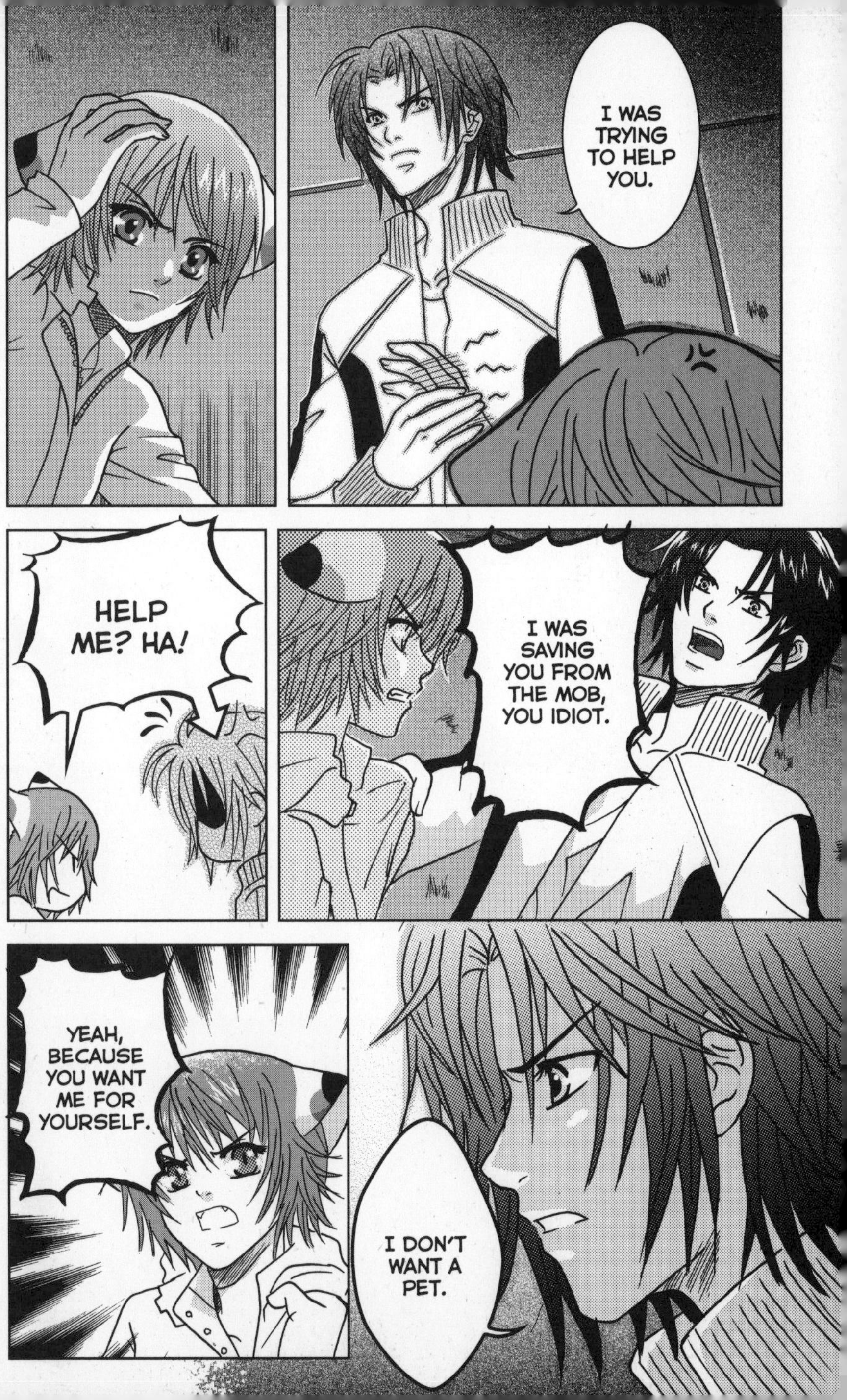
I WAS TRYING TO HELP YOU.
HELP ME? HA!
I WAS SAVING YOU FROM THE MOB, YOU IDIOT.
YEAH, BECAUSE YOU WANT ME FOR YOURSELF.
I DON'T WANT A PET.

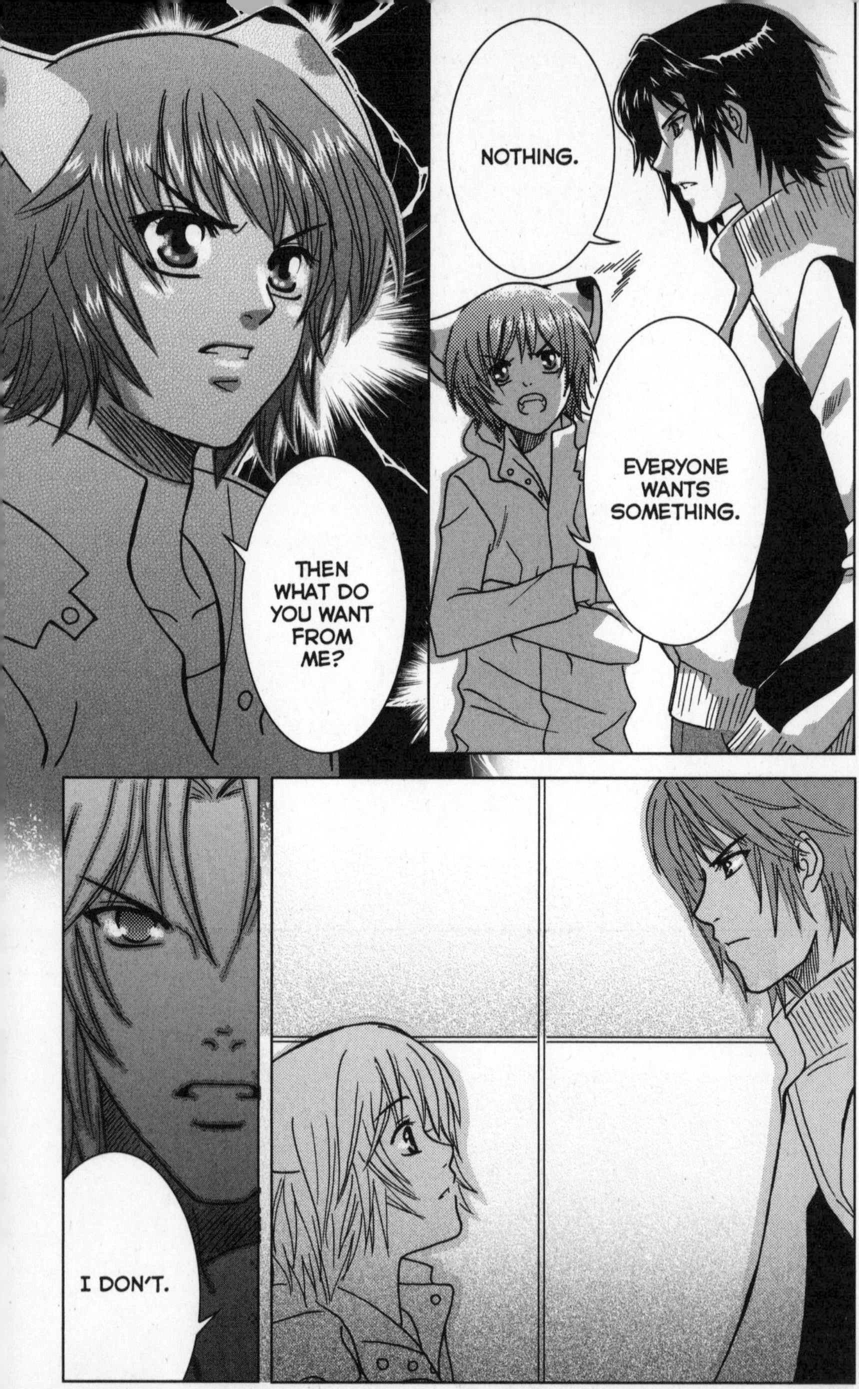
THEN WHAT DO YOU WANT FROM ME?
NOTHING.
EVERYONE WANTS SOMETHING.
I DON'T.

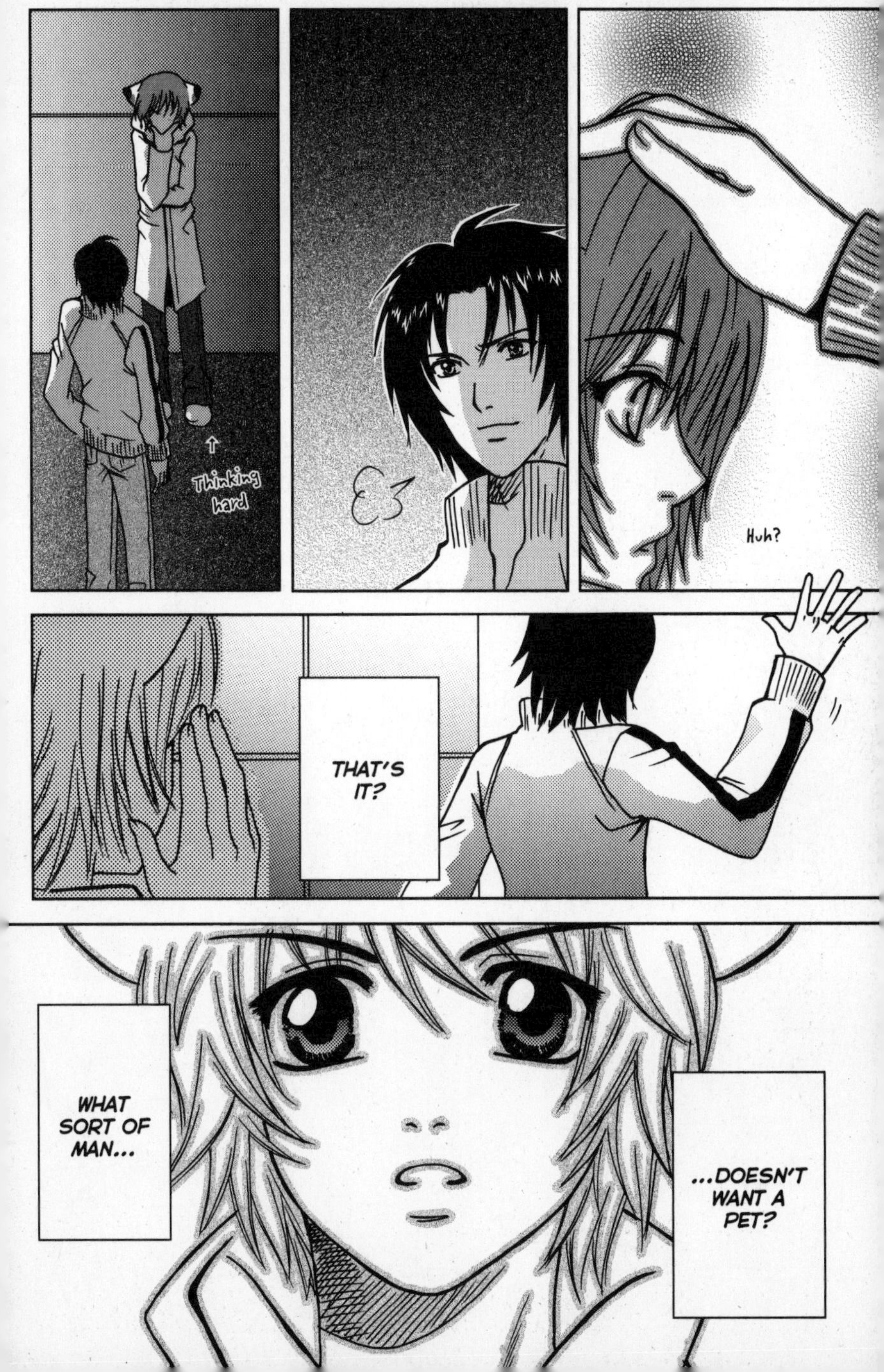
Thinking hard
Huh?
THAT'S IT?
WHAT SORT OF MAN...
...DOESN'T WANT A PET?

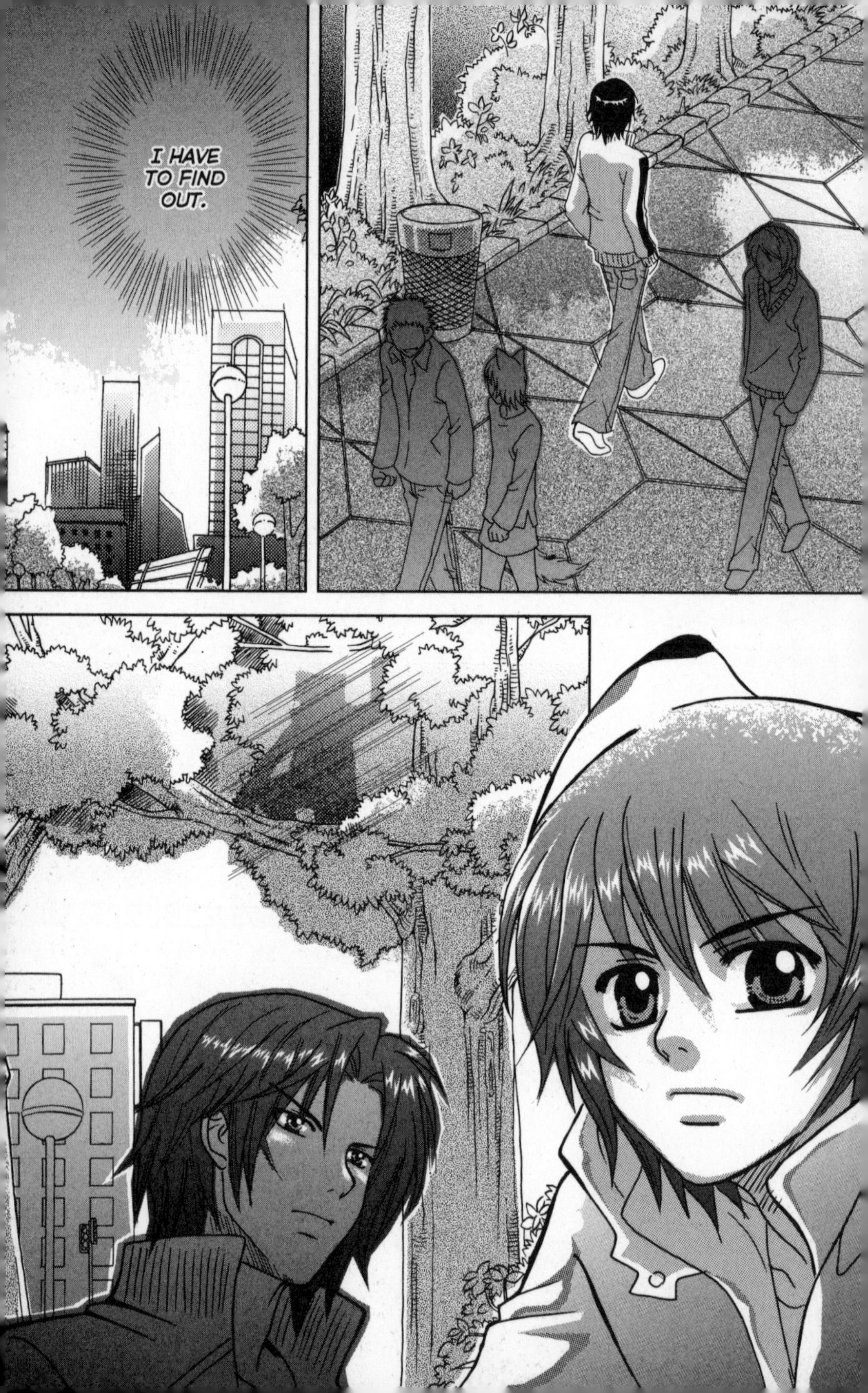
I HAVE TO FIND OUT.

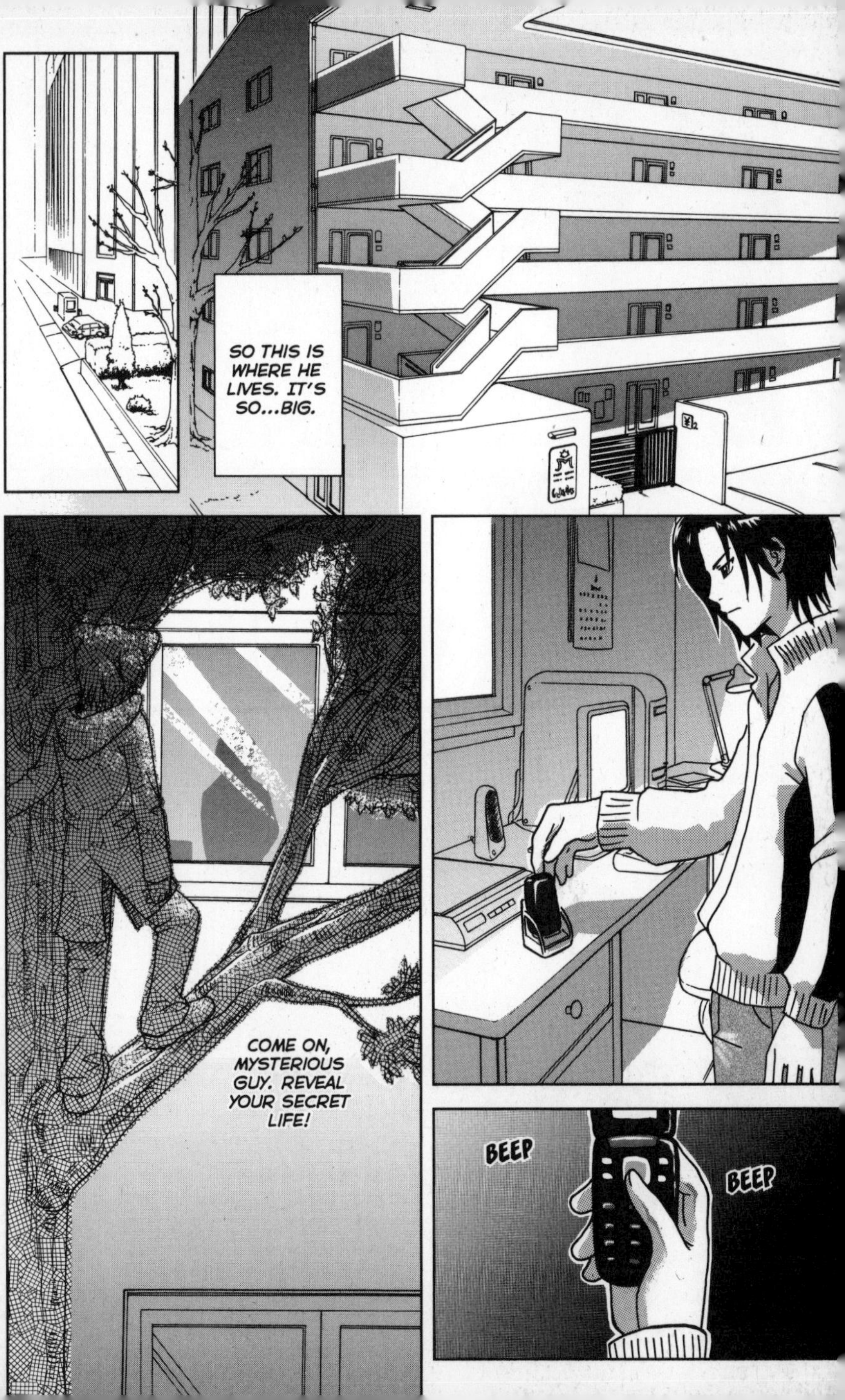
SO THIS IS WHERE HE LIVES. IT'S SO...BIG.
COME ON, MYSTERIOUS GUY. REVEAL YOUR SECRET LIFE!
BEEP
BEEP

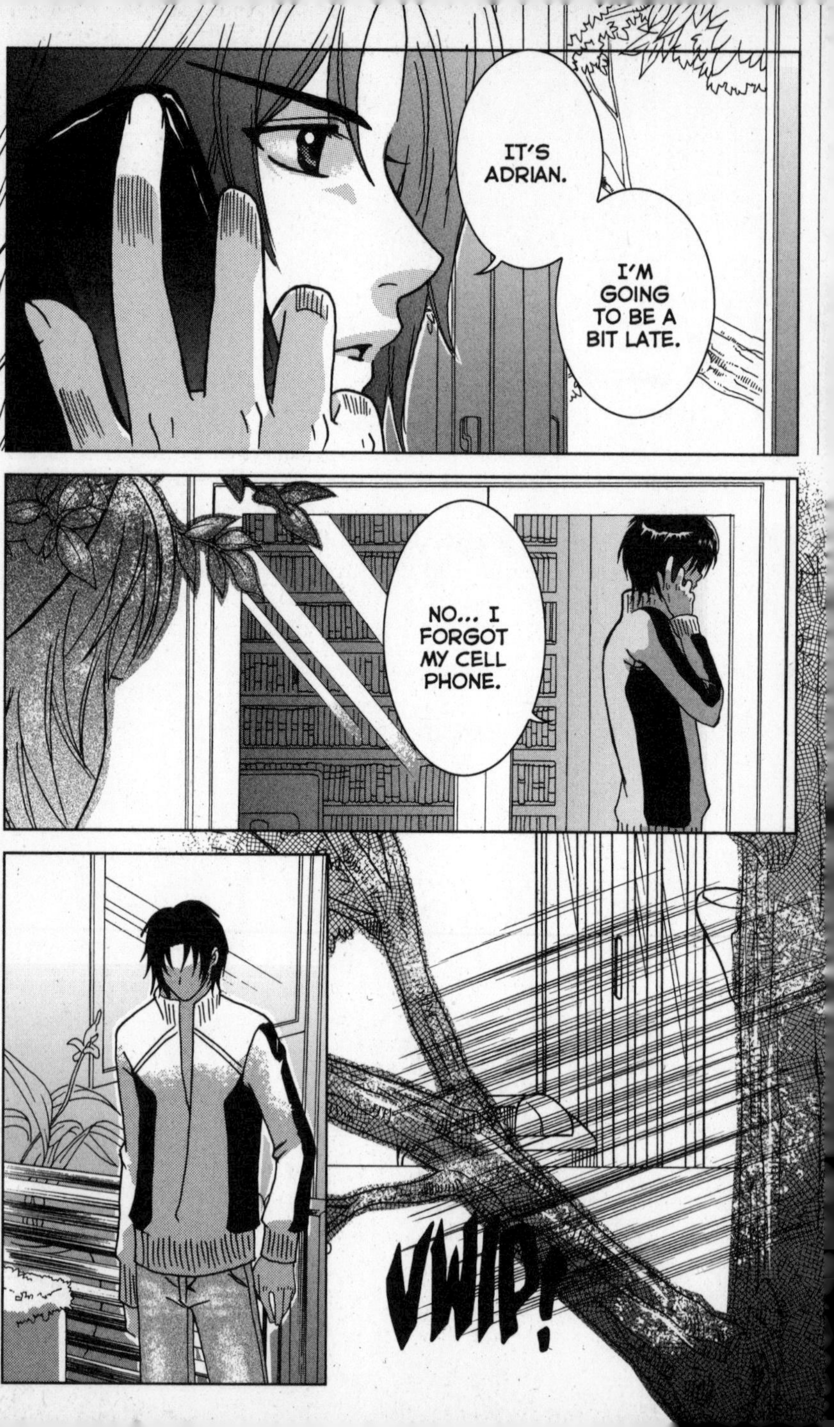
IT'S ADRIAN.
I'M GOING TO BE A BIT LATE.
NO... I FORGOT MY CELL PHONE.
VWIP!

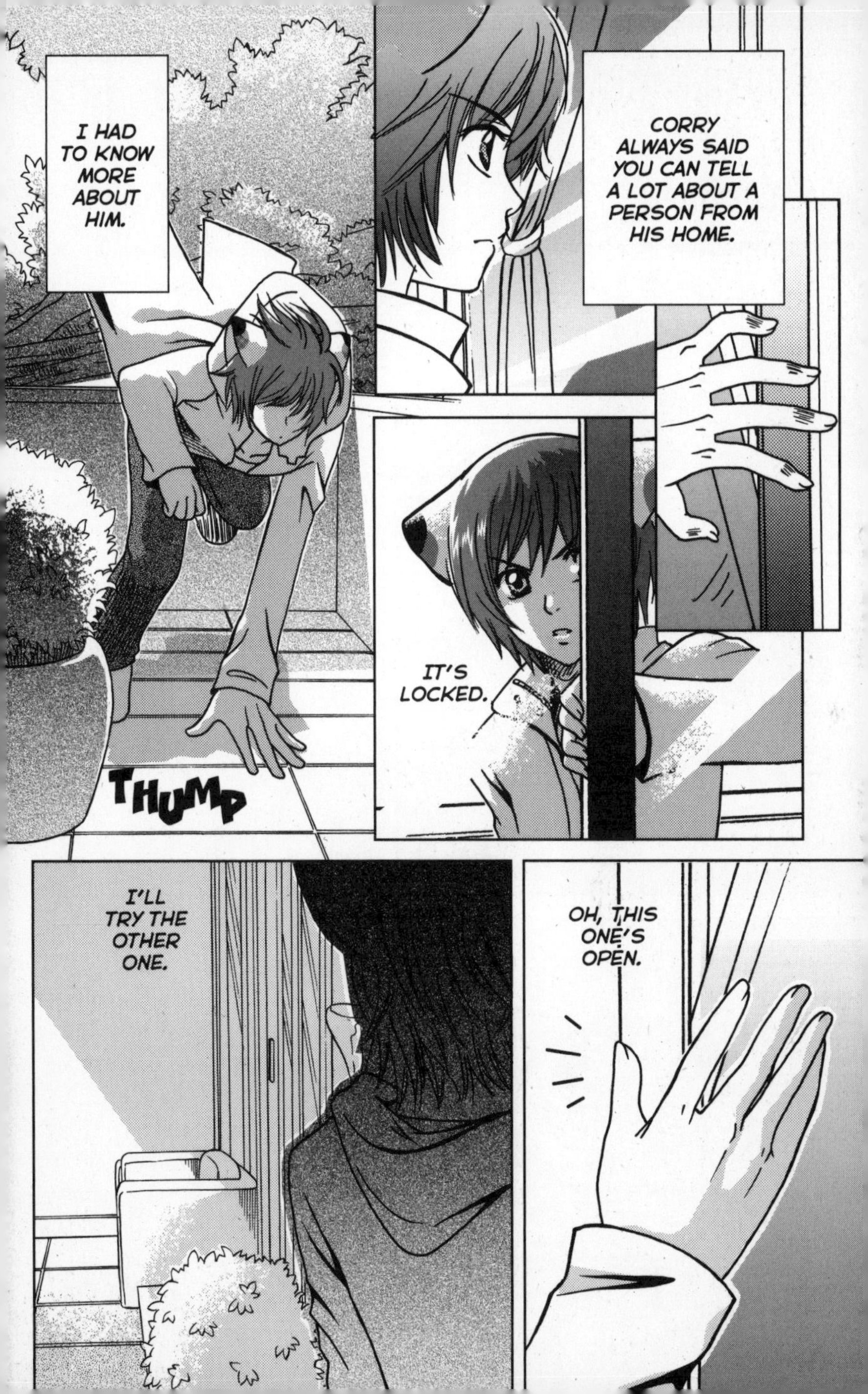
I HAD TO KNOW MORE ABOUT HIM.
THUMP
CORRY ALWAYS SAID YOU CAN TELL A LOT ABOUT A PERSON FROM HIS HOME.
IT'S LOCKED.
I'LL TRY THE OTHER ONE.
OH, THIS ONE'S OPEN.

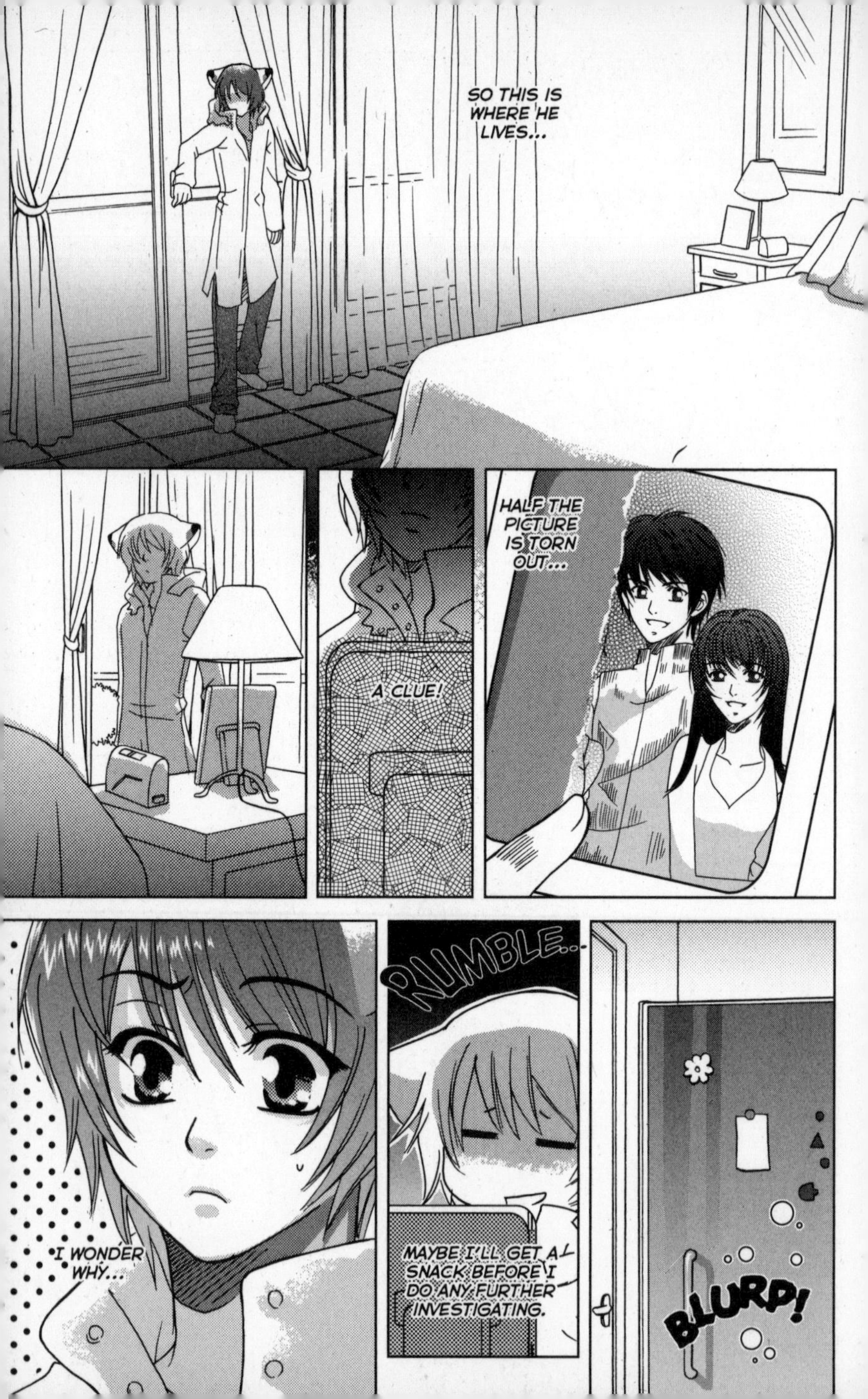
SO THIS IS WHERE HE LIVES...
HALF THE PICTURE IS TORN OUT...
A CLUE!
I WONDER WHY...
RUMBLE...
MAYBE I'LL GET A SNACK BEFORE I DO ANY FURTHER INVESTIGATING.
BLURP!

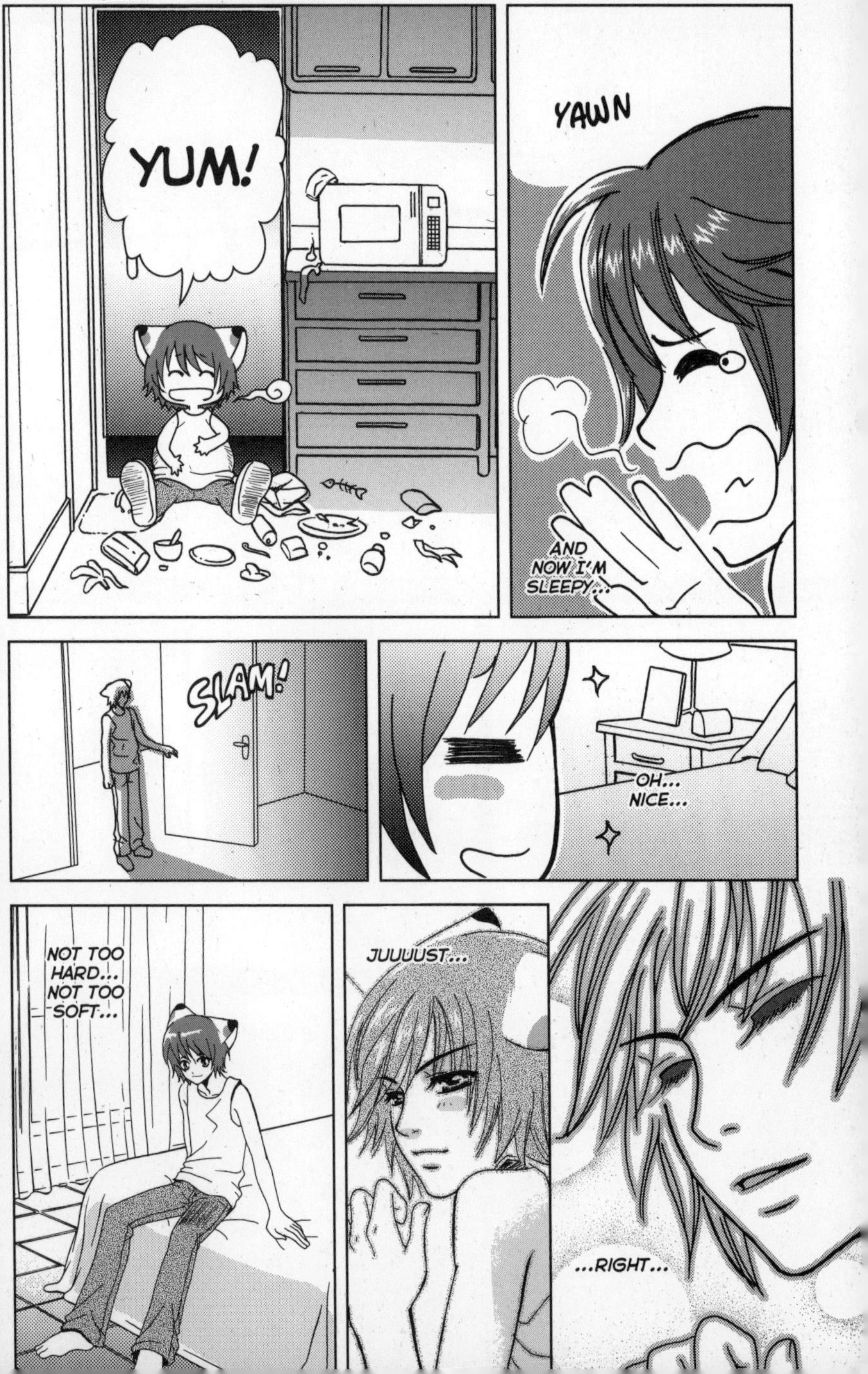
YUM!
YAWN
AND NOW I'M SLEEPY...
SLAM!
OH... NICE...
NOT TOO HARD... NOT TOO SOFT...
JUUUUST...
...RIGHT...

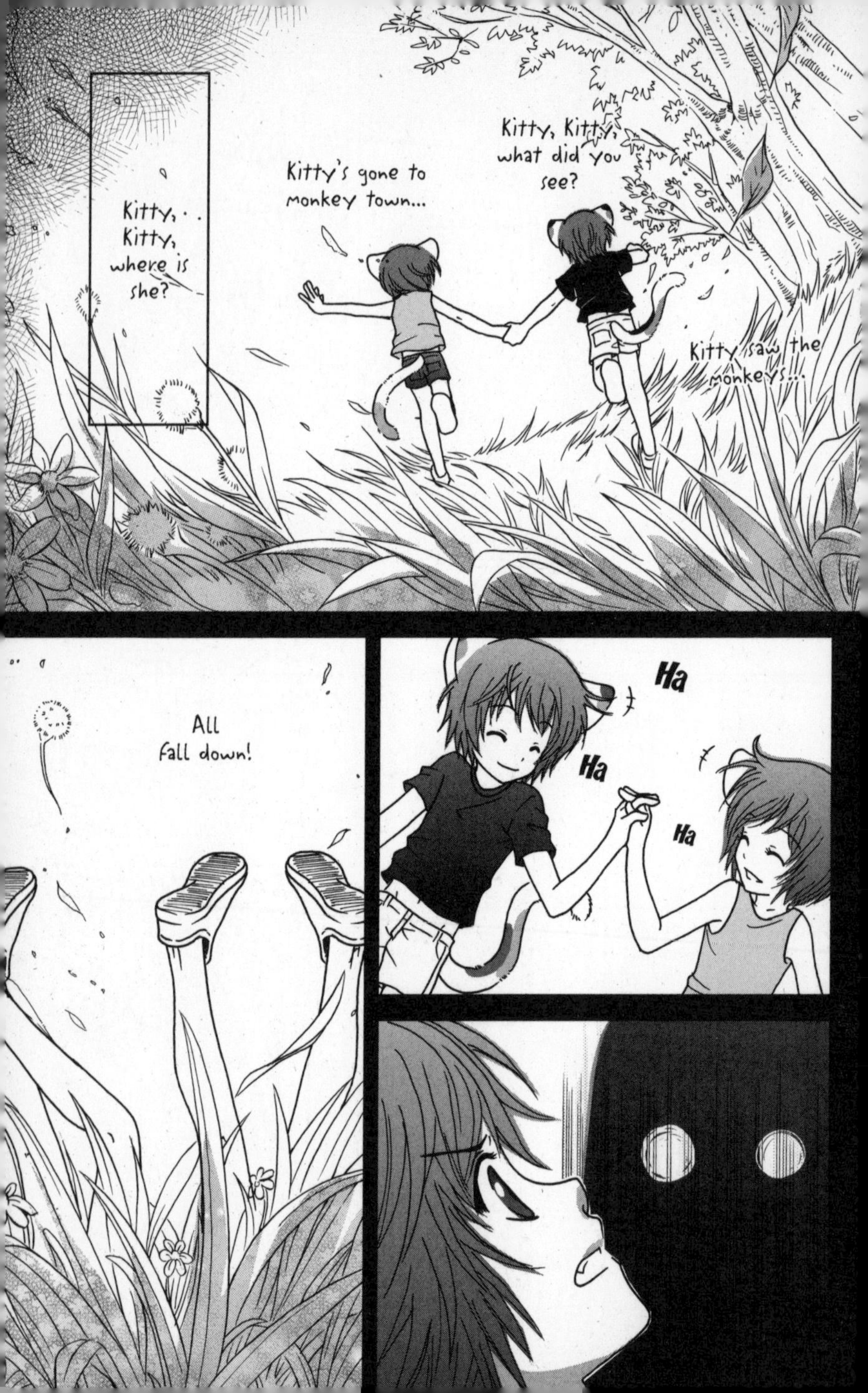
Kitty, Kitty, where is she?
Kitty's gone to monkey town...
Kitty, Kitty, what did you see?
Kitty saw the monkeys...
All fall down!
Ha
Ha
Ha

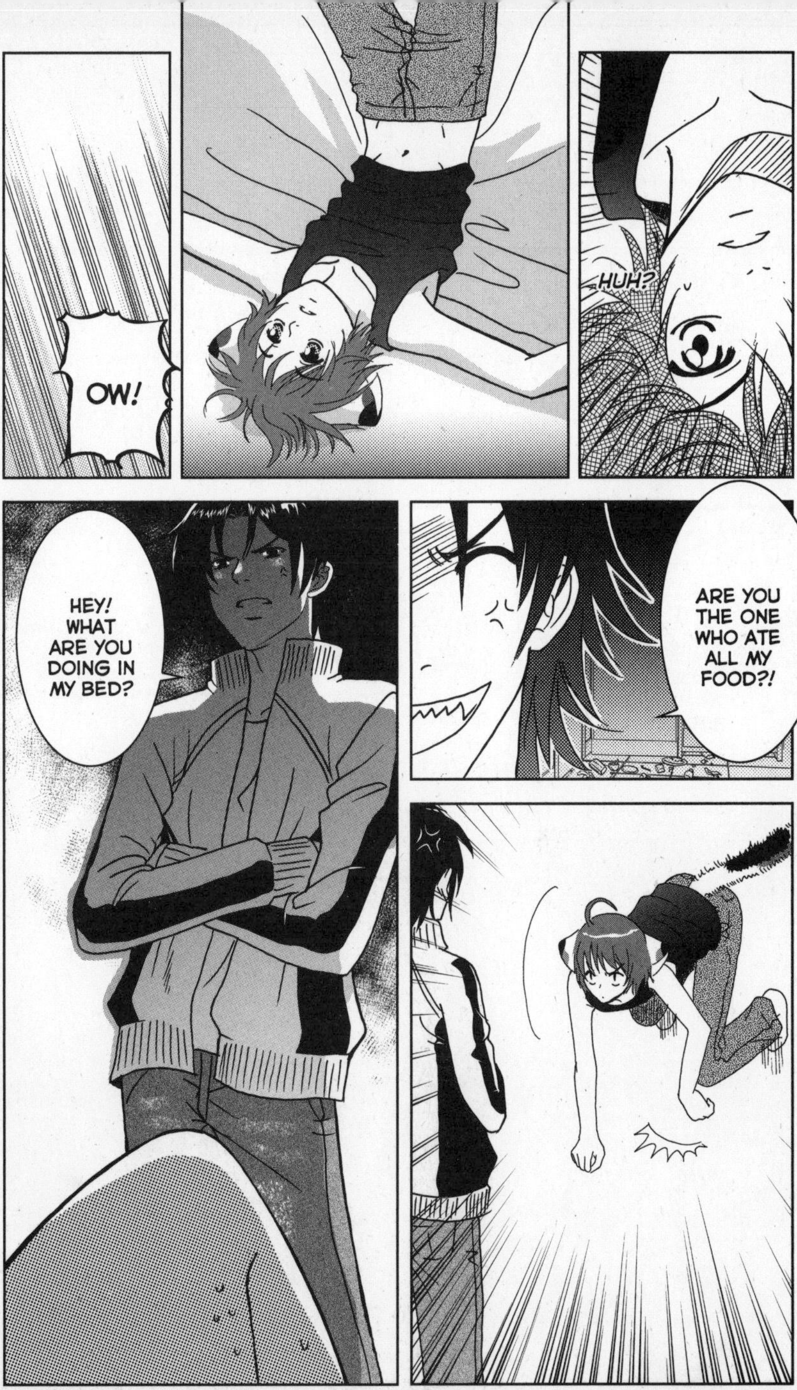
OW!
HUH?
HEY! WHAT ARE YOU DOING IN MY BED?
ARE YOU THE ONE WHO ATE ALL MY FOOD?!

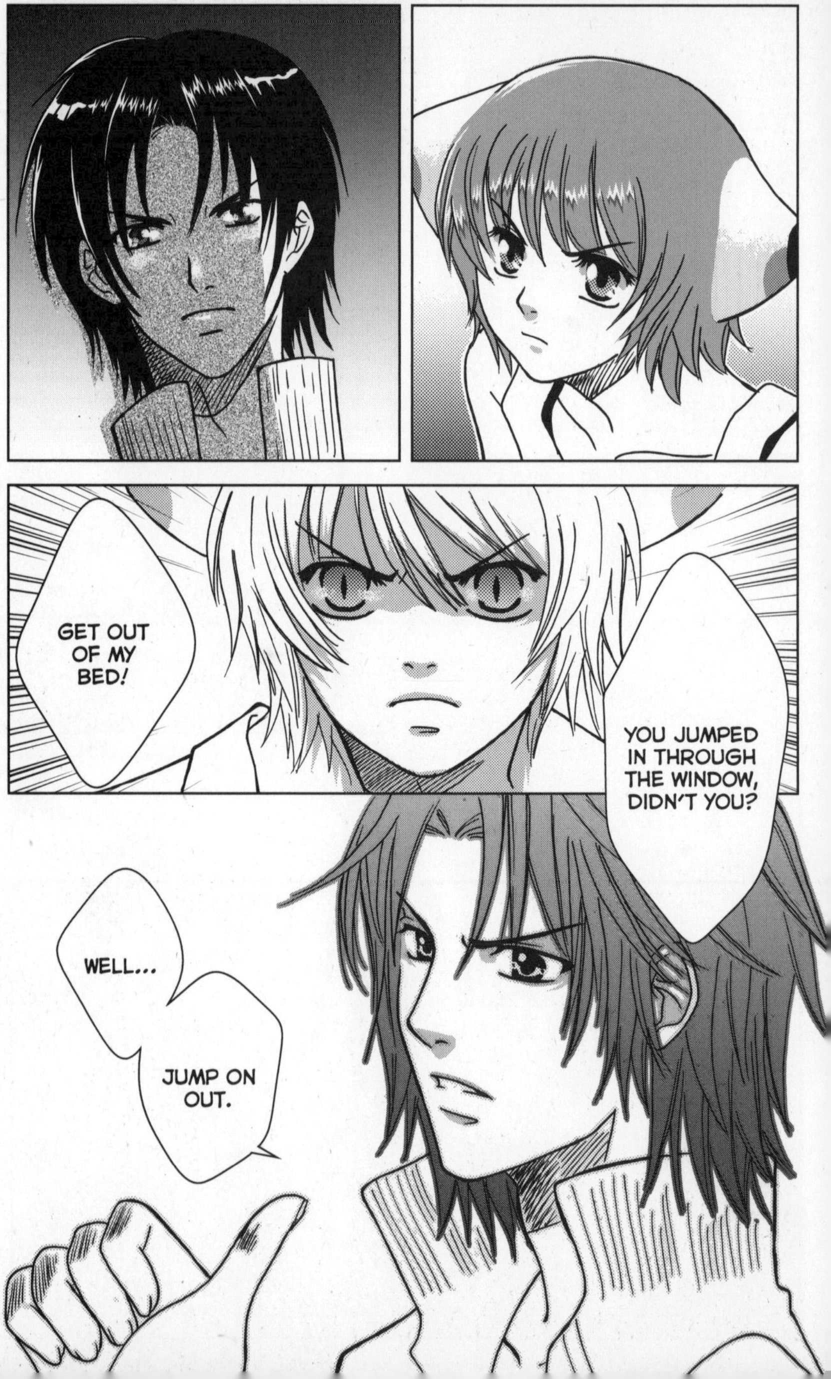
GET OUT OF MY BED!
YOU JUMPED IN THROUGH THE WINDOW, DIDN'T YOU?
WELL...
JUMP ON OUT.

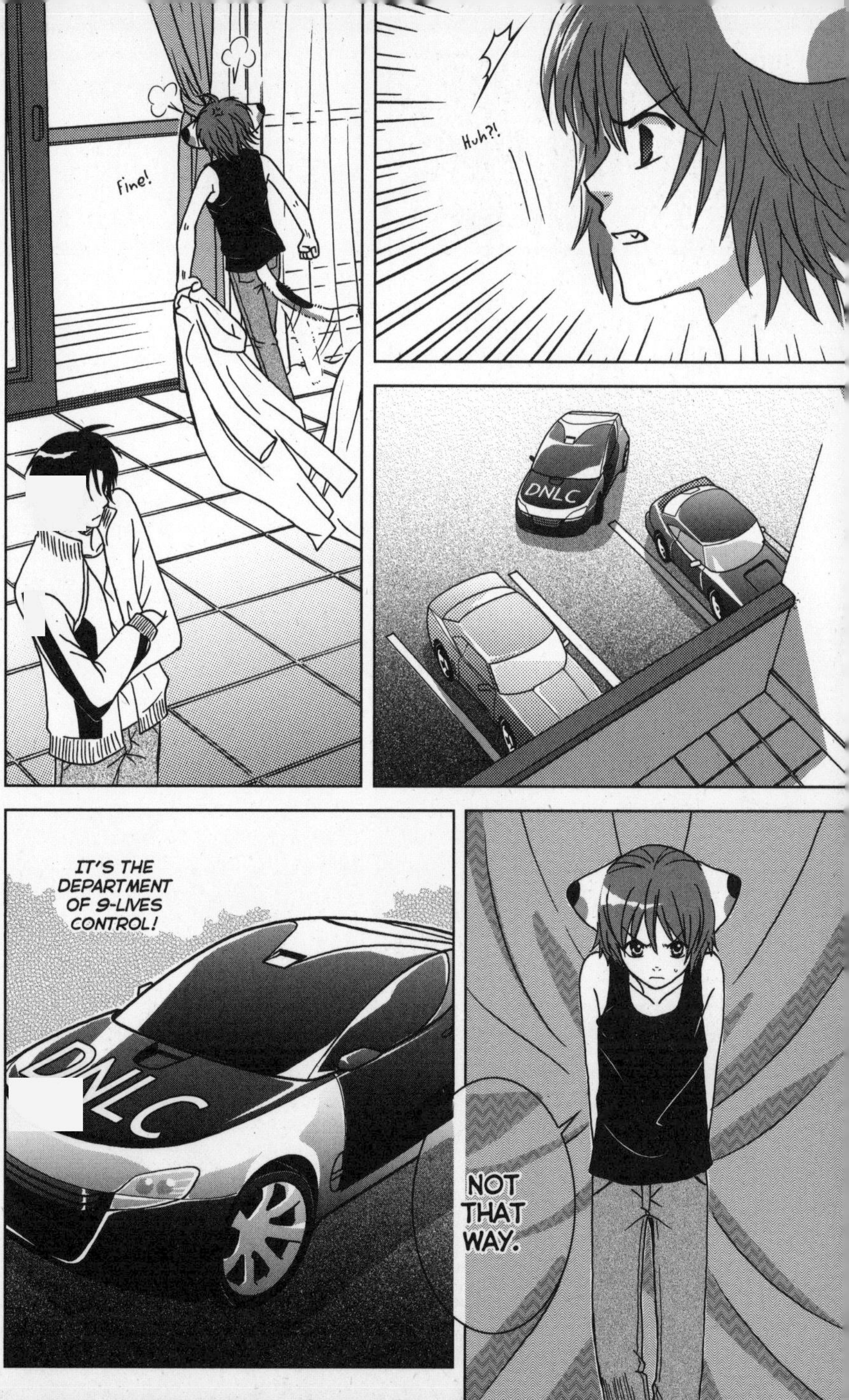
Fine!
Huh?!
DNLC
IT'S THE DEPARTMENT OF 9-LIVES CONTROL!
DNLC
NOT THAT WAY.

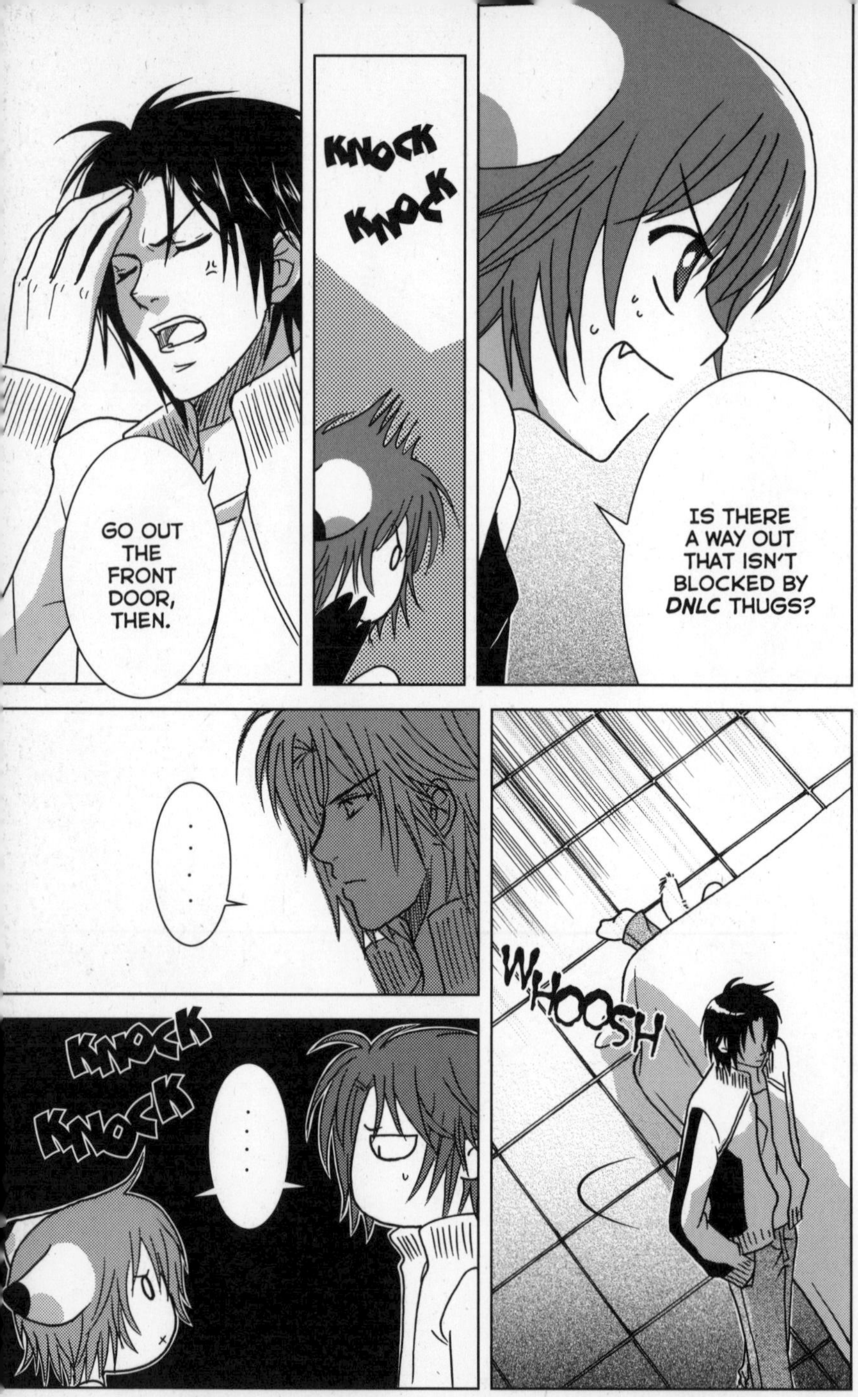
GO OUT THE FRONT DOOR, THEN.
KNOCK KNOCK
IS THERE A WAY OUT THAT ISN'T BLOCKED BY *DNLC* THUGS?
. . . .
WHOOSH
KNOCK KNOCK
. . . .

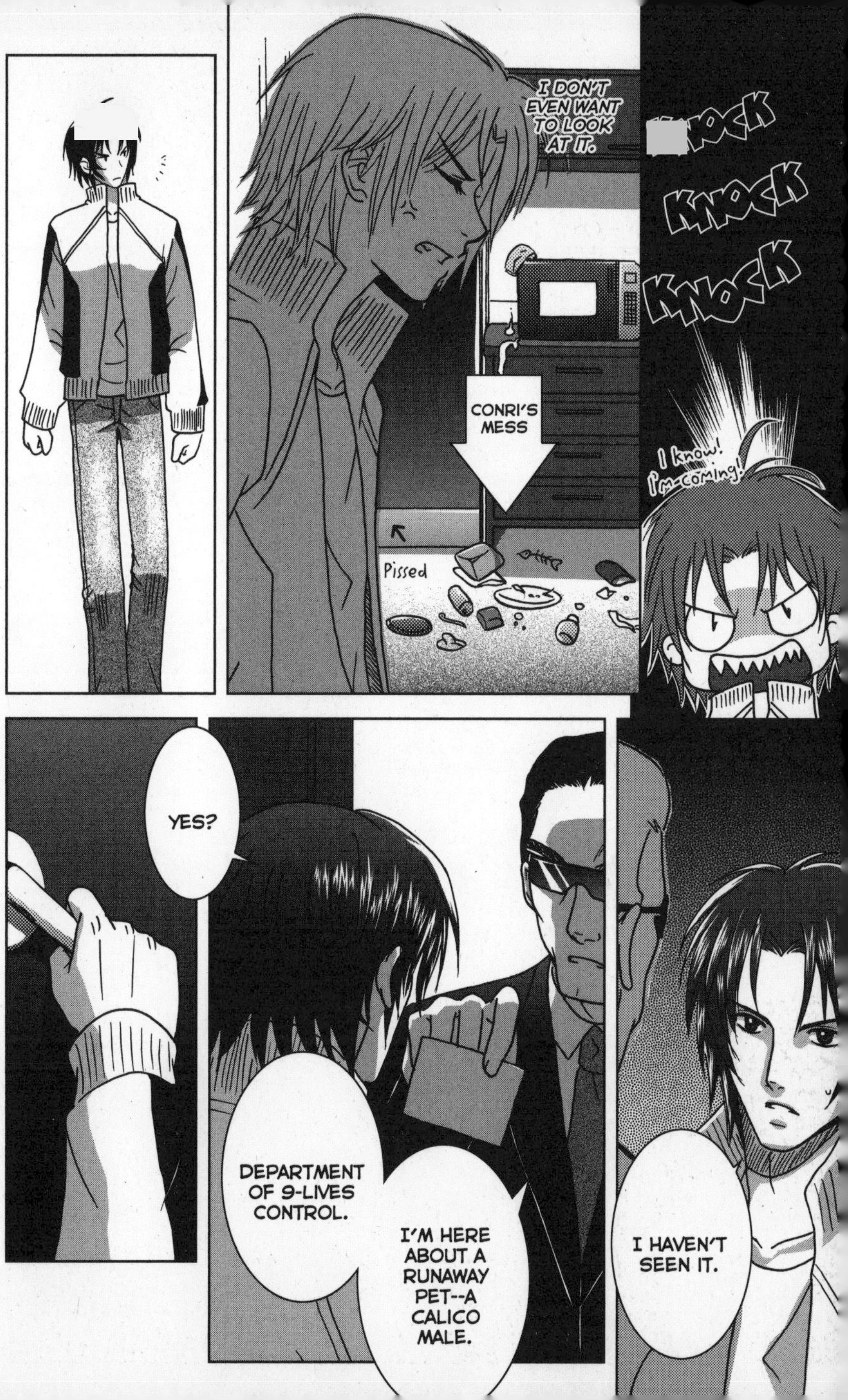
I DON'T EVEN WANT TO LOOK AT IT.
CONRI'S MESS
Pissed
NOCK
KNOCK
KNOCK
I know! I'm coming!
YES?
DEPARTMENT OF 9-LIVES CONTROL.
I'M HERE ABOUT A RUNAWAY PET--A CALICO MALE.
I HAVEN'T SEEN IT.

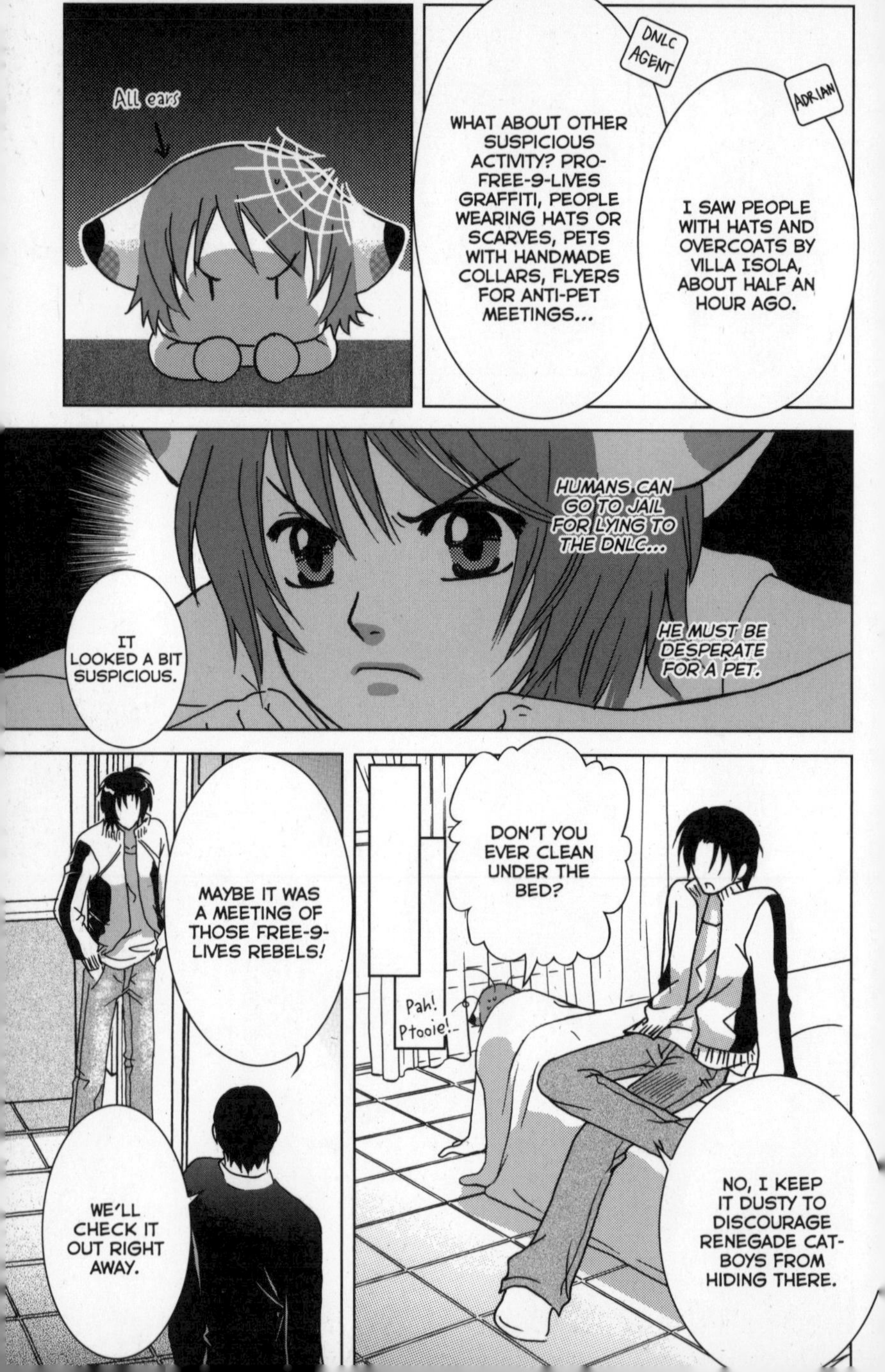
All ears
DNLC AGENT
WHAT ABOUT OTHER SUSPICIOUS ACTIVITY? PRO-FREE-9-LIVES GRAFFITI, PEOPLE WEARING HATS OR SCARVES, PETS WITH HANDMADE COLLARS, FLYERS FOR ANTI-PET MEETINGS...
ADRIAN
I SAW PEOPLE WITH HATS AND OVERCOATS BY VILLA ISOLA, ABOUT HALF AN HOUR AGO.
IT LOOKED A BIT SUSPICIOUS.
HUMANS CAN GO TO JAIL FOR LYING TO THE DNLC...
HE MUST BE DESPERATE FOR A PET.
MAYBE IT WAS A MEETING OF THOSE FREE-9-LIVES REBELS!
WE'LL CHECK IT OUT RIGHT AWAY.
DON'T YOU EVER CLEAN UNDER THE BED?
Pah! Ptooie!
NO, I KEEP IT DUSTY TO DISCOURAGE RENEGADE CAT-BOYS FROM HIDING THERE.

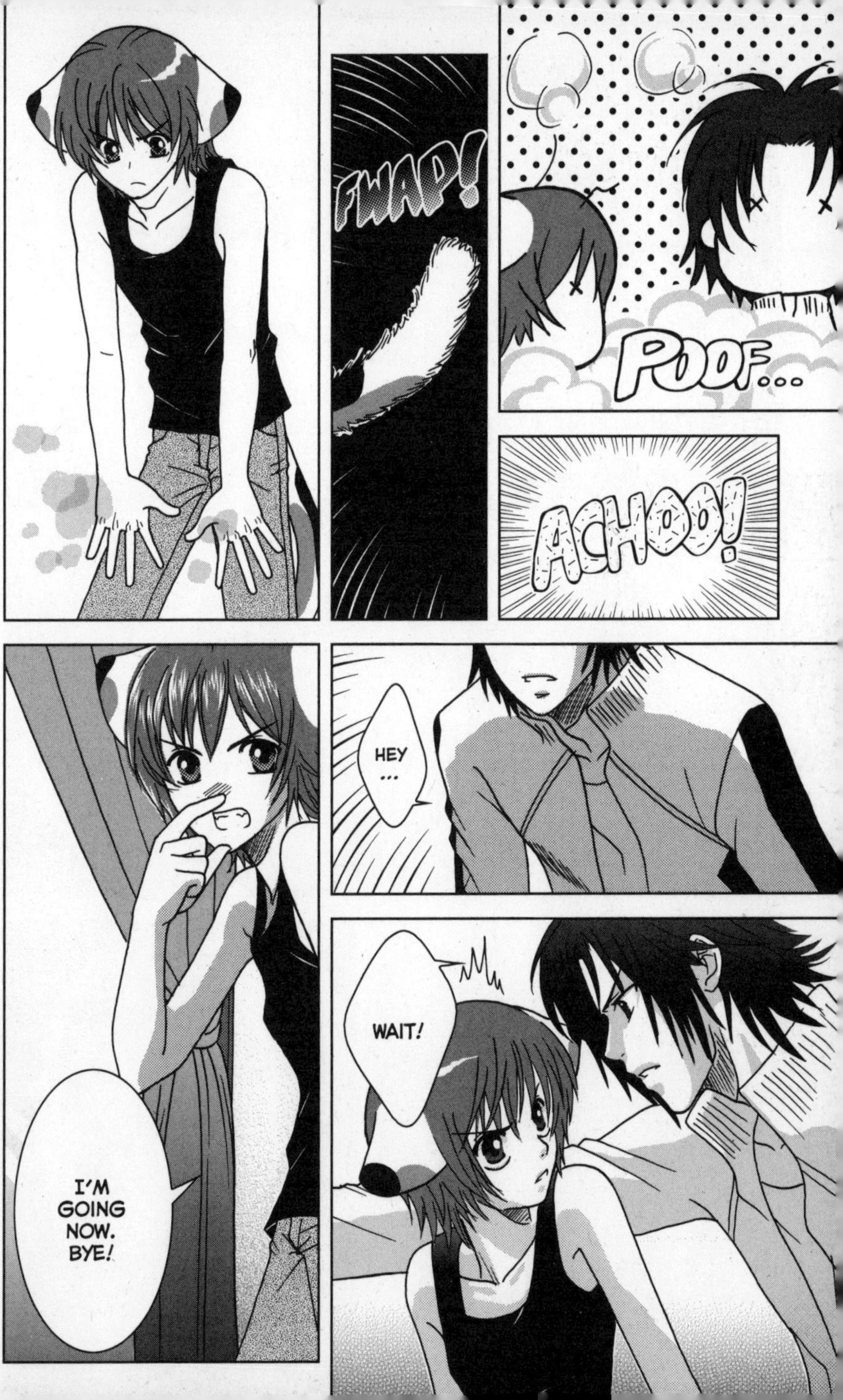
FWAP!
POOF...
ACHOO!
I'M GOING NOW. BYE!
HEY ...
WAIT!

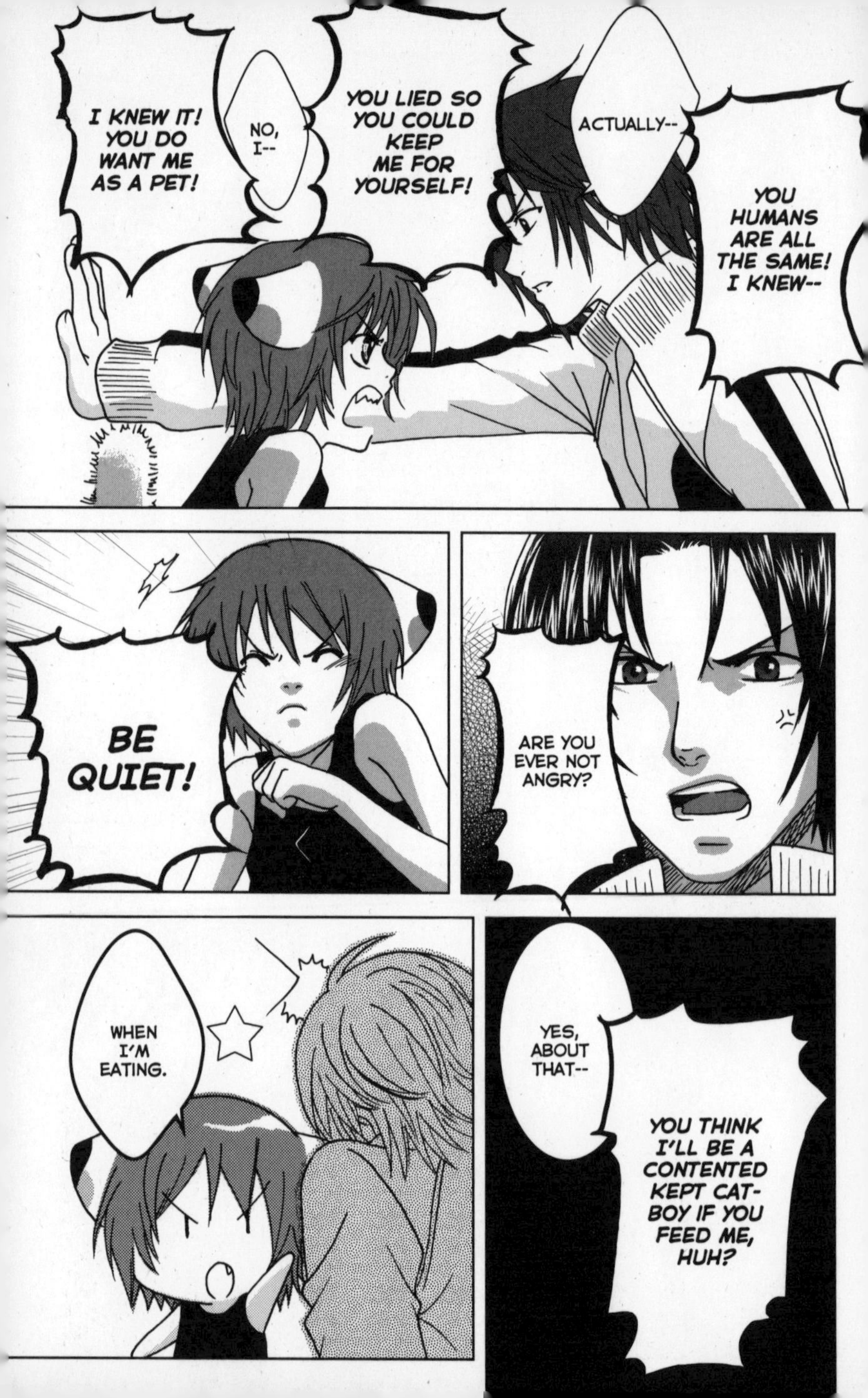
I KNEW IT! YOU DO WANT ME AS A PET!
NO, I--
YOU LIED SO YOU COULD KEEP ME FOR YOURSELF!
ACTUALLY--
YOU HUMANS ARE ALL THE SAME! I KNEW--
BE QUIET!
ARE YOU EVER NOT ANGRY?
WHEN I'M EATING.
YES, ABOUT THAT--
YOU THINK I'LL BE A CONTENTED KEPT CAT-BOY IF YOU FEED ME, HUH?

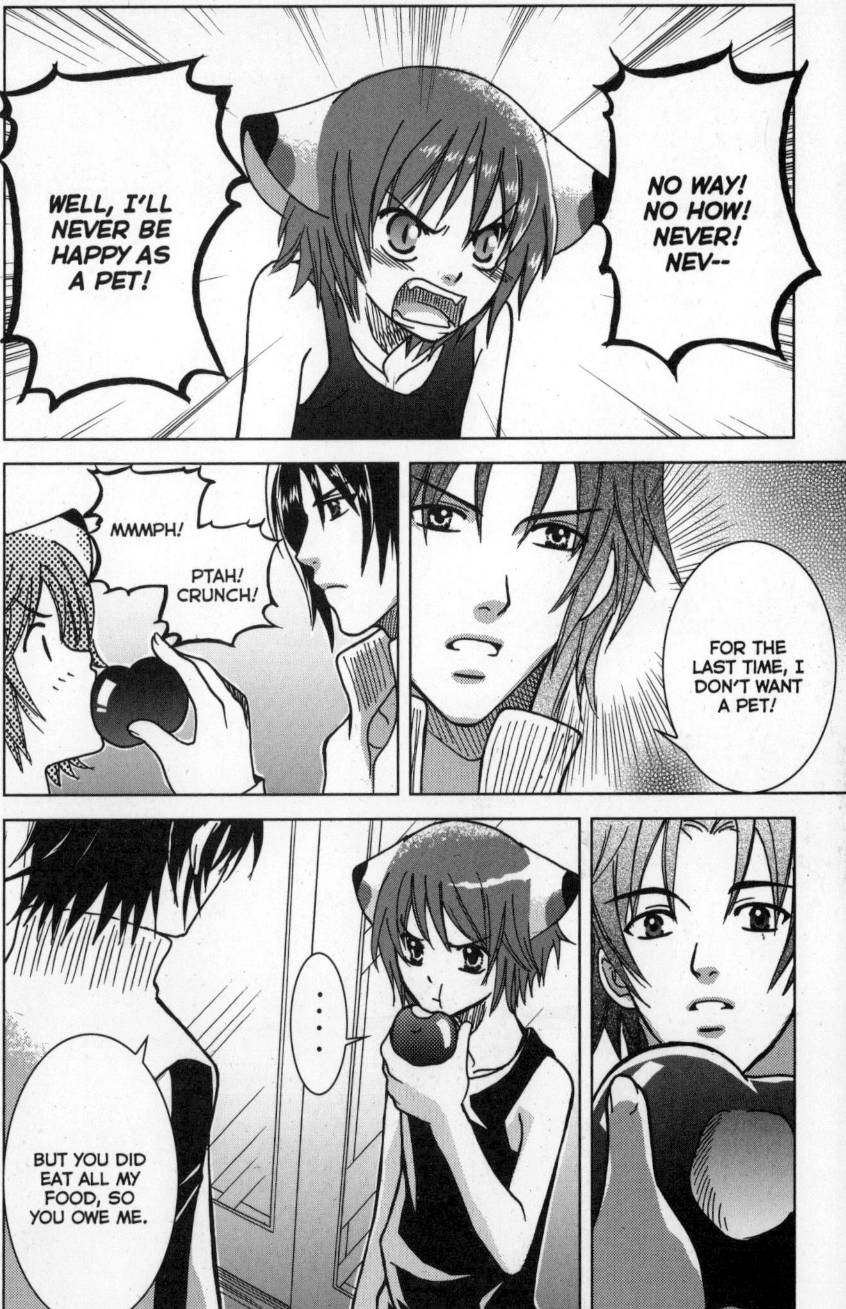
WELL, I'LL NEVER BE HAPPY AS A PET!
NO WAY! NO HOW! NEVER! NEV--
MMMPH!
PTAH! CRUNCH!
FOR THE LAST TIME, I DON'T WANT A PET!
BUT YOU DID EAT ALL MY FOOD, SO YOU OWE ME.
....

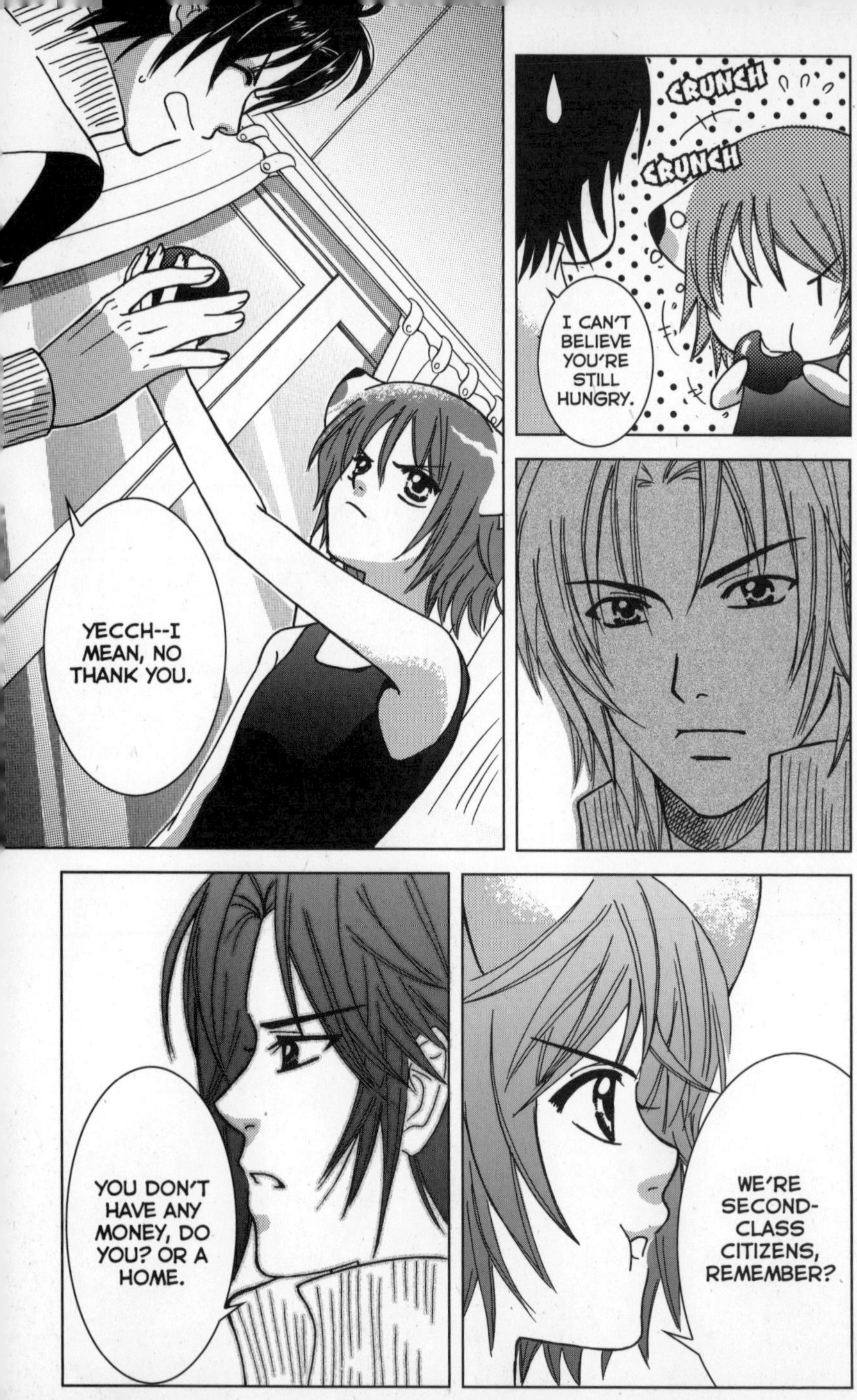
YECCH--I MEAN, NO THANK YOU.
CRUNCH
CRUNCH
I CAN'T BELIEVE YOU'RE STILL HUNGRY.
YOU DON'T HAVE ANY MONEY, DO YOU? OR A HOME.
WE'RE SECOND-CLASS CITIZENS, REMEMBER?

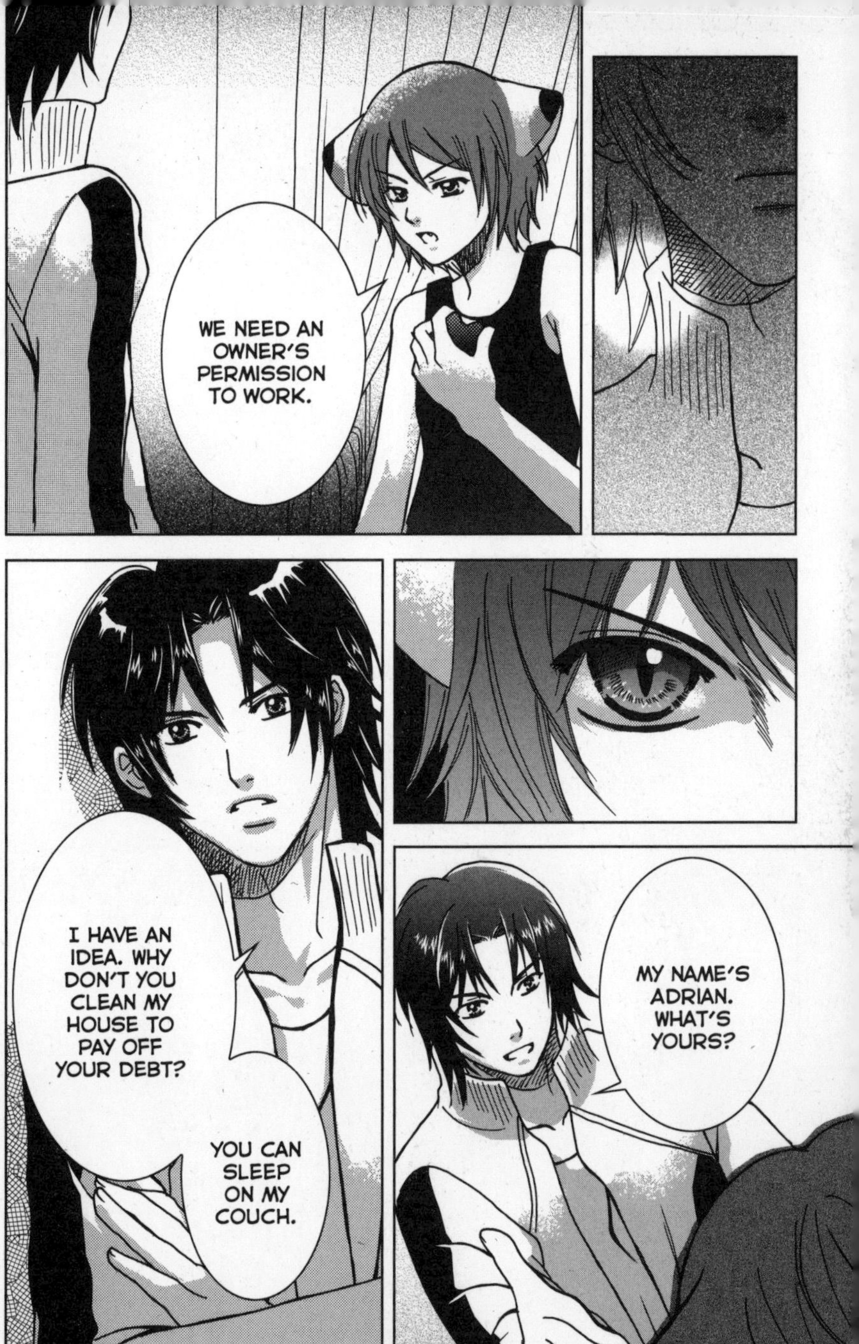
WE NEED AN OWNER'S PERMISSION TO WORK.
I HAVE AN IDEA. WHY DON'T YOU CLEAN MY HOUSE TO PAY OFF YOUR DEBT?
YOU CAN SLEEP ON MY COUCH.
MY NAME'S ADRIAN. WHAT'S YOURS?

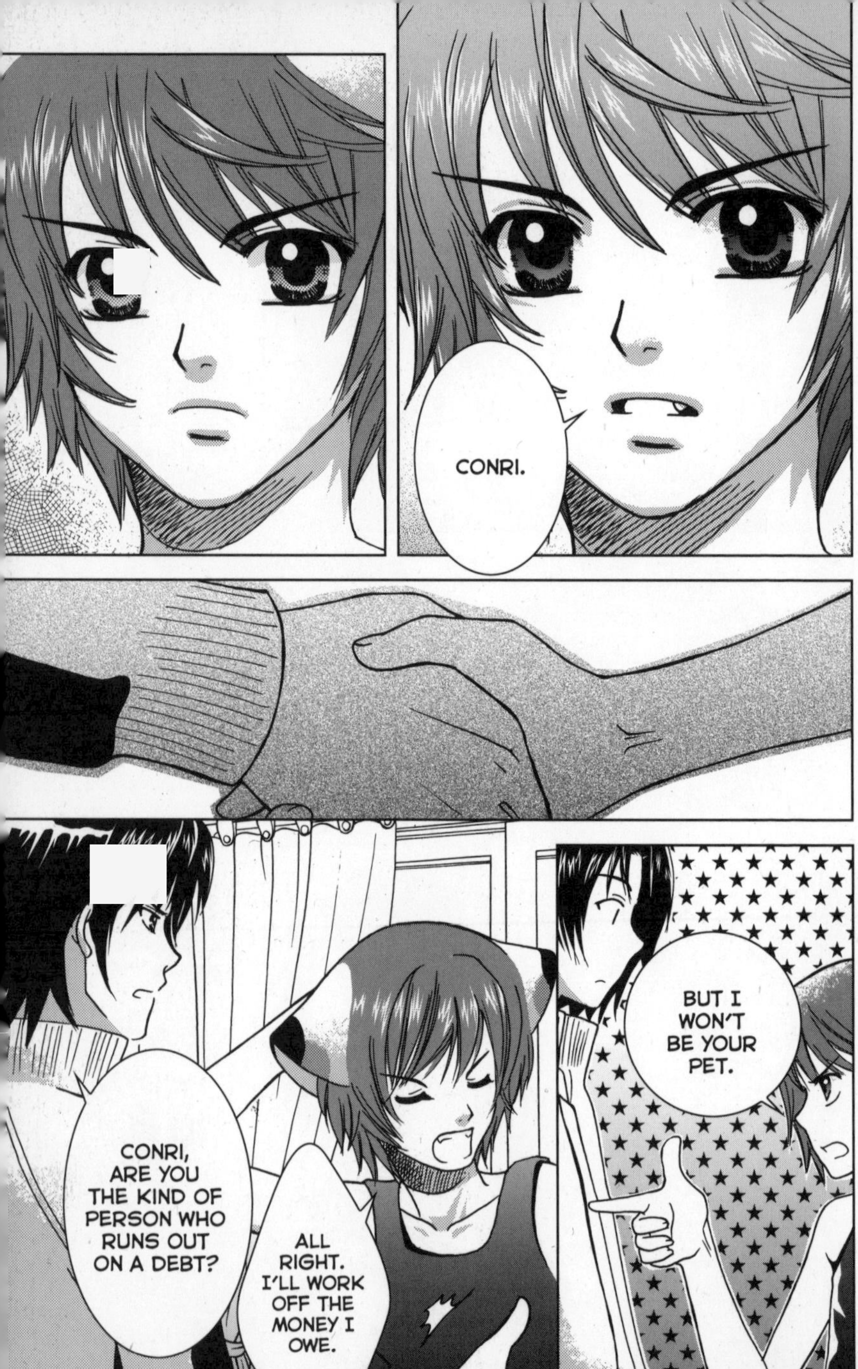
CONRI.
CONRI, ARE YOU THE KIND OF PERSON WHO RUNS OUT ON A DEBT?
ALL RIGHT. I'LL WORK OFF THE MONEY I OWE.
BUT I WON'T BE YOUR PET.

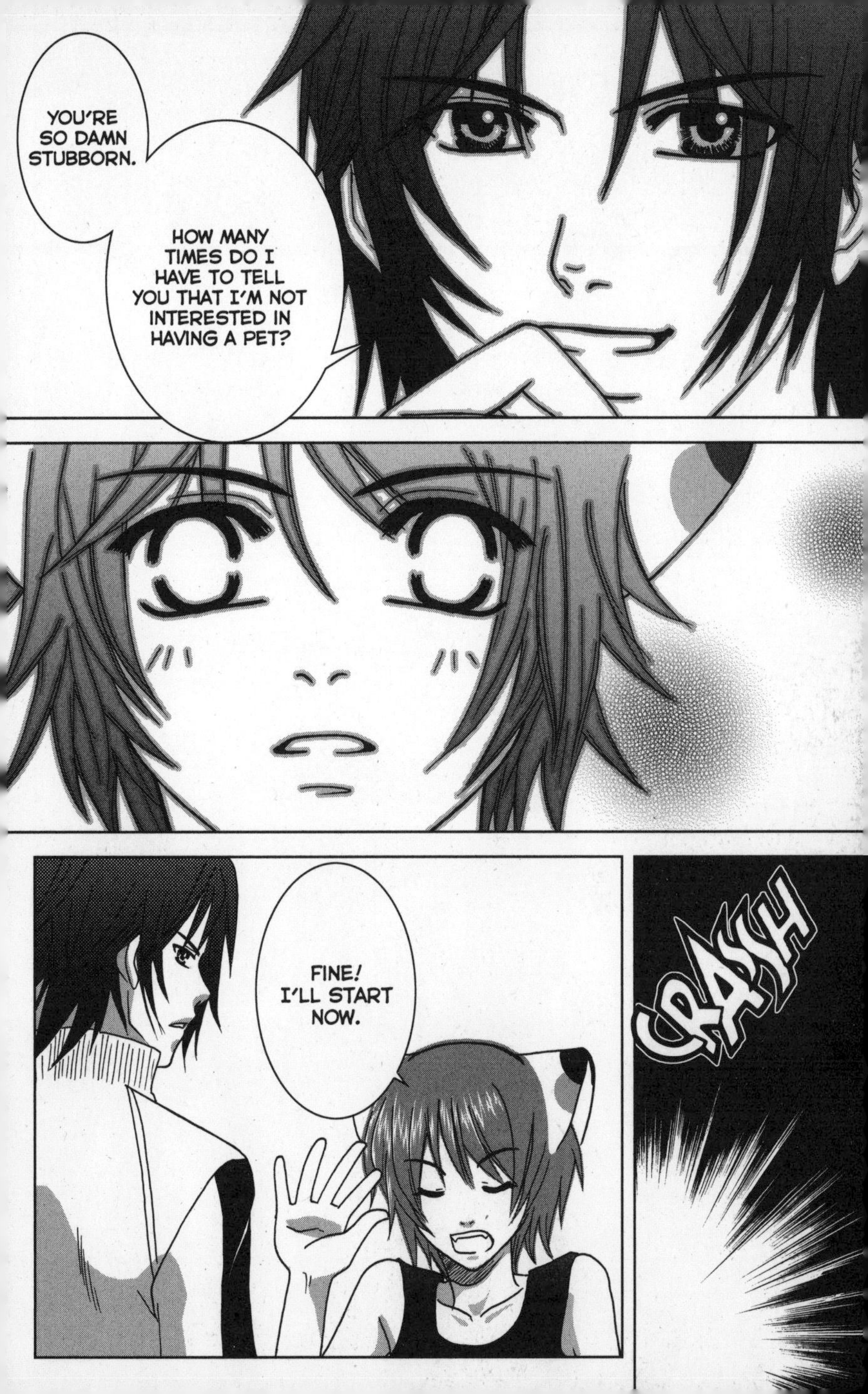
YOU'RE SO DAMN STUBBORN.
HOW MANY TIMES DO I HAVE TO TELL YOU THAT I'M NOT INTERESTED IN HAVING A PET?
CRASH
FINE! I'LL START NOW.

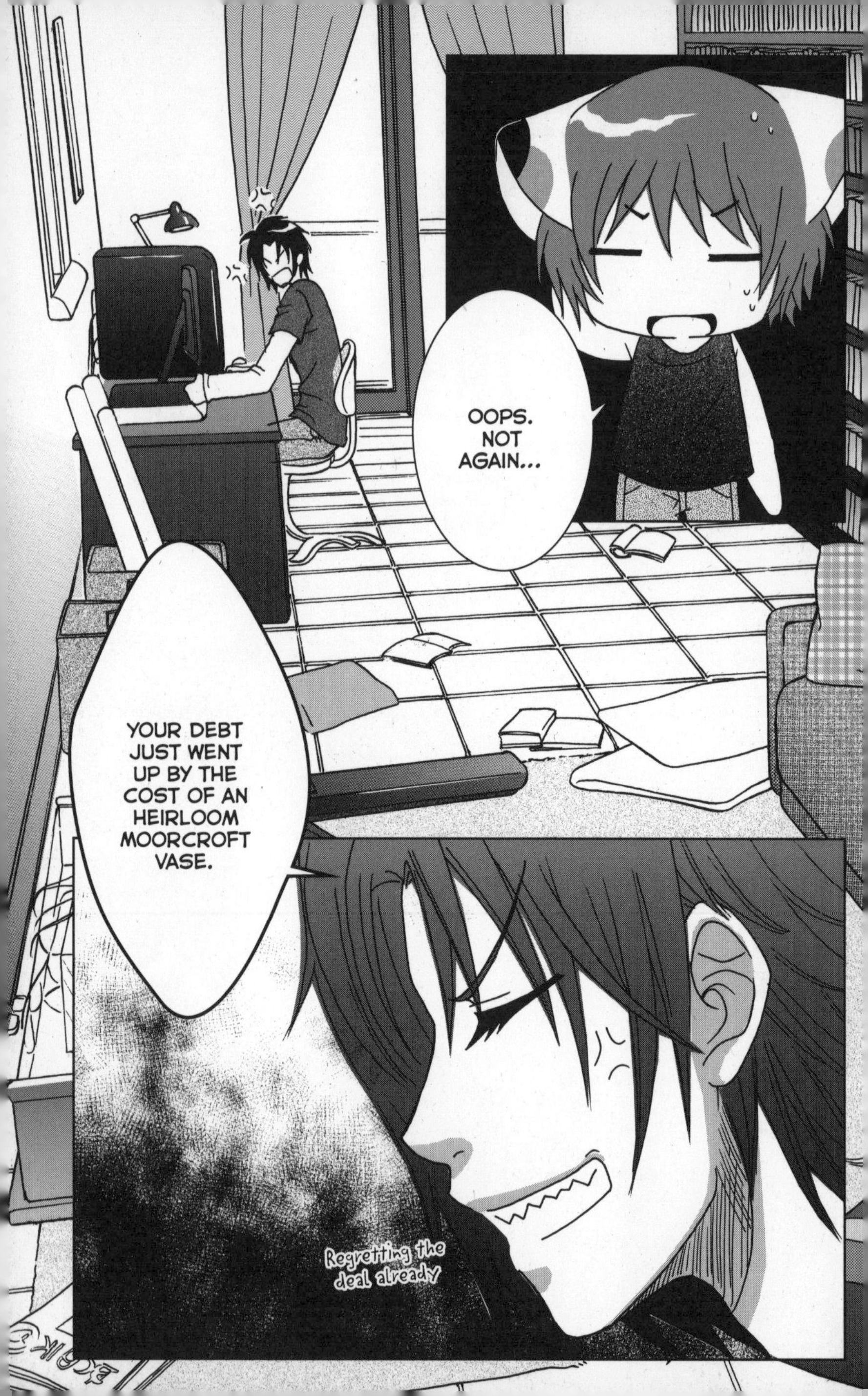
OOPS. NOT AGAIN...
YOUR DEBT JUST WENT UP BY THE COST OF AN HEIRLOOM MOORCROFT VASE.
Regretting the deal already

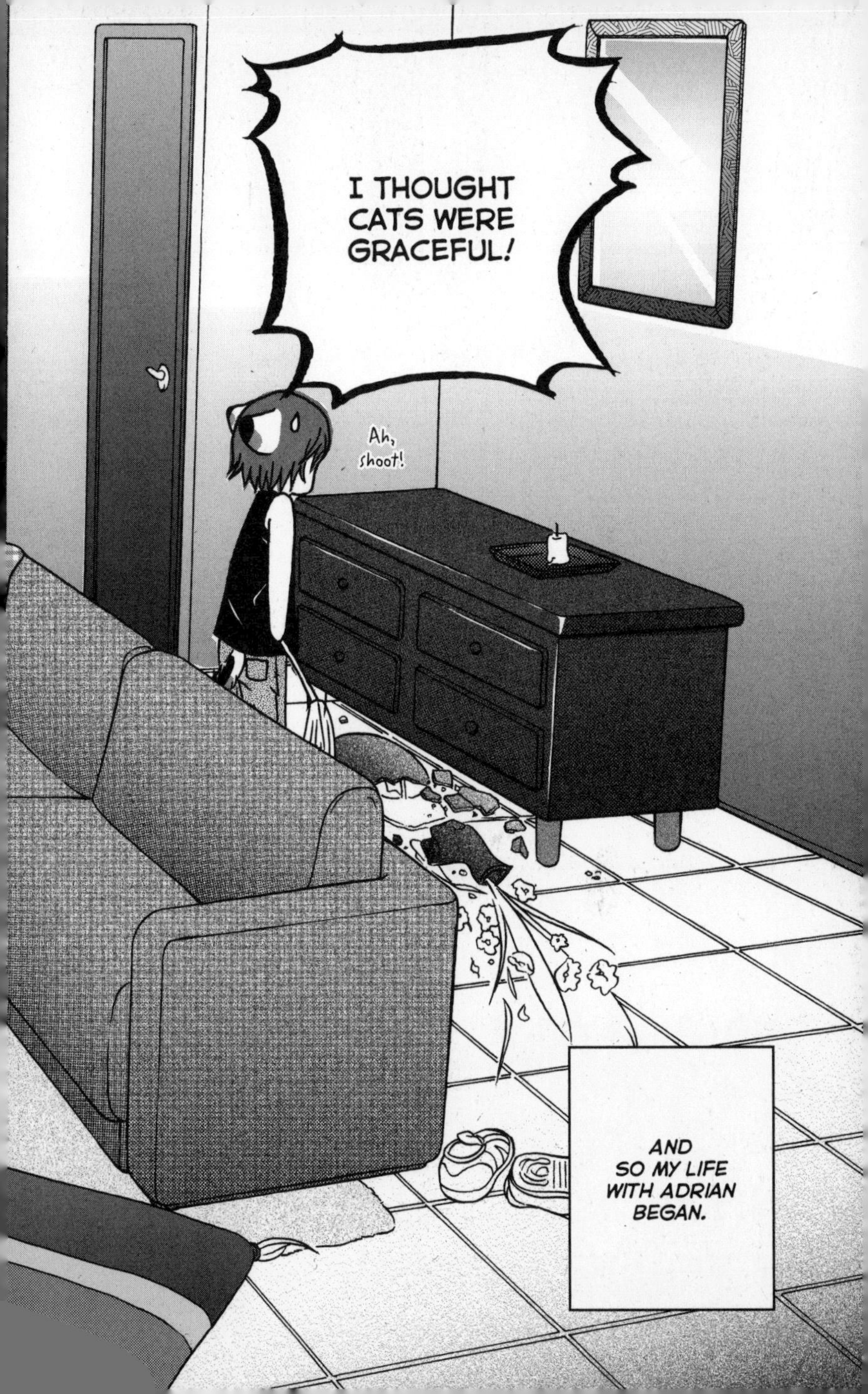
I THOUGHT CATS WERE GRACEFUL!
Ah, shoot!
AND SO MY LIFE WITH ADRIAN BEGAN.

Chapter Two: The Taming of Cat-Boy

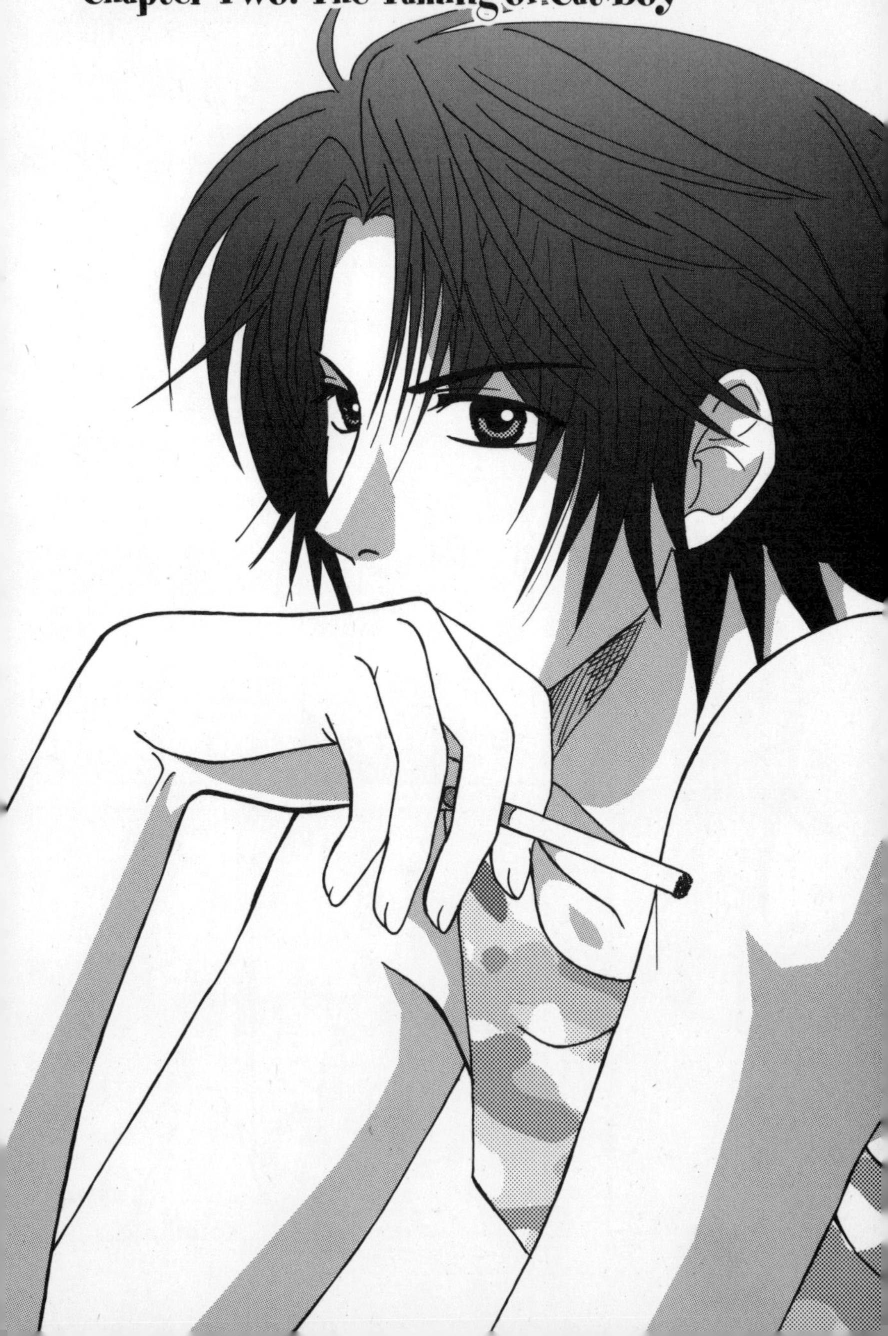

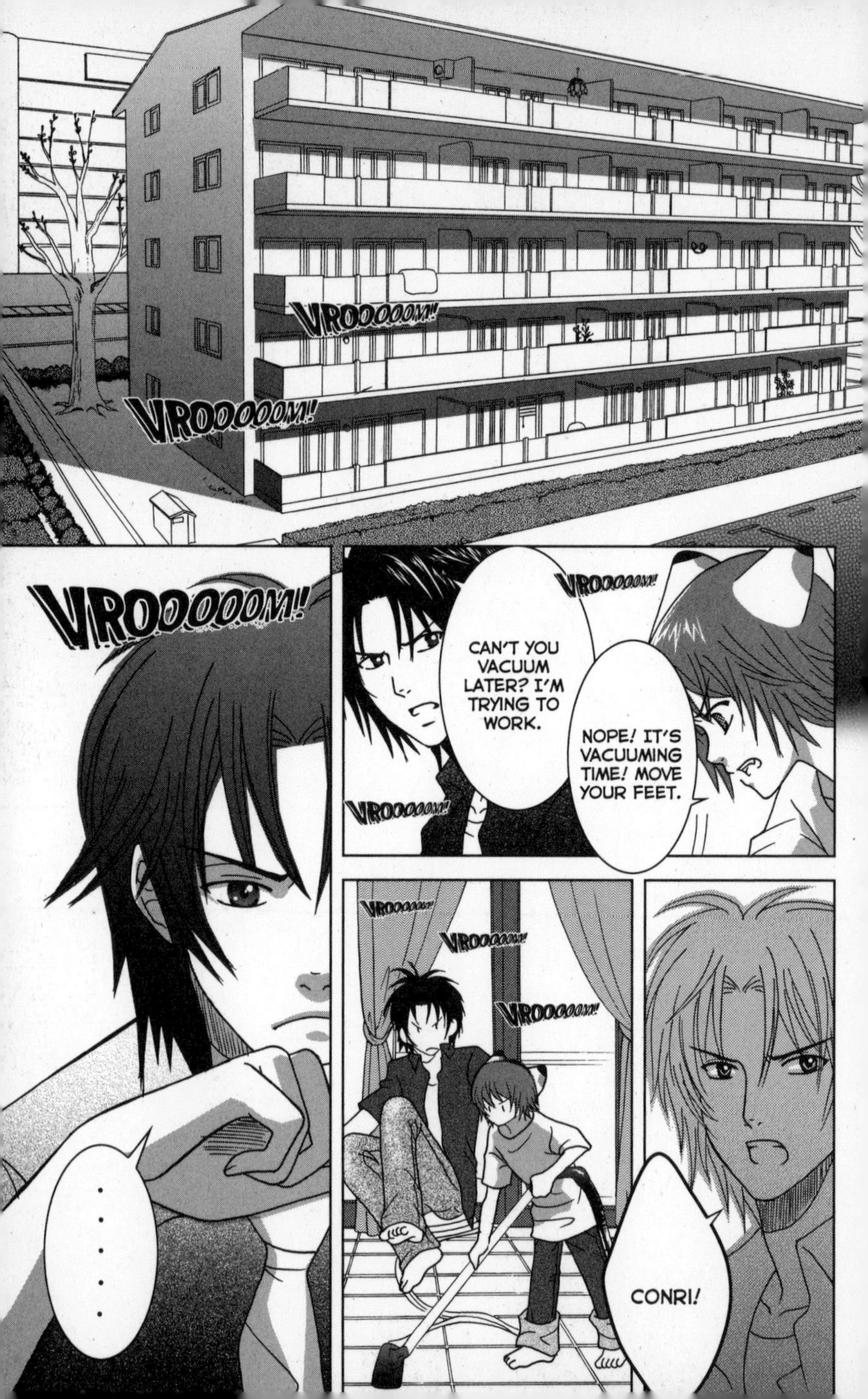
VROOOOOM!!
VROOOOOM!
VROOOOOM!!
...
VROOOOOM!!
CAN'T YOU VACUUM LATER? I'M TRYING TO WORK.
NOPE! IT'S VACUUMING TIME! MOVE YOUR FEET.
VROOOOOM!!
VROOOOOM!!
VROOOOOM!!
VROOOOOM!!
CONRI!

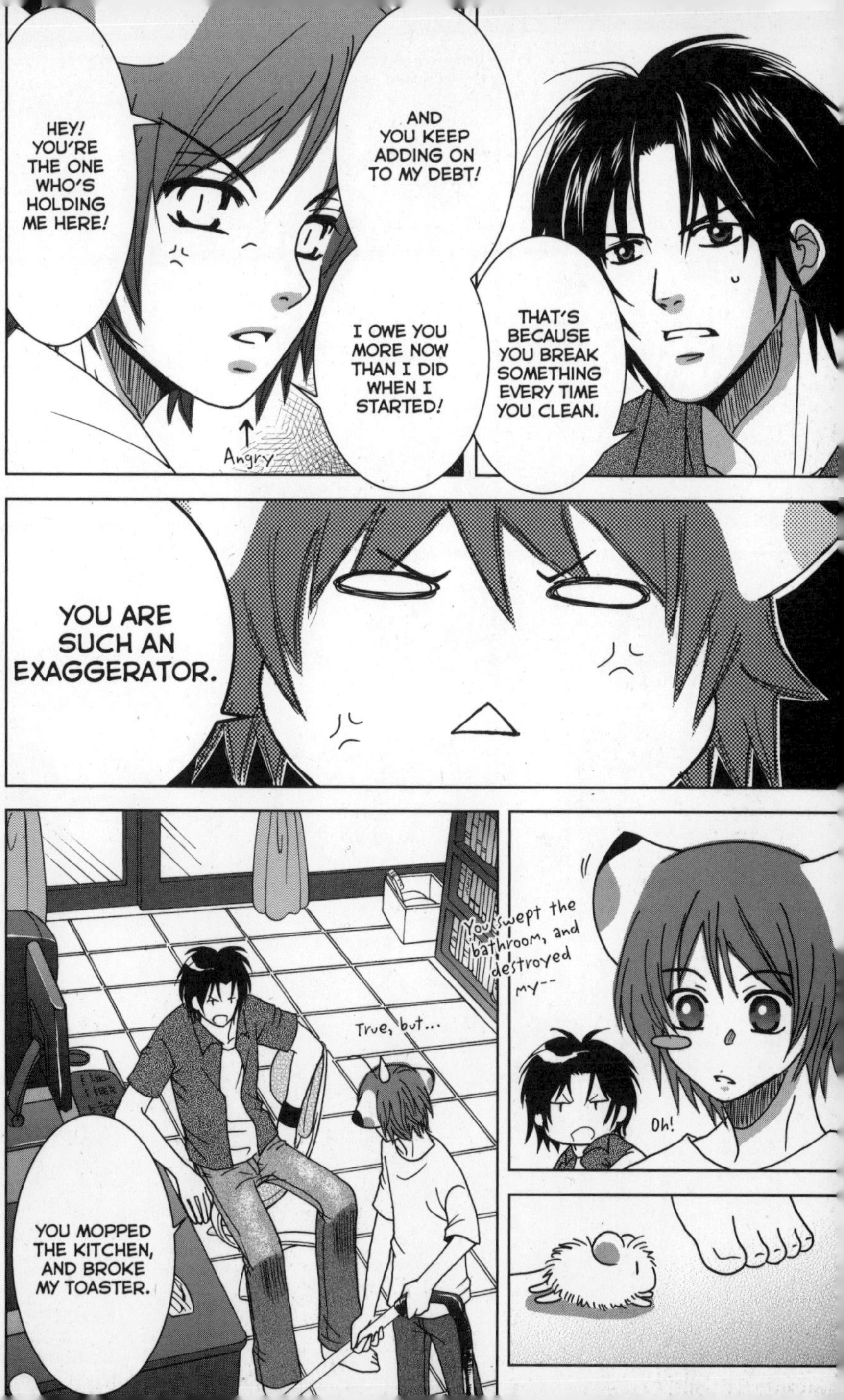
HEY! YOU'RE THE ONE WHO'S HOLDING ME HERE!
Angry
AND YOU KEEP ADDING ON TO MY DEBT!
I OWE YOU MORE NOW THAN I DID WHEN I STARTED!
THAT'S BECAUSE YOU BREAK SOMETHING EVERY TIME YOU CLEAN.
YOU ARE SUCH AN EXAGGERATOR.
YOU MOPPED THE KITCHEN, AND BROKE MY TOASTER.
True, but...
You swept the bathroom, and destroyed my--
Oh!

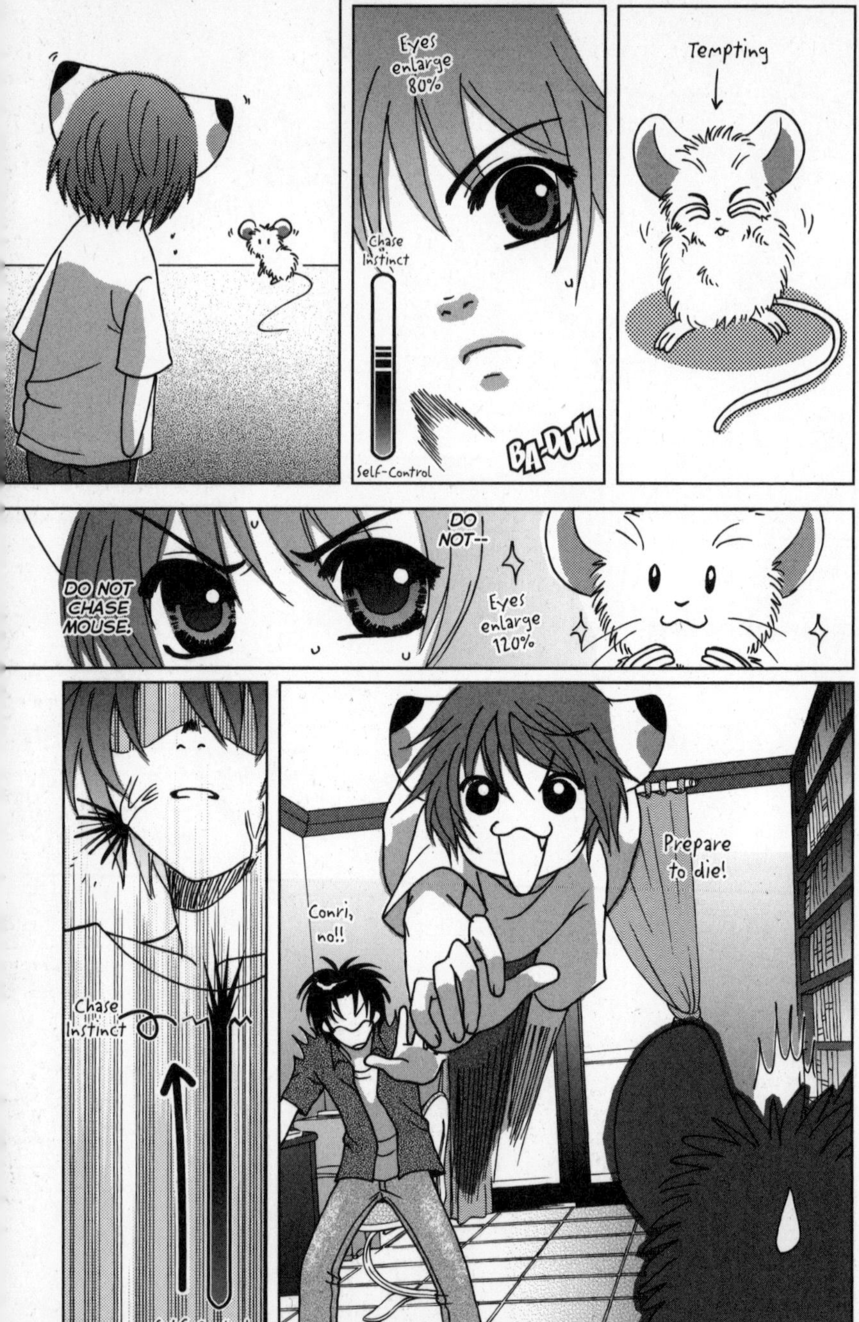
Eyes
enlarge
80%
Chase
Instinct
Self-Control
BA-DUM
Tempting
DO NOT
CHASE
MOUSE.
DO
NOT--
Eyes
enlarge
120%
Chase
Instinct
Self-Control
Conri,
no!!
Prepare
to die!

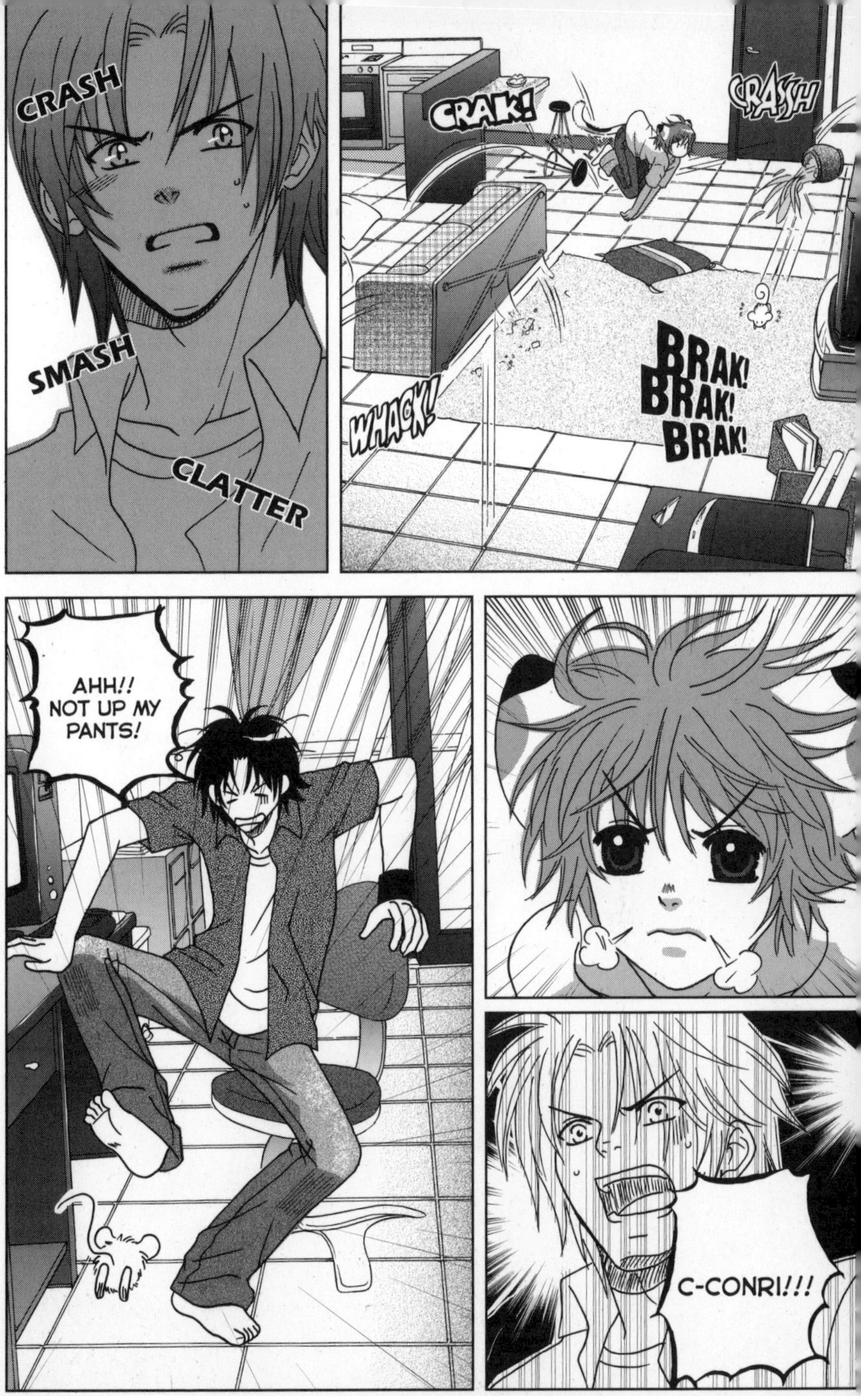
CRASH
SMASH
CLATTER
CRAK!
CRASH
WHACK!
BRAK!
BRAK!
BRAK!
AHH!! NOT UP MY PANTS!
C-CONRI!!!

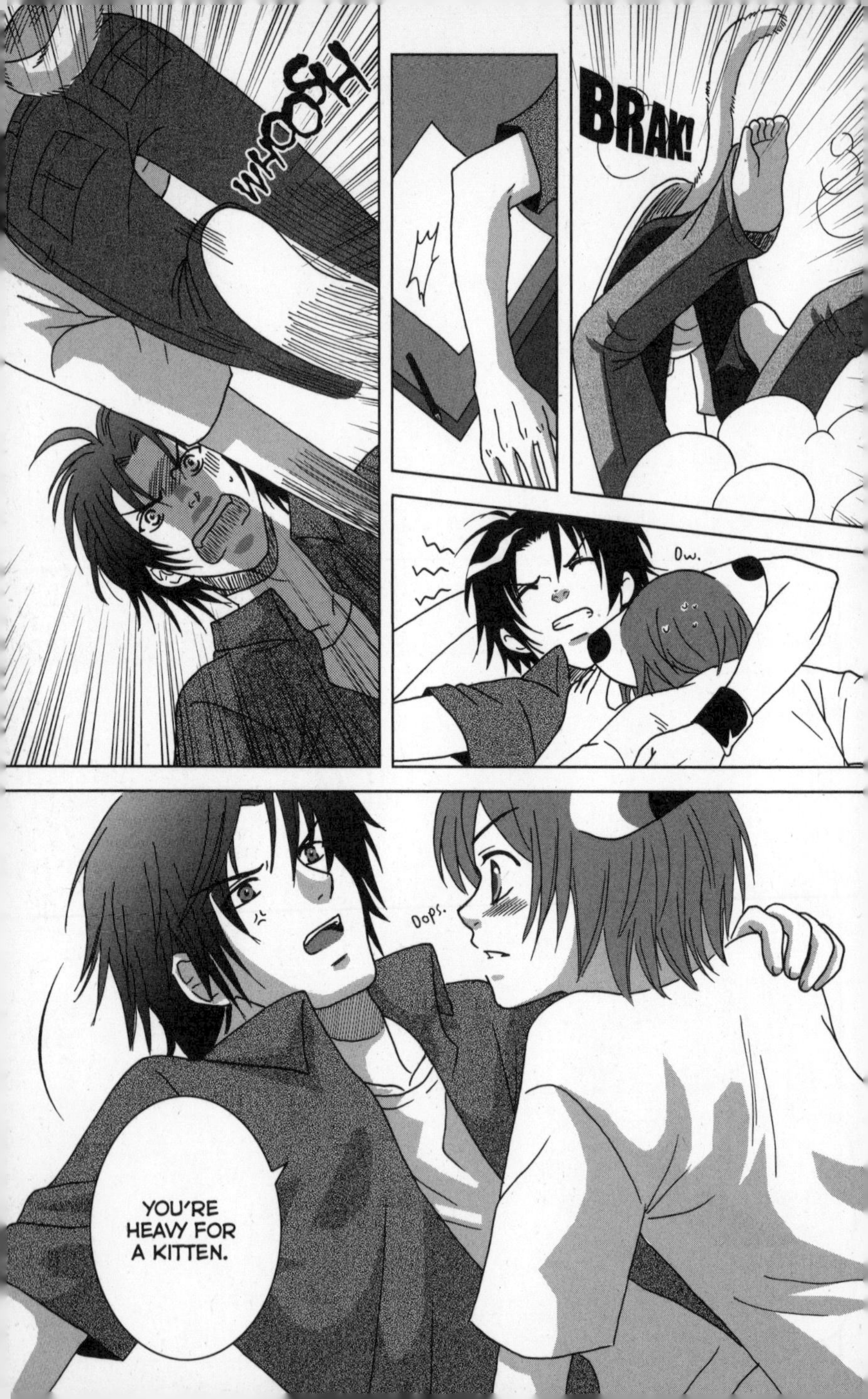
WHOOSH
BRAK!
Ow.
Oops.
YOU'RE HEAVY FOR A KITTEN.

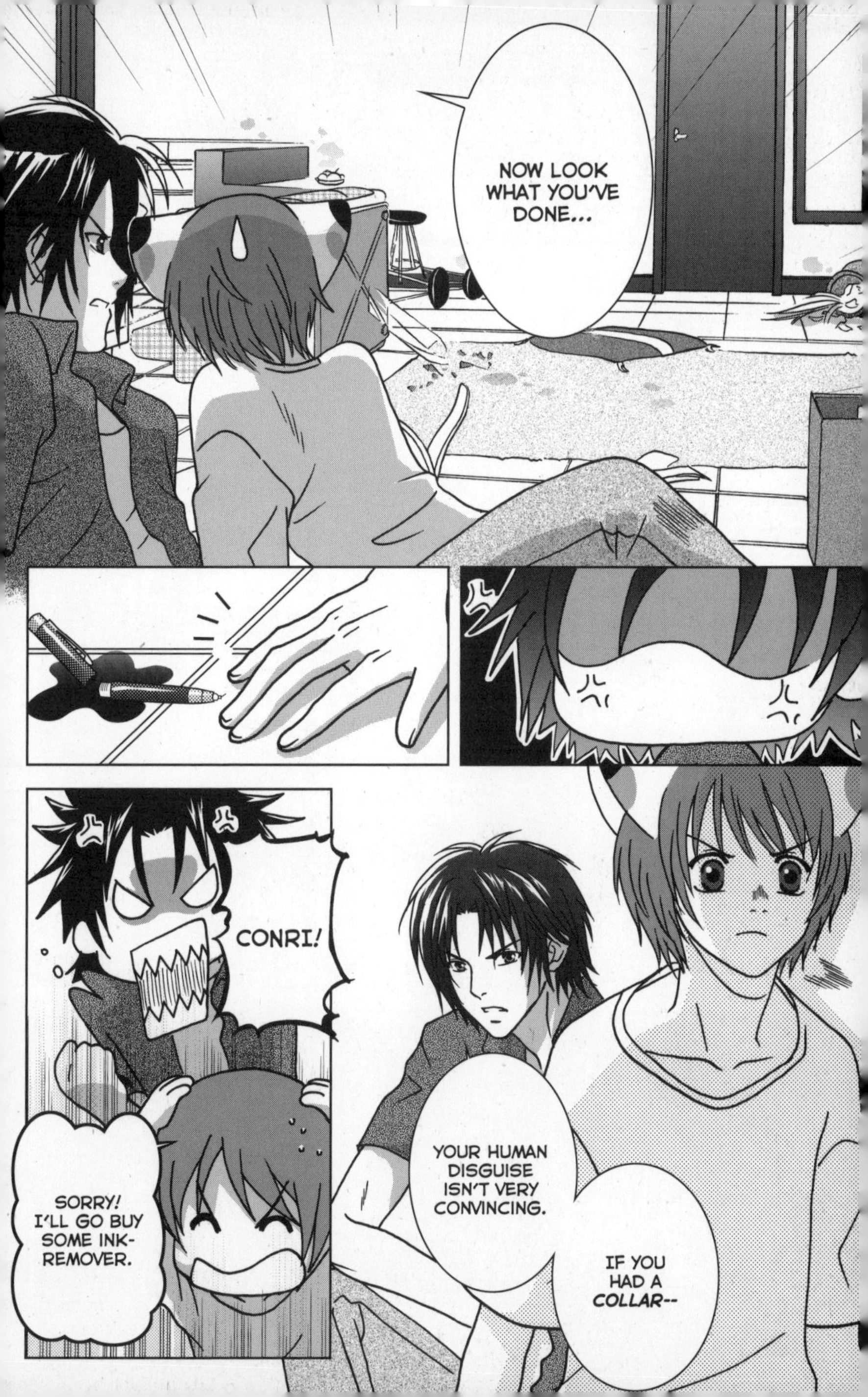
NOW LOOK WHAT YOU'VE DONE...
YOUR HUMAN DISGUISE ISN'T VERY CONVINCING.
IF YOU HAD A *COLLAR*--
CONRI!
SORRY! I'LL GO BUY SOME INK-REMOVER.

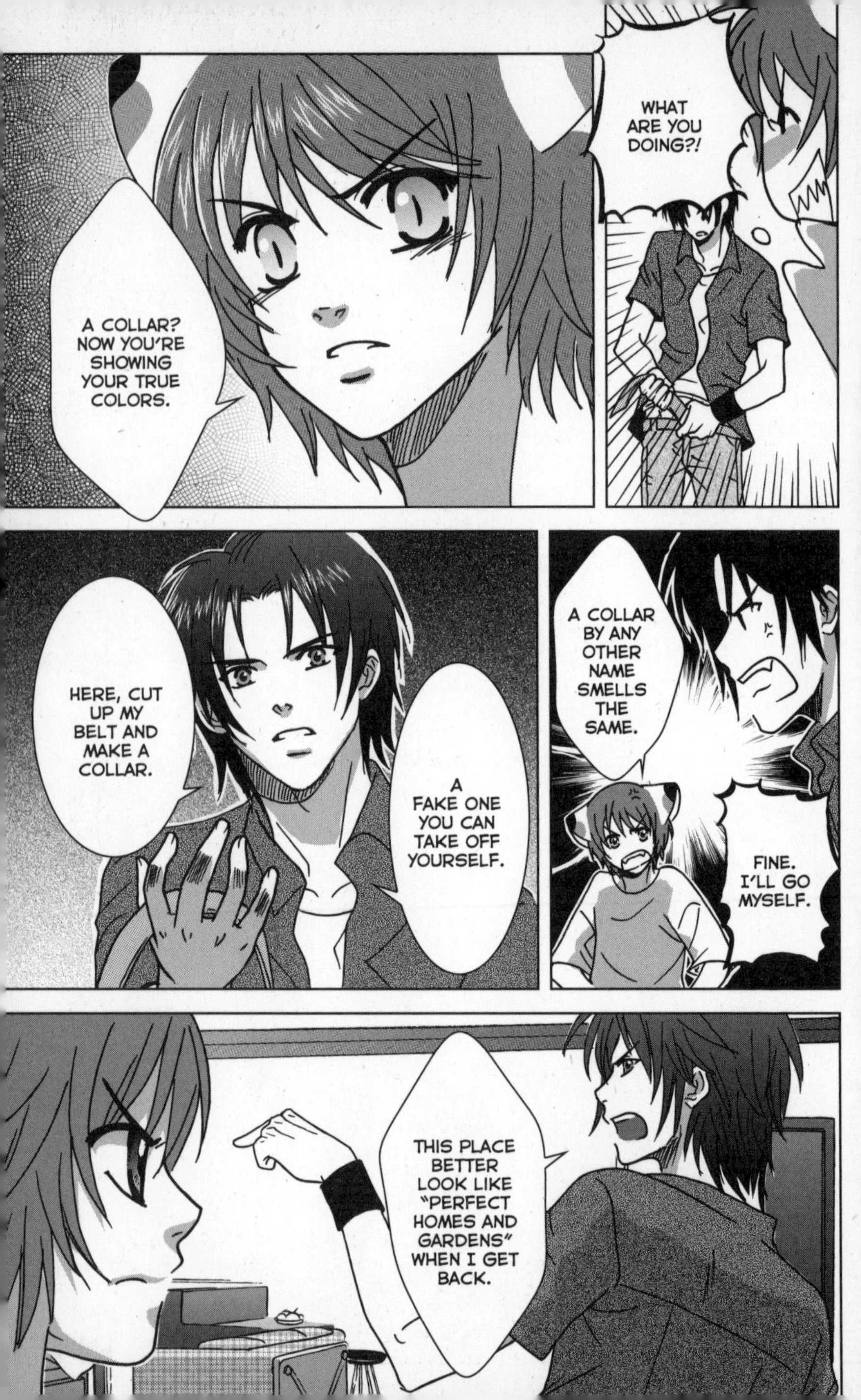

A COLLAR? NOW YOU'RE SHOWING YOUR TRUE COLORS.
WHAT ARE YOU DOING?!
HERE, CUT UP MY BELT AND MAKE A COLLAR.
A FAKE ONE YOU CAN TAKE OFF YOURSELF.
A COLLAR BY ANY OTHER NAME SMELLS THE SAME.
FINE. I'LL GO MYSELF.
THIS PLACE BETTER LOOK LIKE "PERFECT HOMES AND GARDENS" WHEN I GET BACK.

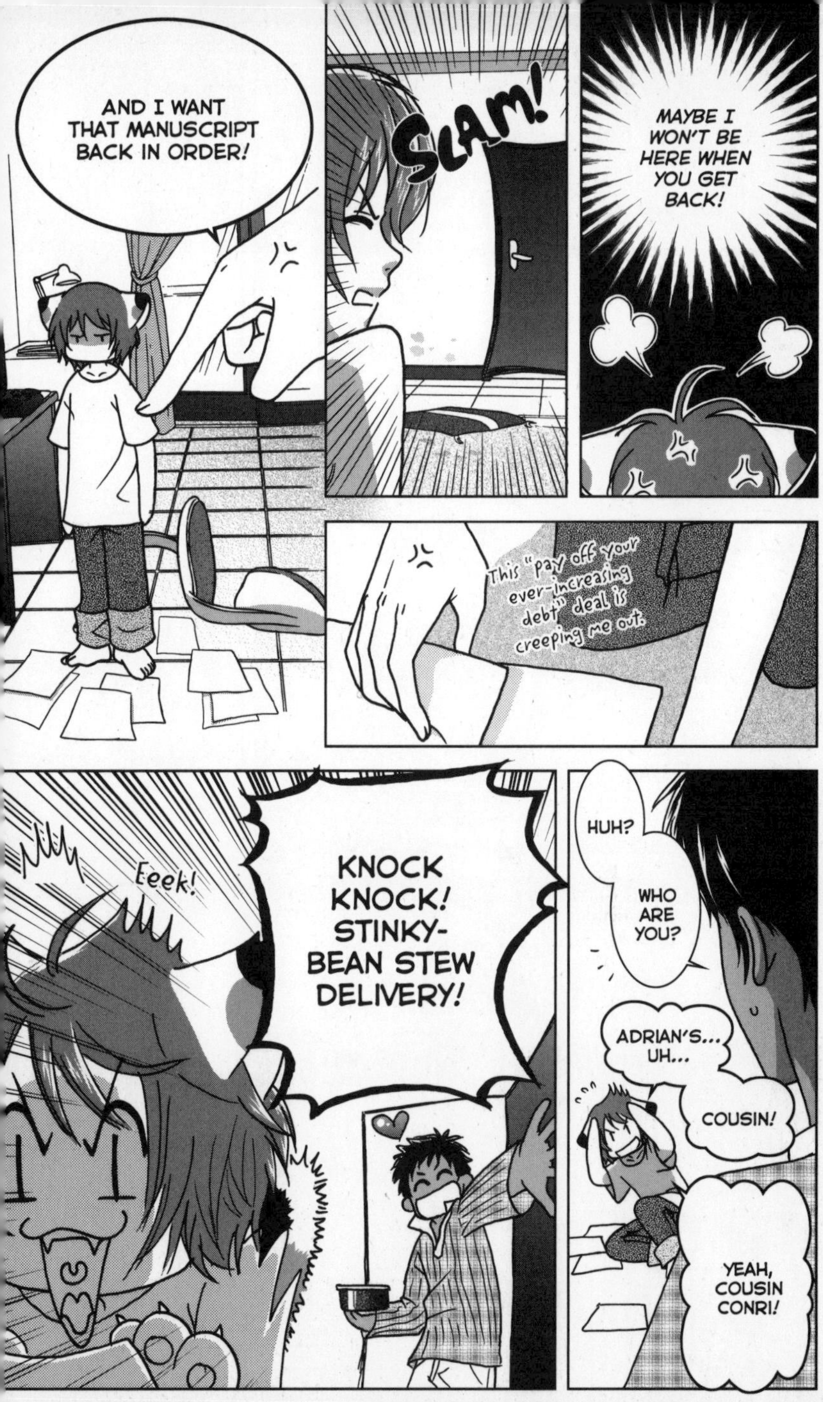
AND I WANT THAT MANUSCRIPT BACK IN ORDER!
SLAM!
MAYBE I WON'T BE HERE WHEN YOU GET BACK!
This "pay off your ever-increasing debt" deal is creeping me out.
Eeek!
KNOCK KNOCK! STINKY-BEAN STEW DELIVERY!
HUH?
WHO ARE YOU?
ADRIAN'S... UH...
COUSIN!
YEAH, COUSIN CONRI!

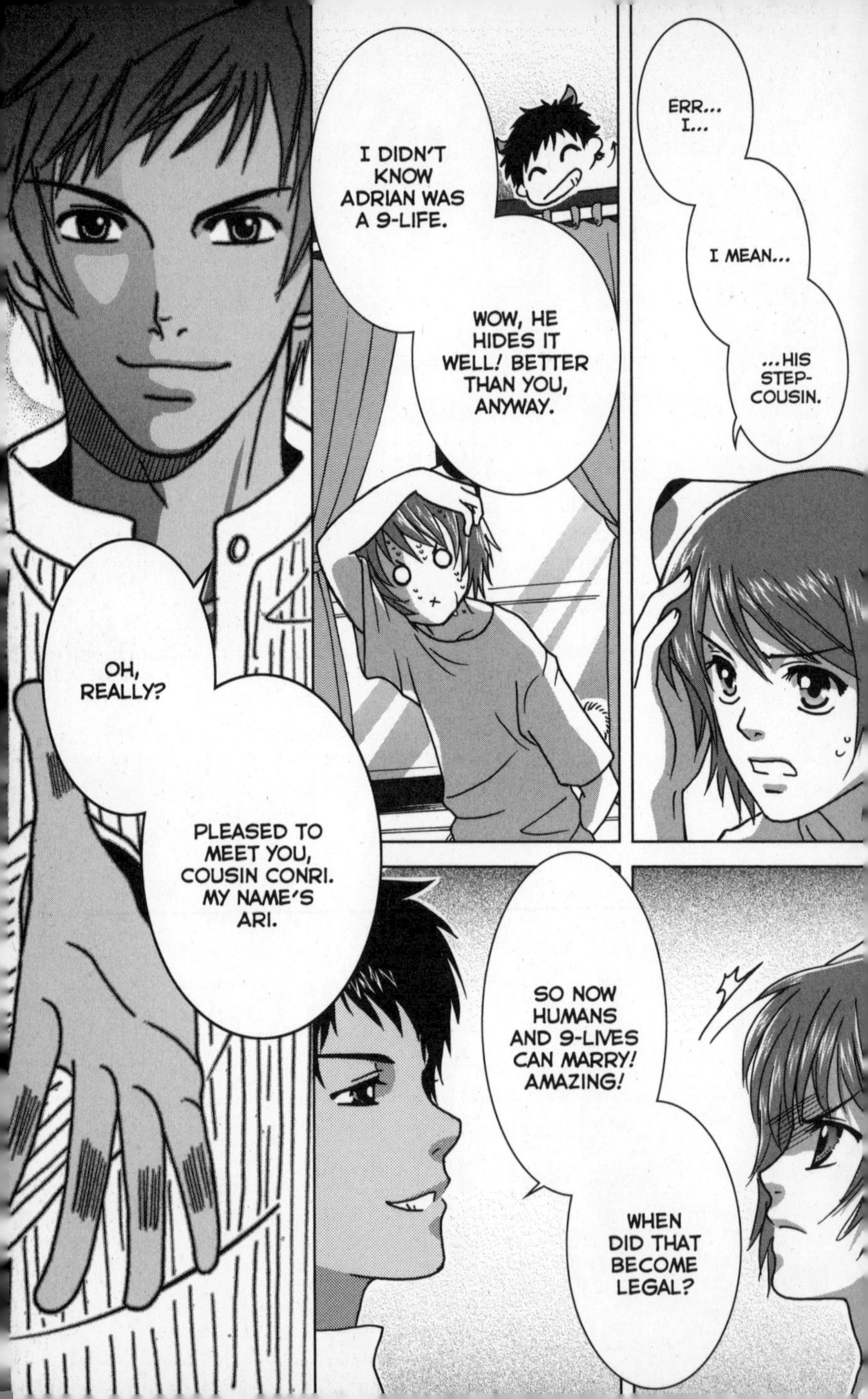
OH, REALLY?
PLEASED TO MEET YOU, COUSIN CONRI. MY NAME'S ARI.
I DIDN'T KNOW ADRIAN WAS A 9-LIFE.
WOW, HE HIDES IT WELL! BETTER THAN YOU, ANYWAY.
ERR... I...
I MEAN...
...HIS STEP-COUSIN.
SO NOW HUMANS AND 9-LIVES CAN MARRY! AMAZING!
WHEN DID THAT BECOME LEGAL?

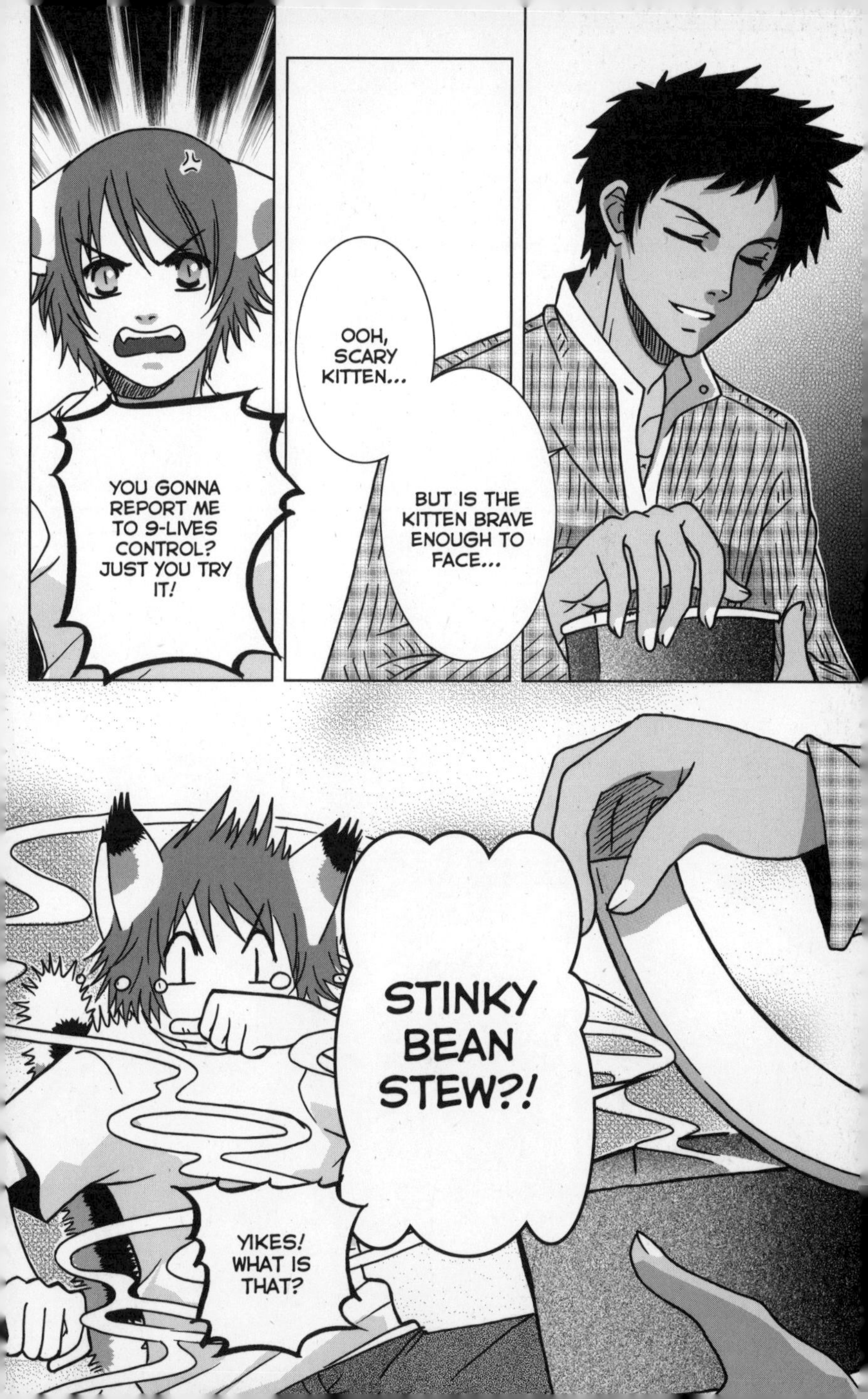
YOU GONNA REPORT ME TO 9-LIVES CONTROL? JUST YOU TRY IT!
OOH, SCARY KITTEN...
BUT IS THE KITTEN BRAVE ENOUGH TO FACE...
STINKY BEAN STEW?!
YIKES! WHAT IS THAT?

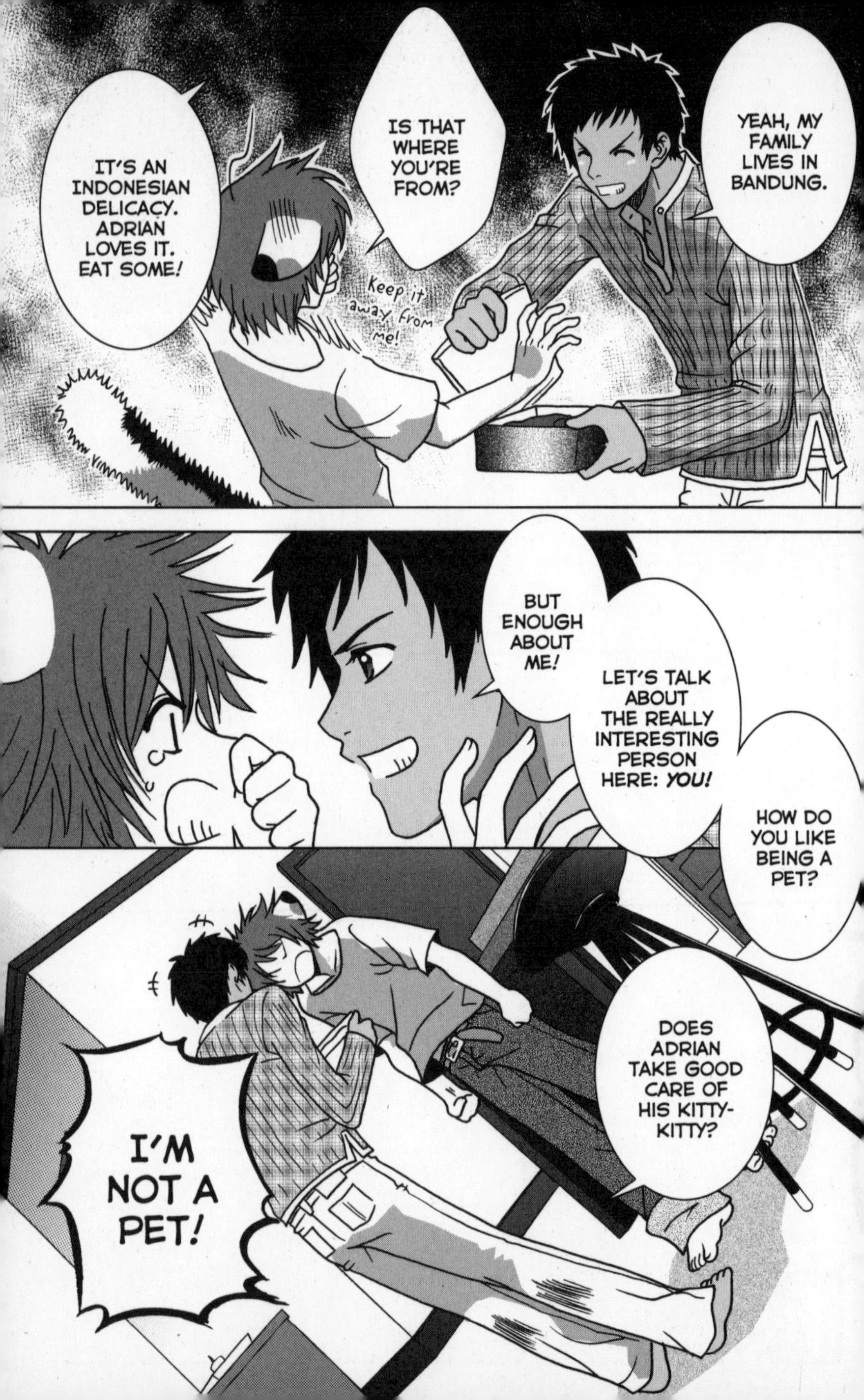
IT'S AN INDONESIAN DELICACY. ADRIAN LOVES IT. EAT SOME!
Keep it away from me!
IS THAT WHERE YOU'RE FROM?
YEAH, MY FAMILY LIVES IN BANDUNG.
BUT ENOUGH ABOUT ME!
LET'S TALK ABOUT THE REALLY INTERESTING PERSON HERE: *YOU!*
HOW DO YOU LIKE BEING A PET?
DOES ADRIAN TAKE GOOD CARE OF HIS KITTY-KITTY?
I'M NOT A PET!

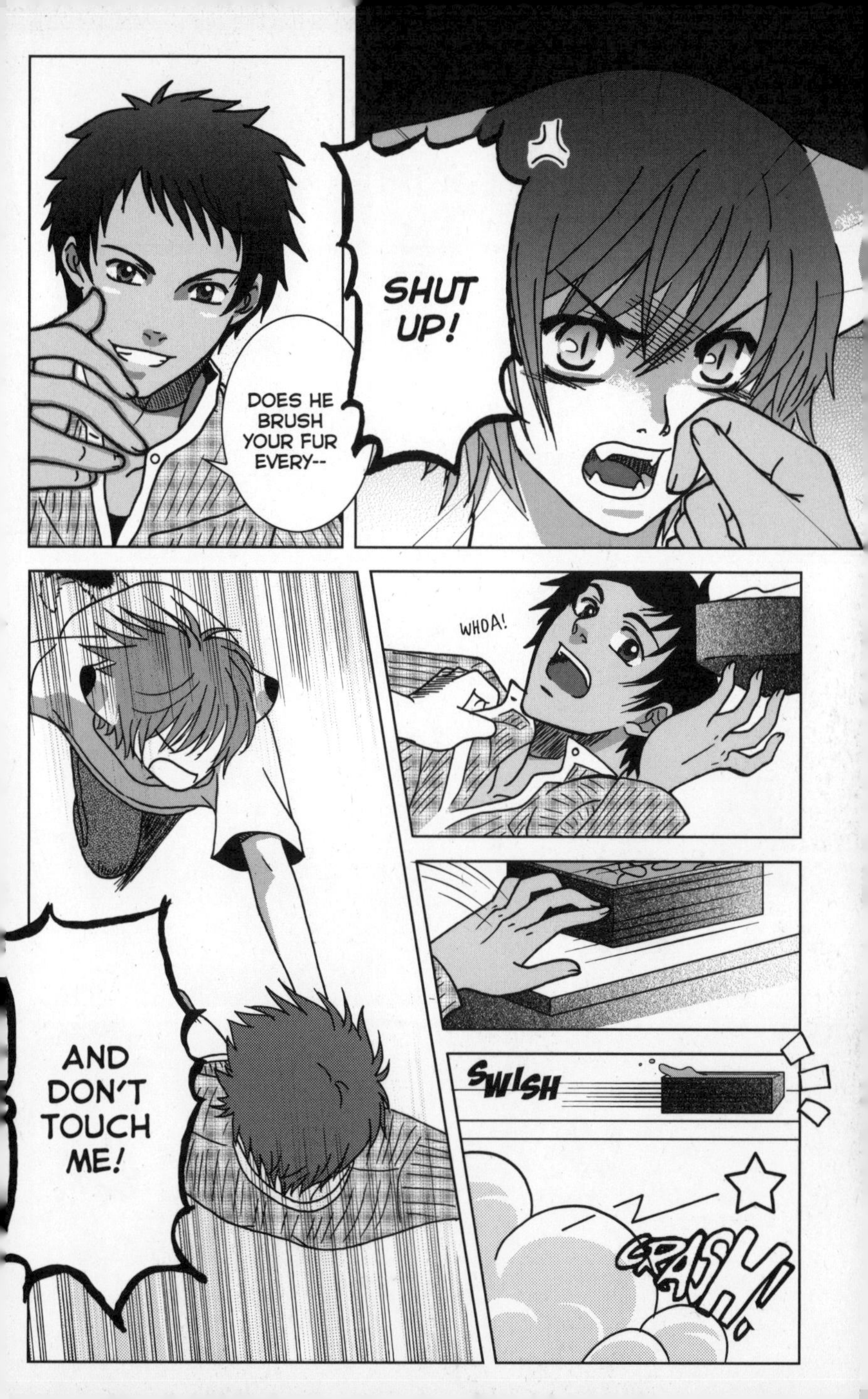
DOES HE BRUSH YOUR FUR EVERY--
SHUT UP!
AND DON'T TOUCH ME!
WHOA!
SWISH
CRASH!

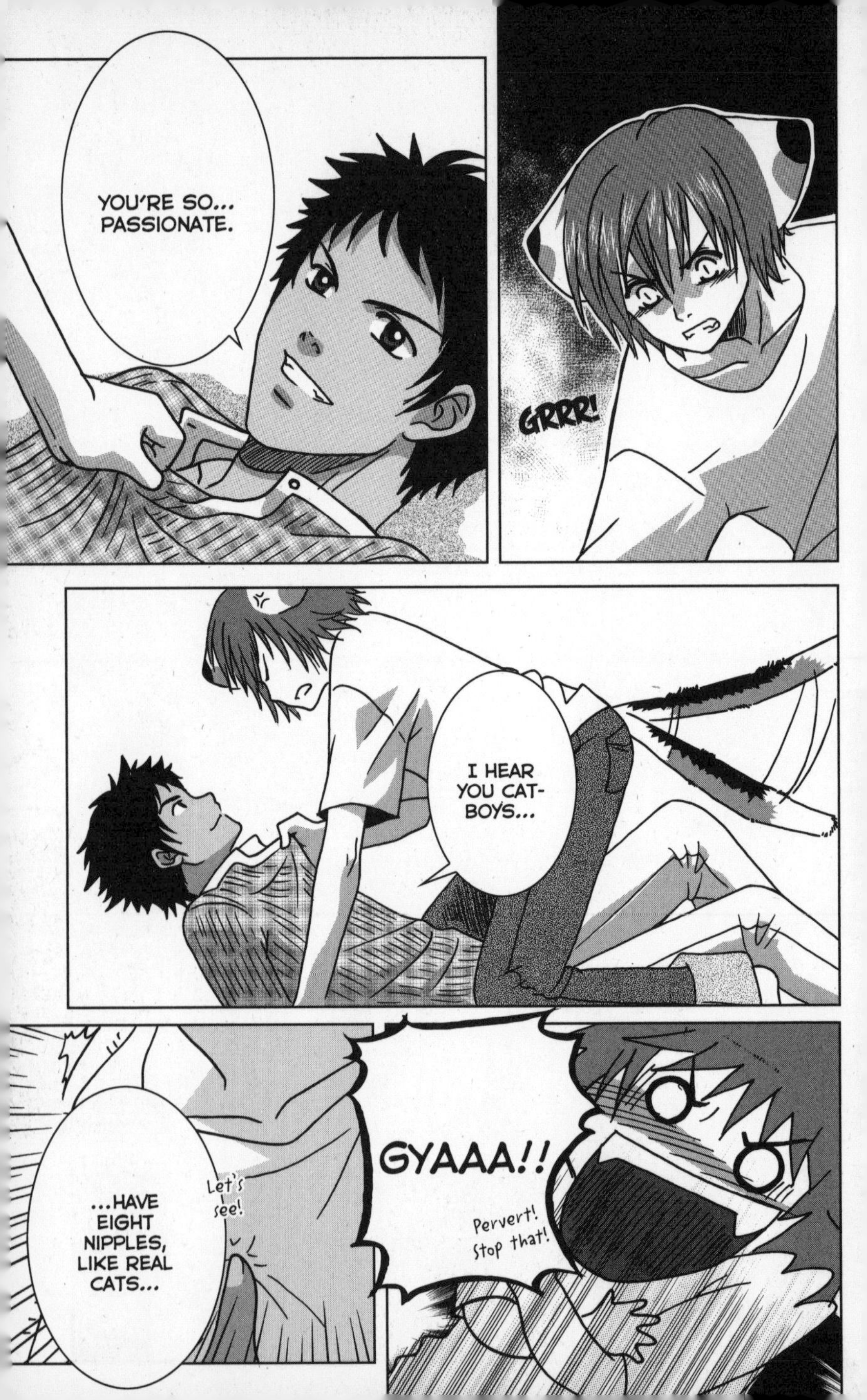

YOU'RE SO... PASSIONATE.
GRRR!
I HEAR YOU CAT-BOYS...
...HAVE EIGHT NIPPLES, LIKE REAL CATS...
Let's see!
GYAAA!!
Pervert! Stop that!

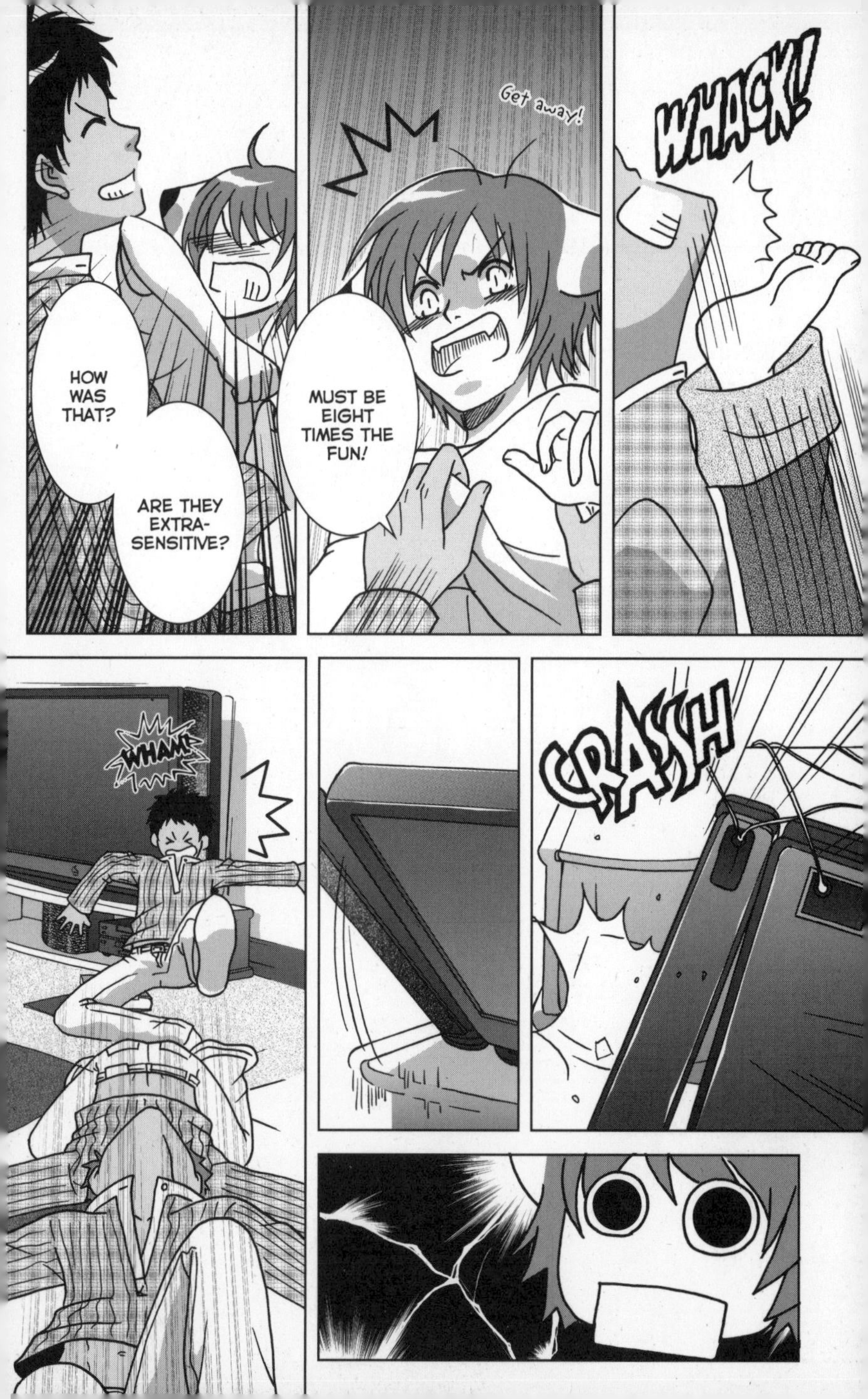
HOW WAS THAT?
ARE THEY EXTRA-SENSITIVE?
Get away!
MUST BE EIGHT TIMES THE FUN!
WHACK!
WHAM!
CRASH

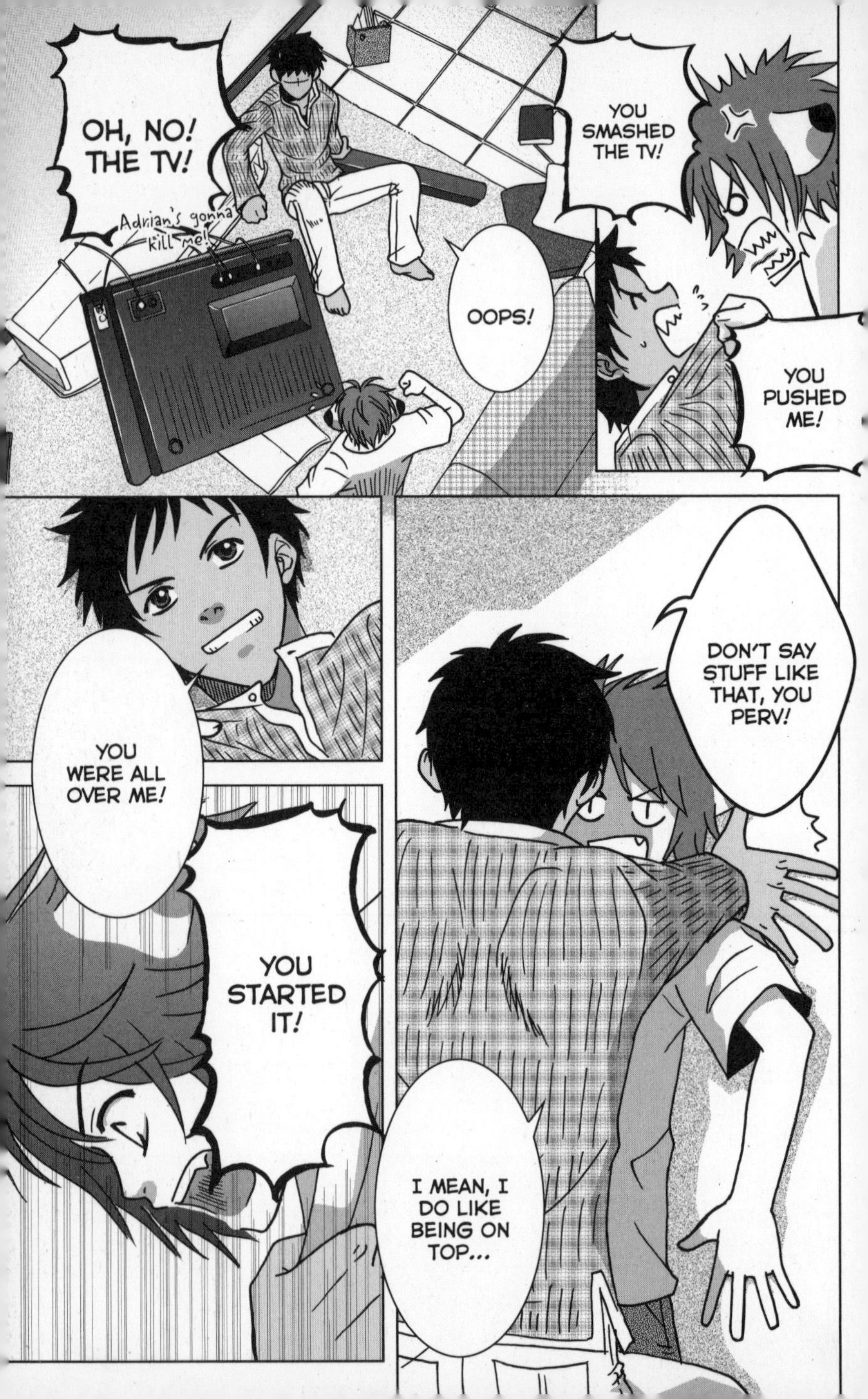
OH, NO! THE TV!
Adrian's gonna kill me!
OOPS!
YOU SMASHED THE TV!
YOU PUSHED ME!
YOU WERE ALL OVER ME!
YOU STARTED IT!
DON'T SAY STUFF LIKE THAT, YOU PERV!
I MEAN, I DO LIKE BEING ON TOP...

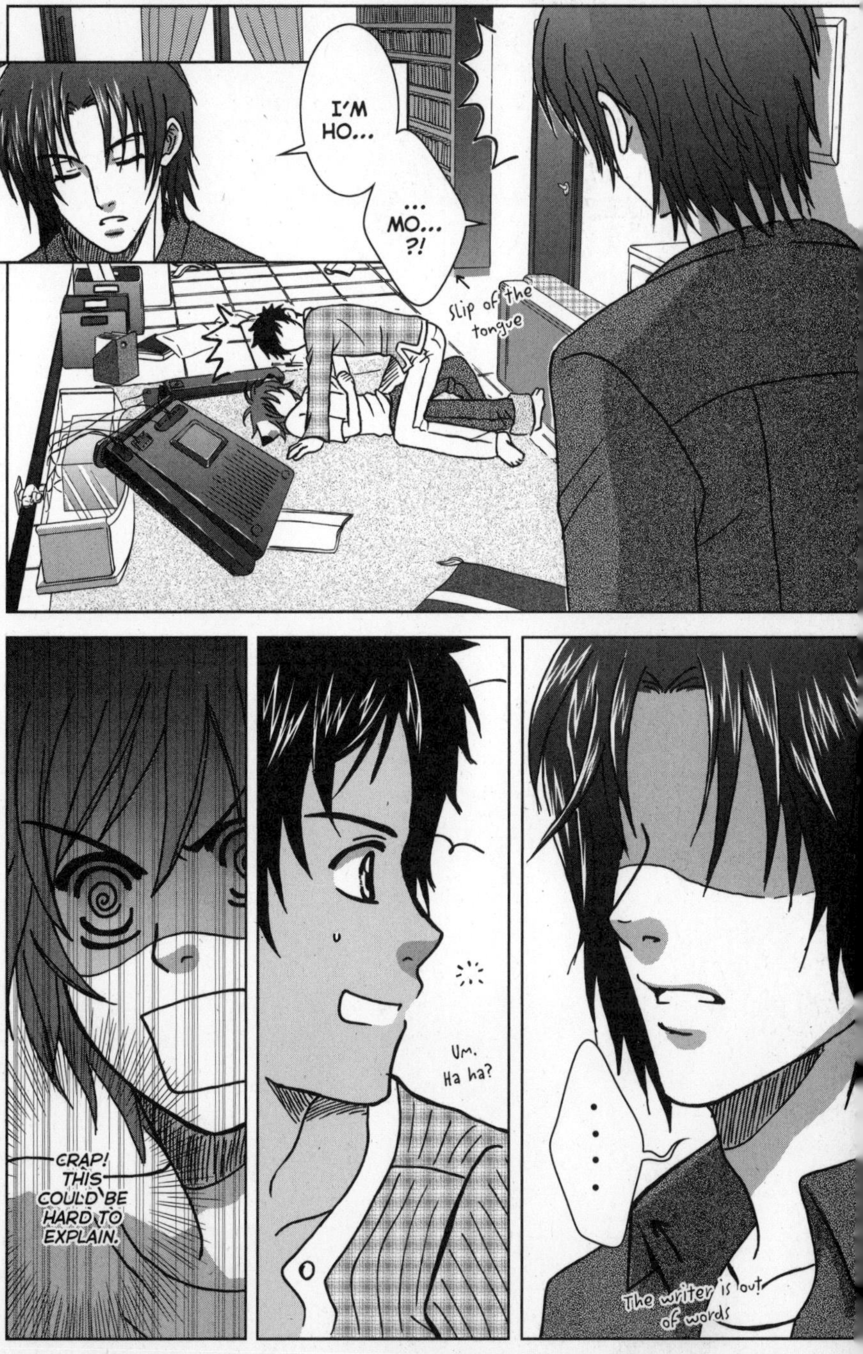
I'M HO...
... MO... ?!
Slip of the tongue
CRAP! THIS COULD BE HARD TO EXPLAIN.
Um. Ha ha?
....
The writer is out of words

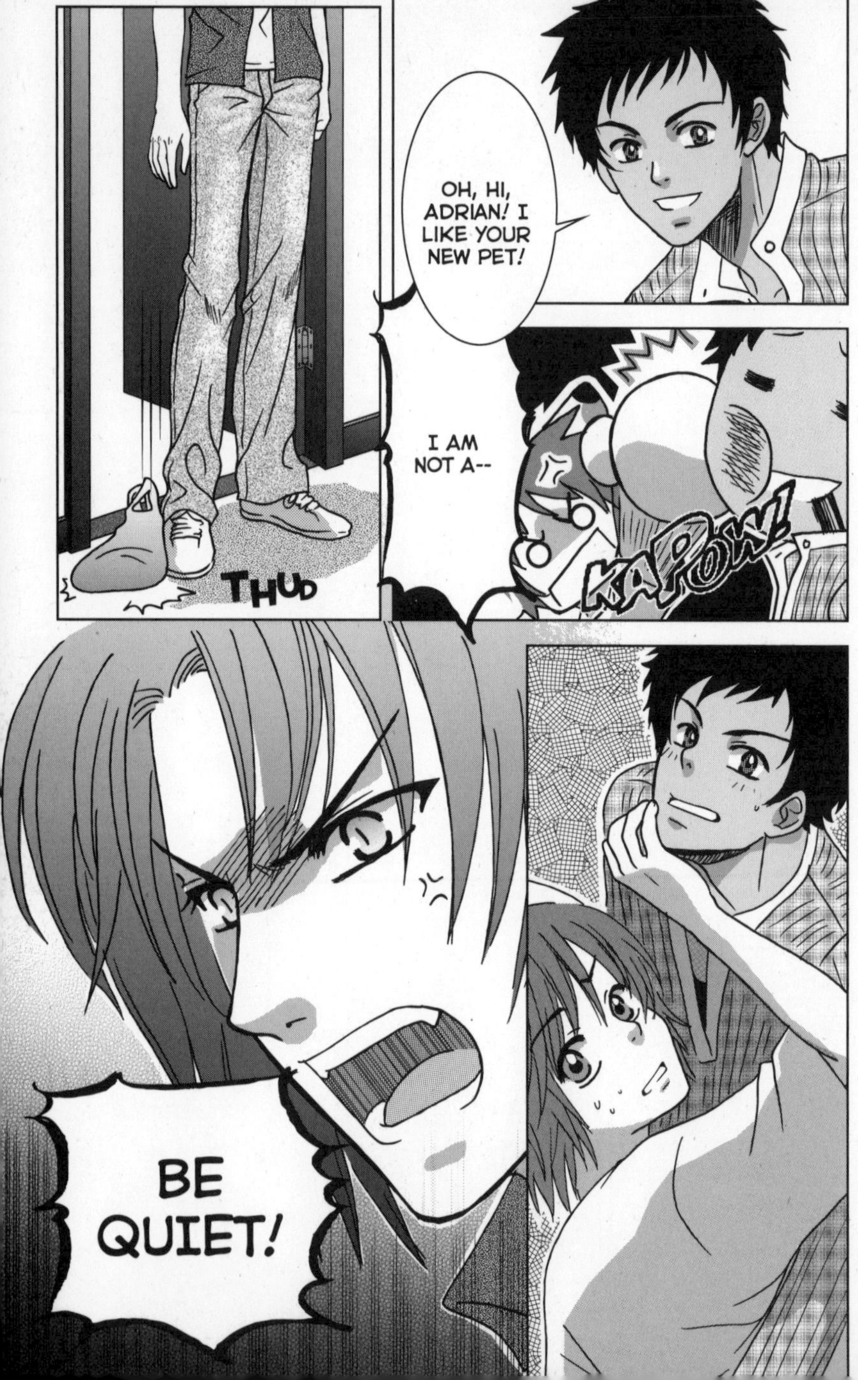
THUD
OH, HI, ADRIAN! I LIKE YOUR NEW PET!
I AM NOT A--
KAPOW!
BE QUIET!

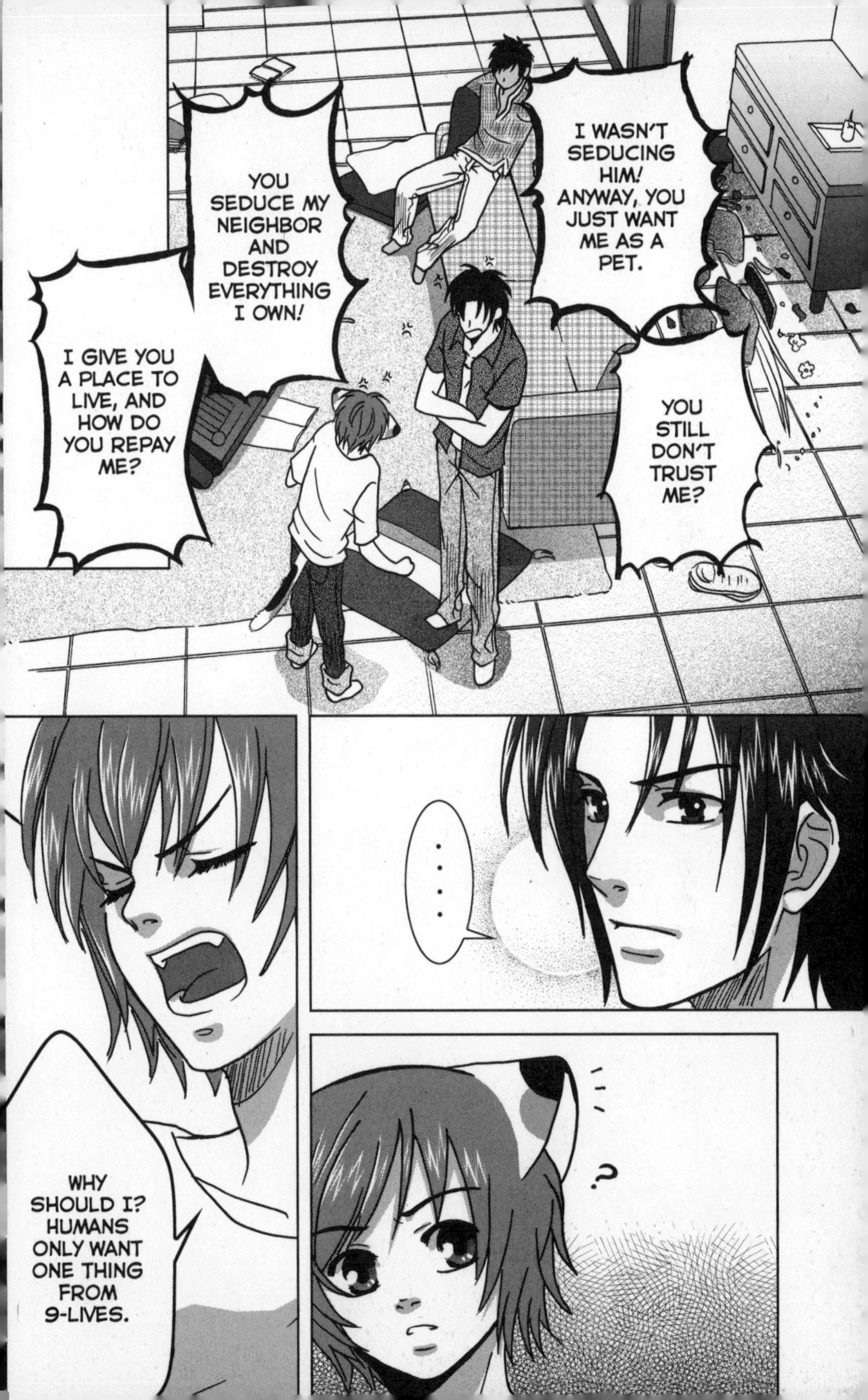
YOU SEDUCE MY NEIGHBOR AND DESTROY EVERYTHING I OWN!
I GIVE YOU A PLACE TO LIVE, AND HOW DO YOU REPAY ME?
I WASN'T SEDUCING HIM! ANYWAY, YOU JUST WANT ME AS A PET.
YOU STILL DON'T TRUST ME?
WHY SHOULD I? HUMANS ONLY WANT ONE THING FROM 9-LIVES.
....
?

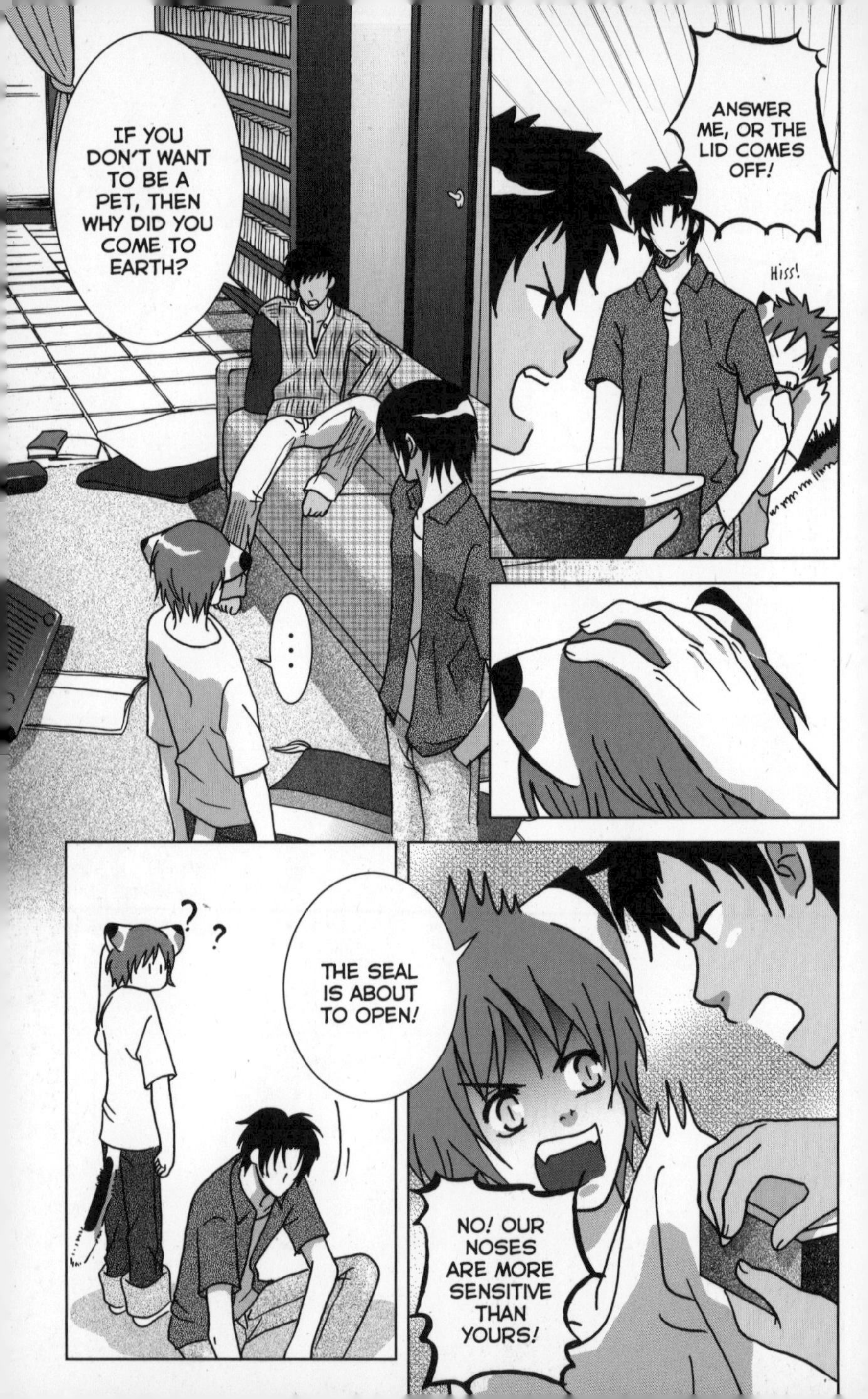
IF YOU DON'T WANT TO BE A PET, THEN WHY DID YOU COME TO EARTH?
...
ANSWER ME, OR THE LID COMES OFF!
Hiss!
??
THE SEAL IS ABOUT TO OPEN!
NO! OUR NOSES ARE MORE SENSITIVE THAN YOURS!

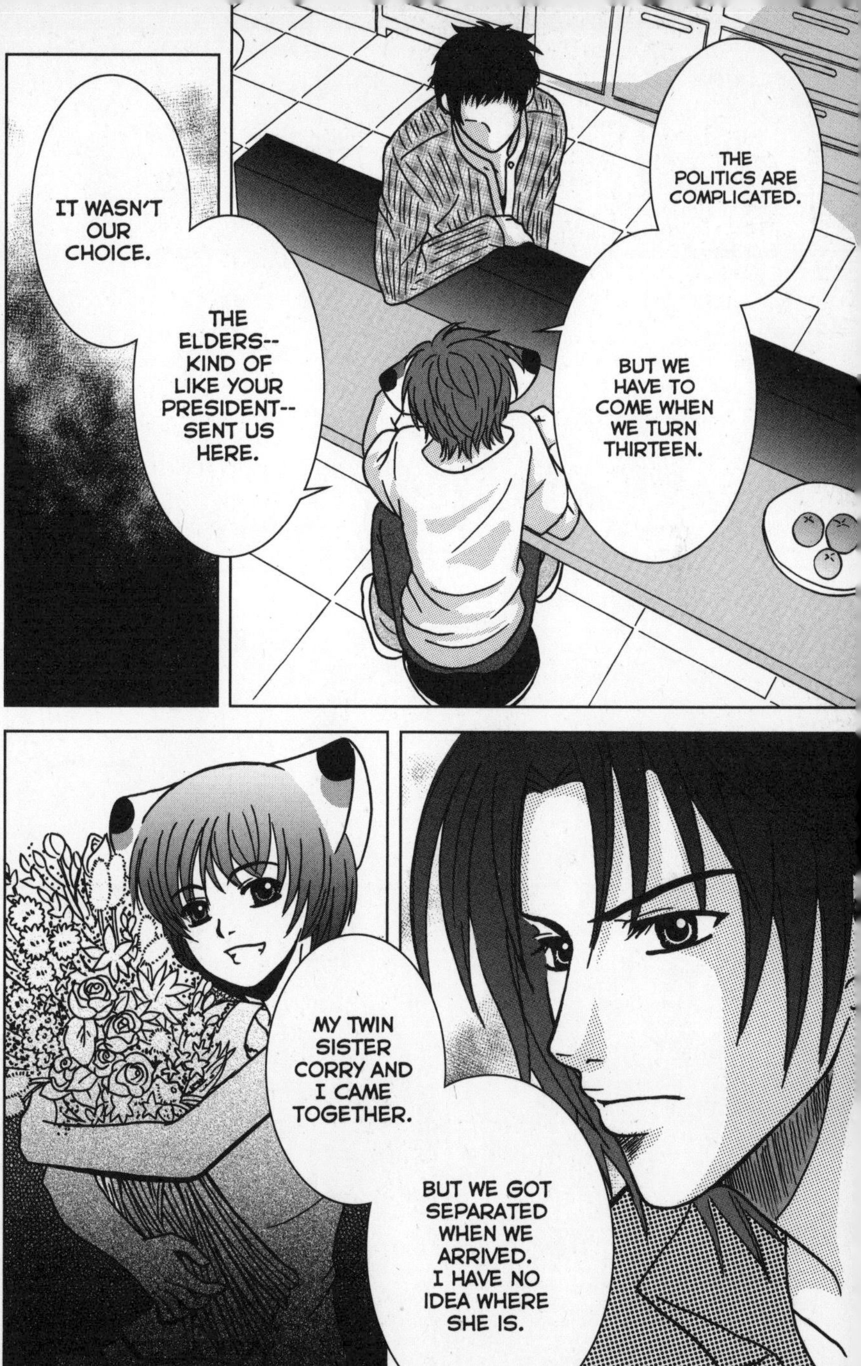
IT WASN'T OUR CHOICE.
THE ELDERS-- KIND OF LIKE YOUR PRESIDENT-- SENT US HERE.
THE POLITICS ARE COMPLICATED.
BUT WE HAVE TO COME WHEN WE TURN THIRTEEN.
MY TWIN SISTER CORRY AND I CAME TOGETHER.
BUT WE GOT SEPARATED WHEN WE ARRIVED. I HAVE NO IDEA WHERE SHE IS.

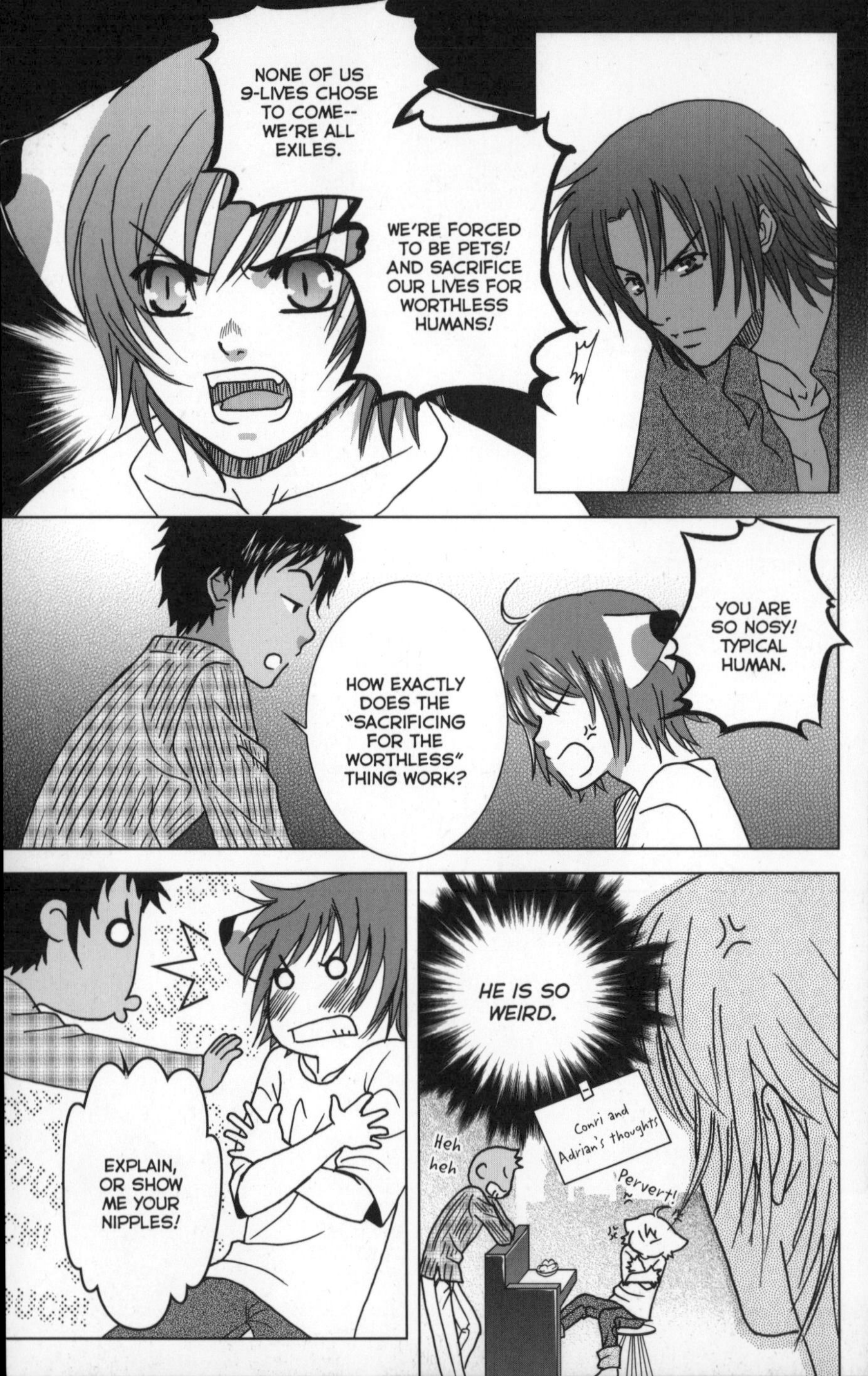
NONE OF US 9-LIVES CHOSE TO COME-- WE'RE ALL EXILES.
WE'RE FORCED TO BE PETS! AND SACRIFICE OUR LIVES FOR WORTHLESS HUMANS!
HOW EXACTLY DOES THE "SACRIFICING FOR THE WORTHLESS" THING WORK?
YOU ARE SO NOSY! TYPICAL HUMAN.
EXPLAIN, OR SHOW ME YOUR NIPPLES!
HE IS SO WEIRD.
Conri and Adrian's thoughts
Heh heh
Pervert!

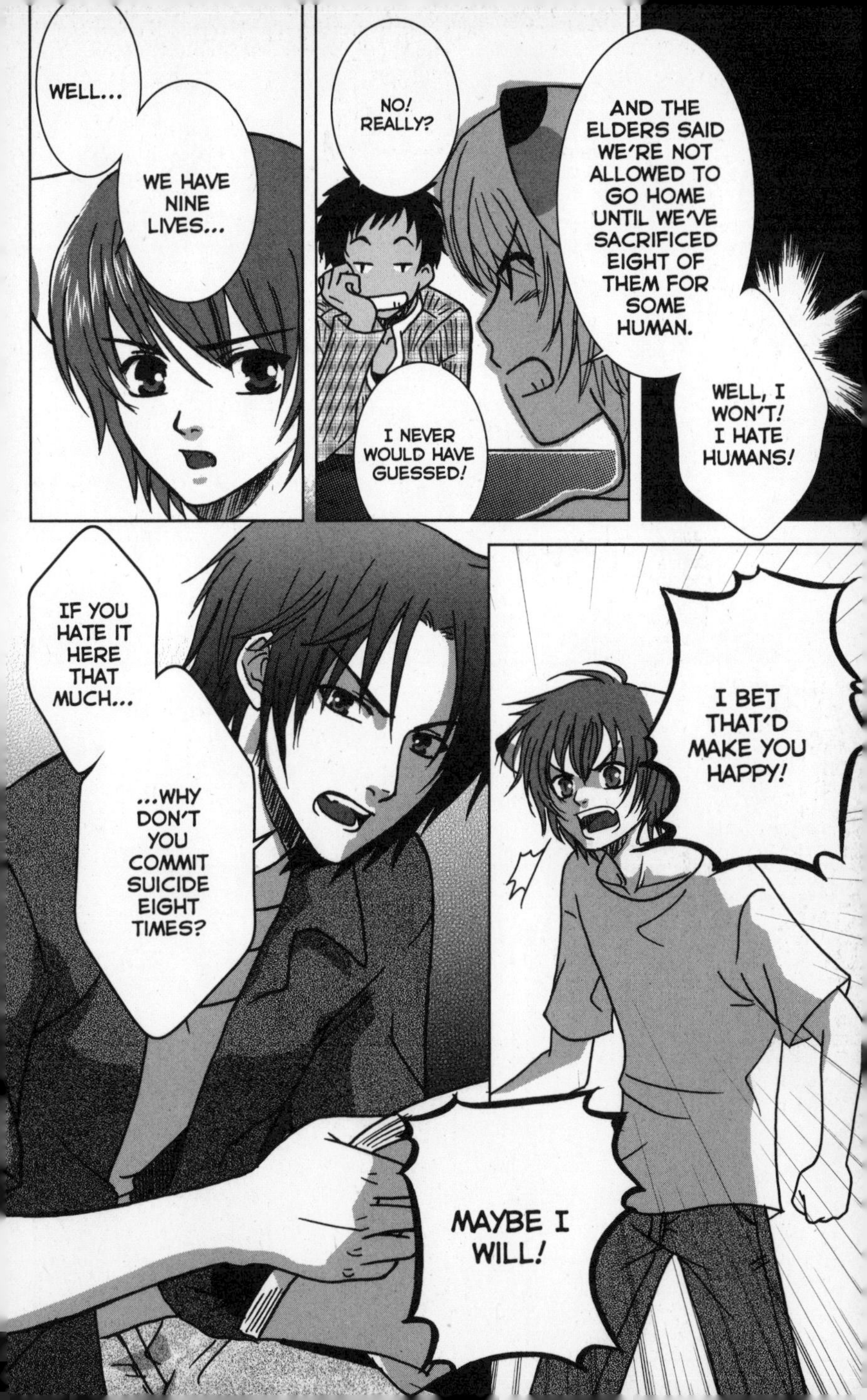
WELL...
WE HAVE NINE LIVES...
NO! REALLY?
I NEVER WOULD HAVE GUESSED!
AND THE ELDERS SAID WE'RE NOT ALLOWED TO GO HOME UNTIL WE'VE SACRIFICED EIGHT OF THEM FOR SOME HUMAN.
WELL, I WON'T! I HATE HUMANS!
IF YOU HATE IT HERE THAT MUCH...
...WHY DON'T YOU COMMIT SUICIDE EIGHT TIMES?
I BET THAT'D MAKE YOU HAPPY!
MAYBE I WILL!

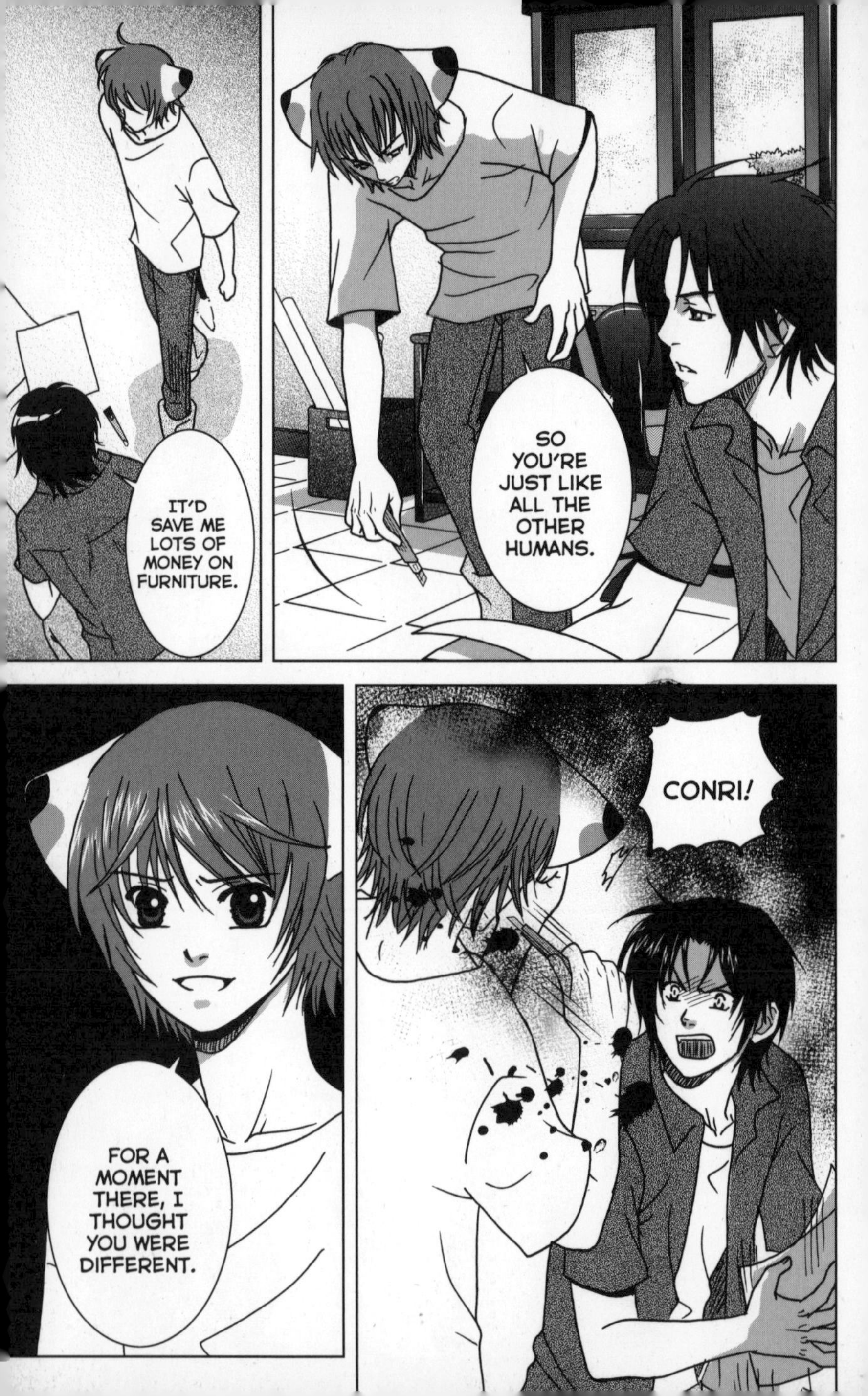
IT'D SAVE ME LOTS OF MONEY ON FURNITURE.
SO YOU'RE JUST LIKE ALL THE OTHER HUMANS.
FOR A MOMENT THERE, I THOUGHT YOU WERE DIFFERENT.
CONRI!

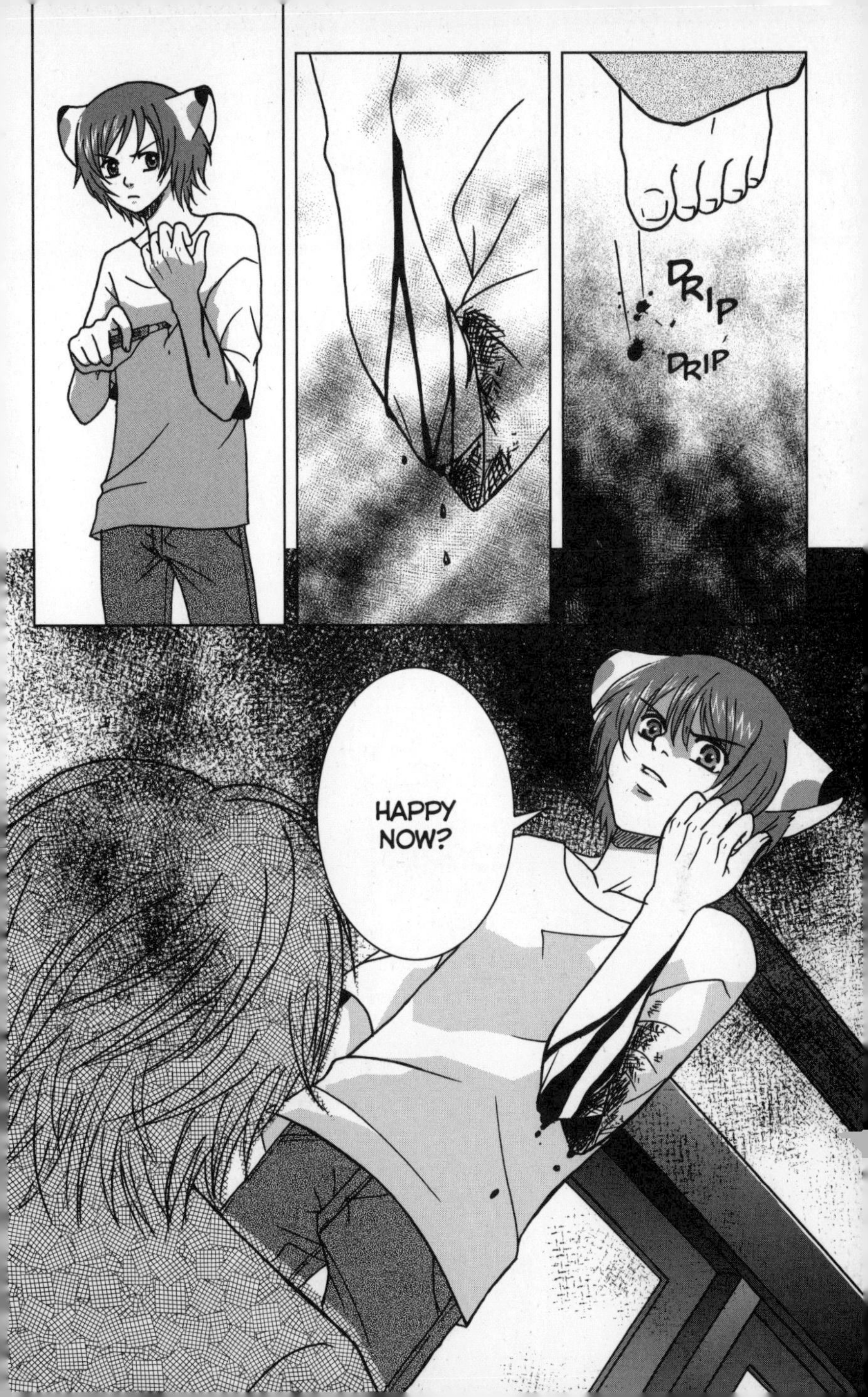
DRIP
DRIP
HAPPY NOW?

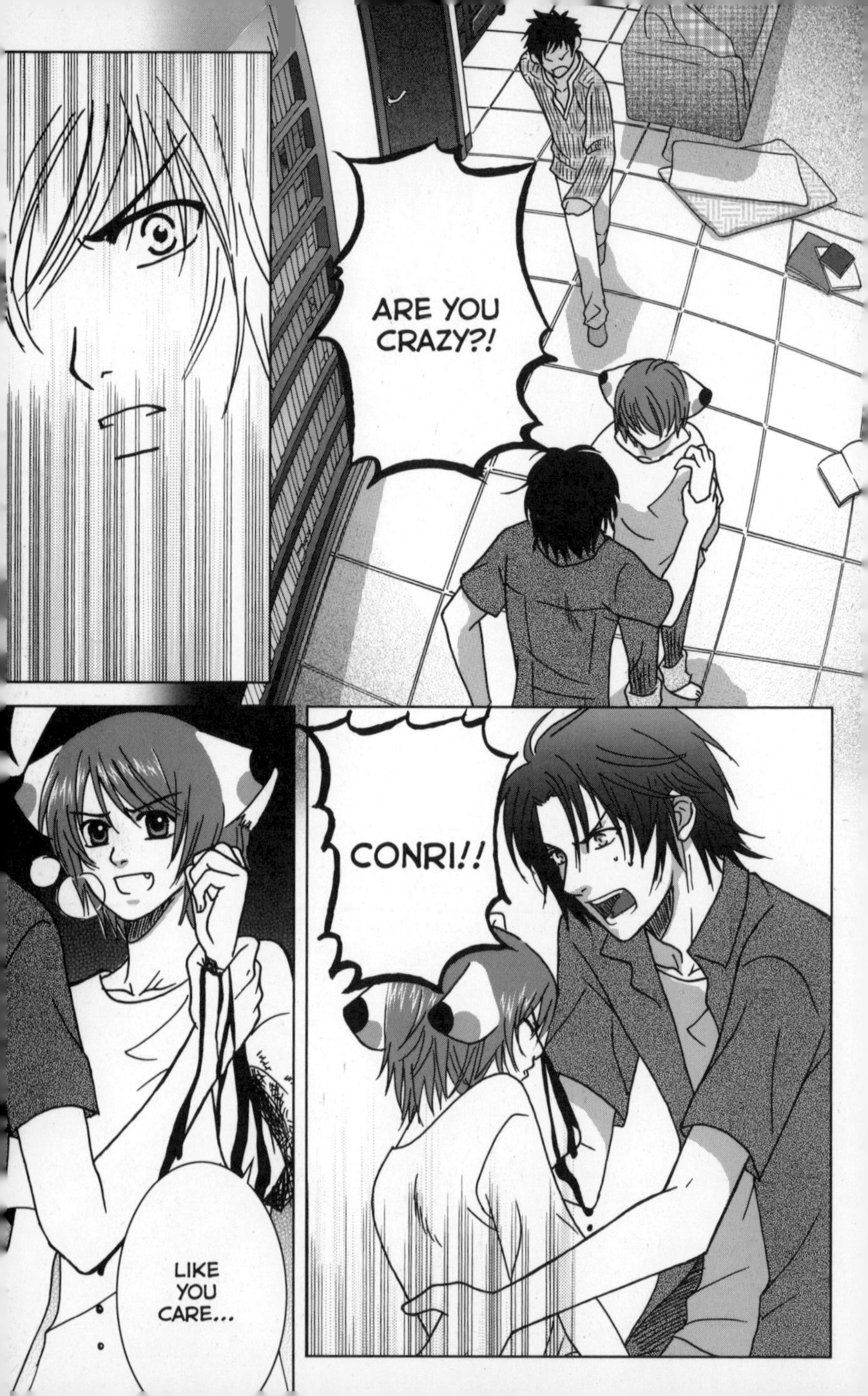
ARE YOU CRAZY?!
LIKE YOU CARE...
CONRI!!

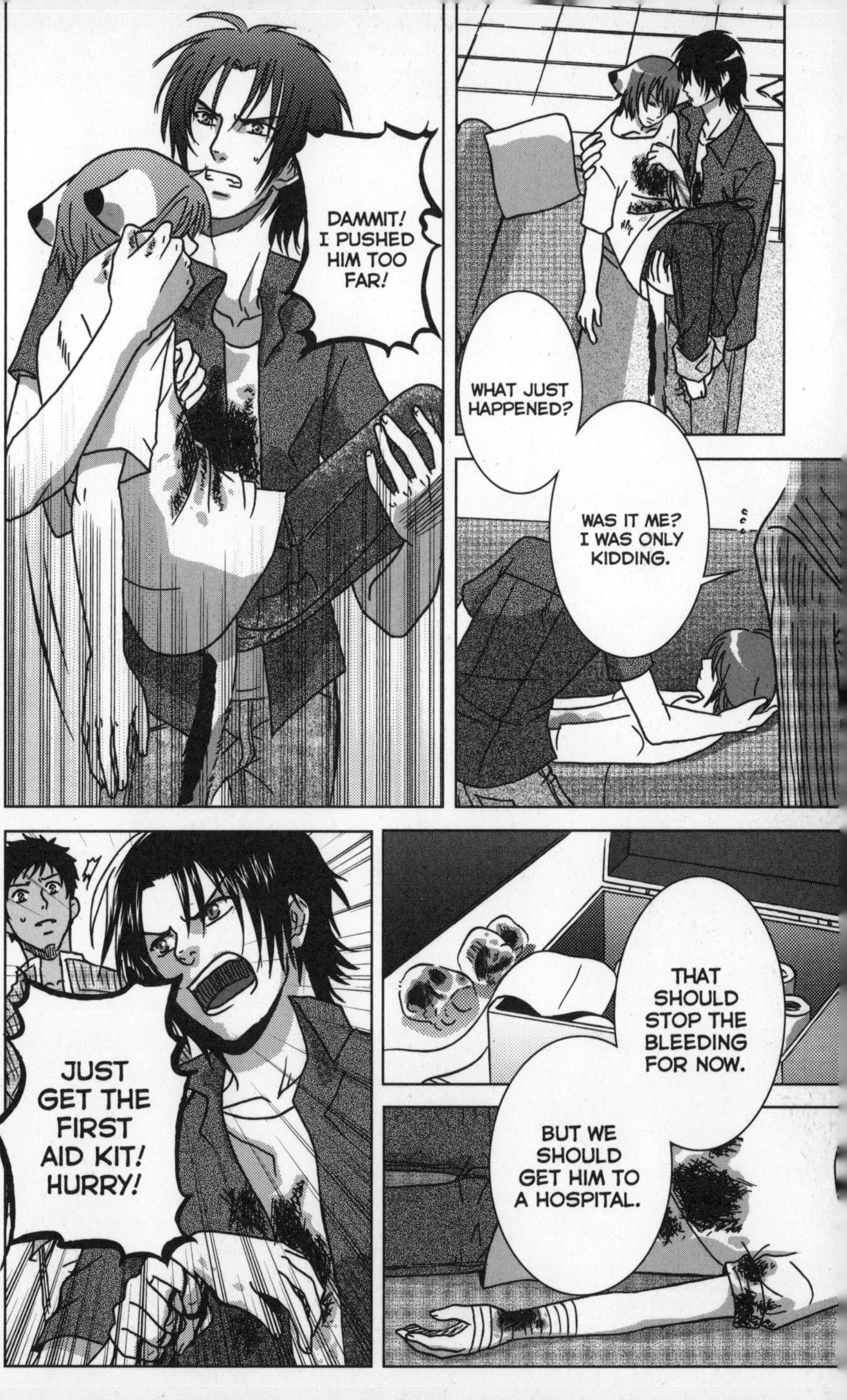
DAMMIT! I PUSHED HIM TOO FAR!
WHAT JUST HAPPENED?
WAS IT ME? I WAS ONLY KIDDING.
JUST GET THE FIRST AID KIT! HURRY!
THAT SHOULD STOP THE BLEEDING FOR NOW.
BUT WE SHOULD GET HIM TO A HOSPITAL.

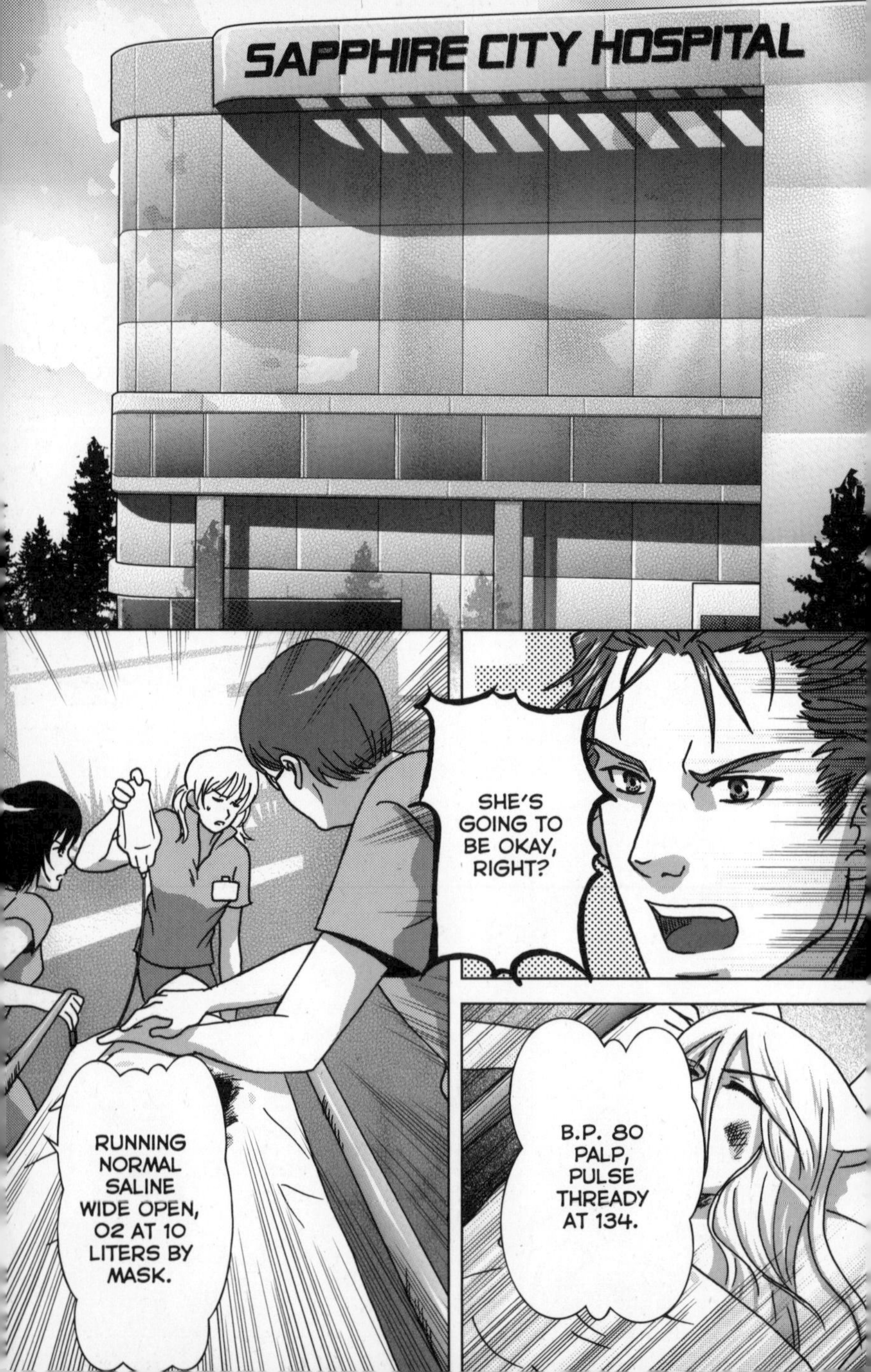
SAPPHIRE CITY HOSPITAL
SHE'S GOING TO BE OKAY, RIGHT?
RUNNING NORMAL SALINE WIDE OPEN, O2 AT 10 LITERS BY MASK.
B.P. 80 PALP, PULSE THREADY AT 134.

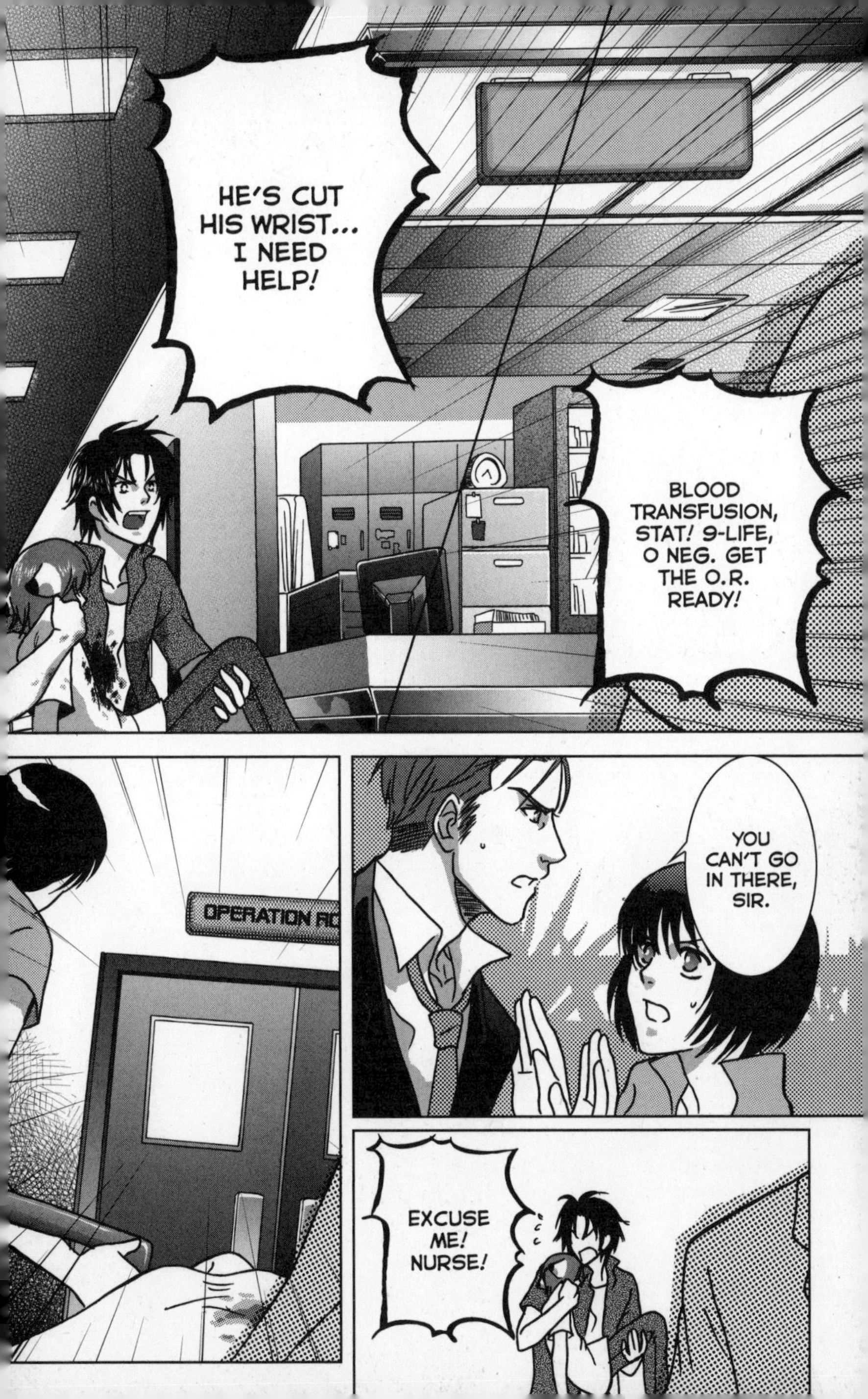
HE'S CUT HIS WRIST... I NEED HELP!
BLOOD TRANSFUSION, STAT! 9-LIFE, O NEG. GET THE O.R. READY!
OPERATION RO
YOU CAN'T GO IN THERE, SIR.
EXCUSE ME! NURSE!

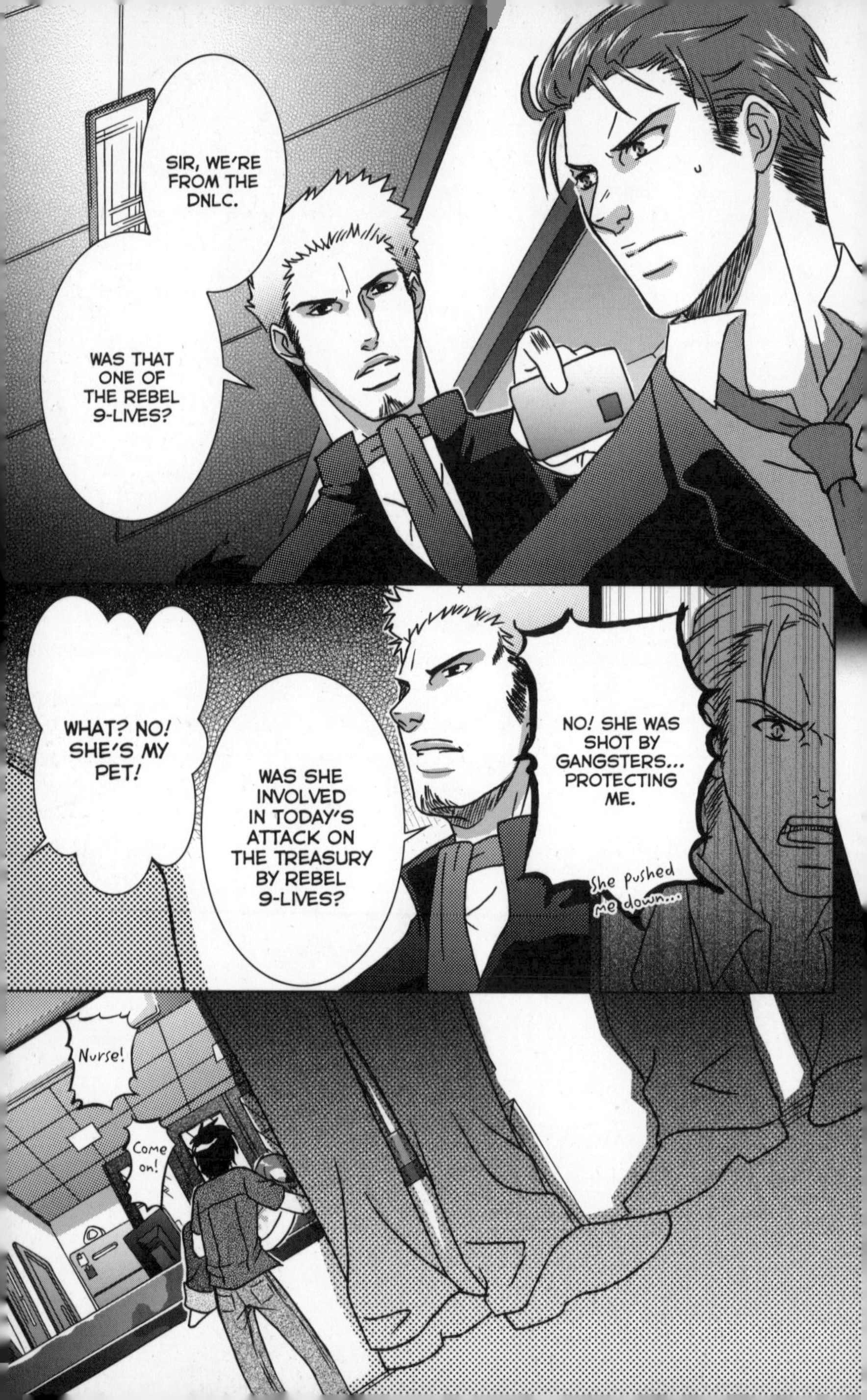
SIR, WE'RE FROM THE DNLC.
WAS THAT ONE OF THE REBEL 9-LIVES?
WHAT? NO! SHE'S MY PET!
WAS SHE INVOLVED IN TODAY'S ATTACK ON THE TREASURY BY REBEL 9-LIVES?
NO! SHE WAS SHOT BY GANGSTERS... PROTECTING ME.
She pushed me down...
Nurse!
Come on!

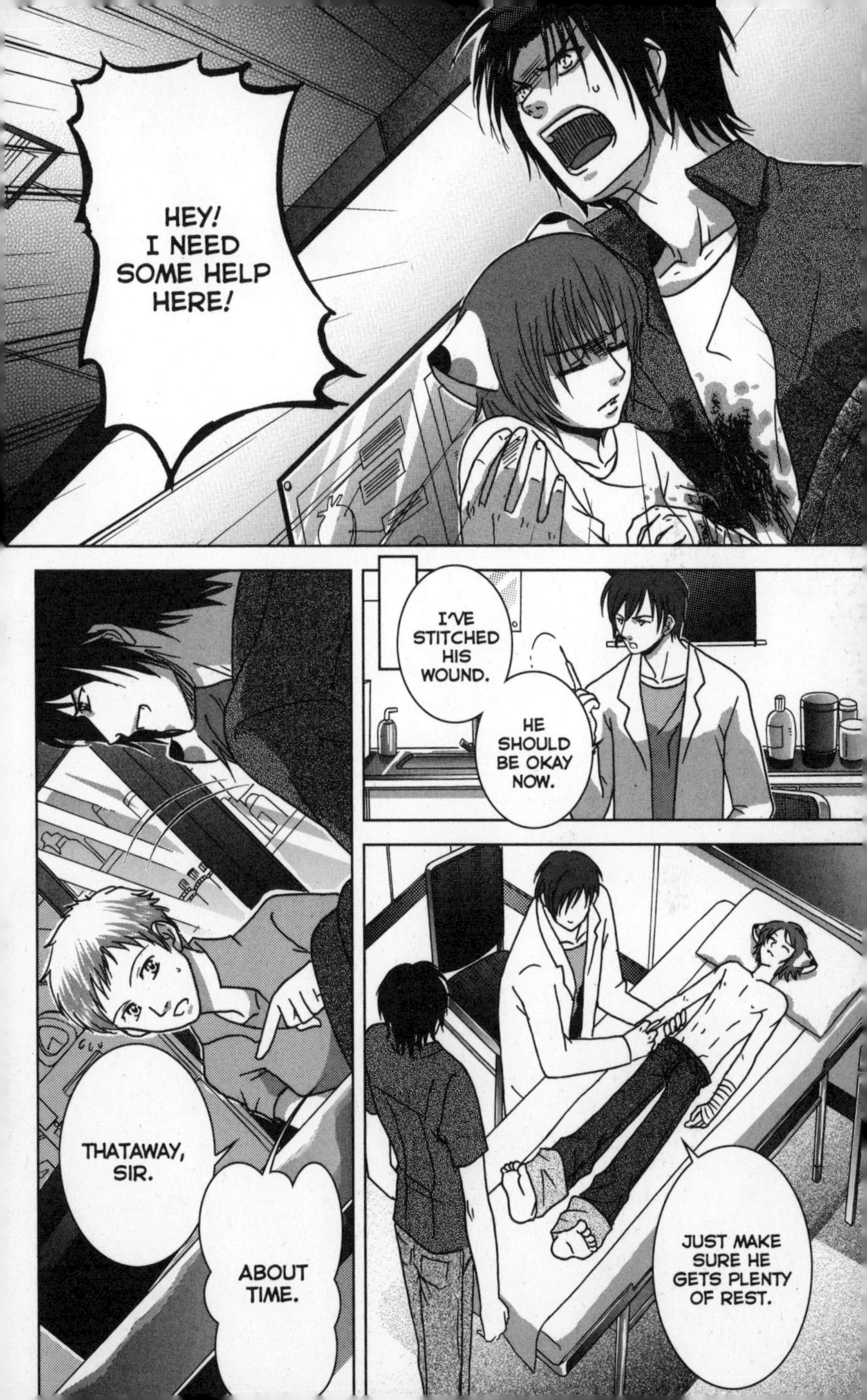
HEY! I NEED SOME HELP HERE!
THATAWAY, SIR.
ABOUT TIME.
I'VE STITCHED HIS WOUND.
HE SHOULD BE OKAY NOW.
JUST MAKE SURE HE GETS PLENTY OF REST.

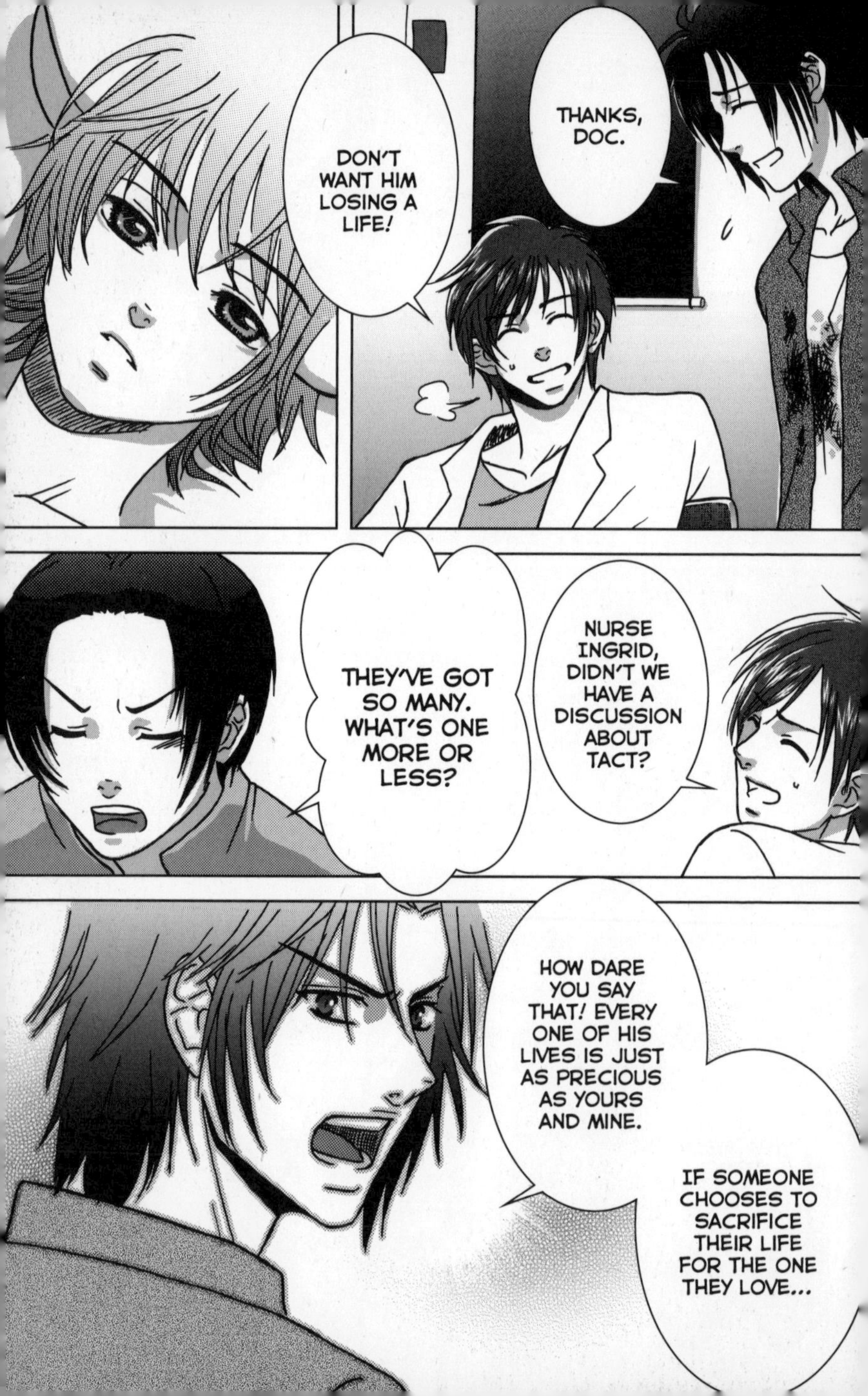
DON'T WANT HIM LOSING A LIFE!
THANKS, DOC.
THEY'VE GOT SO MANY. WHAT'S ONE MORE OR LESS?
NURSE INGRID, DIDN'T WE HAVE A DISCUSSION ABOUT TACT?
HOW DARE YOU SAY THAT! EVERY ONE OF HIS LIVES IS JUST AS PRECIOUS AS YOURS AND MINE.
IF SOMEONE CHOOSES TO SACRIFICE THEIR LIFE FOR THE ONE THEY LOVE...

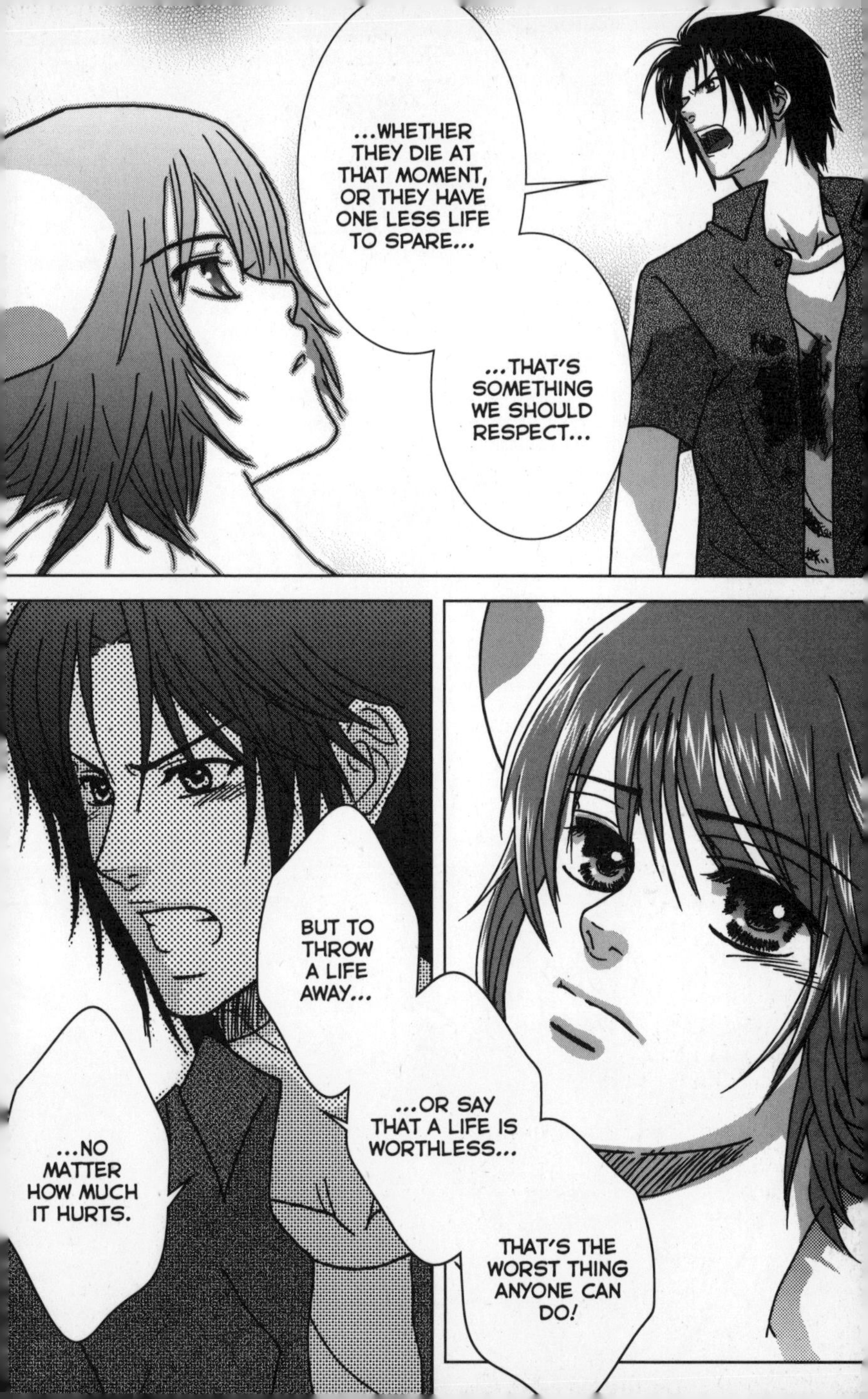
...WHETHER THEY DIE AT THAT MOMENT, OR THEY HAVE ONE LESS LIFE TO SPARE...
...THAT'S SOMETHING WE SHOULD RESPECT...
...NO MATTER HOW MUCH IT HURTS.
BUT TO THROW A LIFE AWAY...
...OR SAY THAT A LIFE IS WORTHLESS...
THAT'S THE WORST THING ANYONE CAN DO!

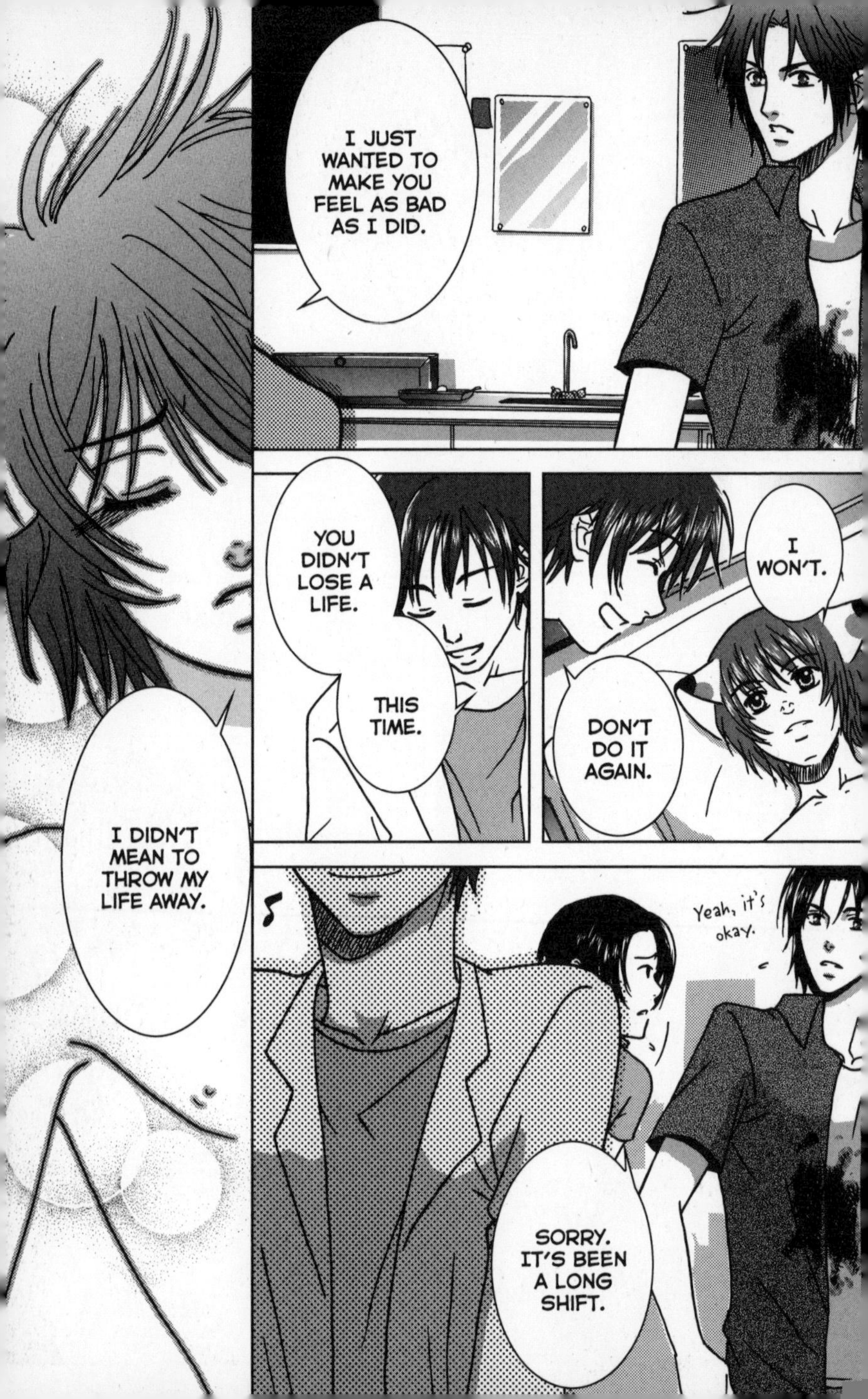
I DIDN'T MEAN TO THROW MY LIFE AWAY.
I JUST WANTED TO MAKE YOU FEEL AS BAD AS I DID.
YOU DIDN'T LOSE A LIFE.
THIS TIME.
I WON'T.
DON'T DO IT AGAIN.
Yeah, it's okay.
SORRY. IT'S BEEN A LONG SHIFT.

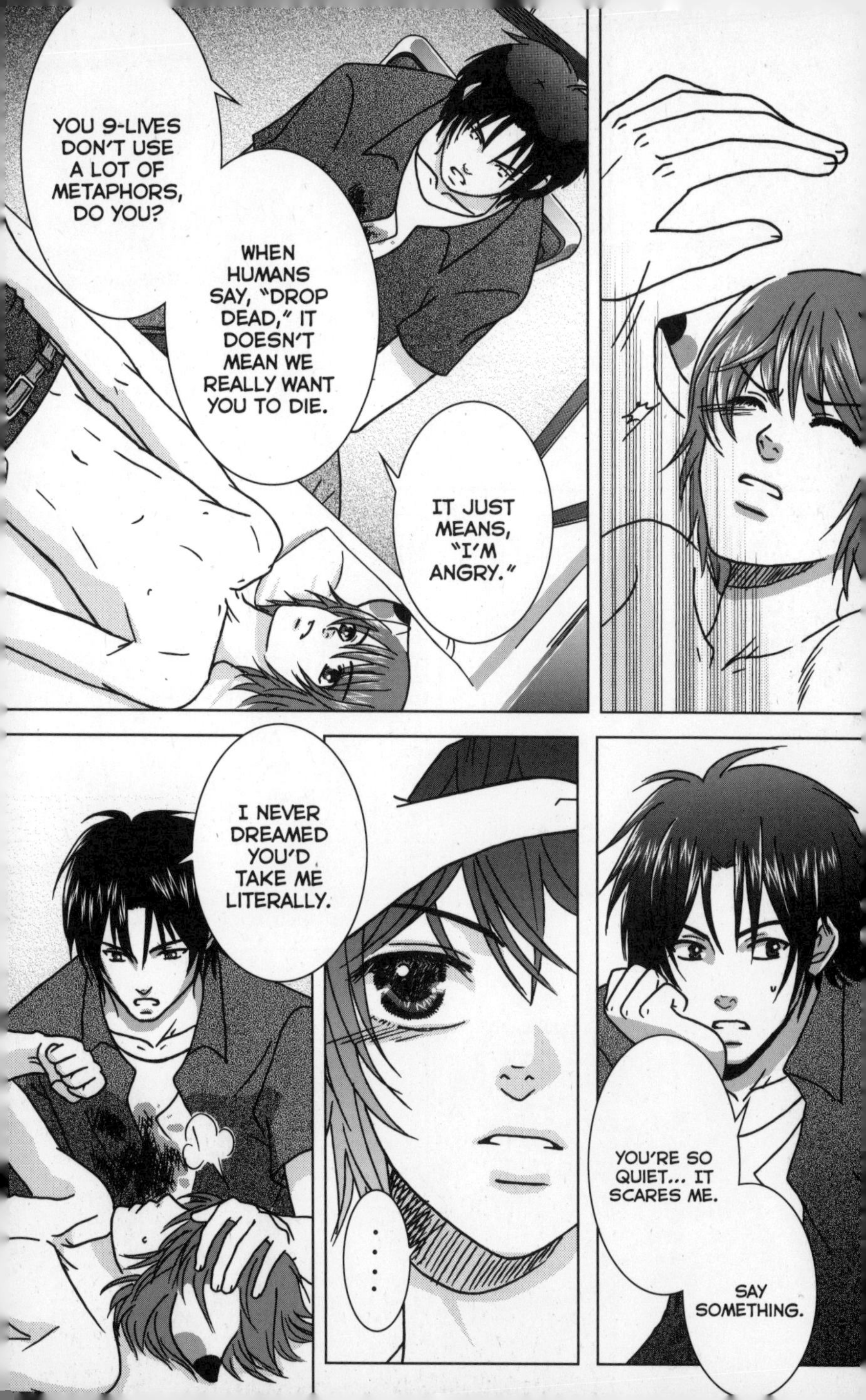
YOU 9-LIVES DON'T USE A LOT OF METAPHORS, DO YOU?
WHEN HUMANS SAY, "DROP DEAD," IT DOESN'T MEAN WE REALLY WANT YOU TO DIE.
IT JUST MEANS, "I'M ANGRY."
I NEVER DREAMED YOU'D TAKE ME LITERALLY.
....
YOU'RE SO QUIET... IT SCARES ME.
SAY SOMETHING.

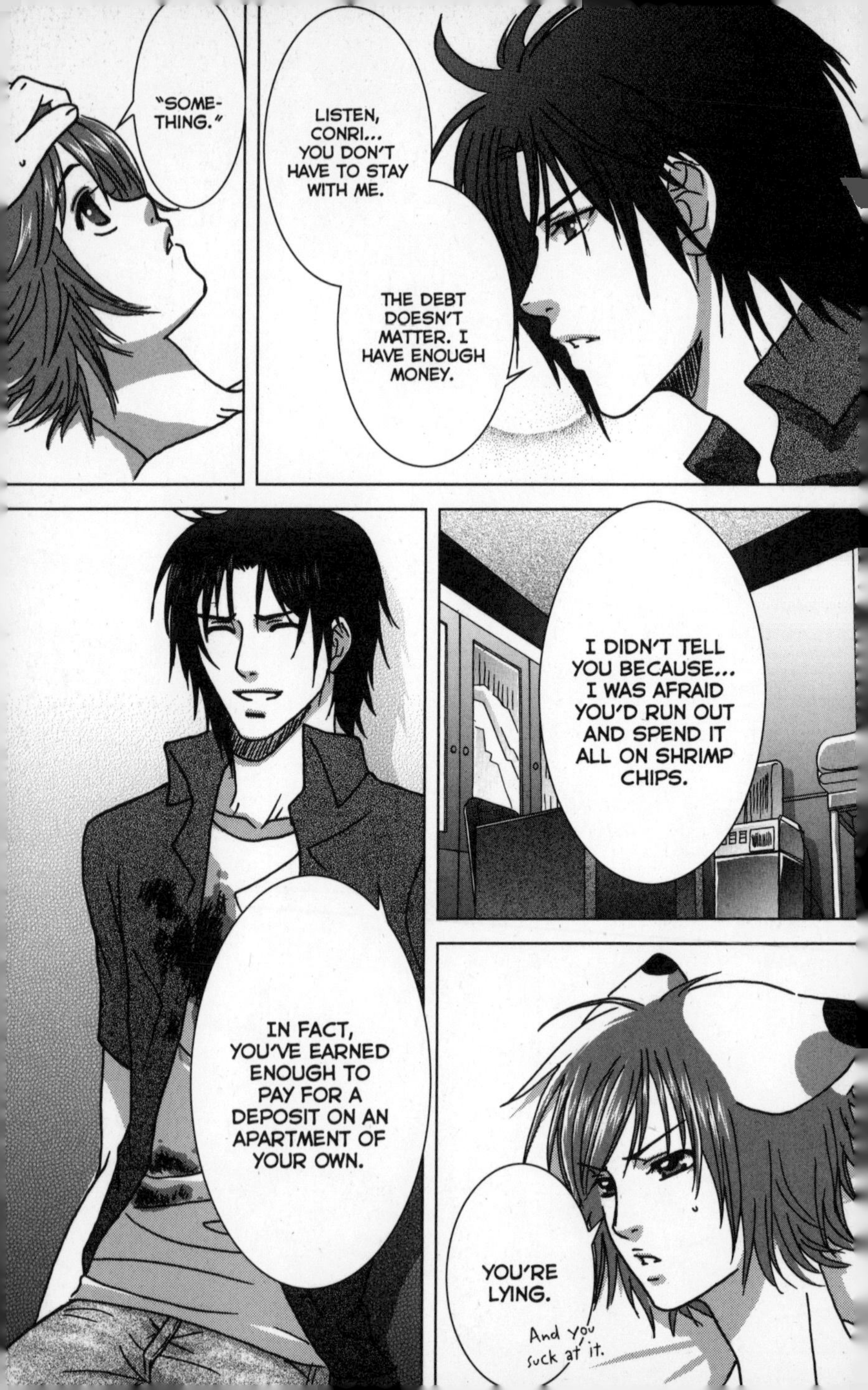
"SOME-THING."
LISTEN, CONRI... YOU DON'T HAVE TO STAY WITH ME.
THE DEBT DOESN'T MATTER. I HAVE ENOUGH MONEY.
IN FACT, YOU'VE EARNED ENOUGH TO PAY FOR A DEPOSIT ON AN APARTMENT OF YOUR OWN.
I DIDN'T TELL YOU BECAUSE... I WAS AFRAID YOU'D RUN OUT AND SPEND IT ALL ON SHRIMP CHIPS.
YOU'RE LYING.
And you suck at it.

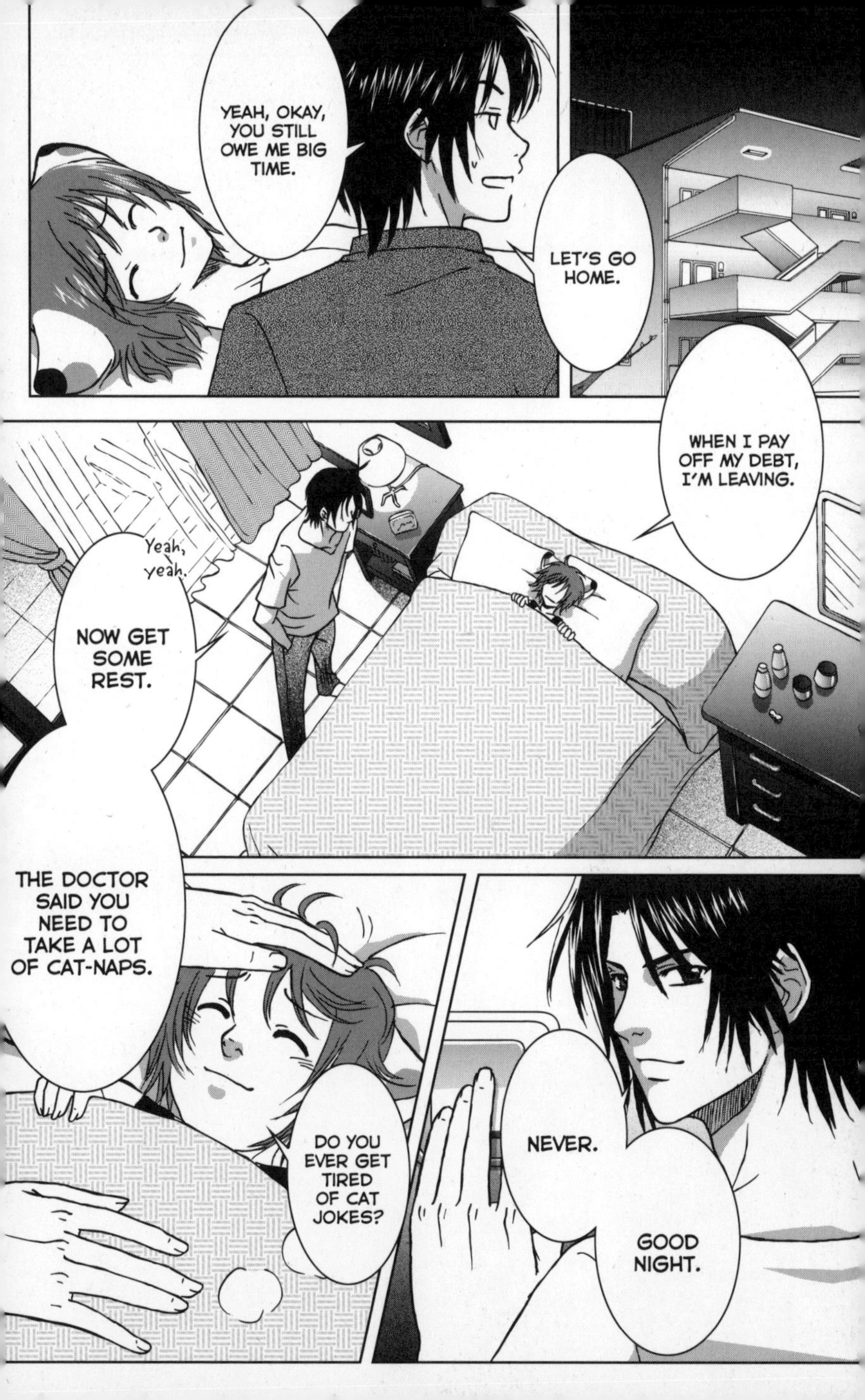
YEAH, OKAY, YOU STILL OWE ME BIG TIME.
LET'S GO HOME.
WHEN I PAY OFF MY DEBT, I'M LEAVING.
Yeah, yeah.
NOW GET SOME REST.
THE DOCTOR SAID YOU NEED TO TAKE A LOT OF CAT-NAPS.
DO YOU EVER GET TIRED OF CAT JOKES?
NEVER.
GOOD NIGHT.

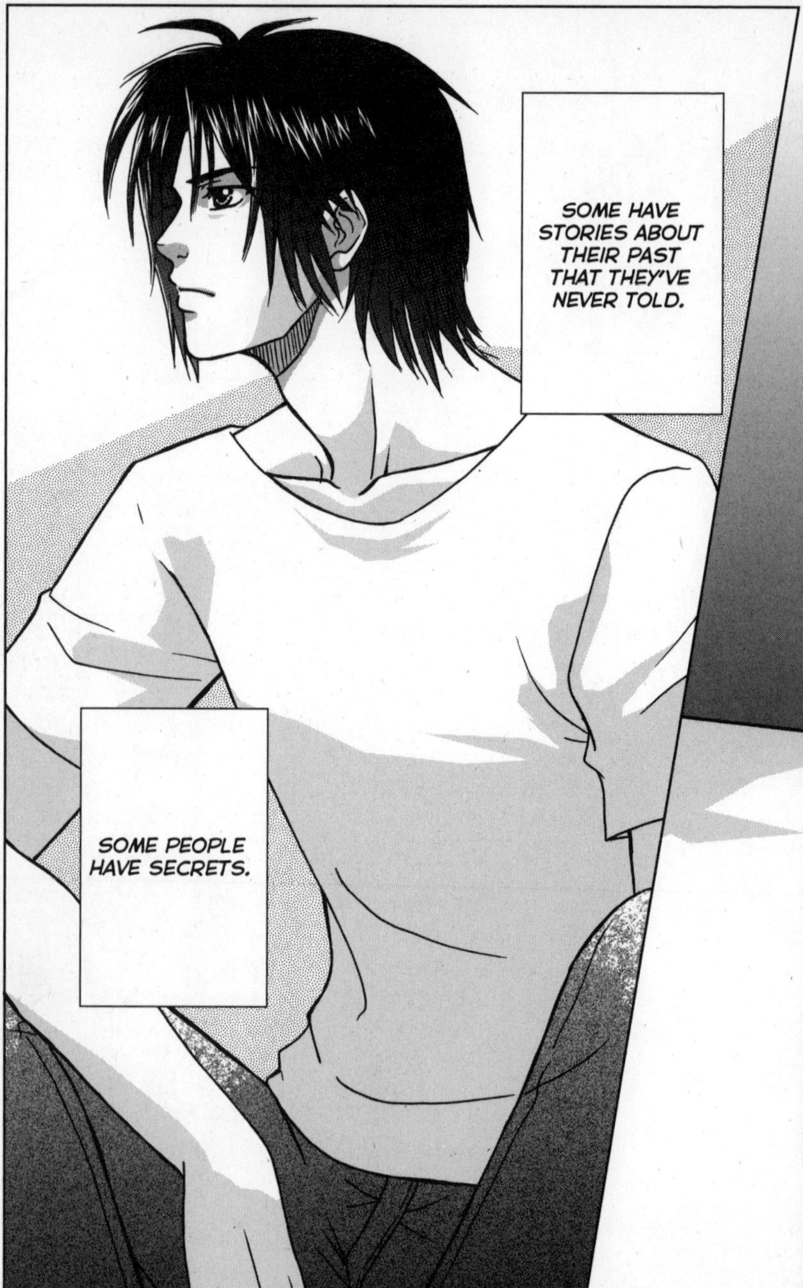
SOME HAVE STORIES ABOUT THEIR PAST THAT THEY'VE NEVER TOLD.
SOME PEOPLE HAVE SECRETS.

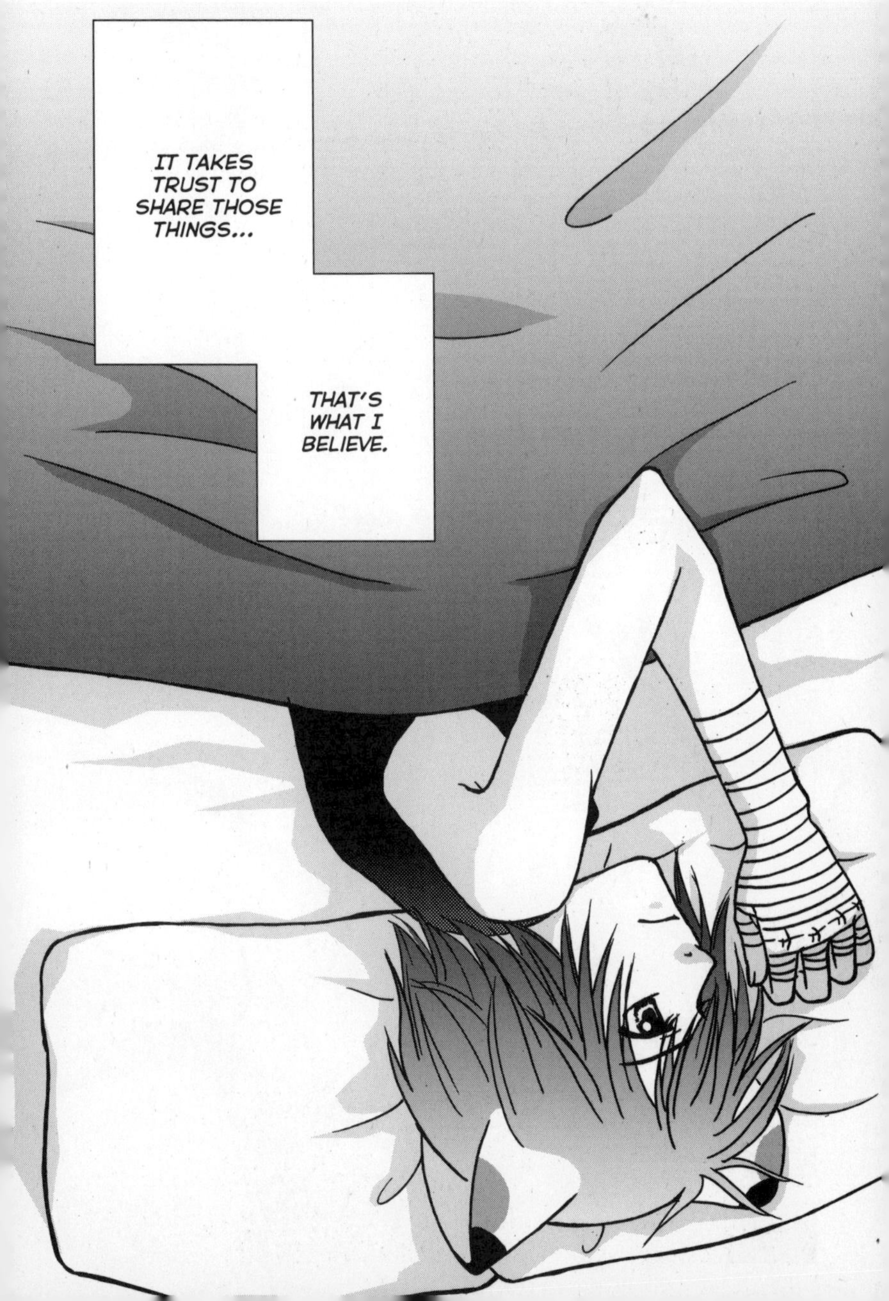
IT TAKES TRUST TO SHARE THOSE THINGS...
THAT'S WHAT I BELIEVE.

Chapter Three: Cat-Boy Get Your Gun

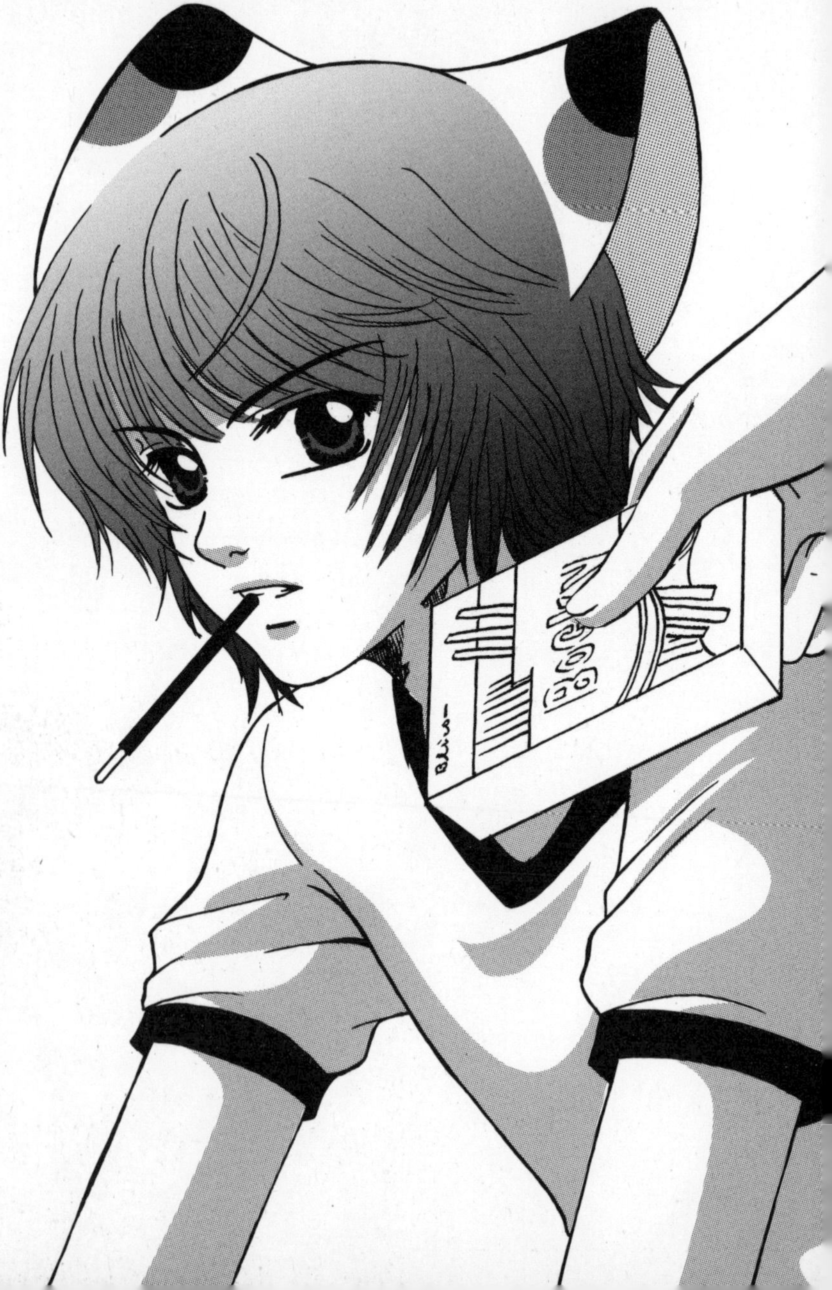

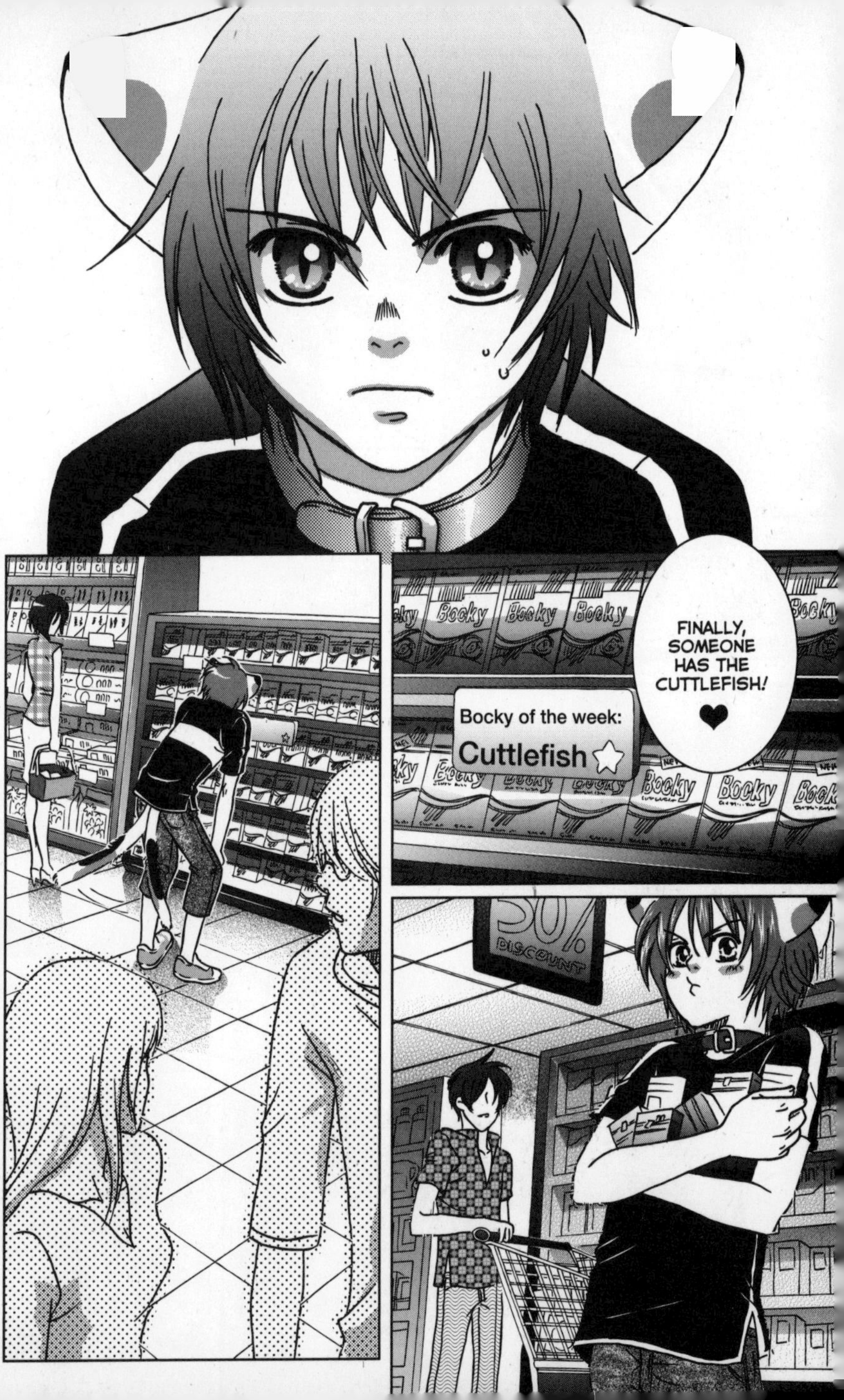
Bocky
Bocky of the week:
Cuttlefish
FINALLY, SOMEONE HAS THE CUTTLEFISH! ♥
DISCOUNT

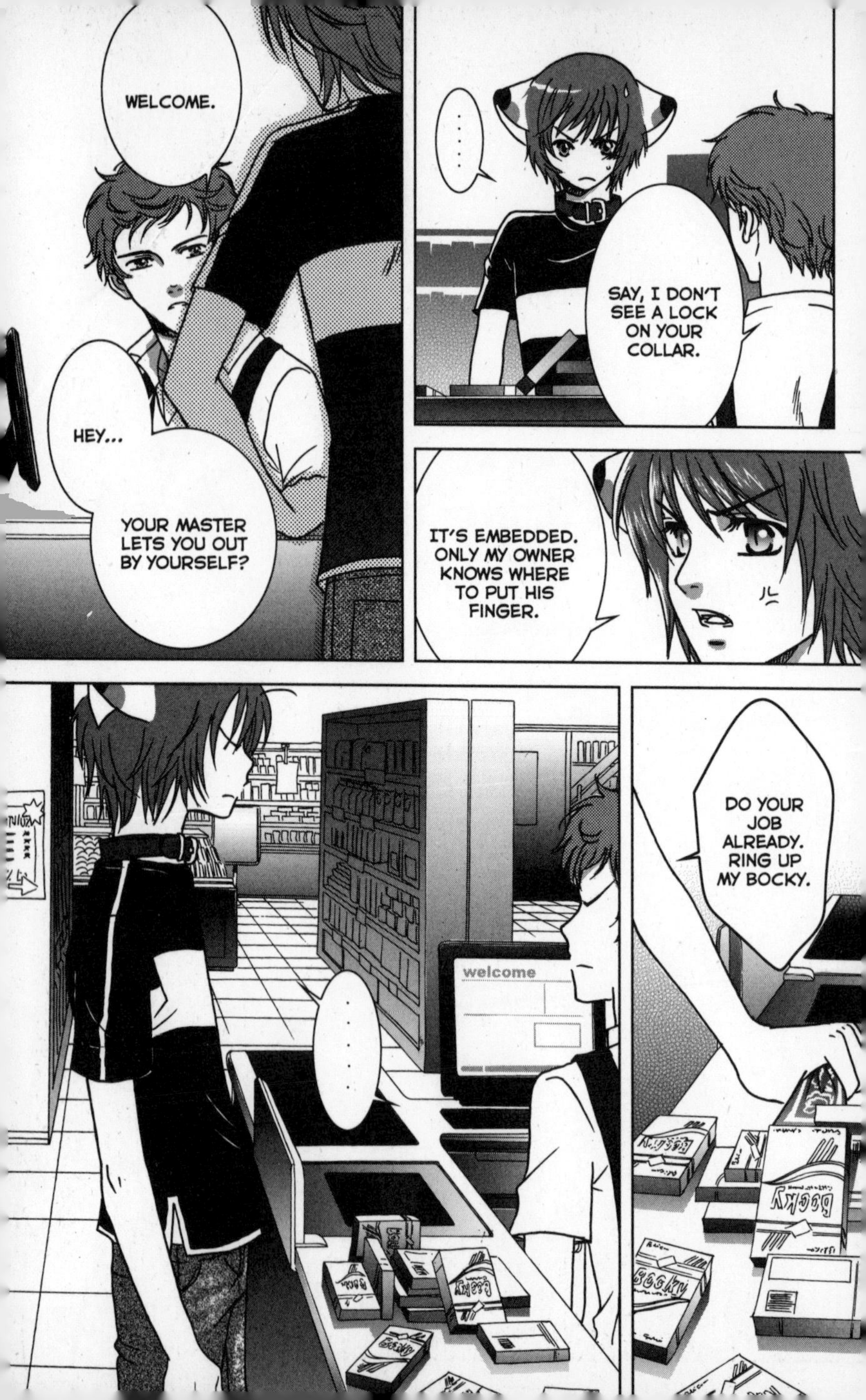
WELCOME.
HEY...
YOUR MASTER LETS YOU OUT BY YOURSELF?
......
SAY, I DON'T SEE A LOCK ON YOUR COLLAR.
IT'S EMBEDDED. ONLY MY OWNER KNOWS WHERE TO PUT HIS FINGER.
......
welcome
DO YOUR JOB ALREADY. RING UP MY BOCKY.

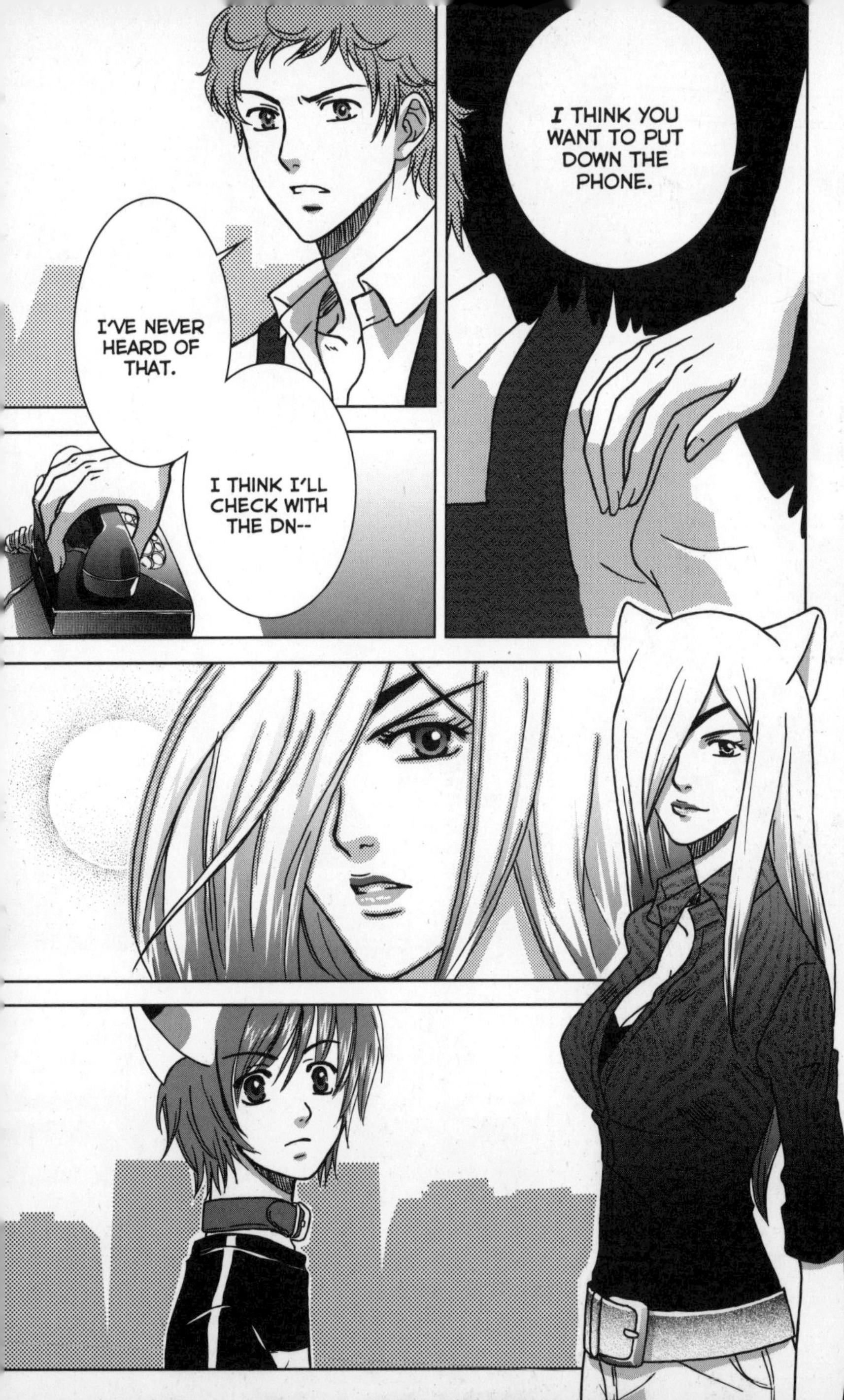
I'VE NEVER HEARD OF THAT.
I THINK I'LL CHECK WITH THE DN--
I THINK YOU WANT TO PUT DOWN THE PHONE.

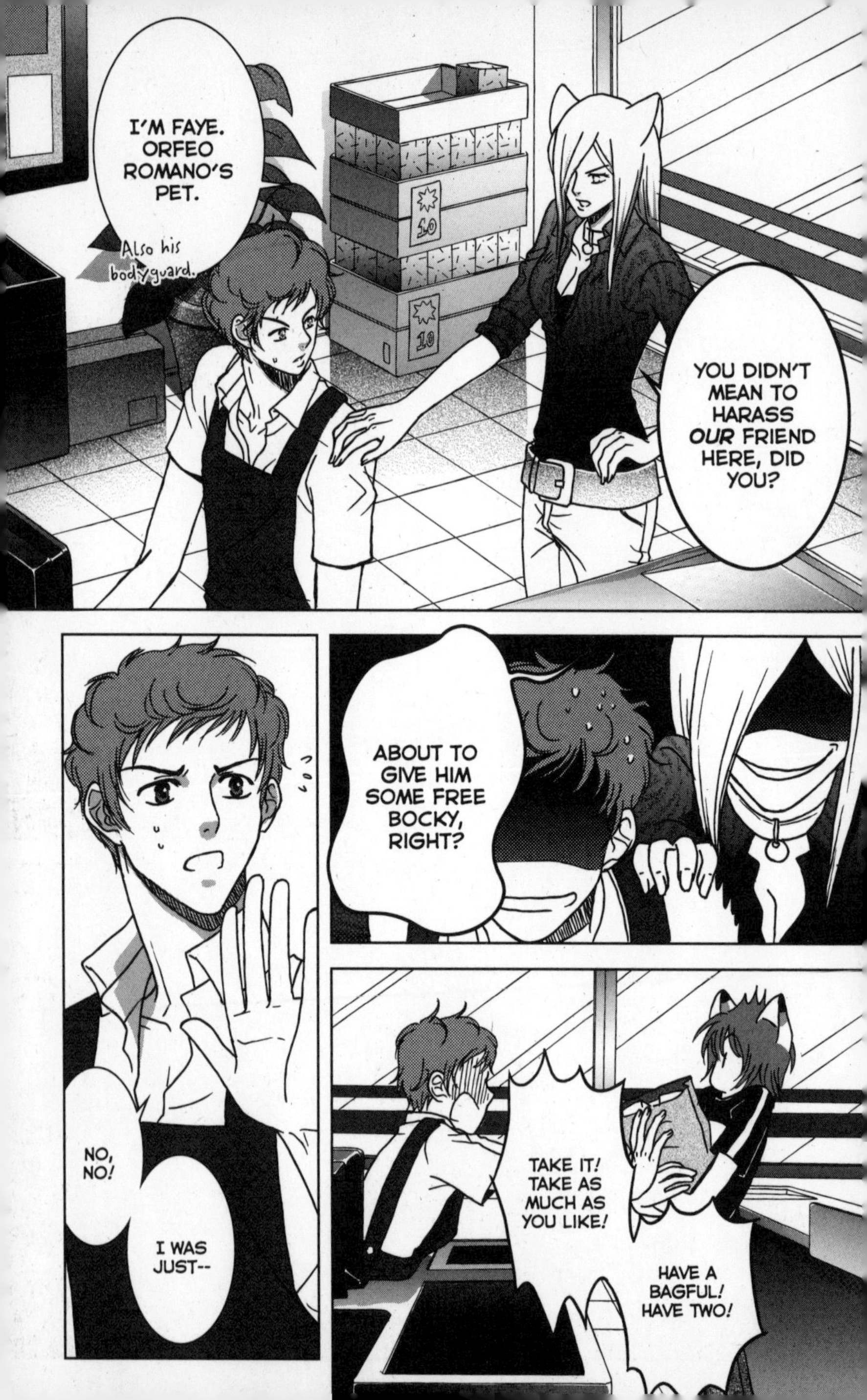
I'M FAYE. ORFEO ROMANO'S PET.
Also his bodyguard.
YOU DIDN'T MEAN TO HARASS *OUR* FRIEND HERE, DID YOU?
NO, NO!
I WAS JUST--
ABOUT TO GIVE HIM SOME FREE BOCKY, RIGHT?
TAKE IT! TAKE AS MUCH AS YOU LIKE!
HAVE A BAGFUL! HAVE TWO!

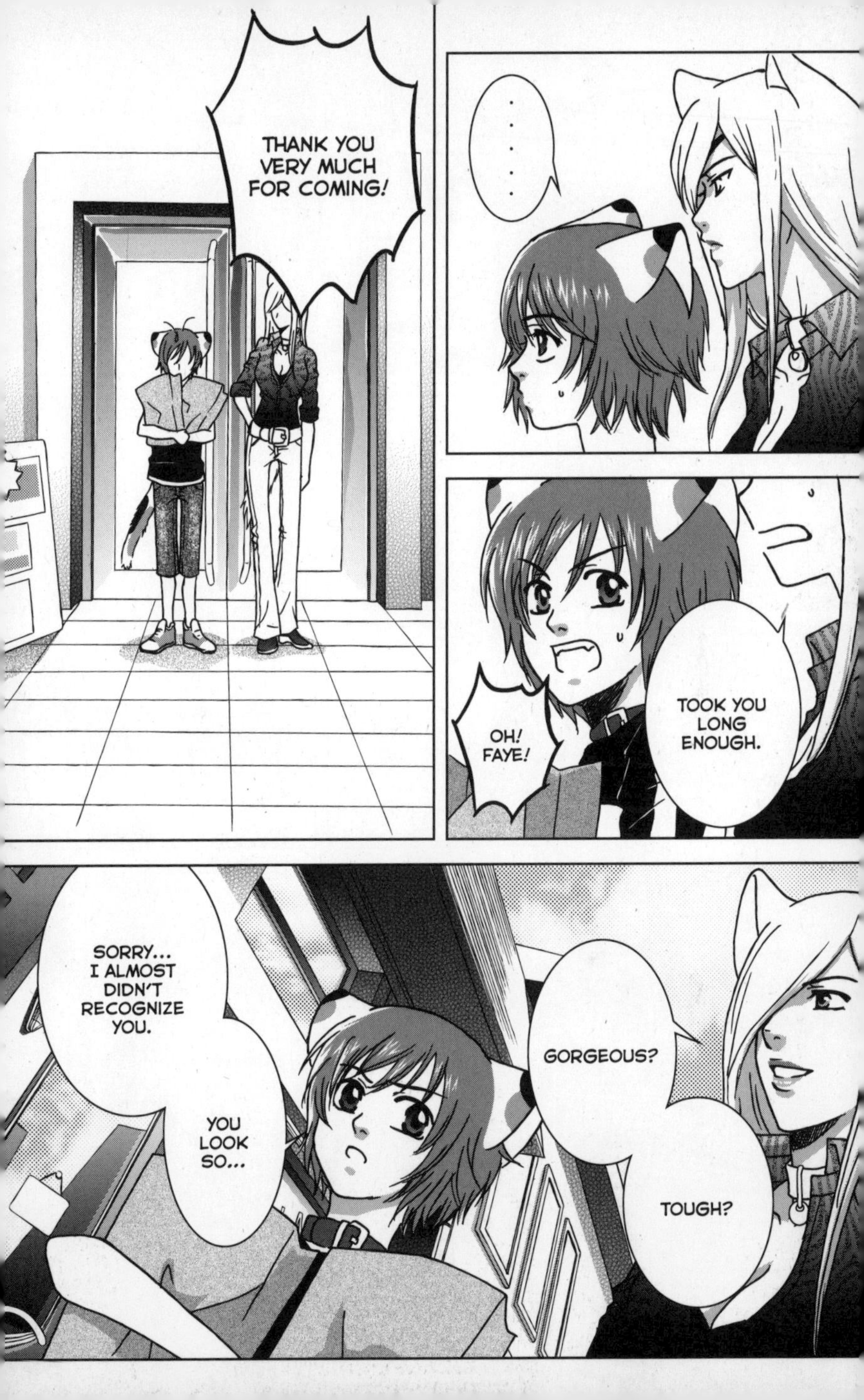
THANK YOU VERY MUCH FOR COMING!
.....
OH! FAYE!
TOOK YOU LONG ENOUGH.
SORRY... I ALMOST DIDN'T RECOGNIZE YOU.
YOU LOOK SO...
GORGEOUS?
TOUGH?

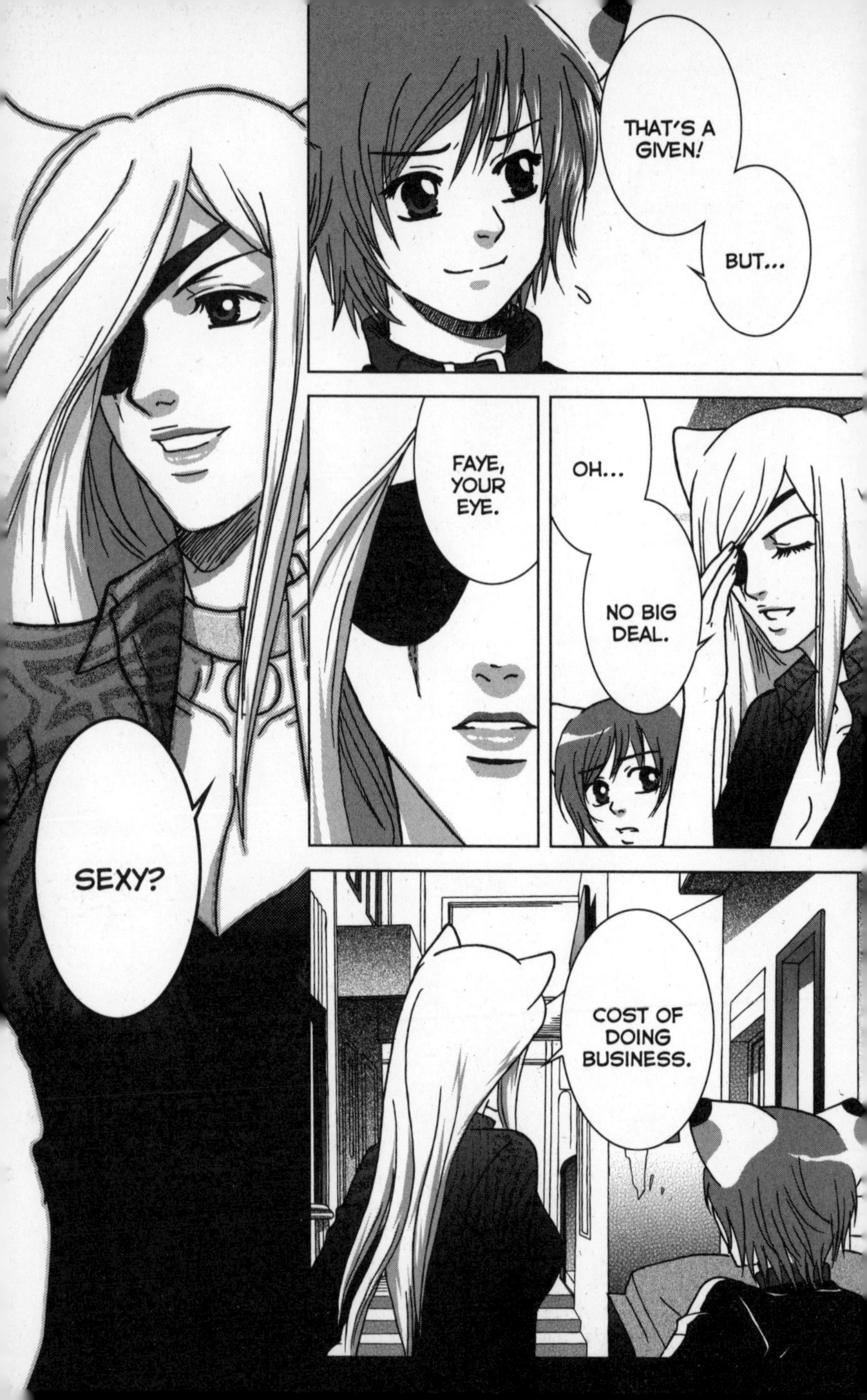
SEXY?
THAT'S A GIVEN!
BUT...
FAYE, YOUR EYE.
OH...
NO BIG DEAL.
COST OF DOING BUSINESS.

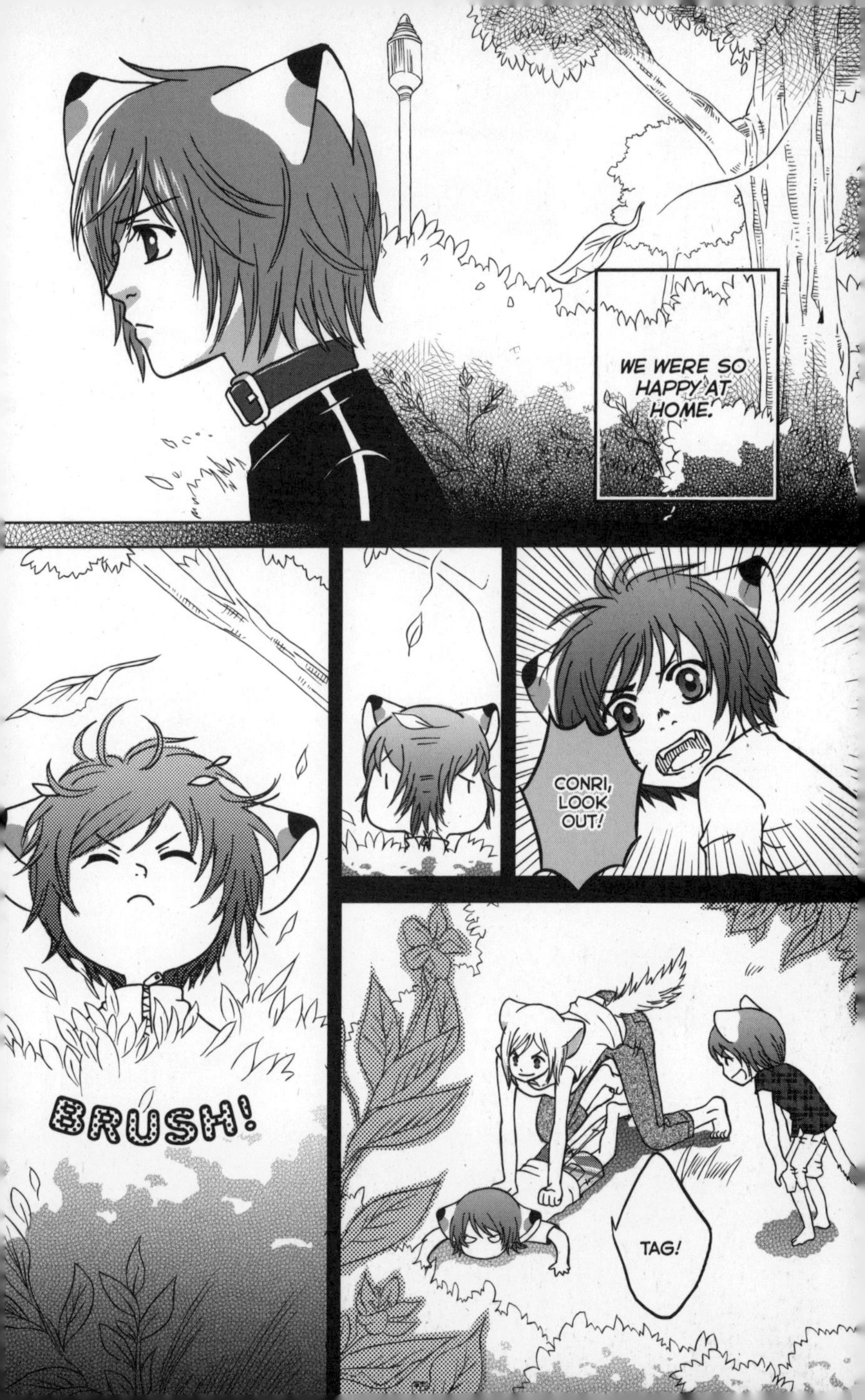
WE WERE SO HAPPY AT HOME.
BRUSH!
CONRI, LOOK OUT!
TAG!

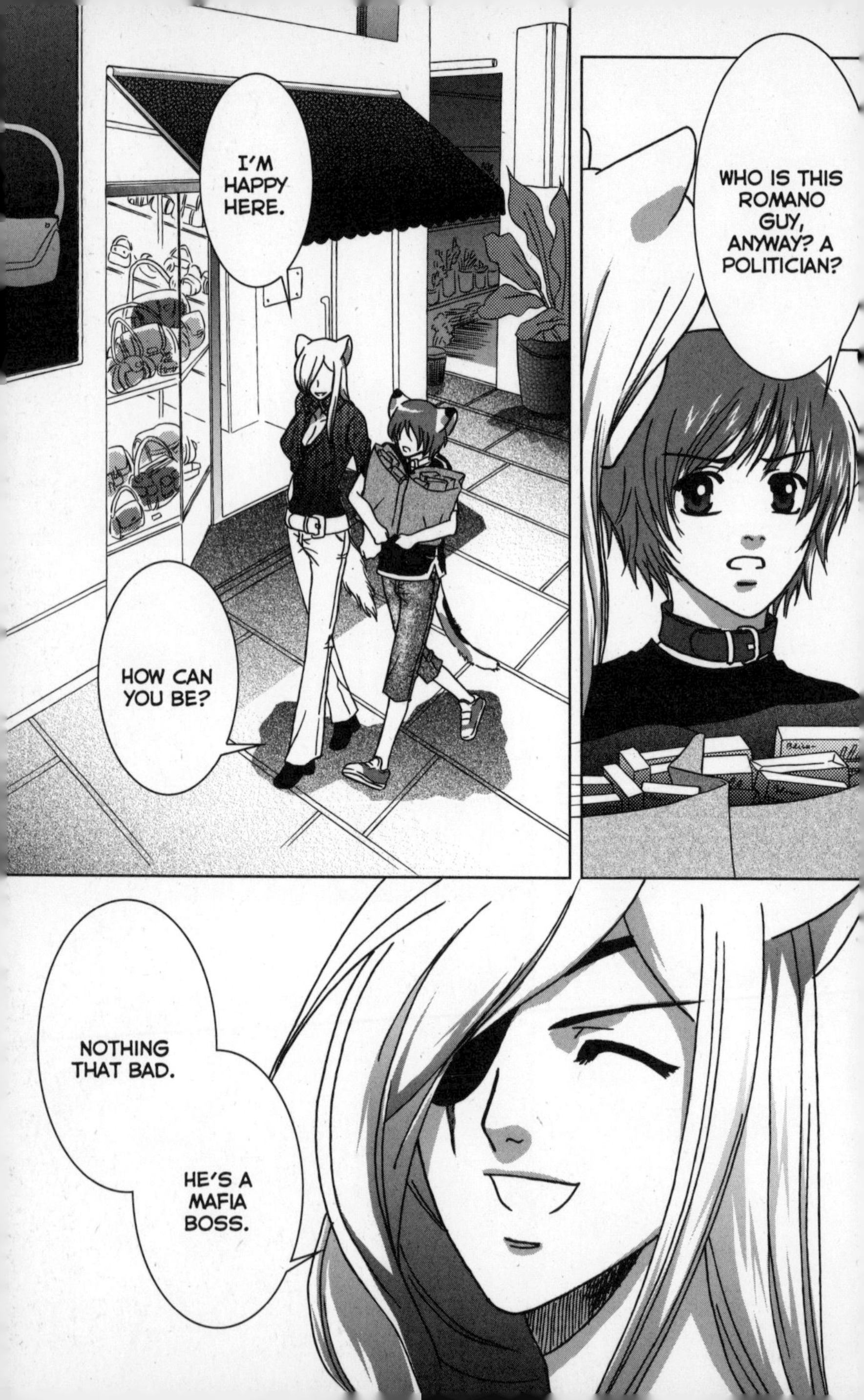
I'M HAPPY HERE.
HOW CAN YOU BE?
WHO IS THIS ROMANO GUY, ANYWAY? A POLITICIAN?
NOTHING THAT BAD.
HE'S A MAFIA BOSS.

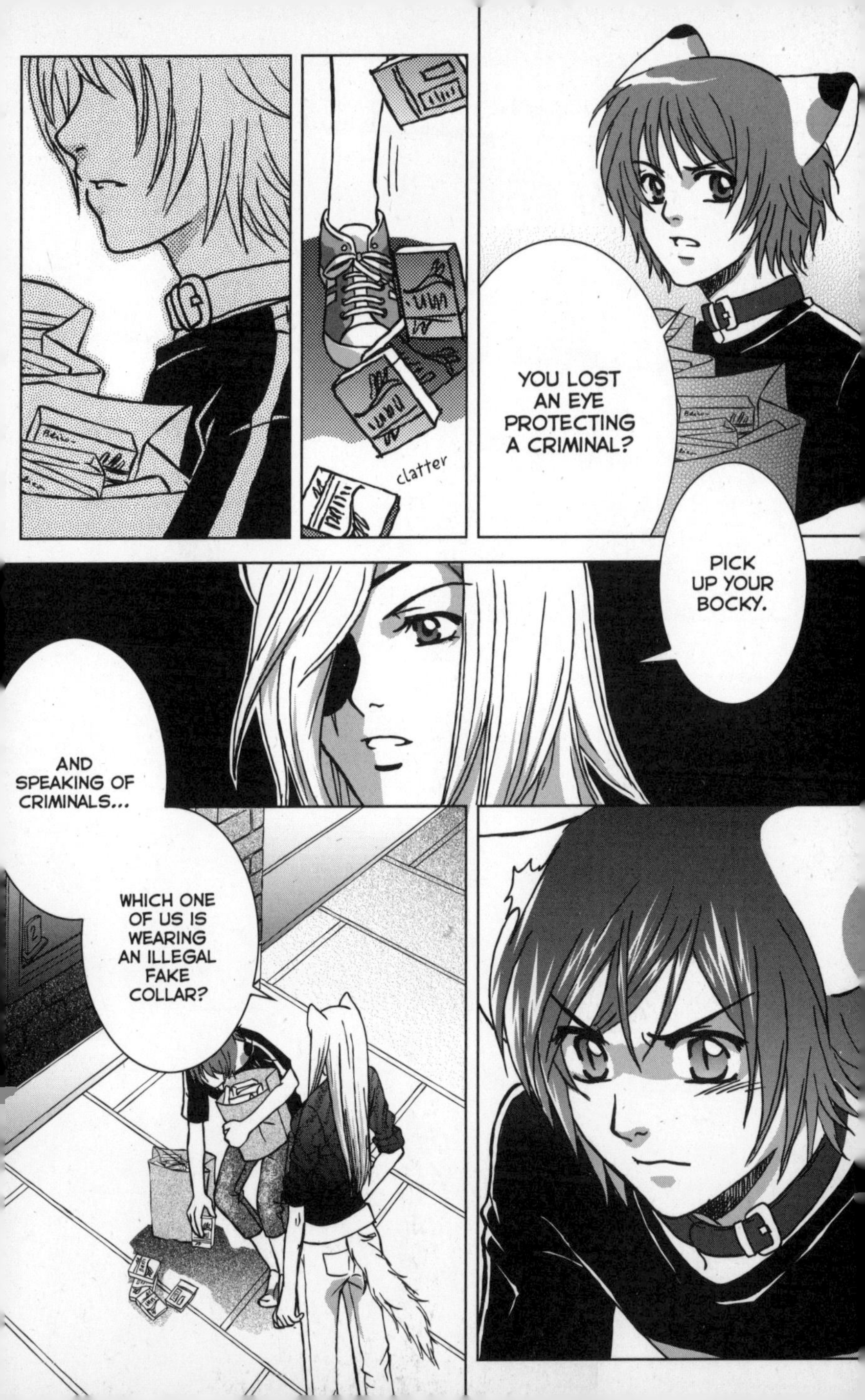
clatter
YOU LOST AN EYE PROTECTING A CRIMINAL?
PICK UP YOUR BOCKY.
AND SPEAKING OF CRIMINALS...
WHICH ONE OF US IS WEARING AN ILLEGAL FAKE COLLAR?

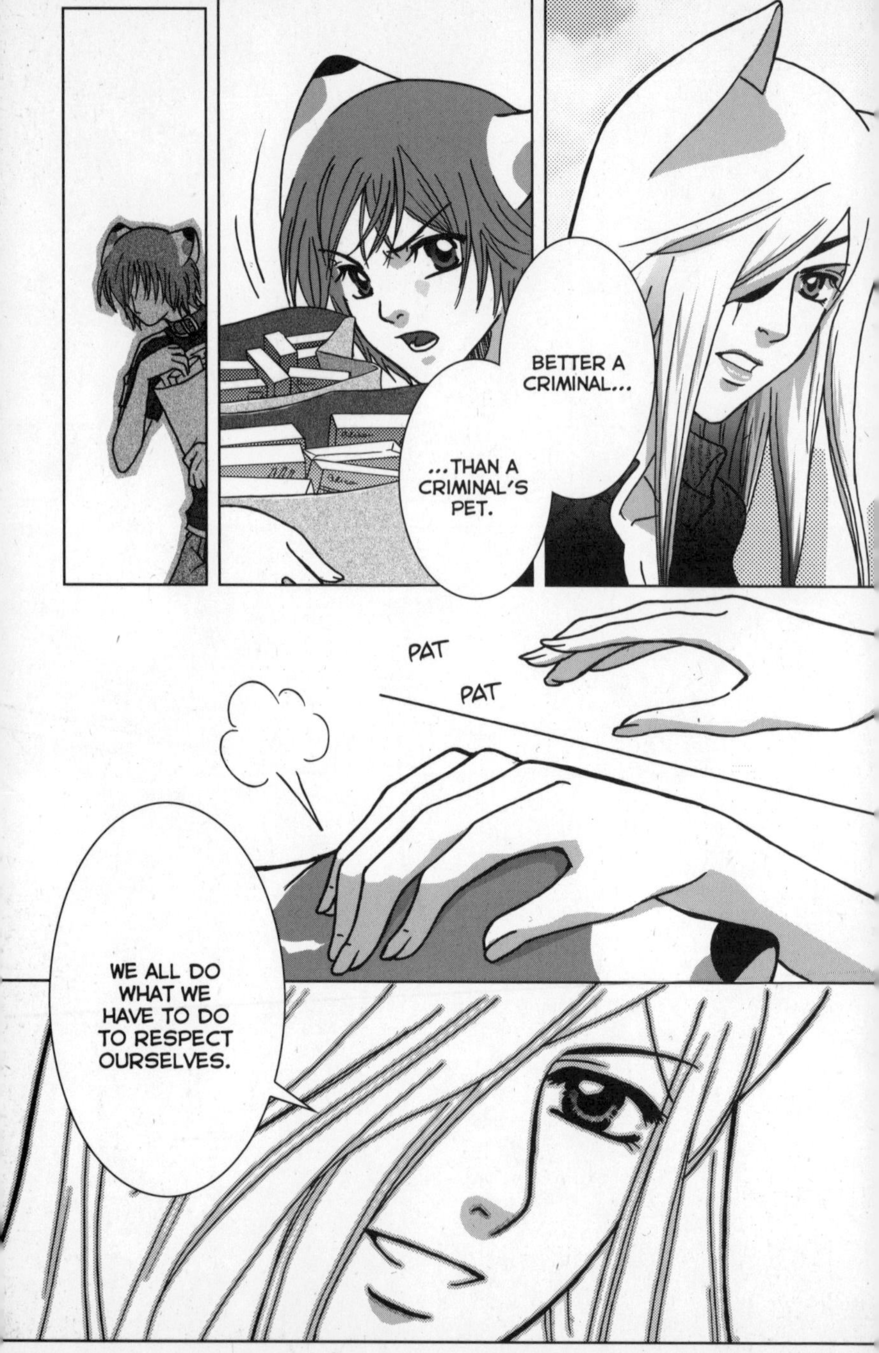
BETTER A CRIMINAL...
...THAN A CRIMINAL'S PET.
PAT
PAT
WE ALL DO WHAT WE HAVE TO DO TO RESPECT OURSELVES.

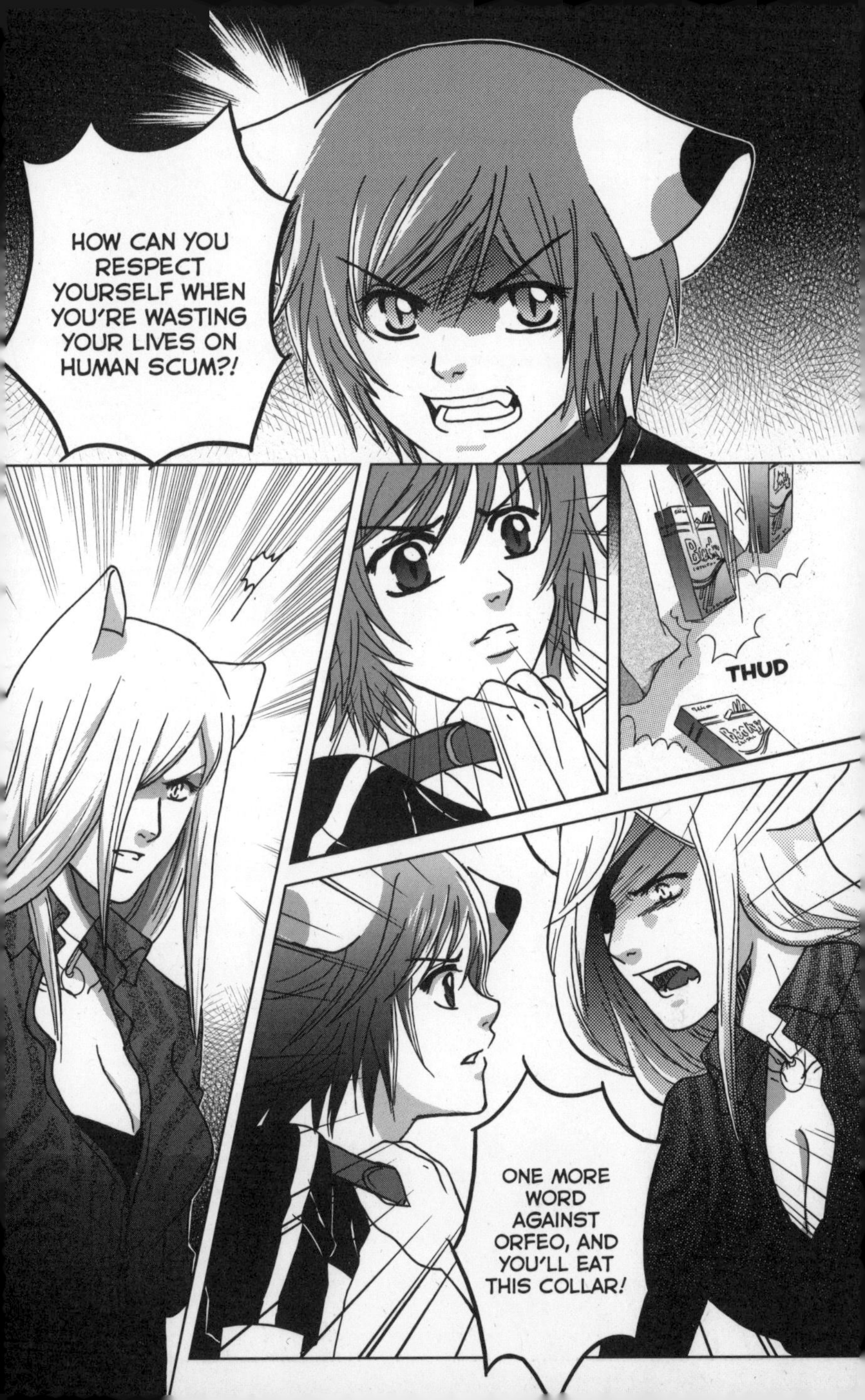
HOW CAN YOU RESPECT YOURSELF WHEN YOU'RE WASTING YOUR LIVES ON HUMAN SCUM?!
THUD
ONE MORE WORD AGAINST ORFEO, AND YOU'LL EAT THIS COLLAR!

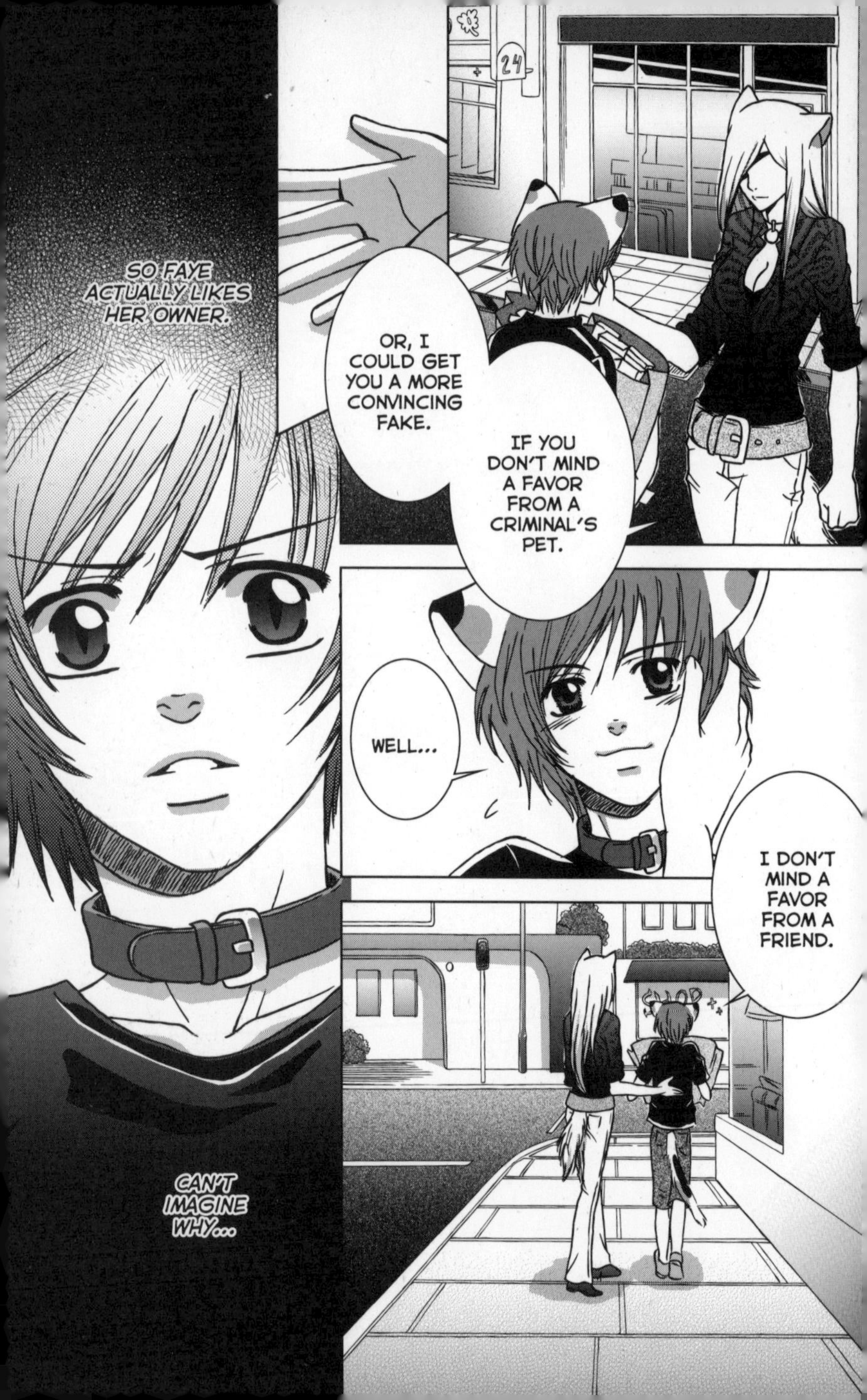
SO FAYE ACTUALLY LIKES HER OWNER.
CAN'T IMAGINE WHY...
OR, I COULD GET YOU A MORE CONVINCING FAKE.
IF YOU DON'T MIND A FAVOR FROM A CRIMINAL'S PET.
WELL...
I DON'T MIND A FAVOR FROM A FRIEND.

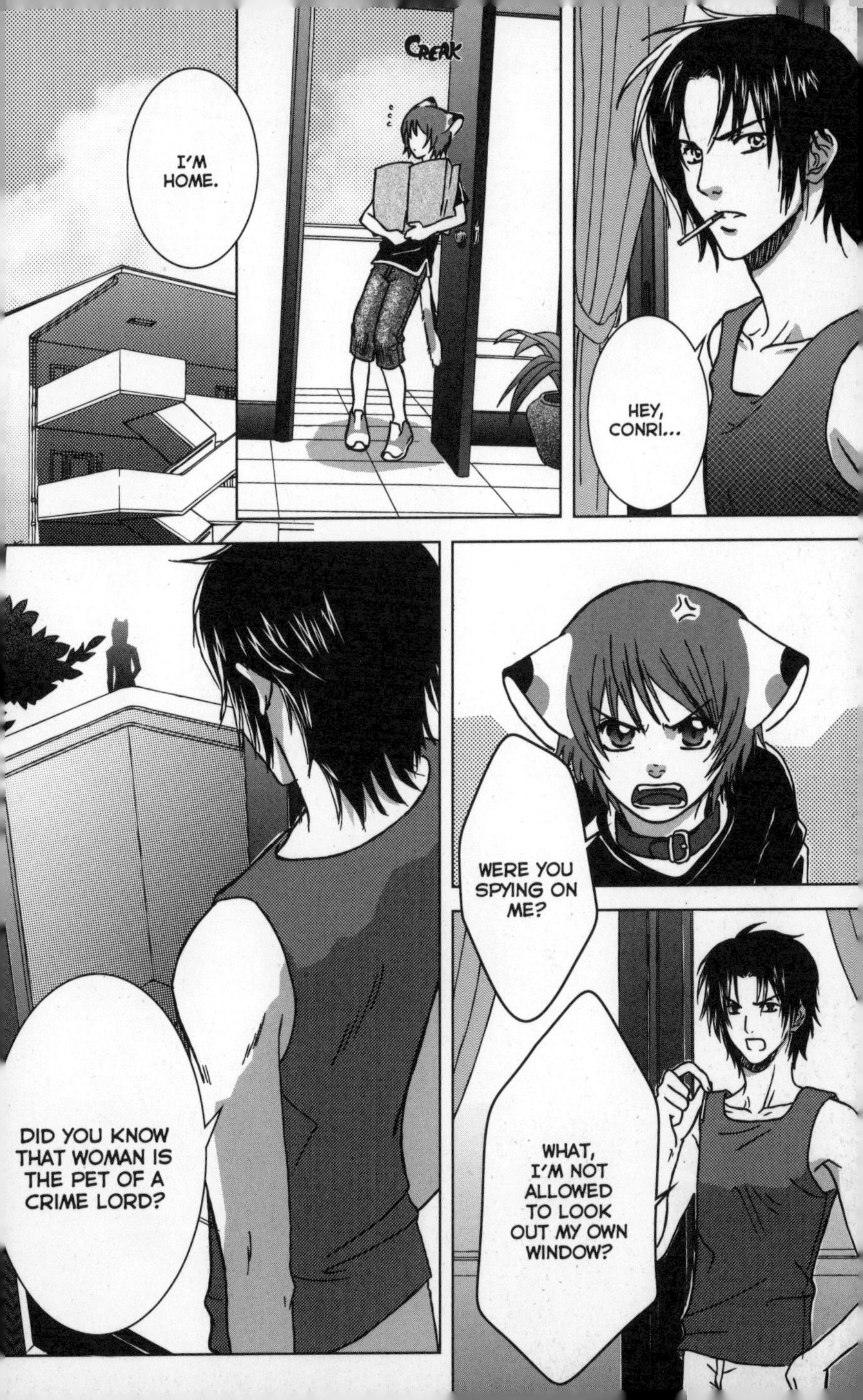
I'M HOME.
CREAK
HEY, CONRI...
DID YOU KNOW THAT WOMAN IS THE PET OF A CRIME LORD?
WERE YOU SPYING ON ME?
WHAT, I'M NOT ALLOWED TO LOOK OUT MY OWN WINDOW?

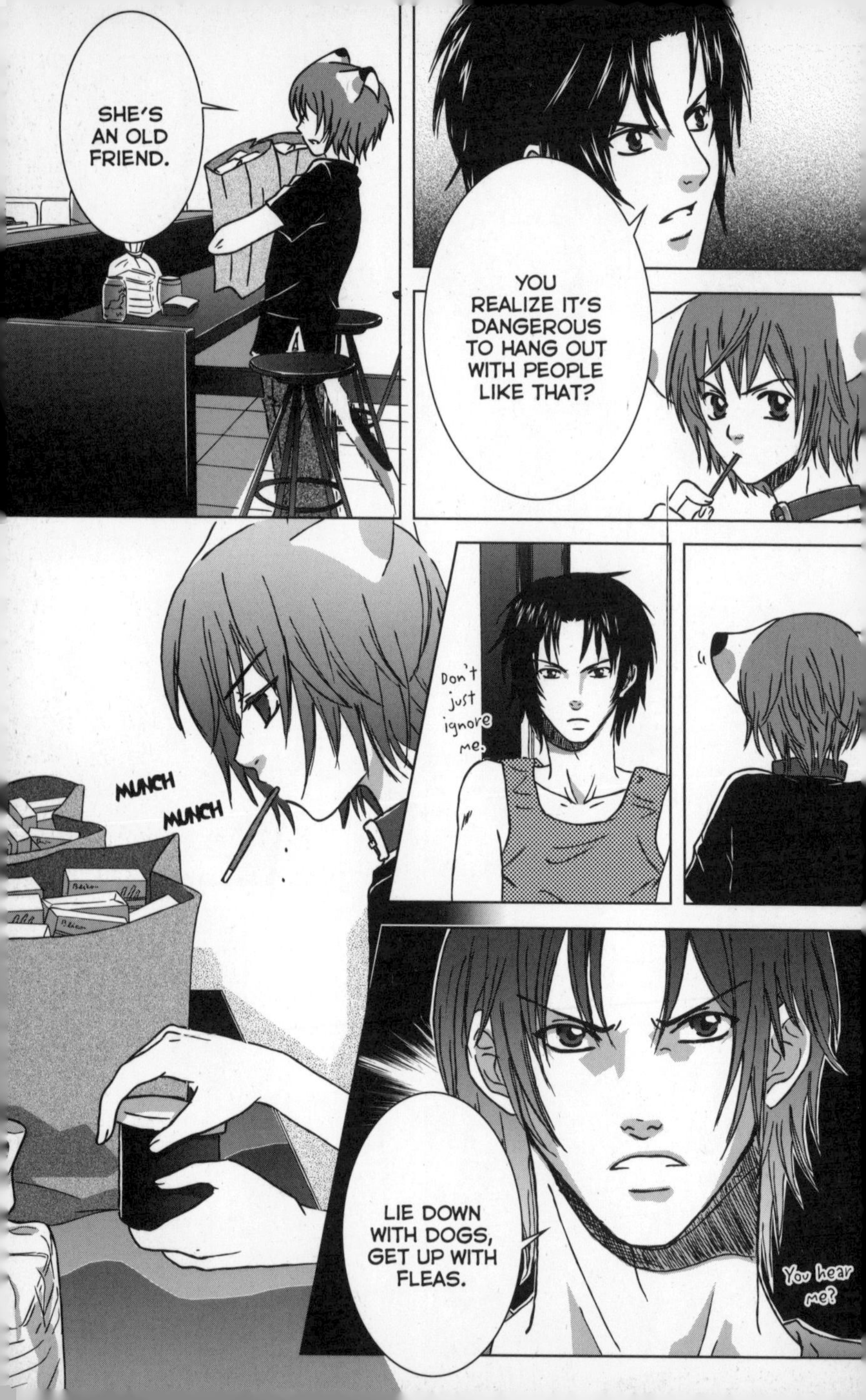
SHE'S AN OLD FRIEND.
YOU REALIZE IT'S DANGEROUS TO HANG OUT WITH PEOPLE LIKE THAT?
MUNCH
MUNCH
Don't just ignore me.
LIE DOWN WITH DOGS, GET UP WITH FLEAS.
You hear me?

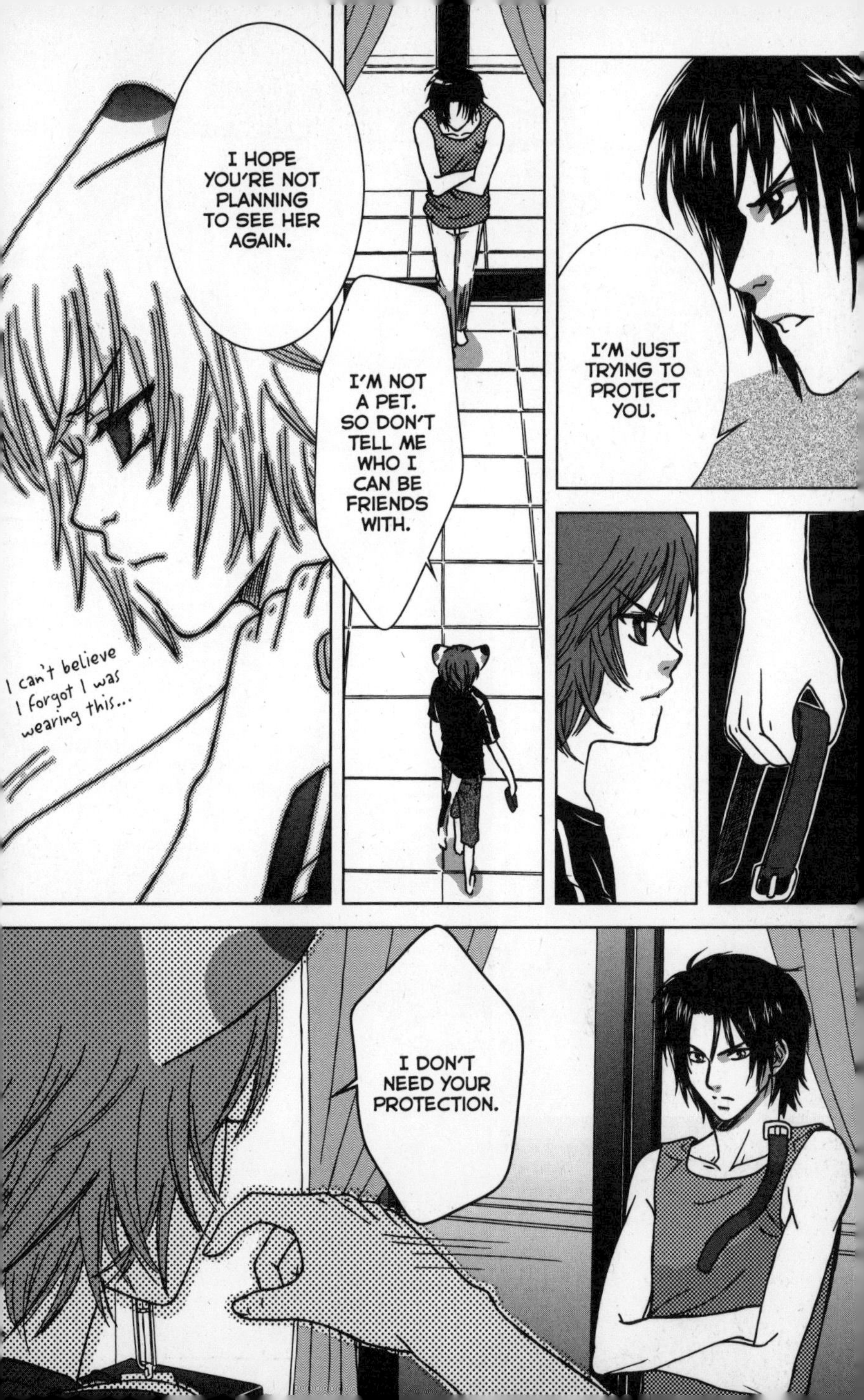
I HOPE YOU'RE NOT PLANNING TO SEE HER AGAIN.
I can't believe I forgot I was wearing this...
I'M NOT A PET. SO DON'T TELL ME WHO I CAN BE FRIENDS WITH.
I'M JUST TRYING TO PROTECT YOU.
I DON'T NEED YOUR PROTECTION.

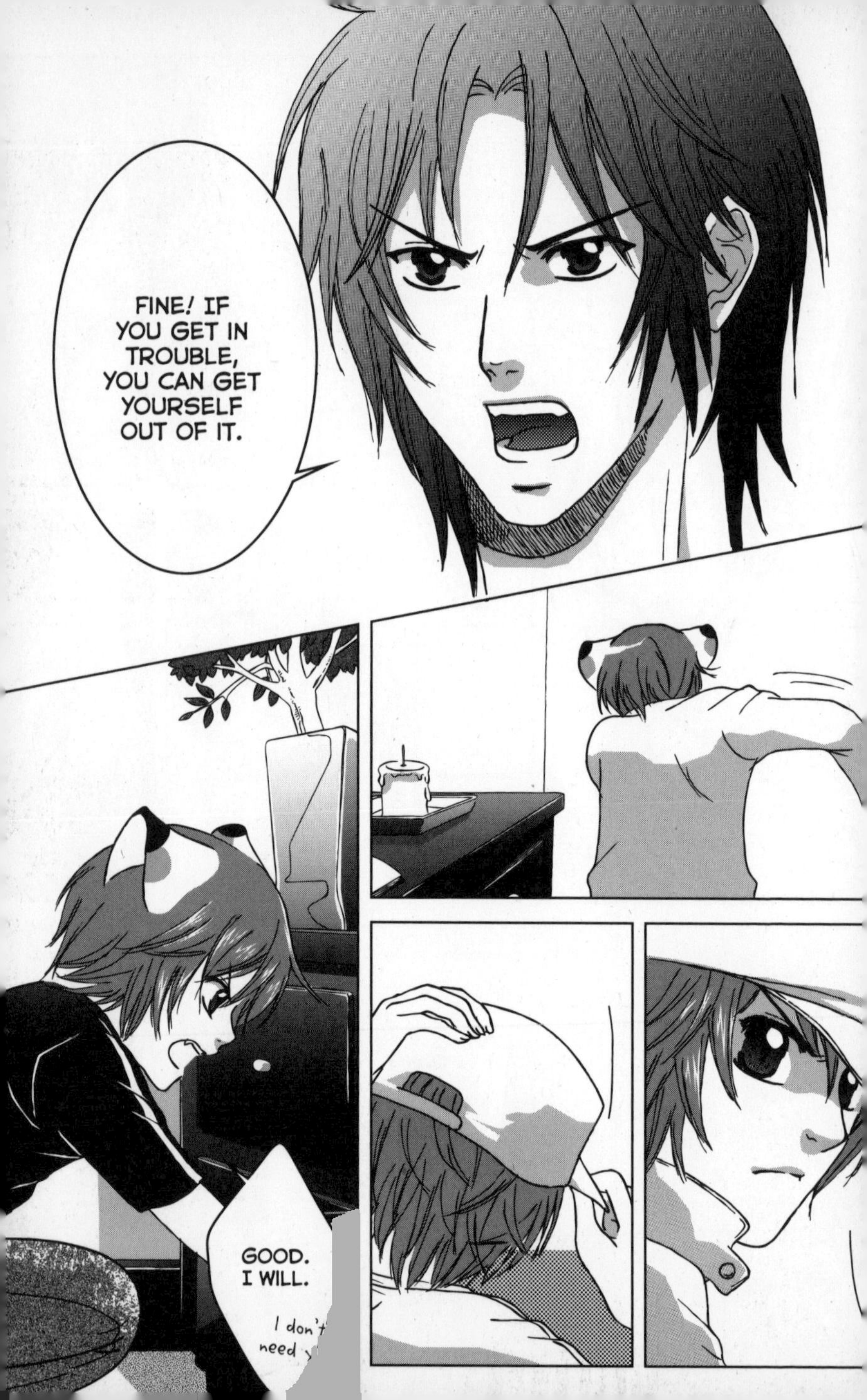
FINE! IF YOU GET IN TROUBLE, YOU CAN GET YOURSELF OUT OF IT.
GOOD. I WILL.
I don't need

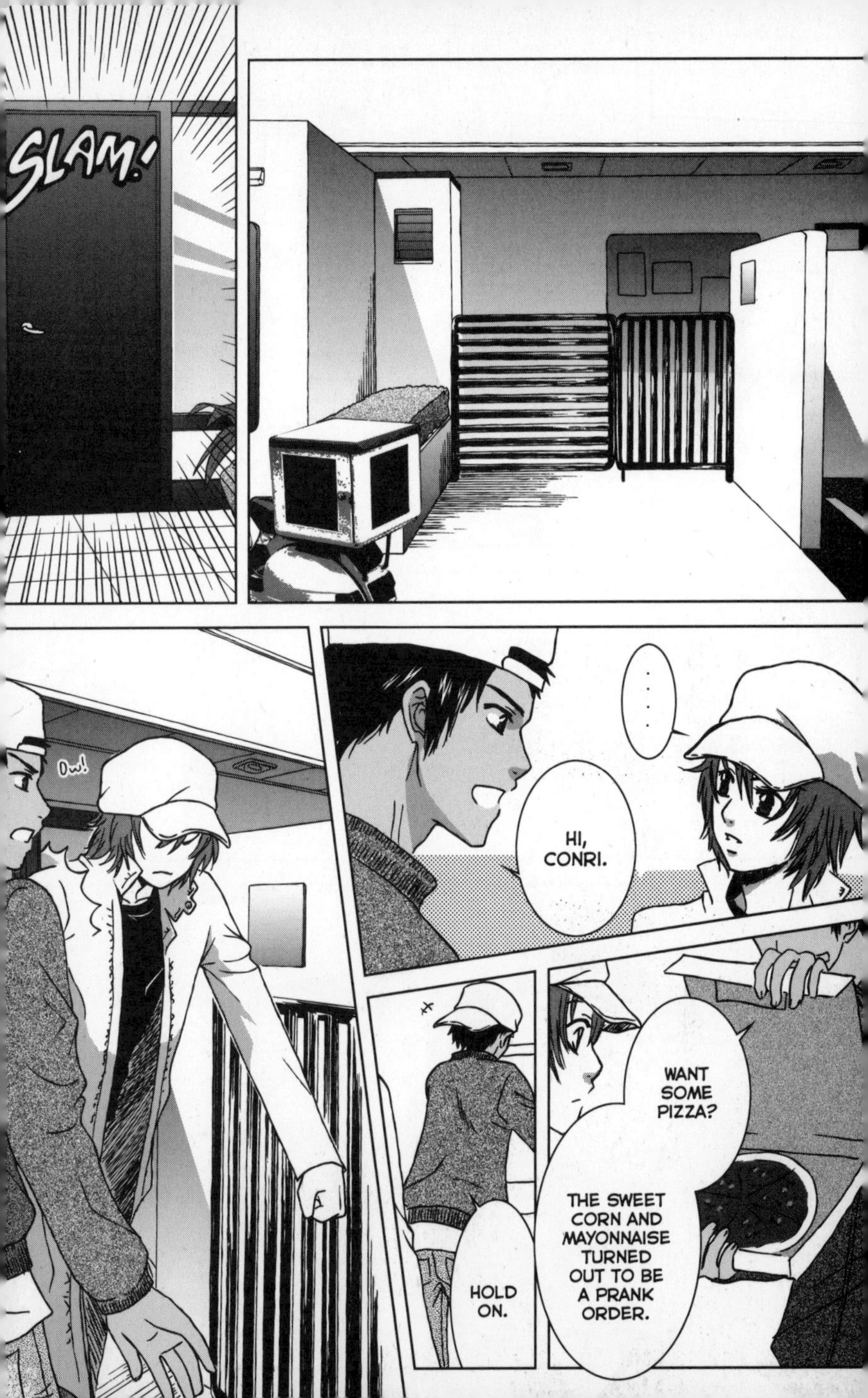
SLAM!
Ow!
. . . . .
HI, CONRI.
HOLD ON.
WANT SOME PIZZA?
THE SWEET CORN AND MAYONNAISE TURNED OUT TO BE A PRANK ORDER.

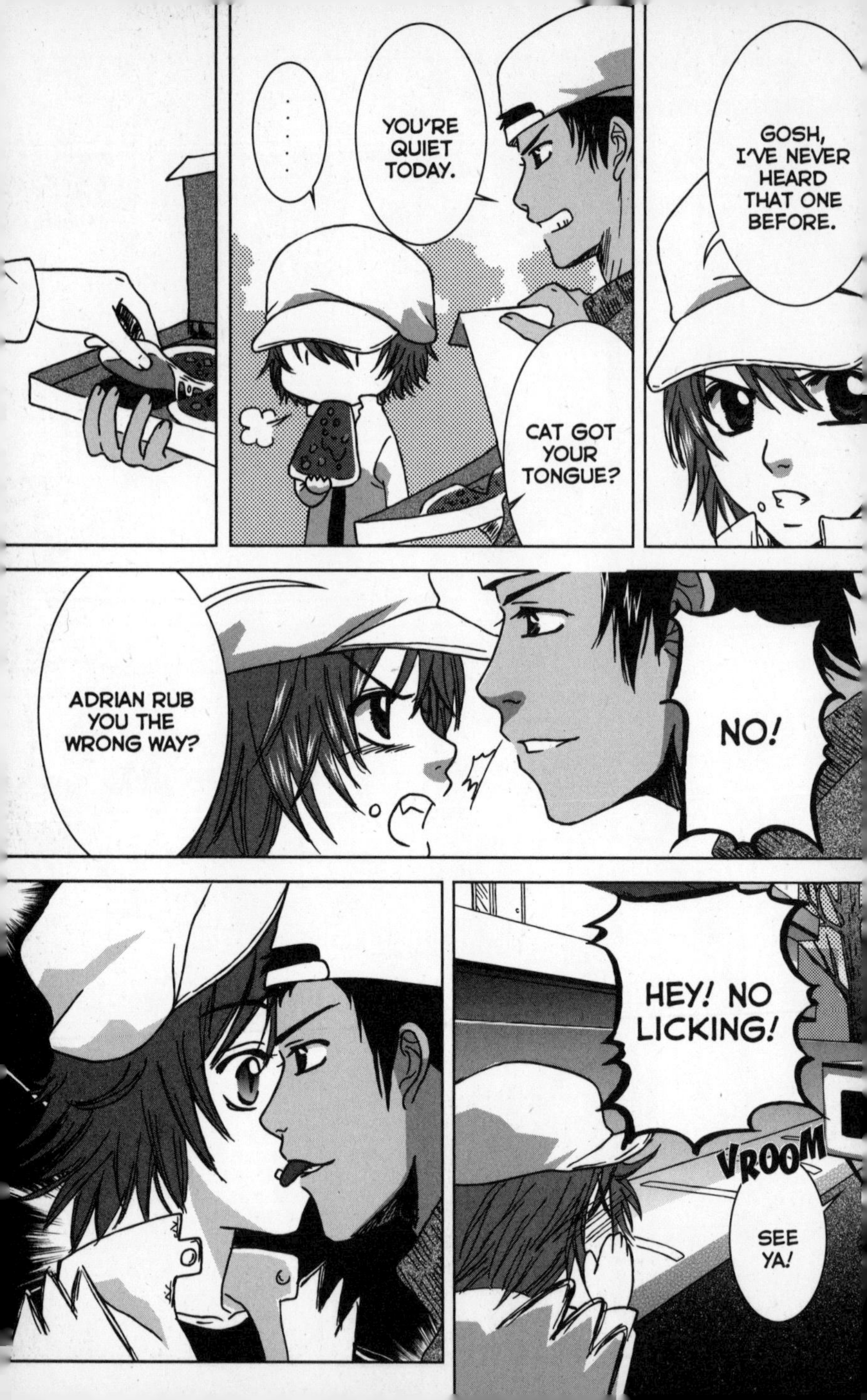
. . . . .
YOU'RE QUIET TODAY.
CAT GOT YOUR TONGUE?
GOSH, I'VE NEVER HEARD THAT ONE BEFORE.
ADRIAN RUB YOU THE WRONG WAY?
NO!
HEY! NO LICKING!
VROOM
SEE YA!

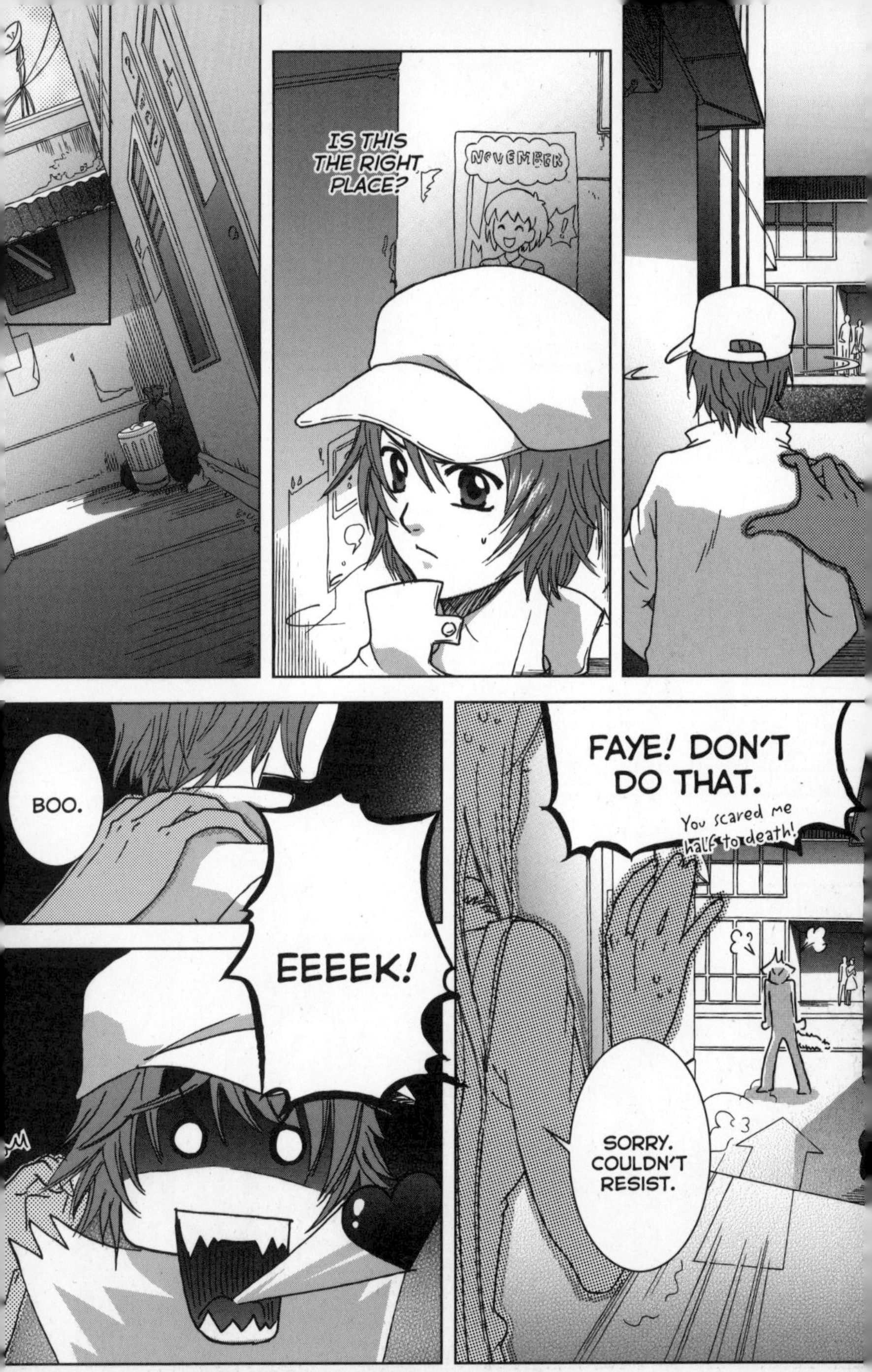
IS THIS THE RIGHT PLACE?
NOVEMBER
BOO.
EEEEK!
FAYE! DON'T DO THAT.
You scared me half to death!
SORRY. COULDN'T RESIST.

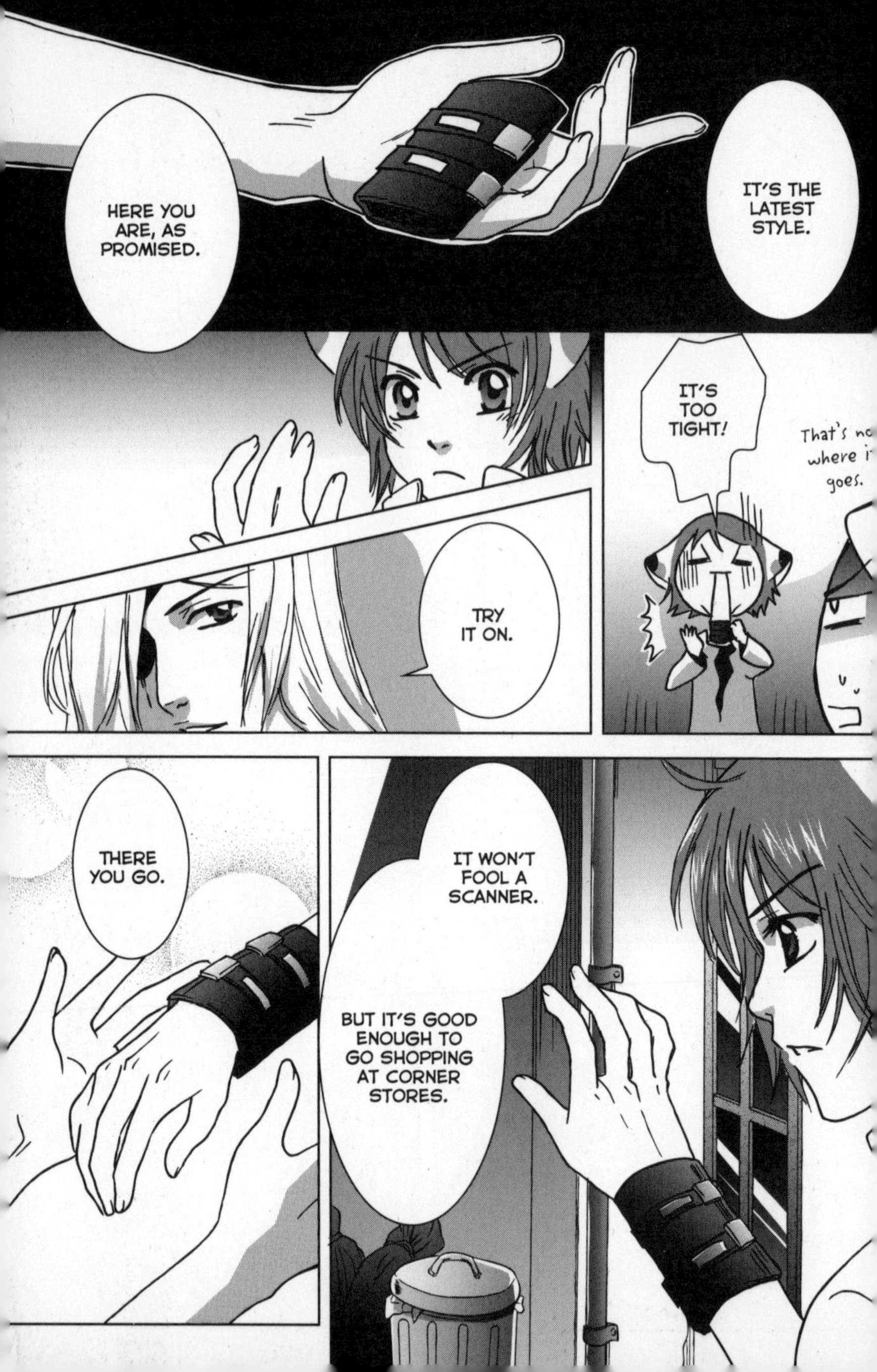
HERE YOU ARE, AS PROMISED.
IT'S THE LATEST STYLE.
TRY IT ON.
IT'S TOO TIGHT!
That's no where i goes.
THERE YOU GO.
IT WON'T FOOL A SCANNER.
BUT IT'S GOOD ENOUGH TO GO SHOPPING AT CORNER STORES.

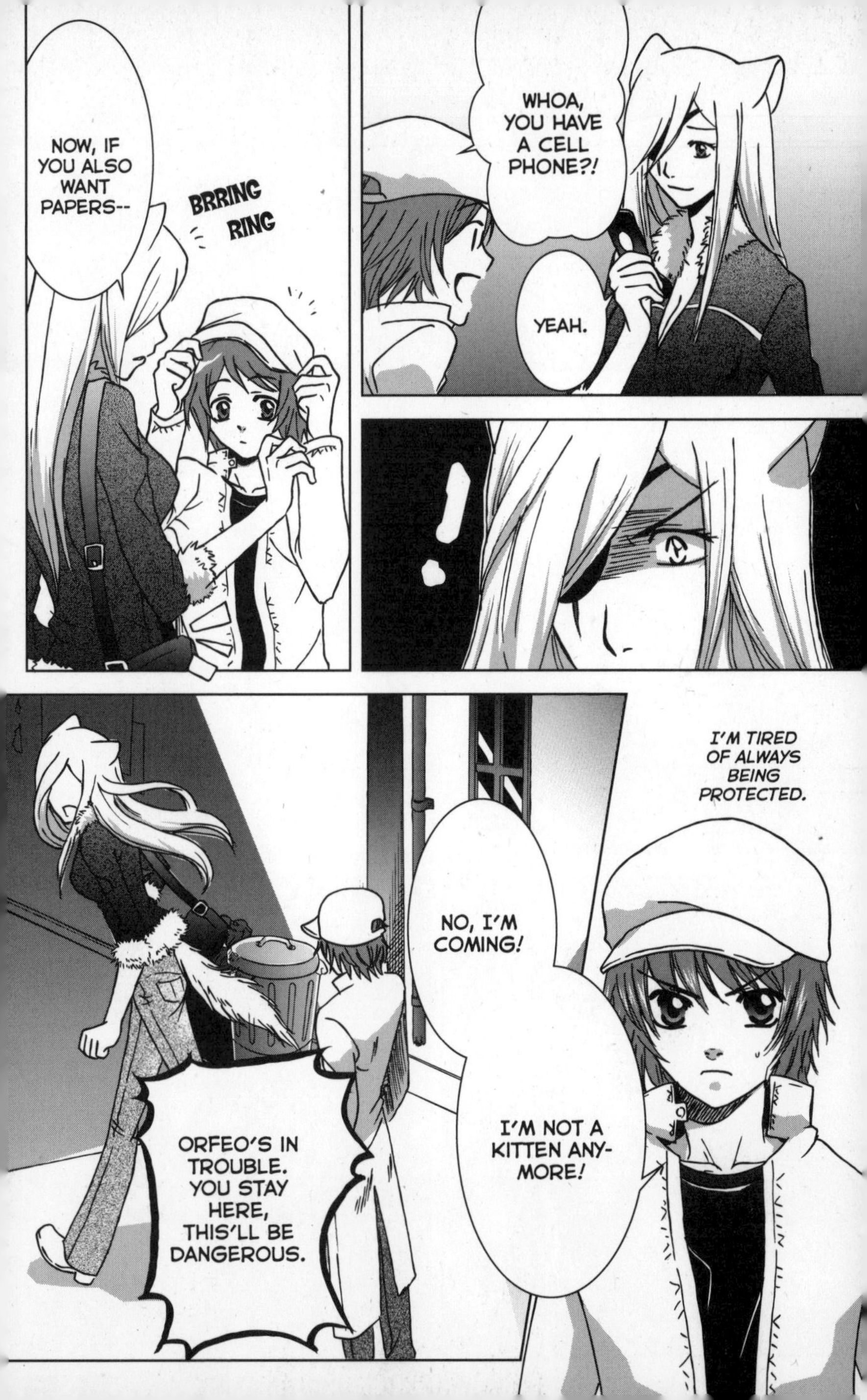
NOW, IF YOU ALSO WANT PAPERS--
BRRING
RING
WHOA, YOU HAVE A CELL PHONE?!
YEAH.
!
ORFEO'S IN TROUBLE. YOU STAY HERE, THIS'LL BE DANGEROUS.
NO, I'M COMING!
I'M NOT A KITTEN ANY-MORE!
I'M TIRED OF ALWAYS BEING PROTECTED.

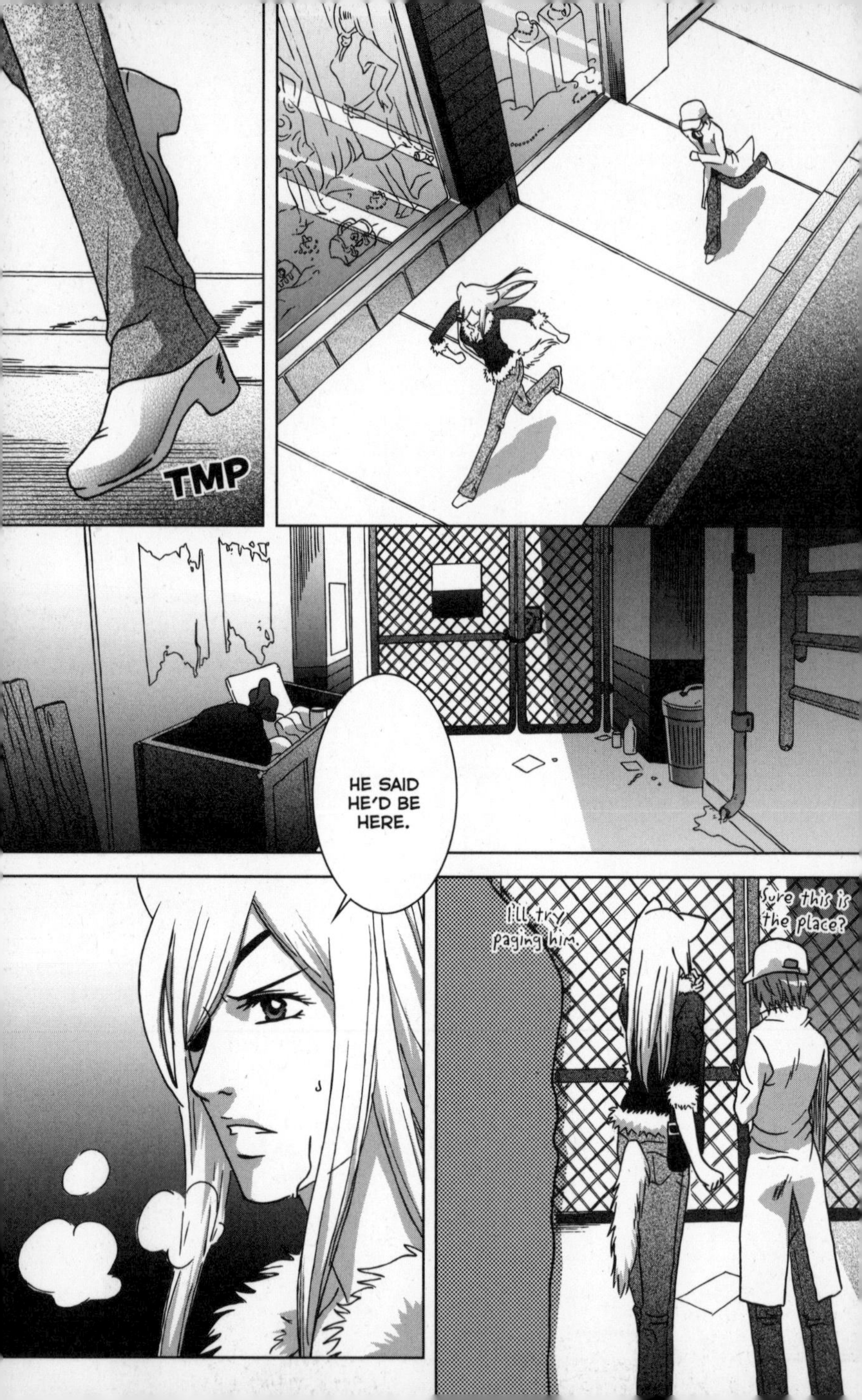
TMP
HE SAID HE'D BE HERE.
Sure this is the place?
I'll try paging him.

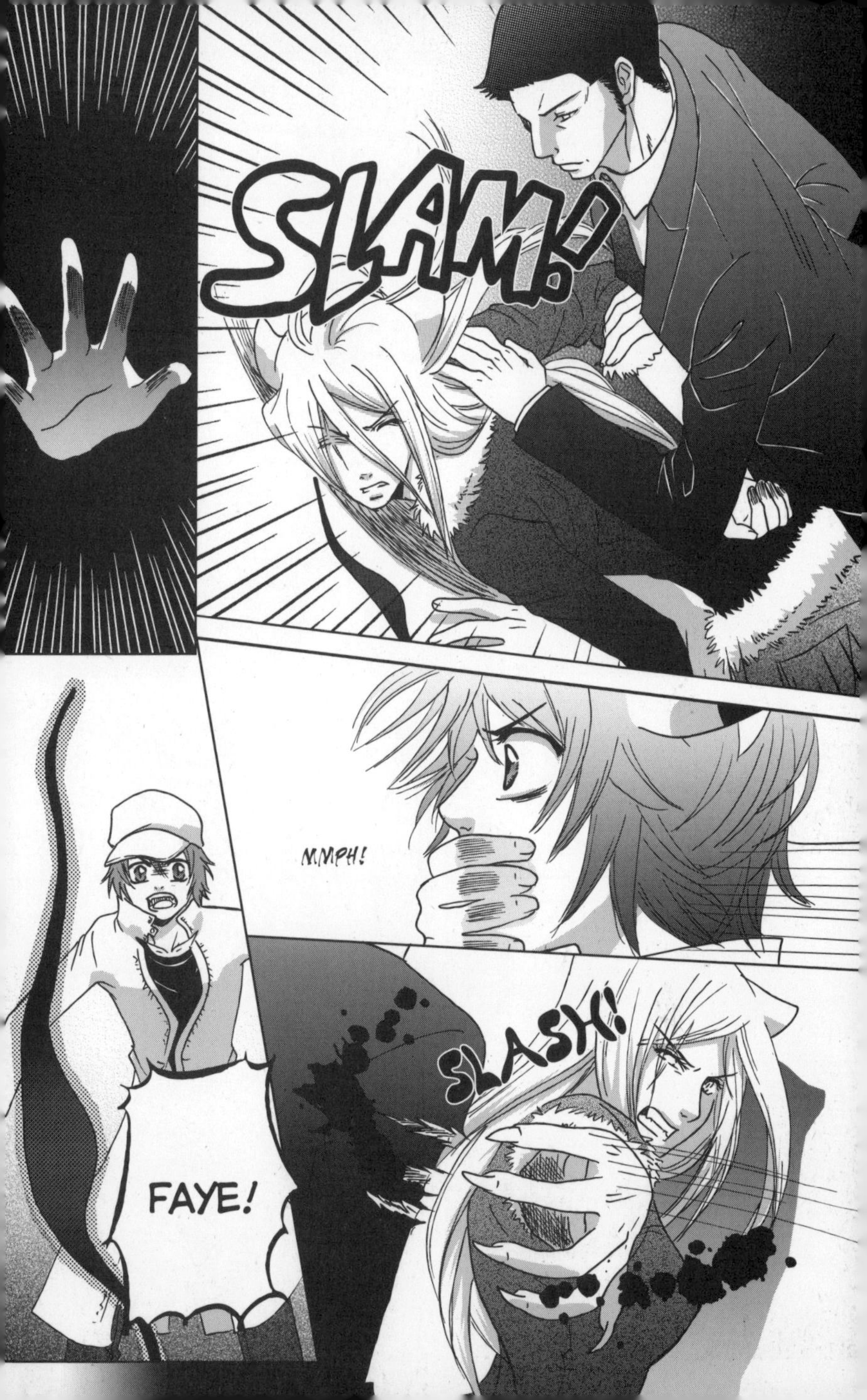
SLAM!
FAYE!
MMPH!
SLASH!

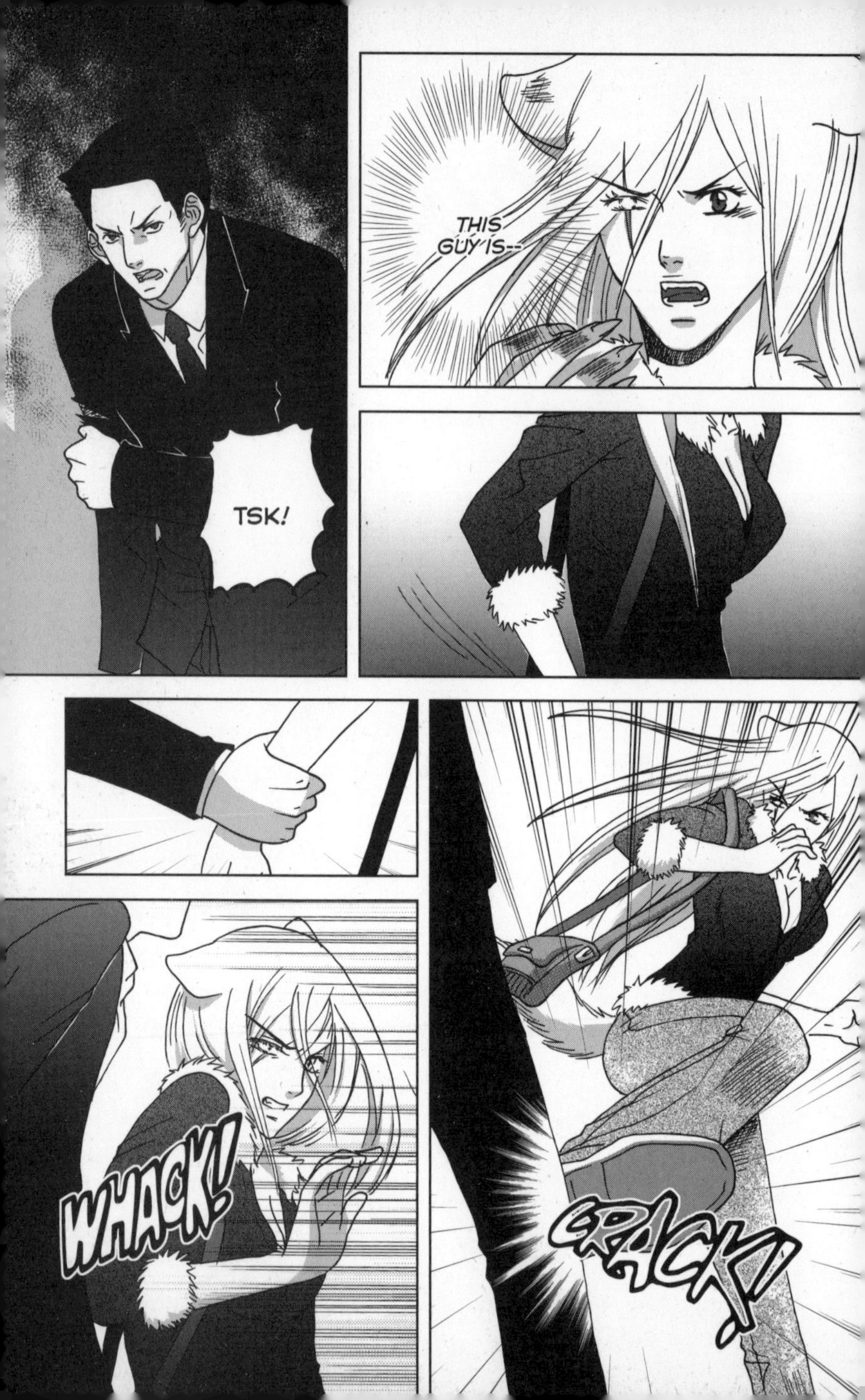
TSK!
THIS GUY IS--
WHACK!
CRACK!

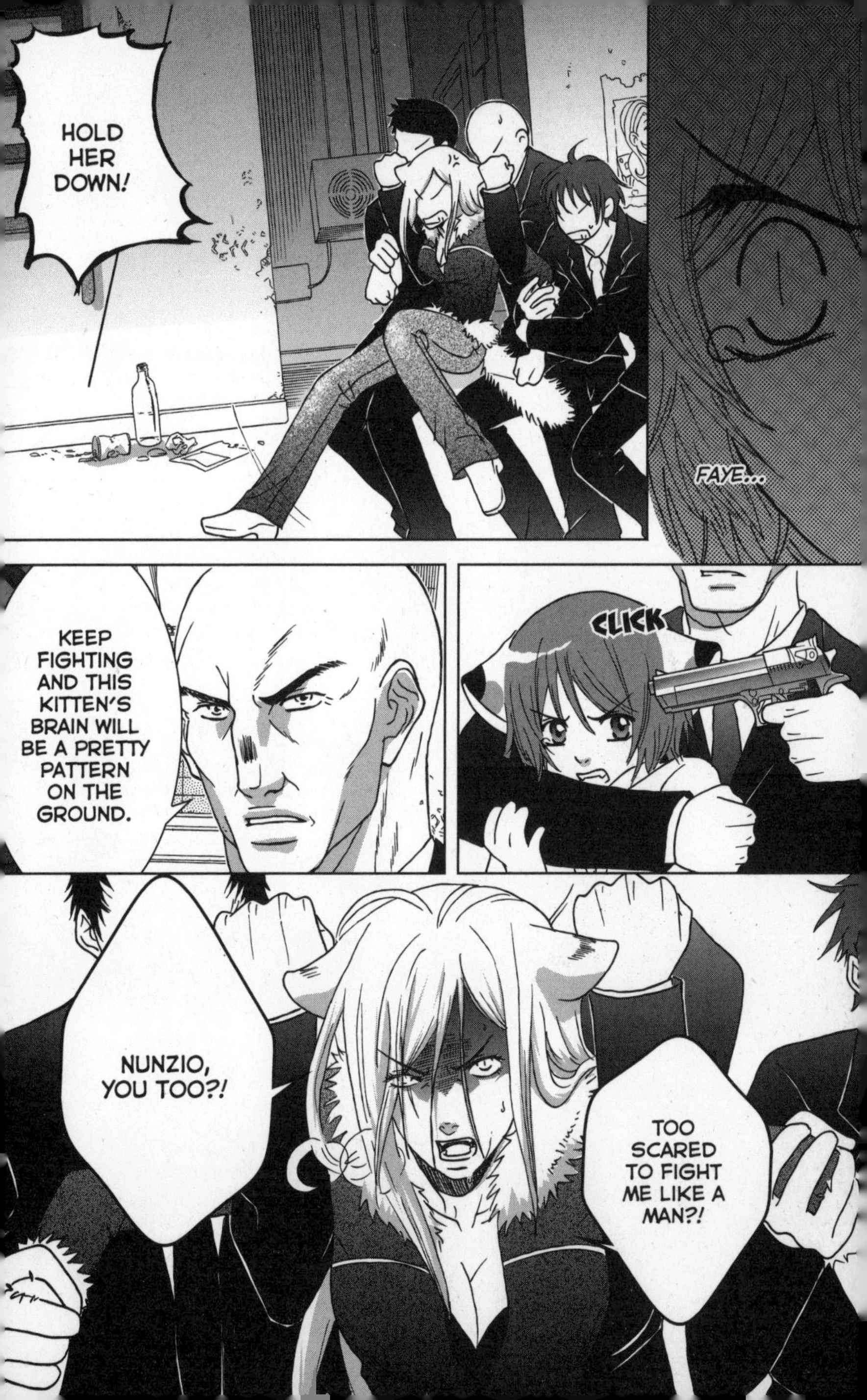

HOLD HER DOWN!
FAYE...
KEEP FIGHTING AND THIS KITTEN'S BRAIN WILL BE A PRETTY PATTERN ON THE GROUND.
CLICK
NUNZIO, YOU TOO?!
TOO SCARED TO FIGHT ME LIKE A MAN?!

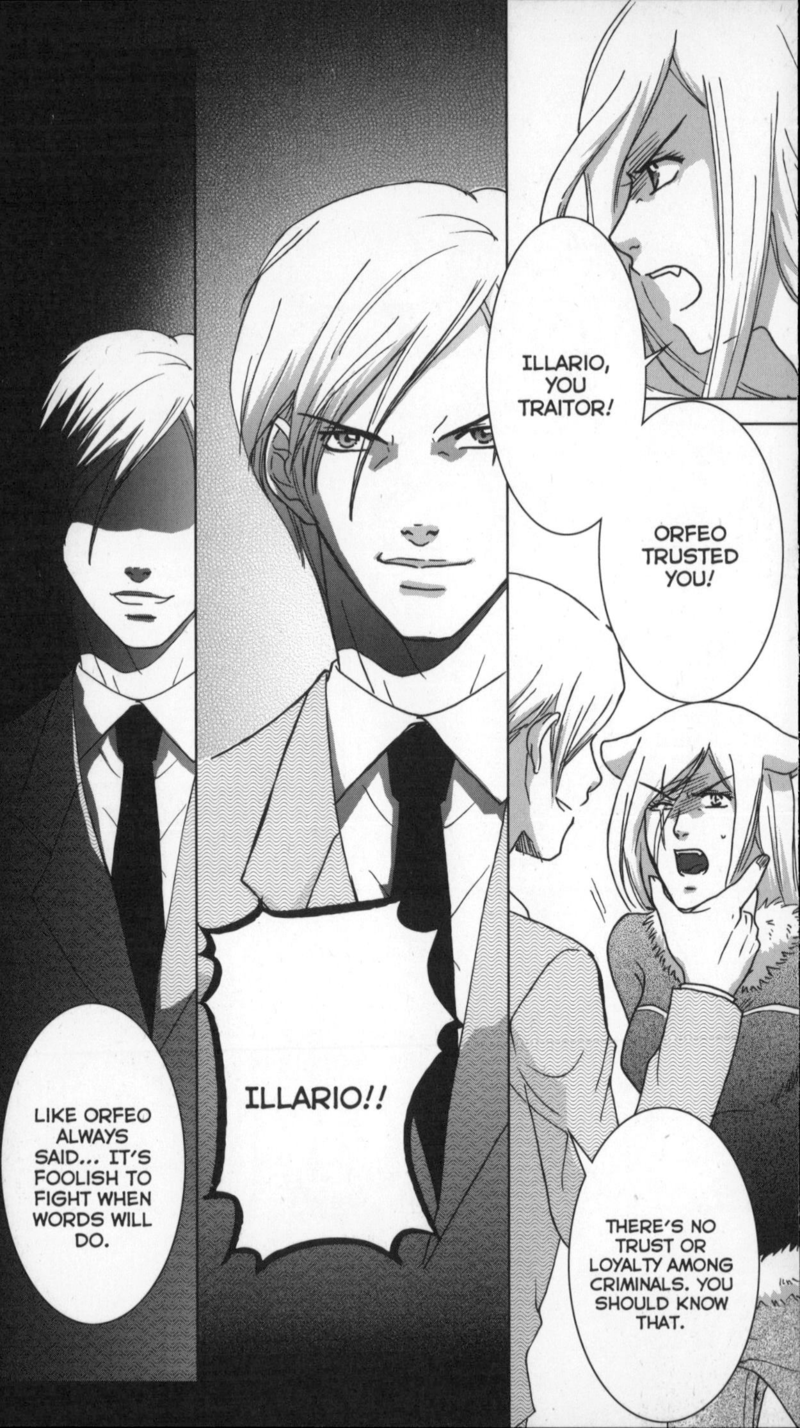
LIKE ORFEO ALWAYS SAID... IT'S FOOLISH TO FIGHT WHEN WORDS WILL DO.
ILLARIO!!
ILLARIO, YOU TRAITOR!
ORFEO TRUSTED YOU!
THERE'S NO TRUST OR LOYALTY AMONG CRIMINALS. YOU SHOULD KNOW THAT.

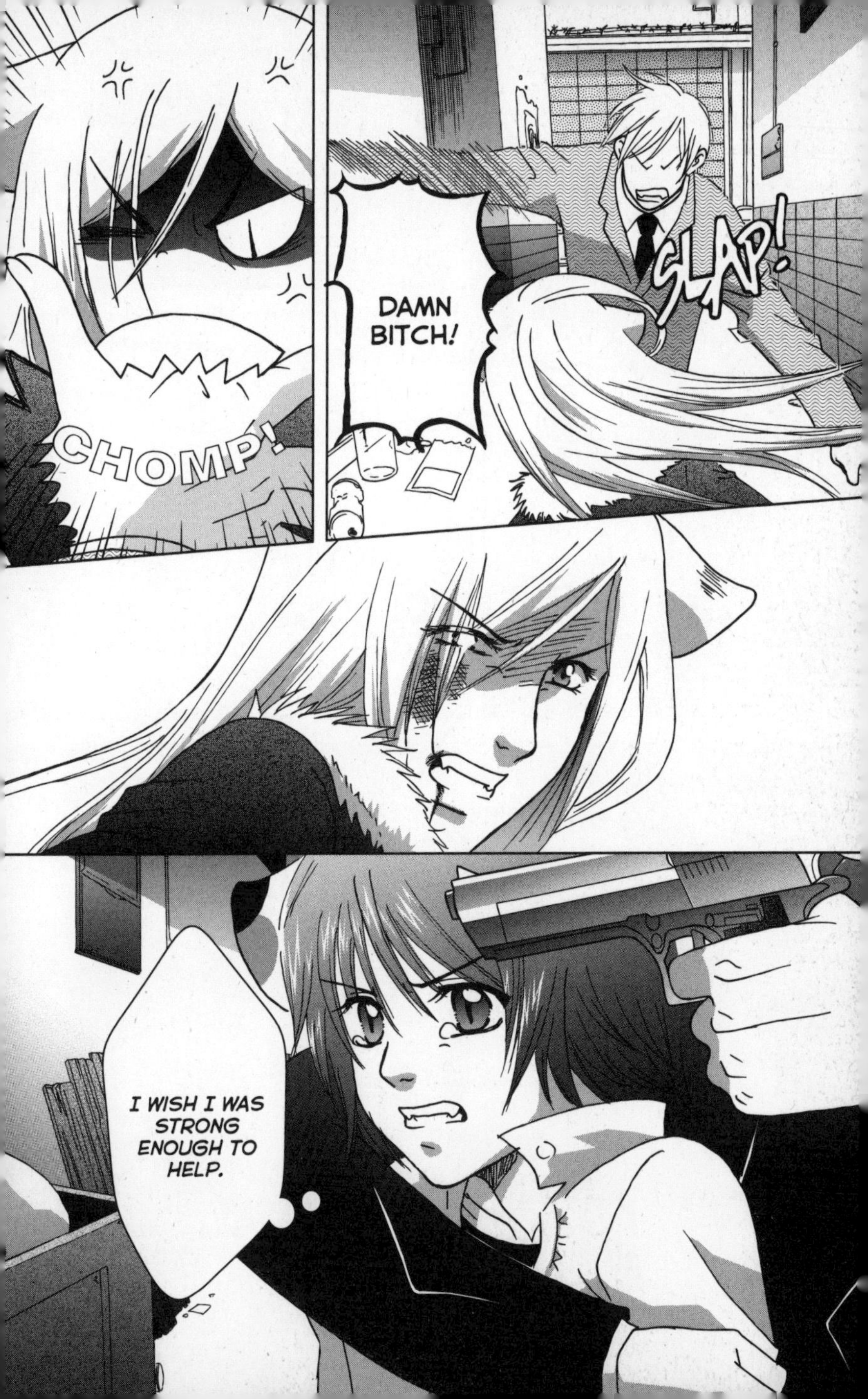
CHOMP!
DAMN BITCH!
SLAP!
I WISH I WAS STRONG ENOUGH TO HELP.

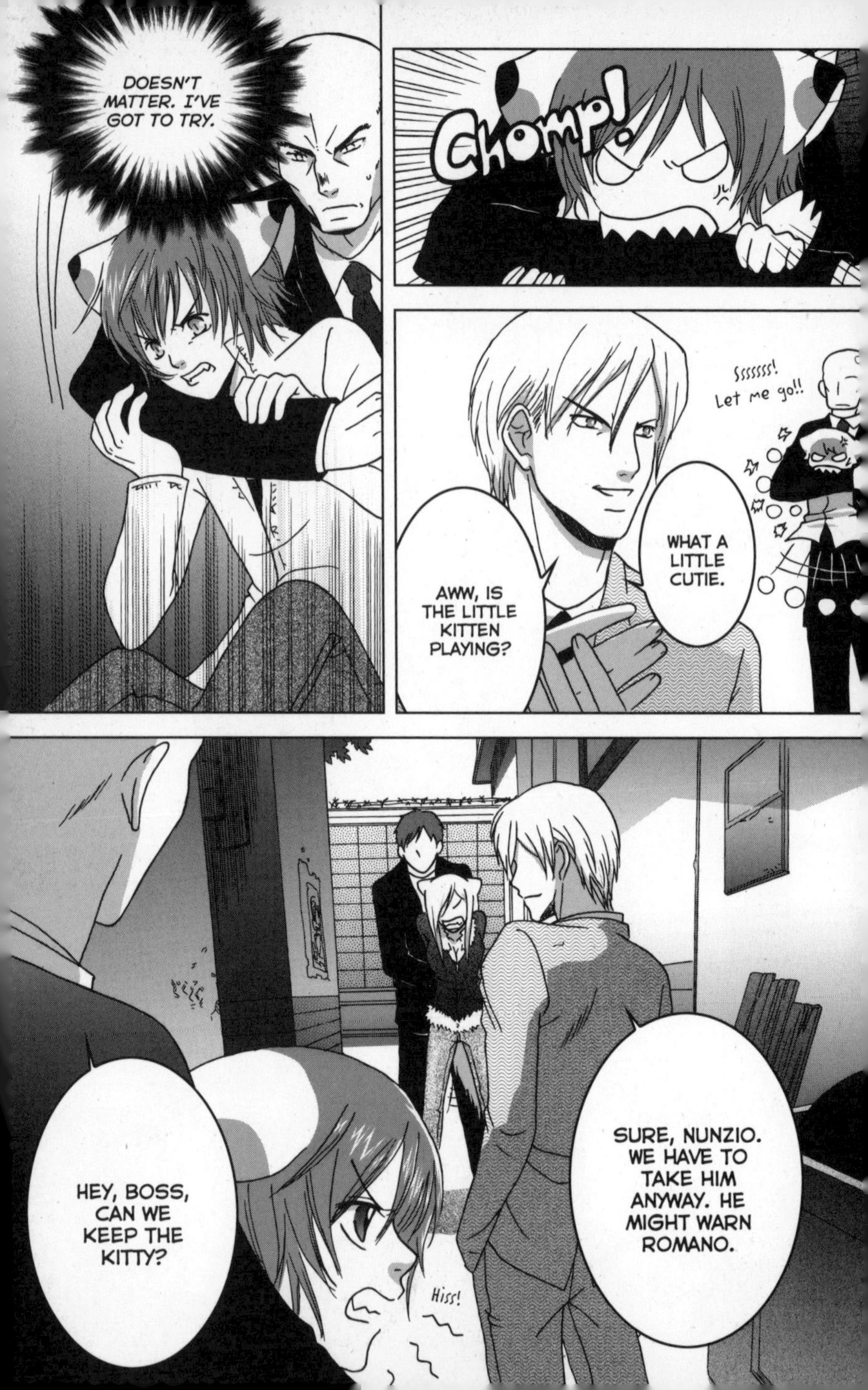
DOESN'T MATTER. I'VE GOT TO TRY.
CHOMP!
AWW, IS THE LITTLE KITTEN PLAYING?
WHAT A LITTLE CUTIE.
Ssssssss! Let me go!!
HEY, BOSS, CAN WE KEEP THE KITTY?
Hiss!
SURE, NUNZIO. WE HAVE TO TAKE HIM ANYWAY. HE MIGHT WARN ROMANO.

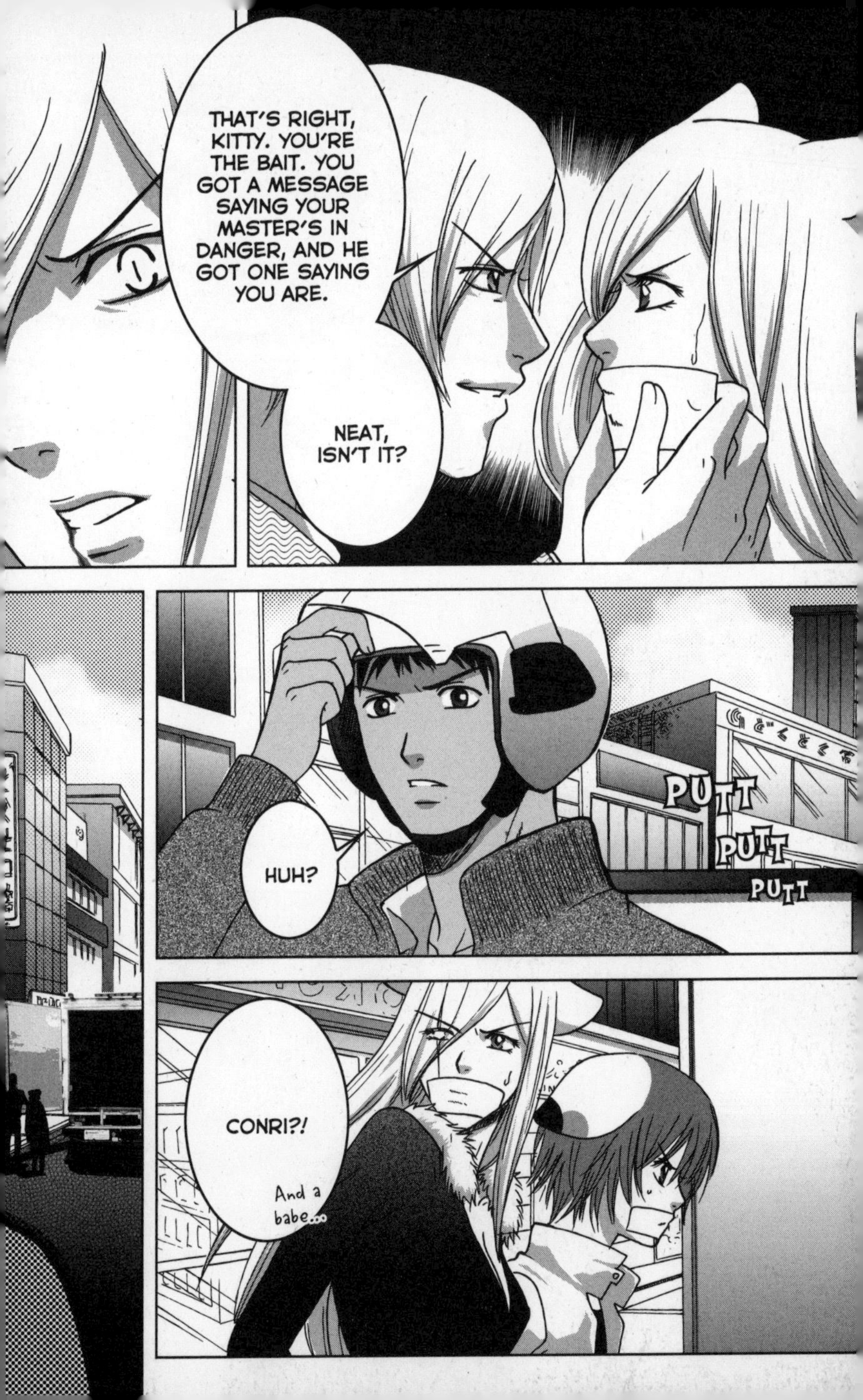
THAT'S RIGHT, KITTY. YOU'RE THE BAIT. YOU GOT A MESSAGE SAYING YOUR MASTER'S IN DANGER, AND HE GOT ONE SAYING YOU ARE.
NEAT, ISN'T IT?
HUH?
PUTT
PUTT
PUTT
CONRI?!
And a babe...

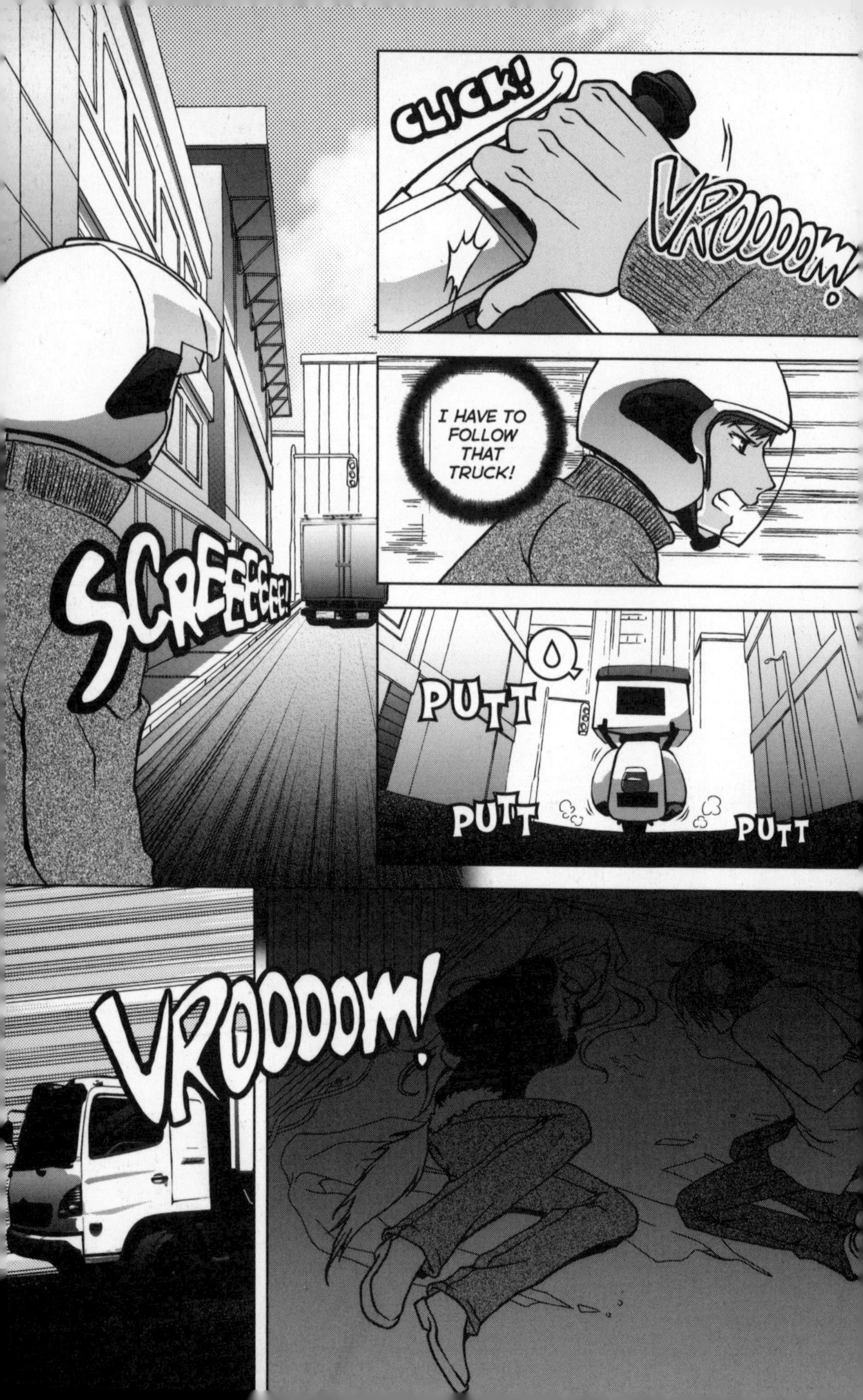
SCREEEEEE!
CLICK!
VROOOOOM!
I HAVE TO FOLLOW THAT TRUCK!
PUTT
PUTT
PUTT
VROOOOM!

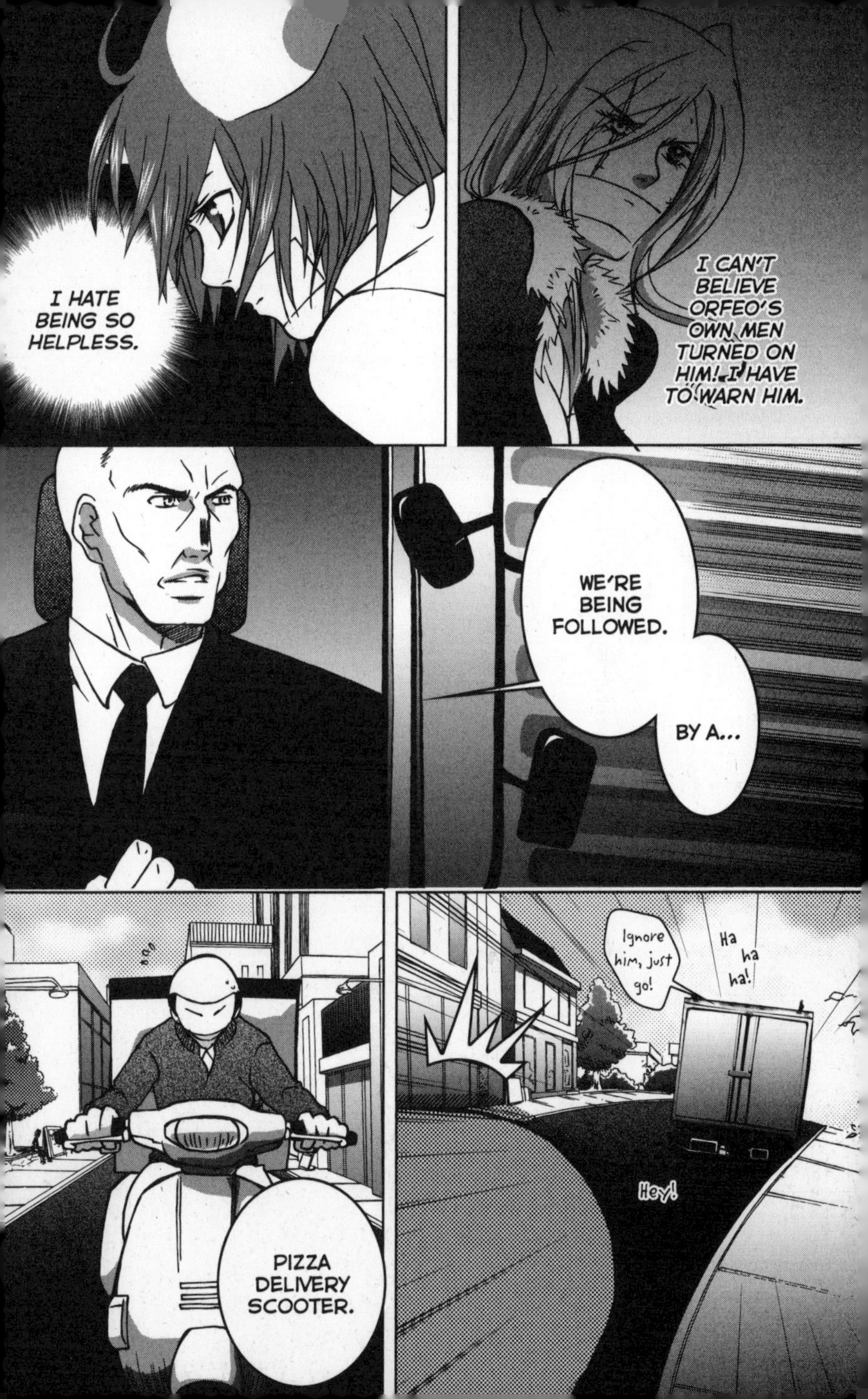
I HATE BEING SO HELPLESS.
I CAN'T BELIEVE ORFEO'S OWN MEN TURNED ON HIM! I HAVE TO WARN HIM.
WE'RE BEING FOLLOWED.
BY A...
PIZZA DELIVERY SCOOTER.
Ignore him, just go!
Ha ha ha!
Hey!

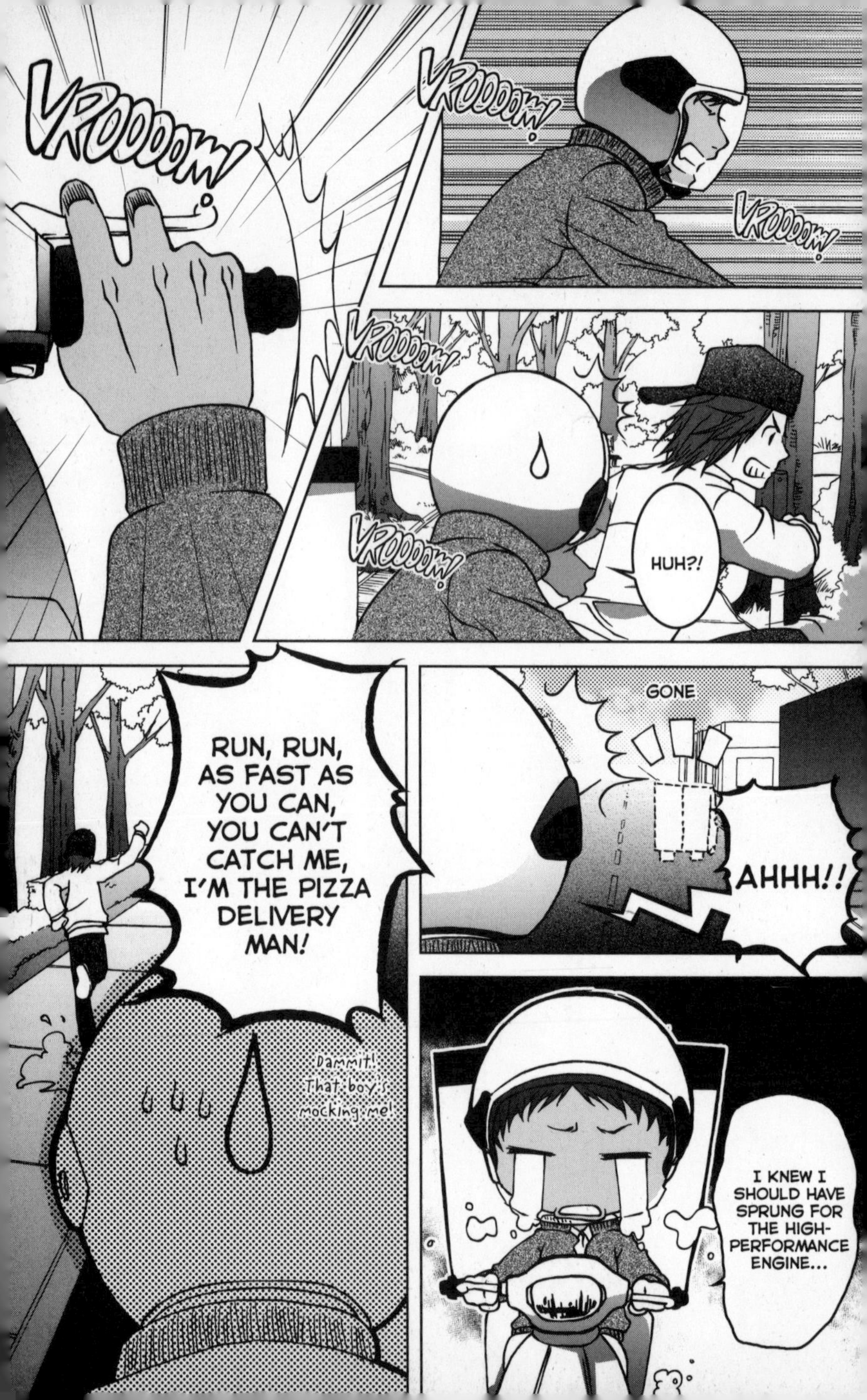
VROOOOOM!
VROOOOM!
VROOOOM!
VROOOOM!
VROOOOM!
HUH?!
RUN, RUN, AS FAST AS YOU CAN, YOU CAN'T CATCH ME, I'M THE PIZZA DELIVERY MAN!
Dammit! That boy's mocking me!
GONE
AHHH!!
I KNEW I SHOULD HAVE SPRUNG FOR THE HIGH-PERFORMANCE ENGINE...

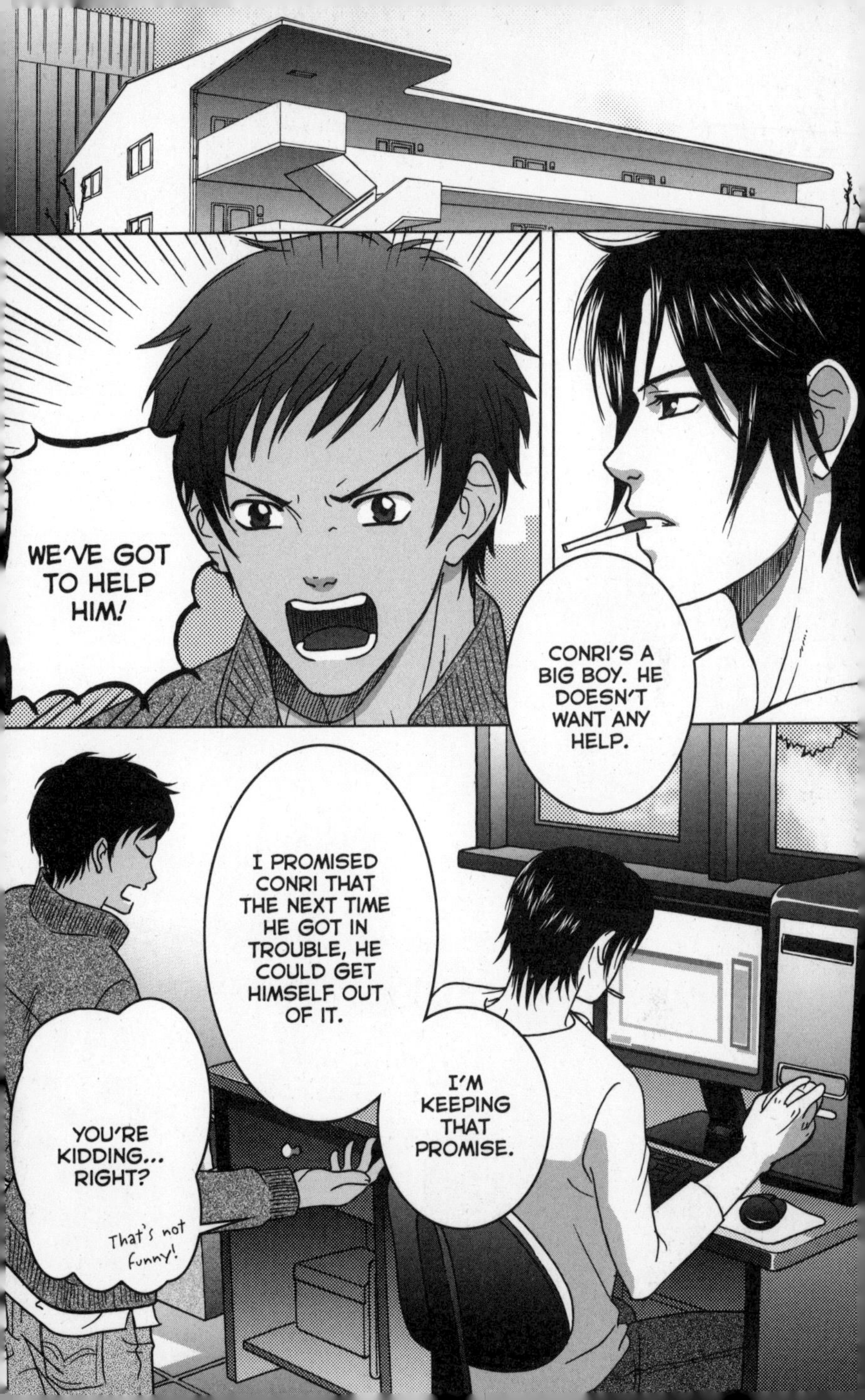
WE'VE GOT TO HELP HIM!
CONRI'S A BIG BOY. HE DOESN'T WANT ANY HELP.
I PROMISED CONRI THAT THE NEXT TIME HE GOT IN TROUBLE, HE COULD GET HIMSELF OUT OF IT.
I'M KEEPING THAT PROMISE.
YOU'RE KIDDING... RIGHT?
That's not funny!

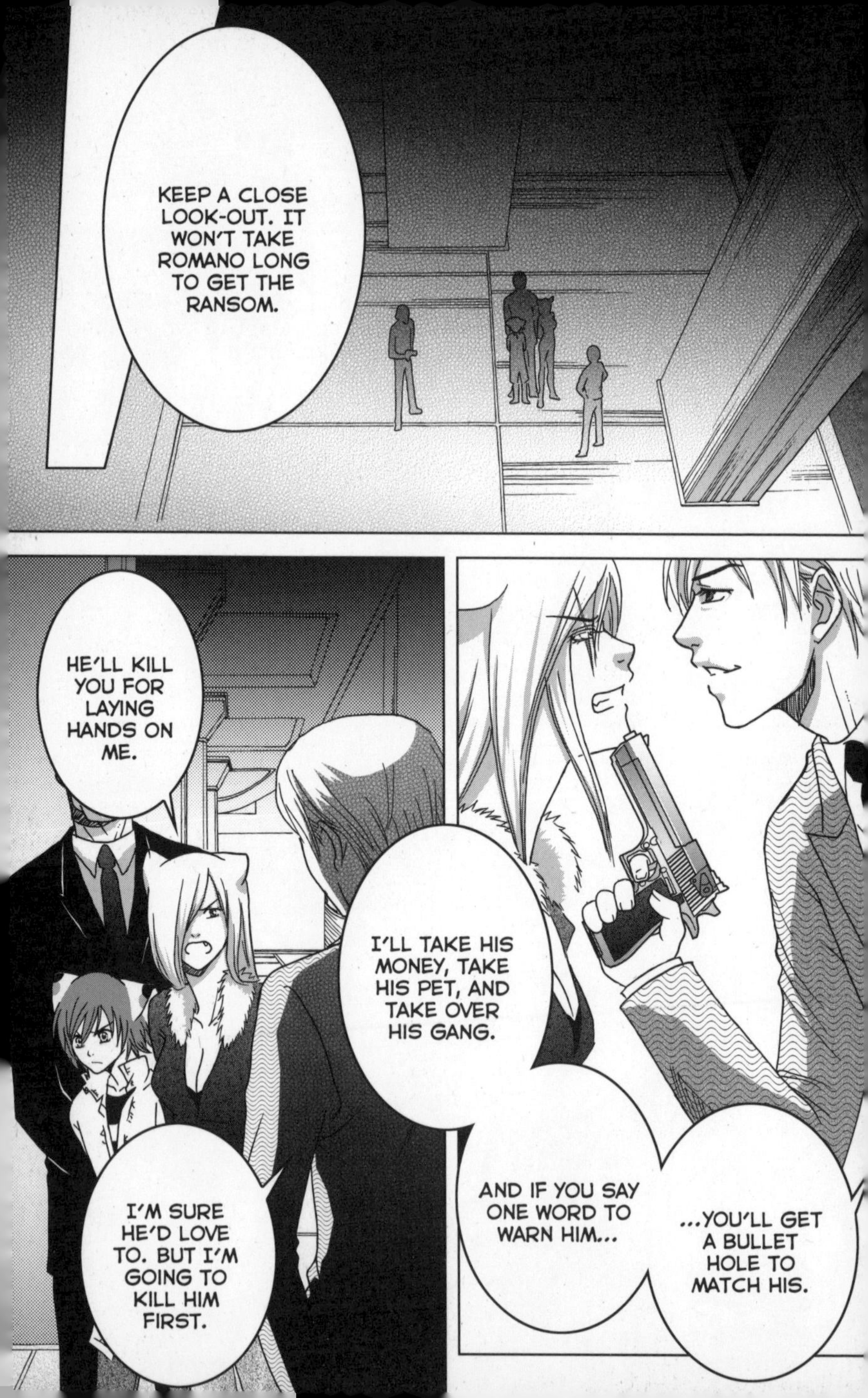
KEEP A CLOSE LOOK-OUT. IT WON'T TAKE ROMANO LONG TO GET THE RANSOM.
HE'LL KILL YOU FOR LAYING HANDS ON ME.
I'M SURE HE'D LOVE TO. BUT I'M GOING TO KILL HIM FIRST.
I'LL TAKE HIS MONEY, TAKE HIS PET, AND TAKE OVER HIS GANG.
AND IF YOU SAY ONE WORD TO WARN HIM...
...YOU'LL GET A BULLET HOLE TO MATCH HIS.

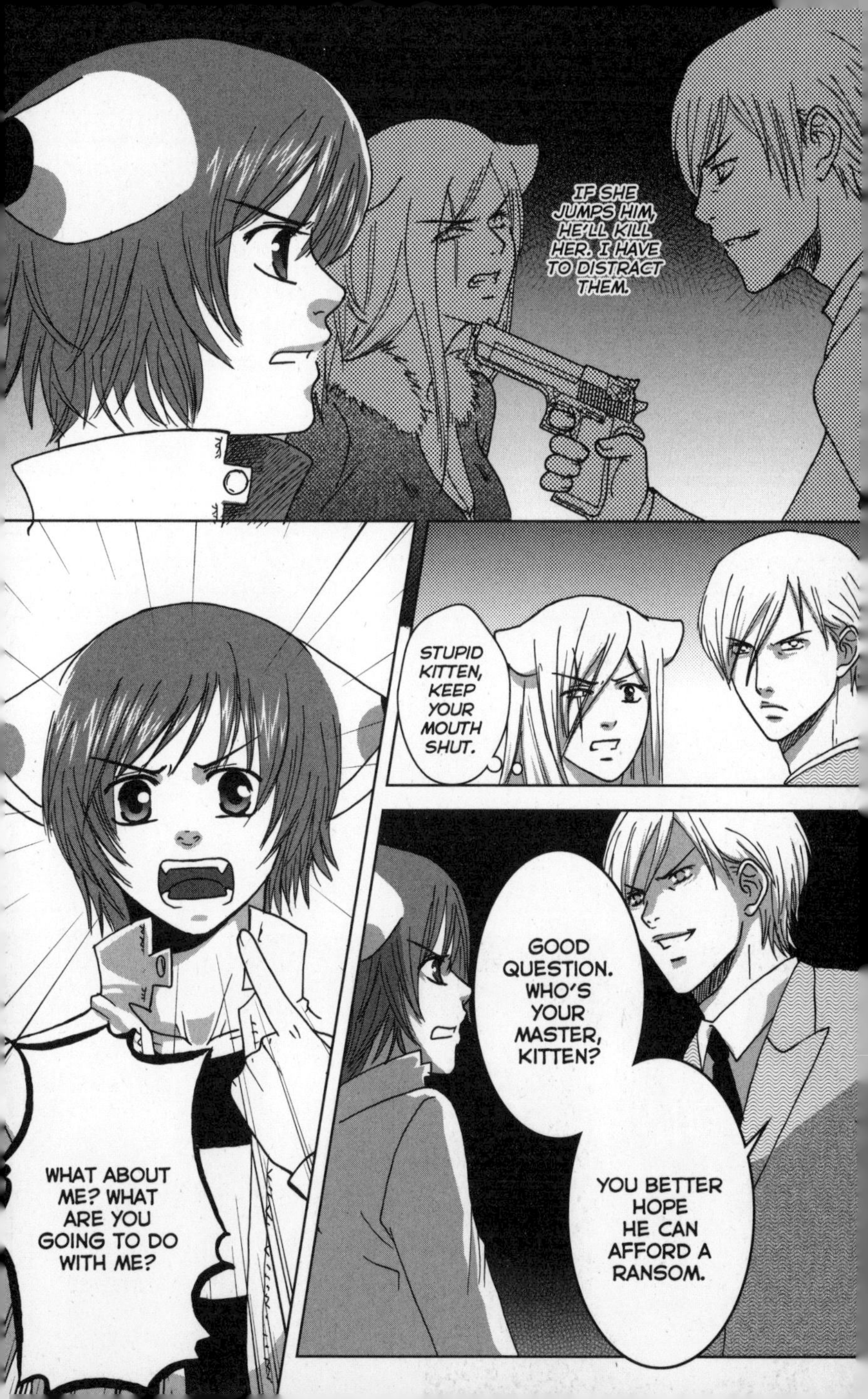
IF SHE JUMPS HIM, HE'LL KILL HER. I HAVE TO DISTRACT THEM.
WHAT ABOUT ME? WHAT ARE YOU GOING TO DO WITH ME?
STUPID KITTEN, KEEP YOUR MOUTH SHUT.
GOOD QUESTION. WHO'S YOUR MASTER, KITTEN?
YOU BETTER HOPE HE CAN AFFORD A RANSOM.

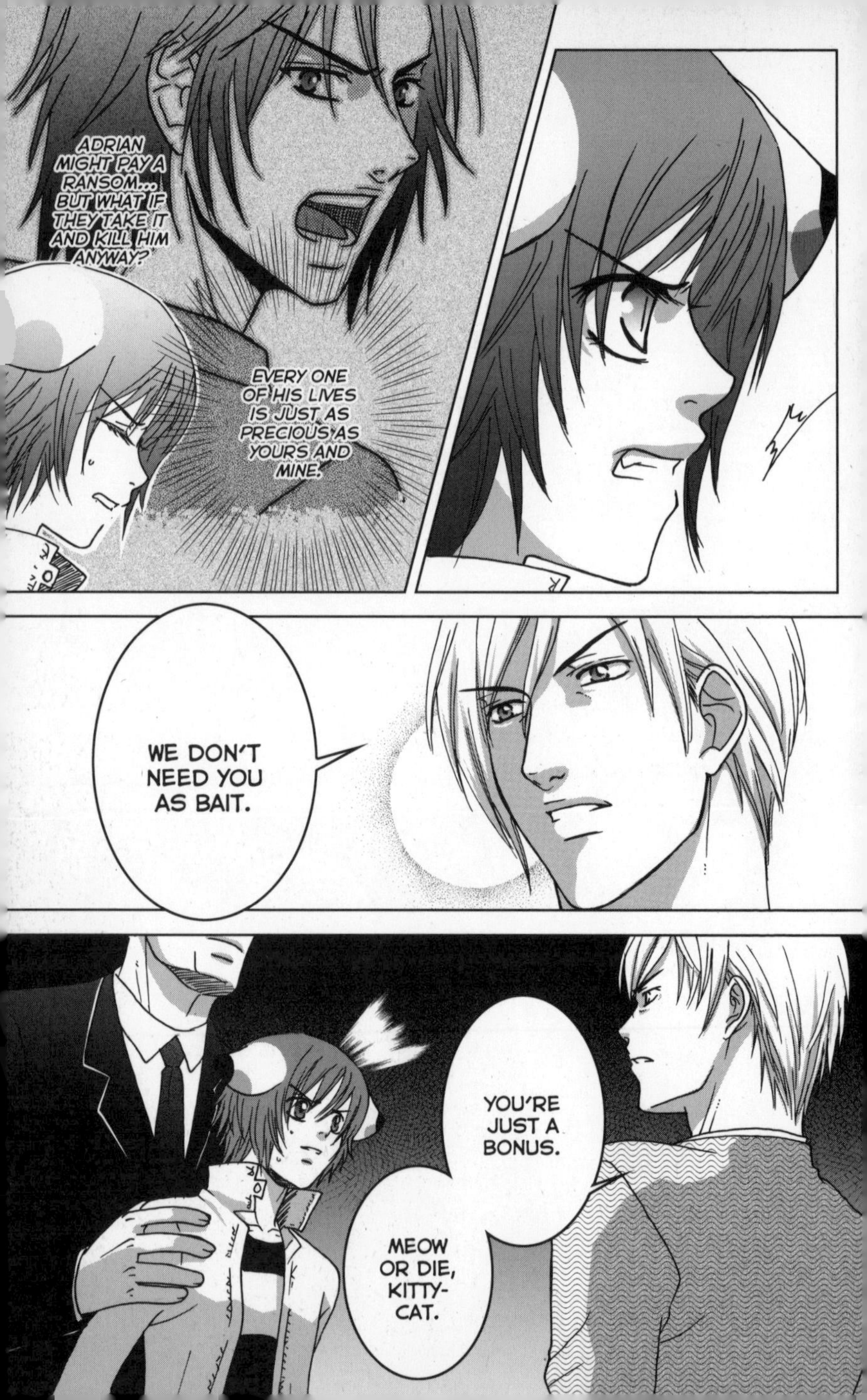
ADRIAN MIGHT PAY A RANSOM... BUT WHAT IF THEY TAKE IT AND KILL HIM ANYWAY?
EVERY ONE OF HIS LIVES IS JUST AS PRECIOUS AS YOURS AND MINE.
WE DON'T NEED YOU AS BAIT.
YOU'RE JUST A BONUS.
MEOW OR DIE, KITTY-CAT.

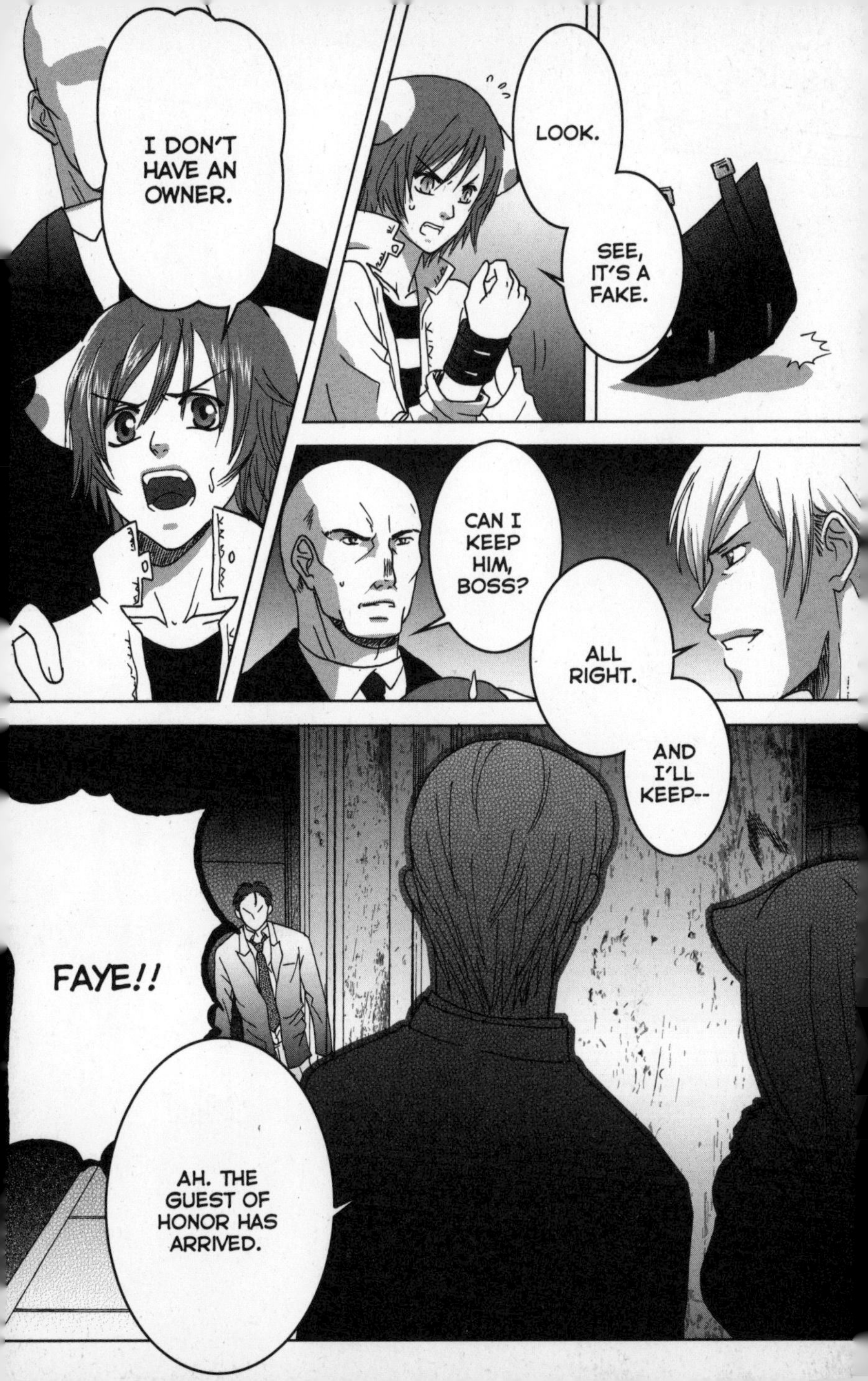
I DON'T HAVE AN OWNER.
LOOK.
SEE, IT'S A FAKE.
CAN I KEEP HIM, BOSS?
ALL RIGHT.
AND I'LL KEEP--
FAYE!!
AH. THE GUEST OF HONOR HAS ARRIVED.

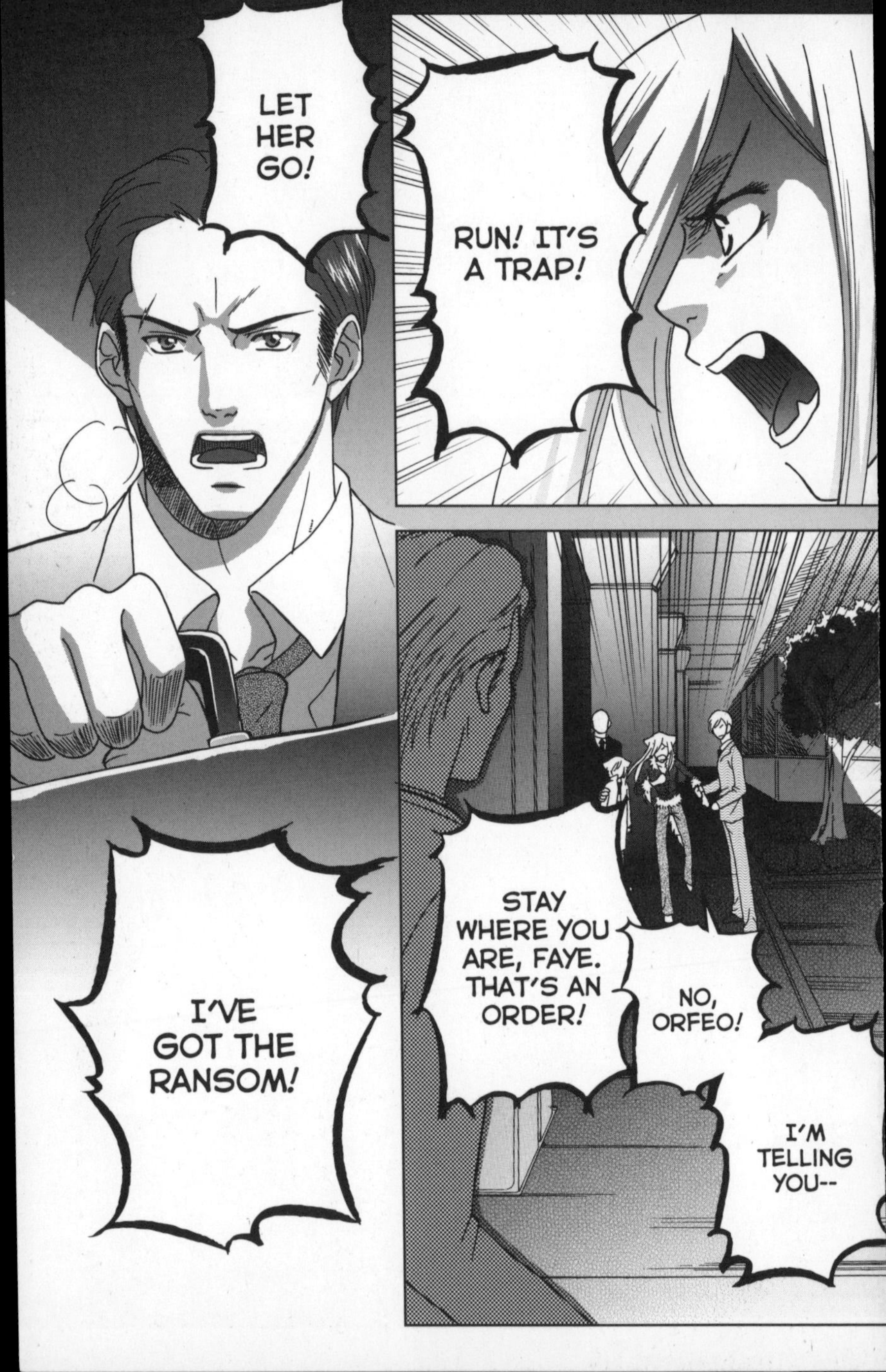
LET HER GO!
RUN! IT'S A TRAP!
I'VE GOT THE RANSOM!
STAY WHERE YOU ARE, FAYE. THAT'S AN ORDER!
NO, ORFEO!
I'M TELLING YOU--

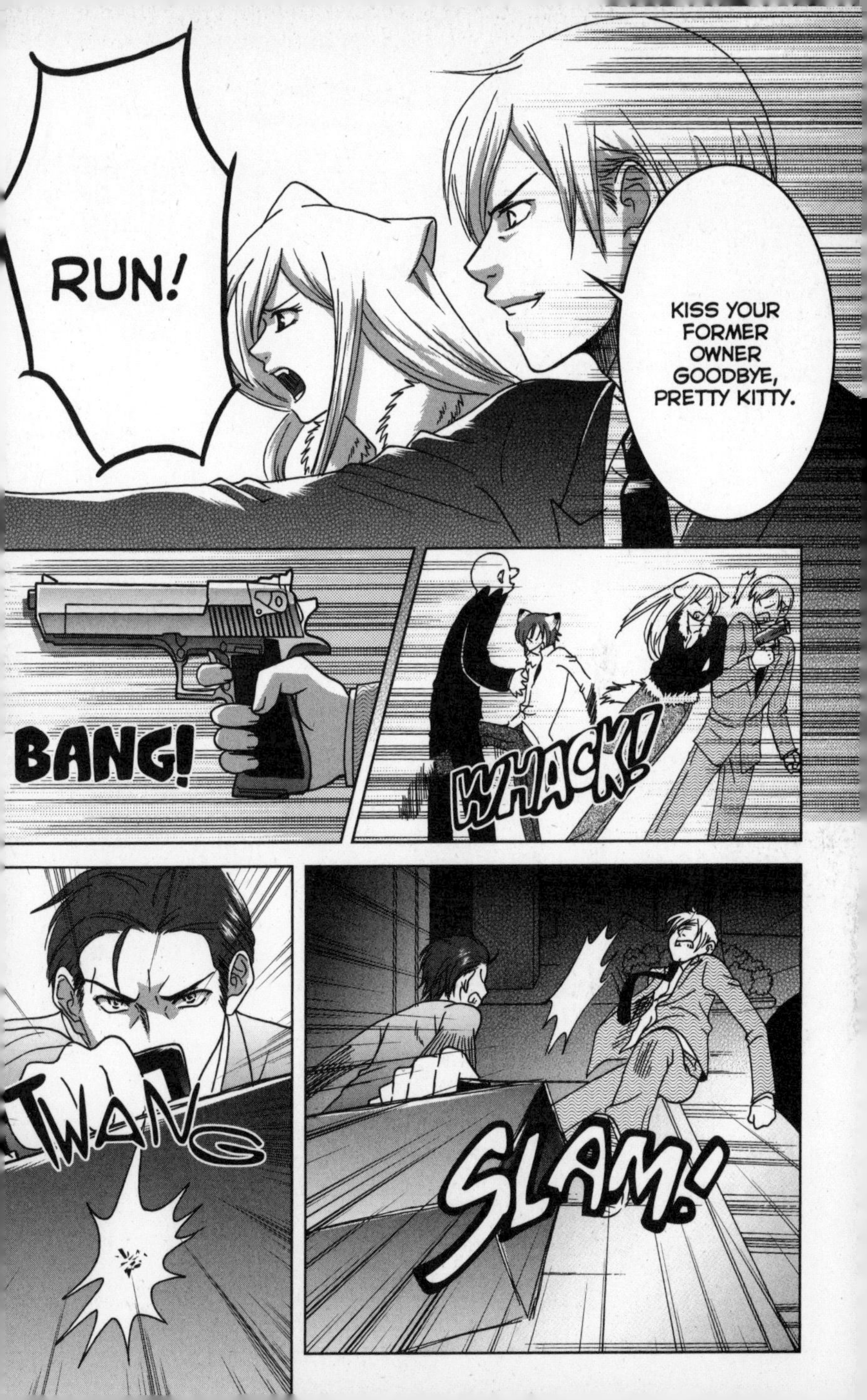
RUN!
KISS YOUR FORMER OWNER GOODBYE, PRETTY KITTY.
BANG!
WHACK!
TWANG
SLAM!

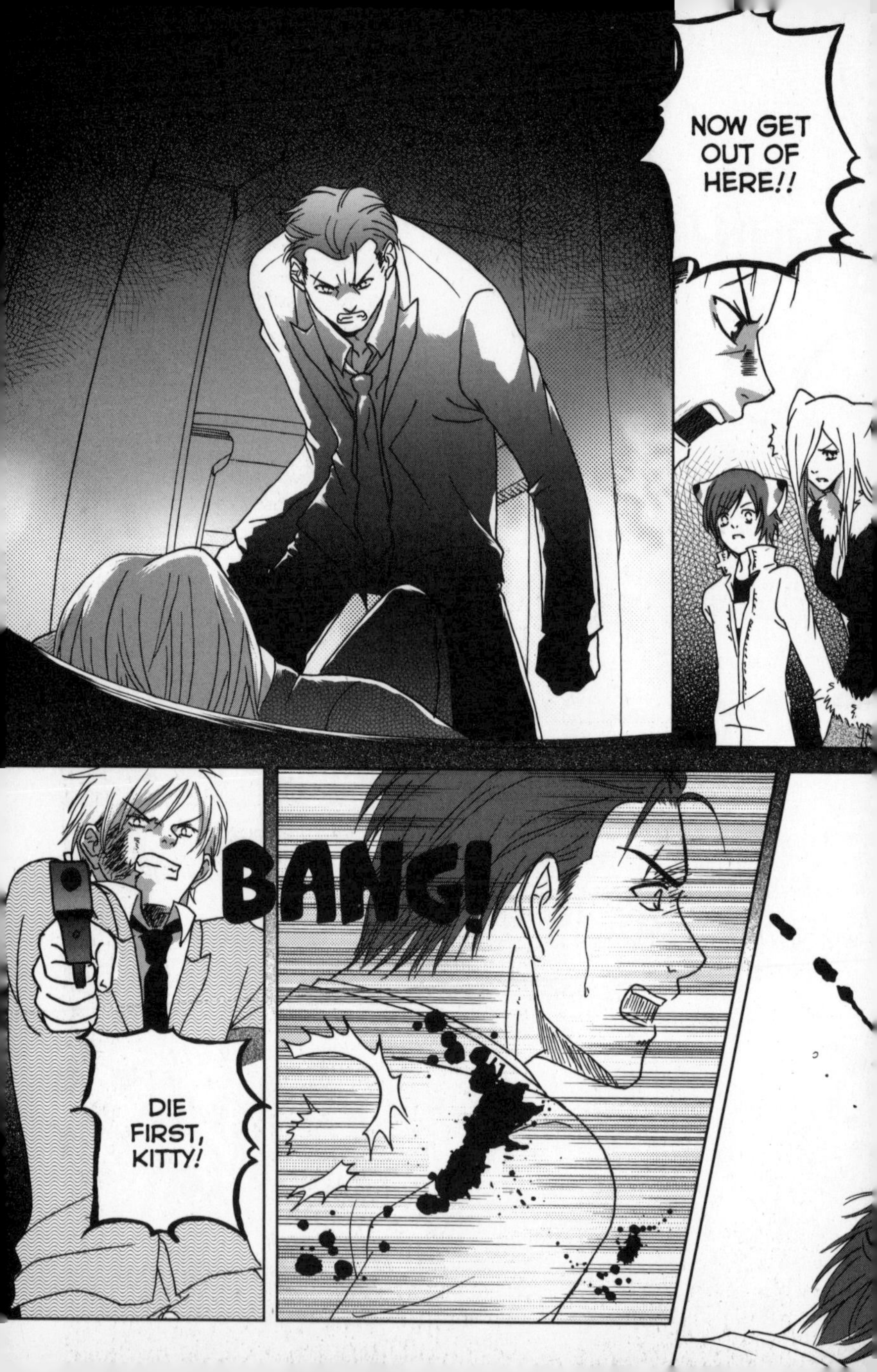
NOW GET OUT OF HERE!!
DIE FIRST, KITTY!
BANG!

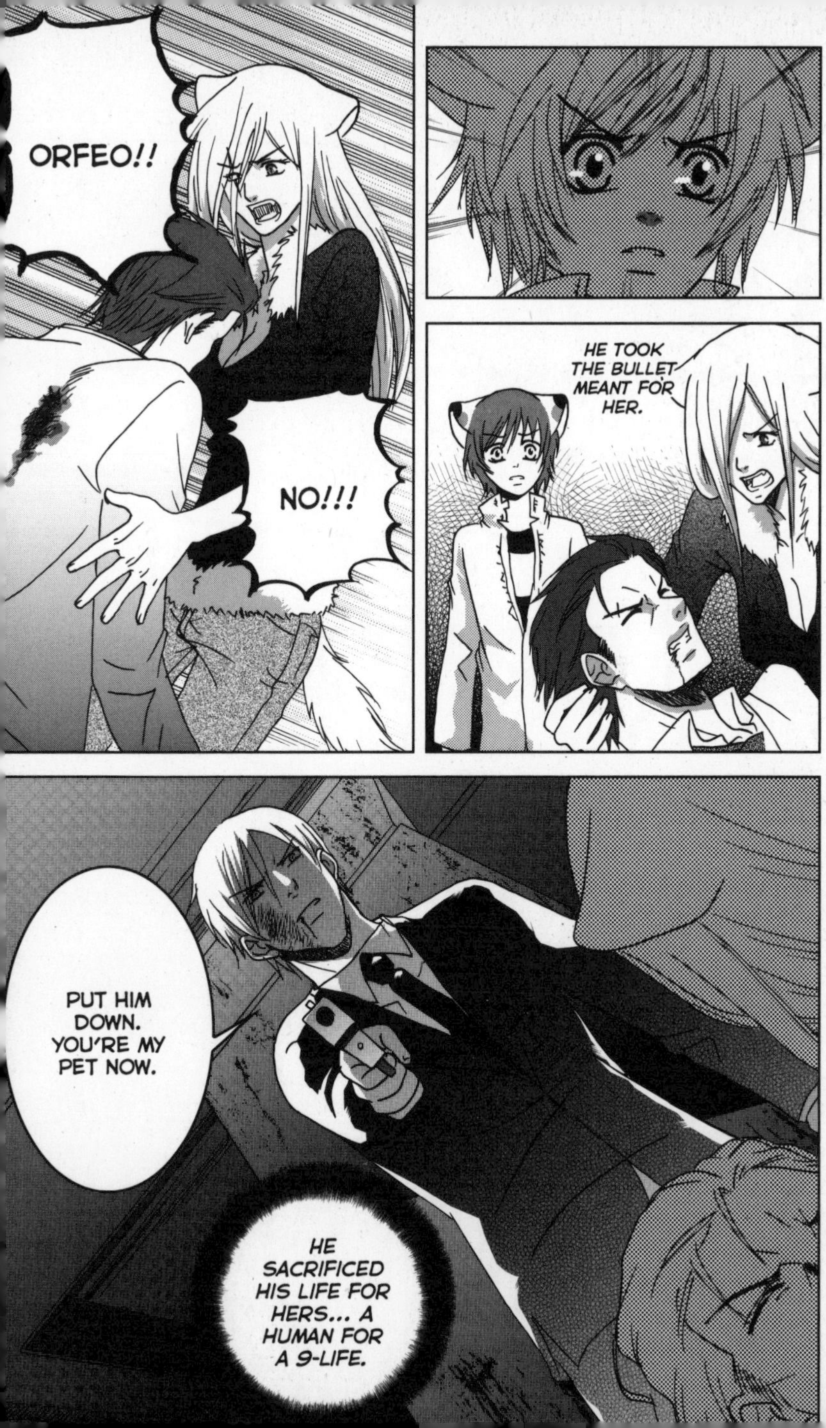
ORFEO!!
NO!!!
HE TOOK THE BULLET MEANT FOR HER.
PUT HIM DOWN. YOU'RE MY PET NOW.
HE SACRIFICED HIS LIFE FOR HERS... A HUMAN FOR A 9-LIFE.

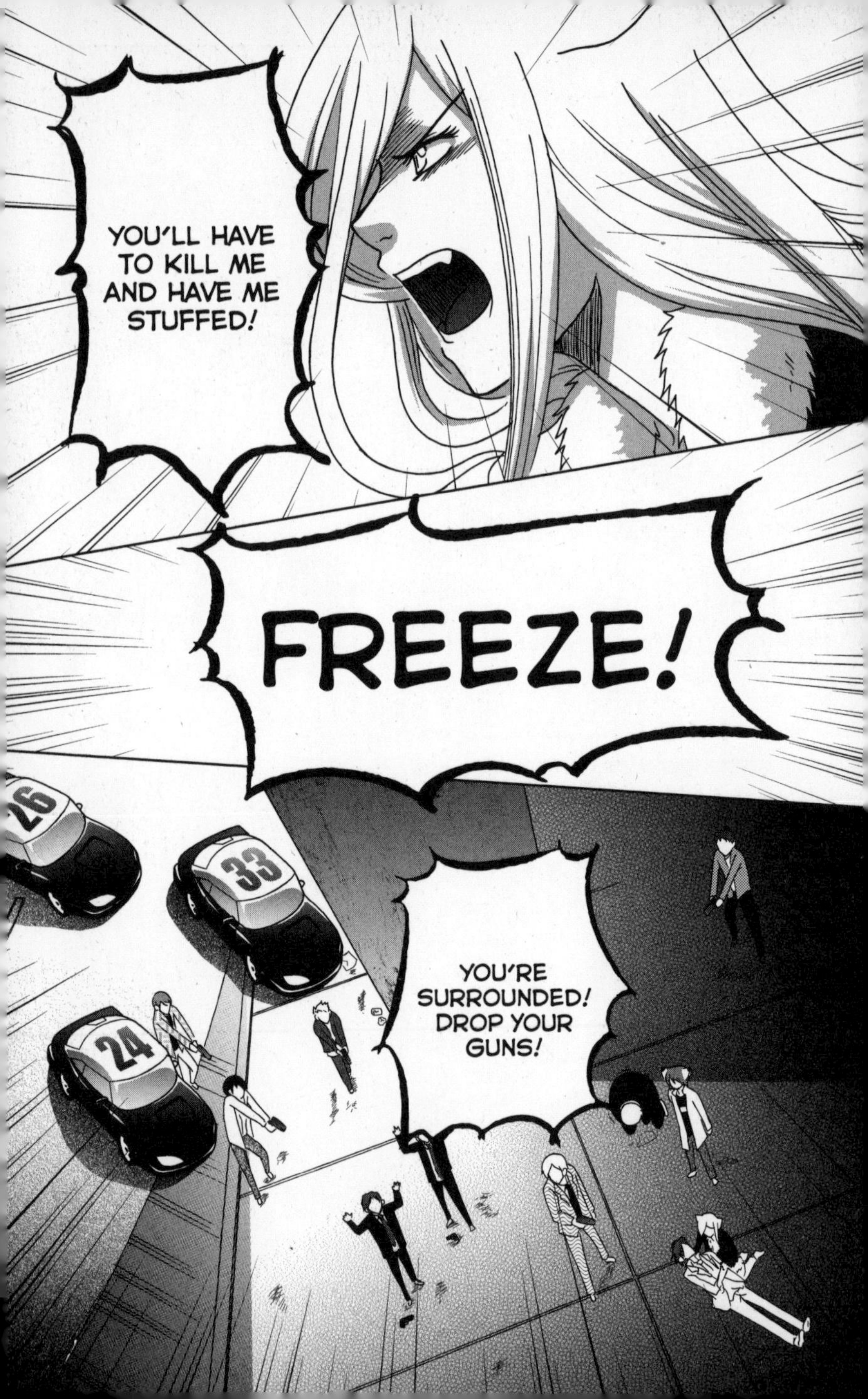
YOU'LL HAVE TO KILL ME AND HAVE ME STUFFED!
FREEZE!
YOU'RE SURROUNDED! DROP YOUR GUNS!
26
33
24

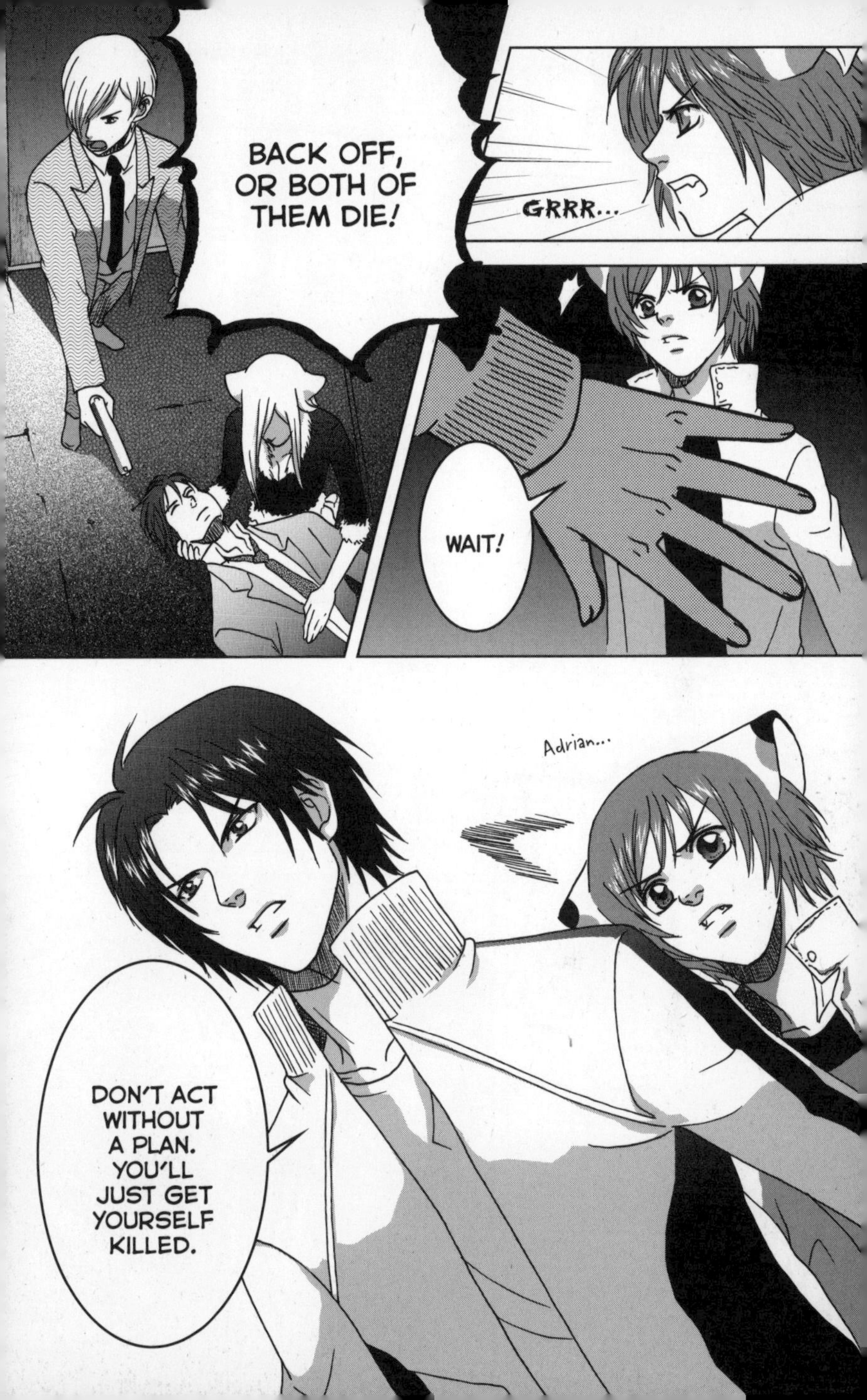
BACK OFF, OR BOTH OF THEM DIE!
GRRR...
WAIT!
Adrian...
DON'T ACT WITHOUT A PLAN. YOU'LL JUST GET YOURSELF KILLED.

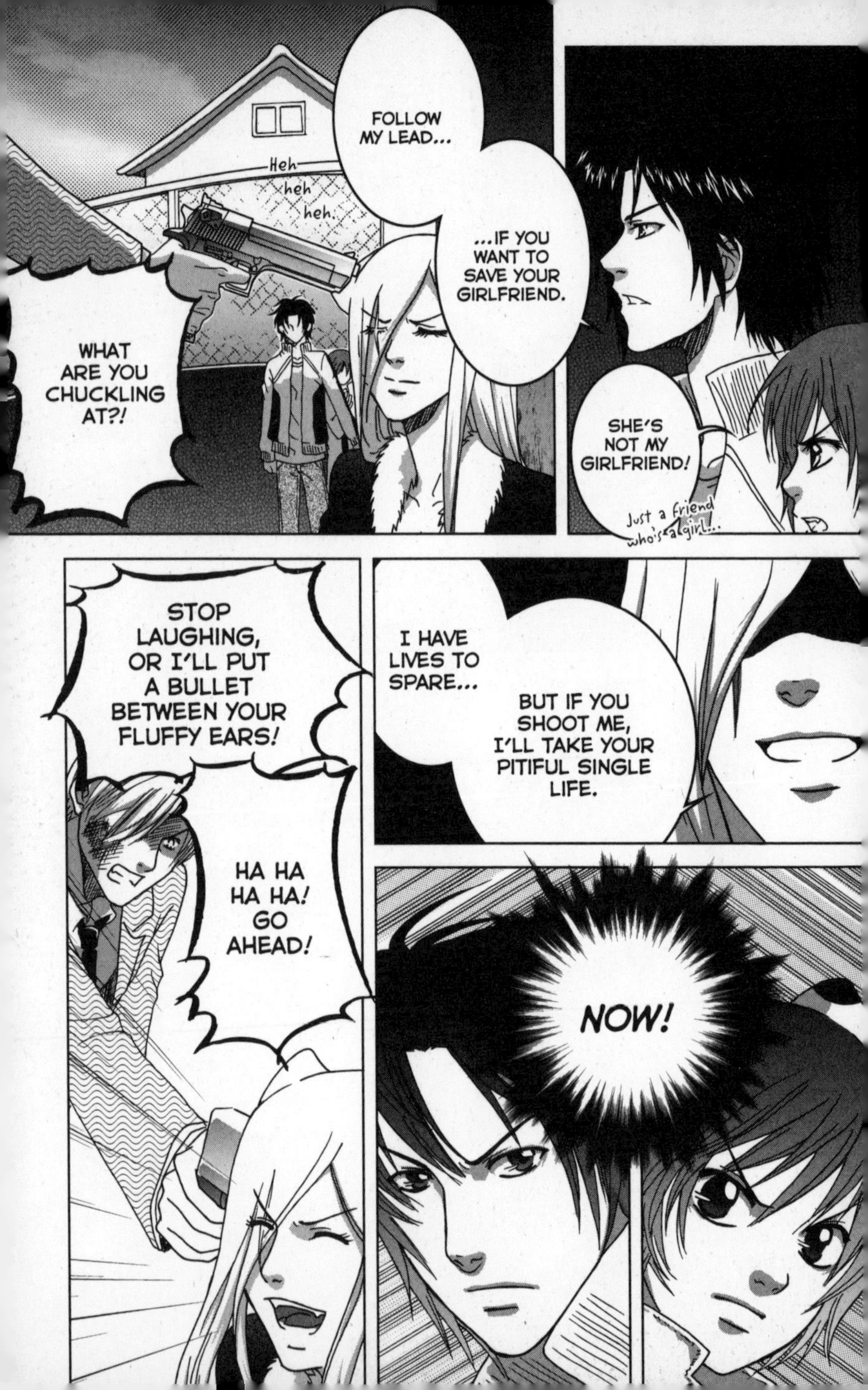
Heh heh heh.
WHAT ARE YOU CHUCKLING AT?!
FOLLOW MY LEAD...
...IF YOU WANT TO SAVE YOUR GIRLFRIEND.
SHE'S NOT MY GIRLFRIEND!
Just a friend who's a girl...
STOP LAUGHING, OR I'LL PUT A BULLET BETWEEN YOUR FLUFFY EARS!
HA HA HA HA! GO AHEAD!
I HAVE LIVES TO SPARE...
BUT IF YOU SHOOT ME, I'LL TAKE YOUR PITIFUL SINGLE LIFE.
NOW!

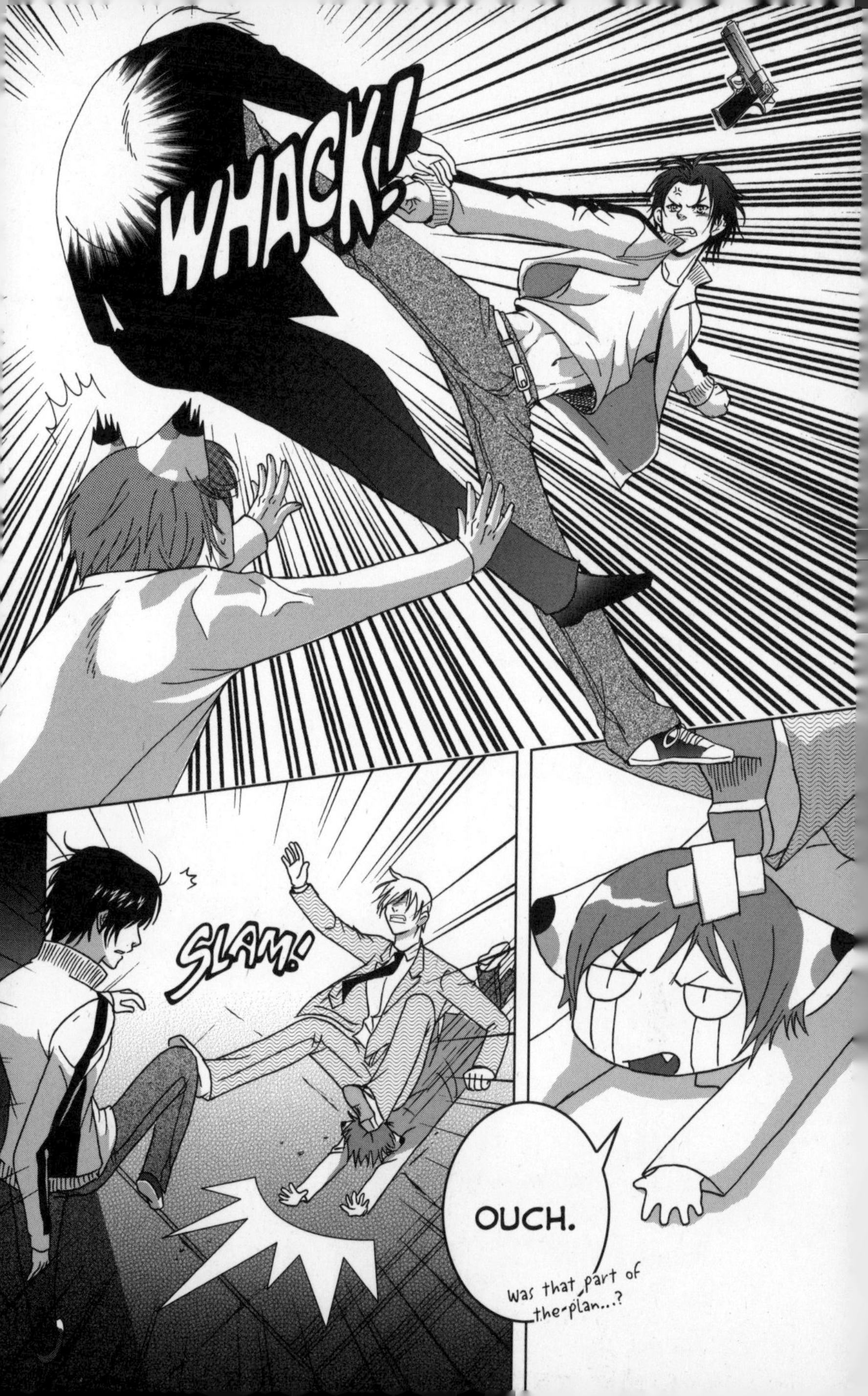
WHACK!
SLAM!
OUCH.
Was that part of the plan...?

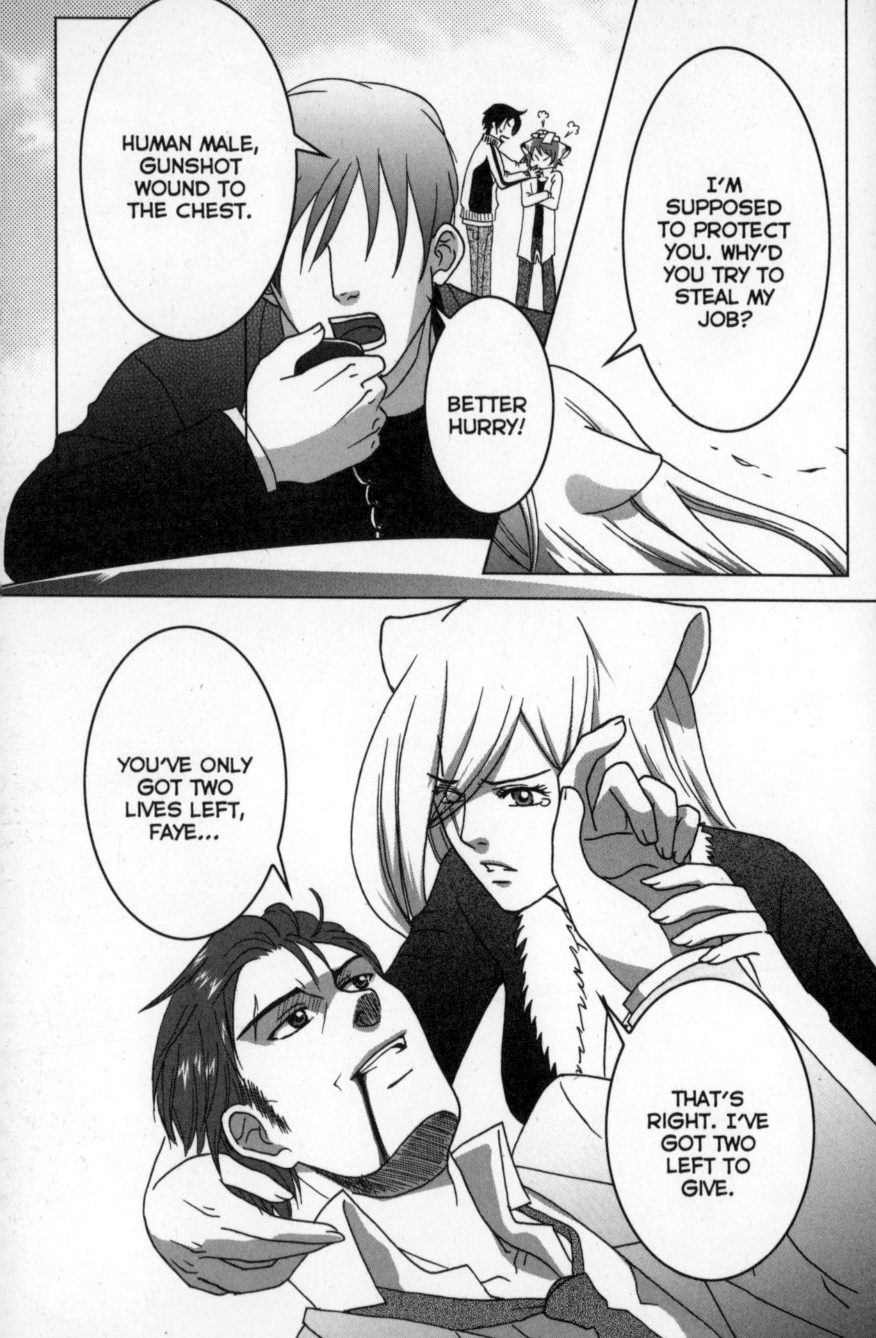
I'M SUPPOSED TO PROTECT YOU. WHY'D YOU TRY TO STEAL MY JOB?
BETTER HURRY!
HUMAN MALE, GUNSHOT WOUND TO THE CHEST.
YOU'VE ONLY GOT TWO LIVES LEFT, FAYE...
THAT'S RIGHT. I'VE GOT TWO LEFT TO GIVE.

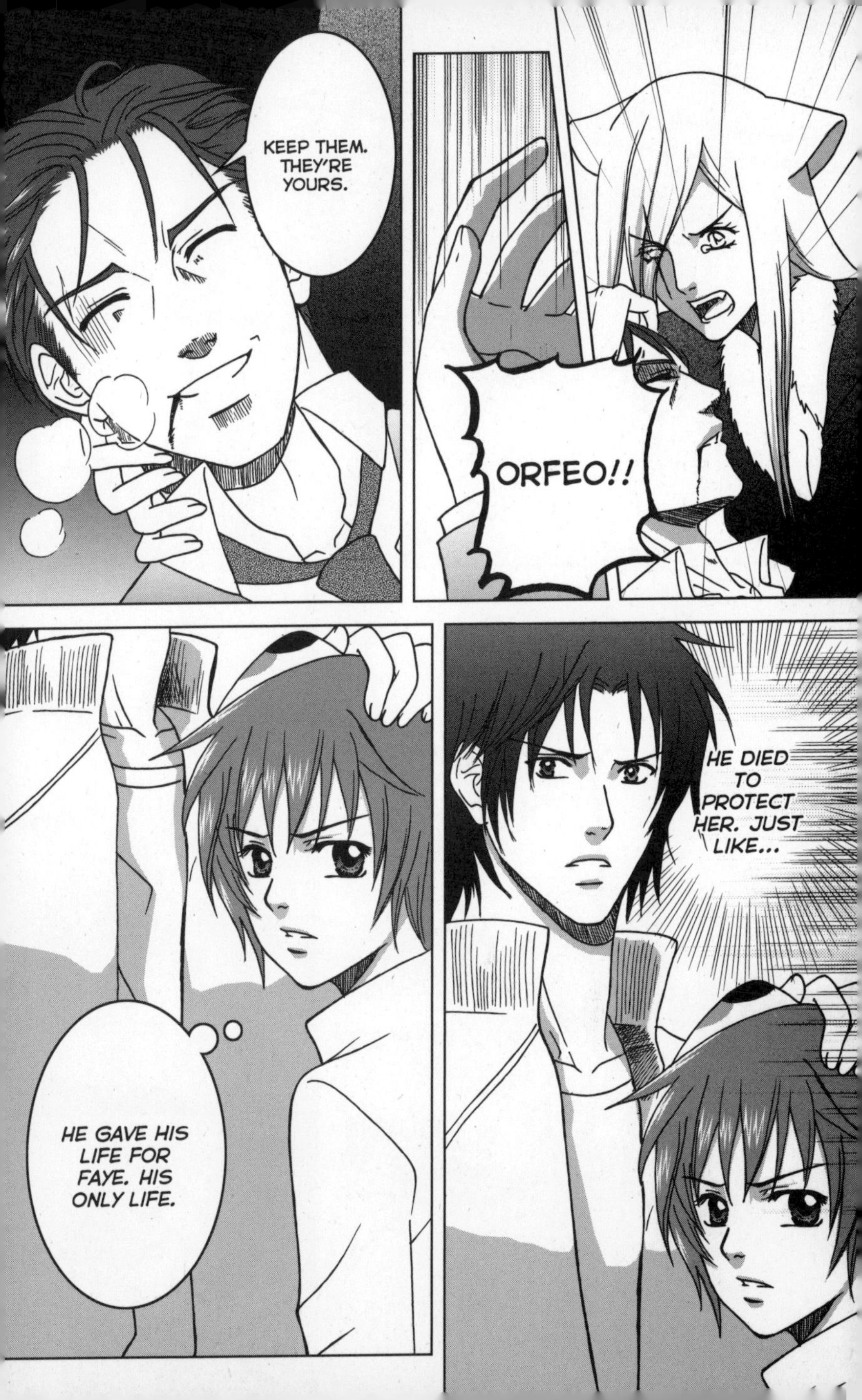
KEEP THEM. THEY'RE YOURS.
ORFEO!!
HE GAVE HIS LIFE FOR FAYE. HIS ONLY LIFE.
HE DIED TO PROTECT HER. JUST LIKE...

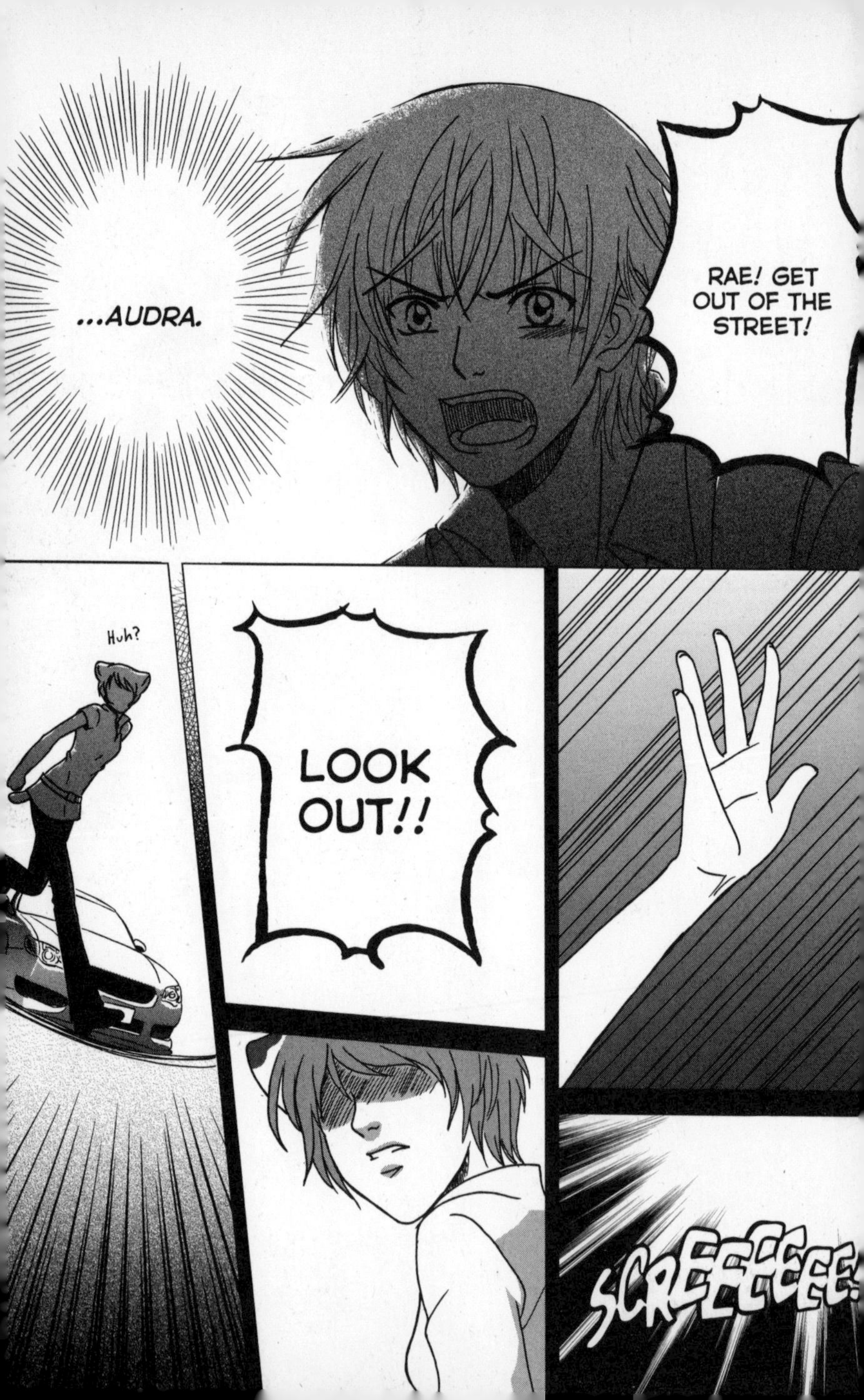
...AUDRA.
RAE! GET OUT OF THE STREET!
Huh?
LOOK OUT!!
SCREEEEEE

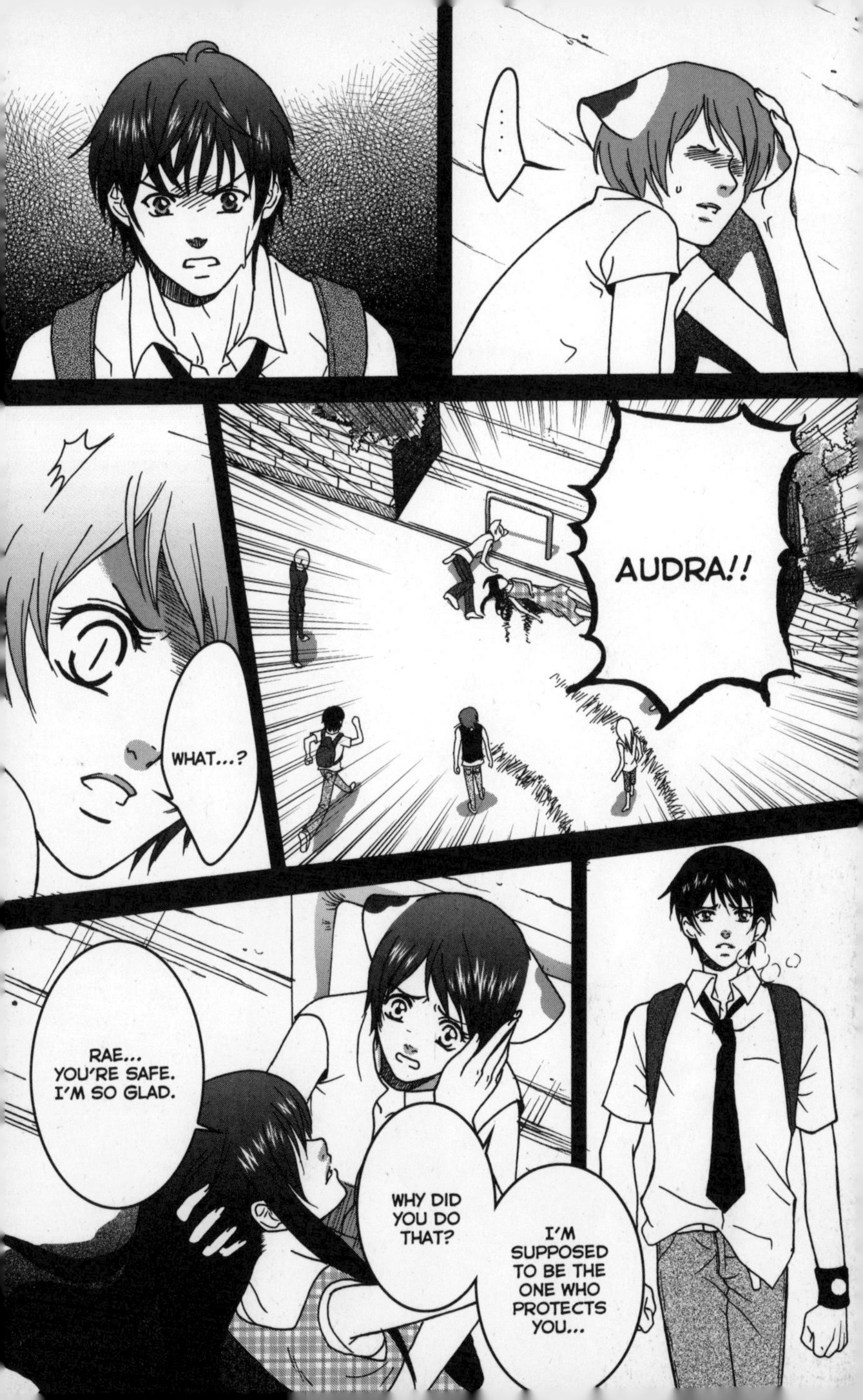
...
WHAT...?
AUDRA!!
RAE...
YOU'RE SAFE.
I'M SO GLAD.
WHY DID
YOU DO
THAT?
I'M
SUPPOSED
TO BE THE
ONE WHO
PROTECTS
YOU...

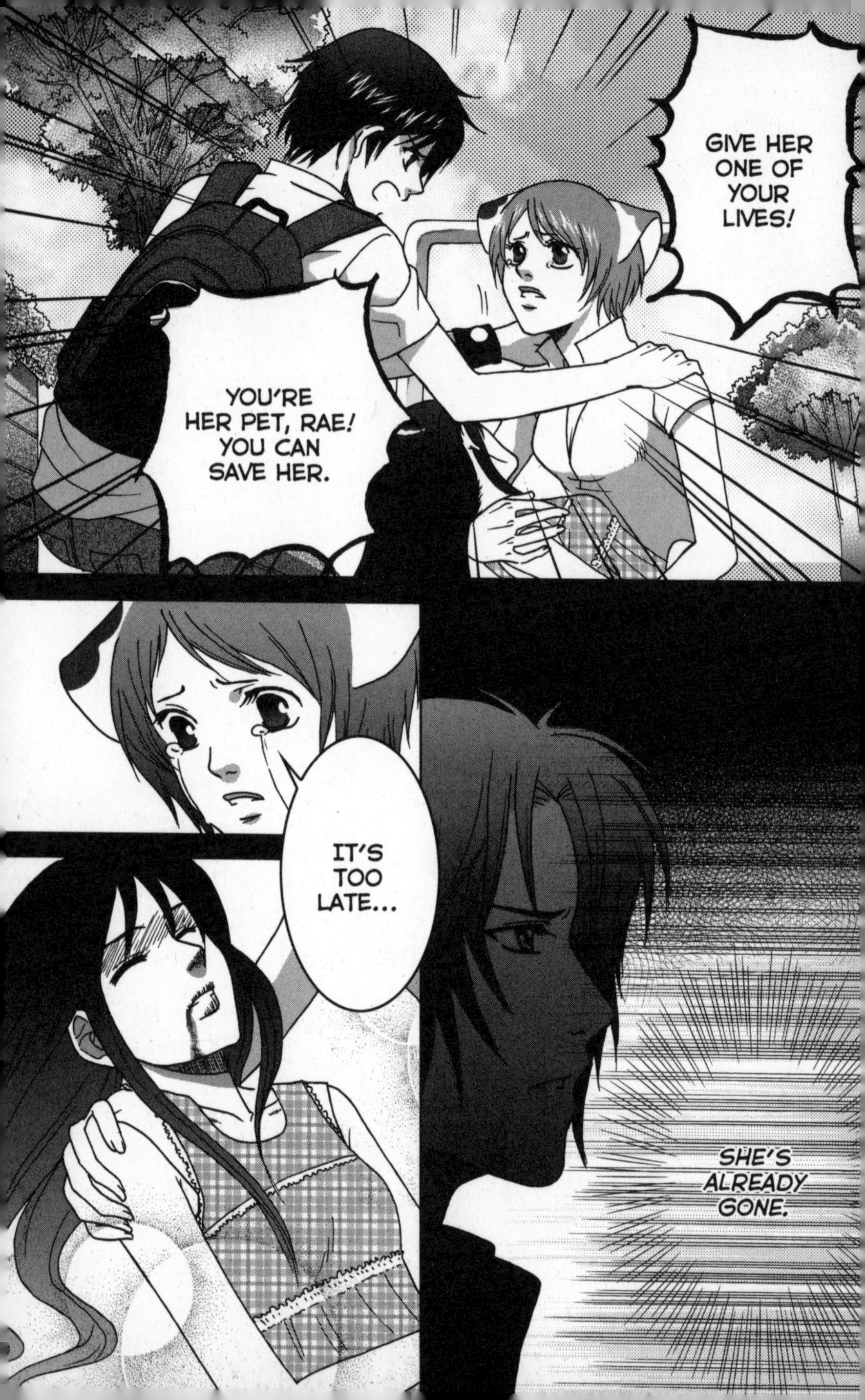
YOU'RE HER PET, RAE! YOU CAN SAVE HER.
GIVE HER ONE OF YOUR LIVES!
IT'S TOO LATE...
SHE'S ALREADY GONE.

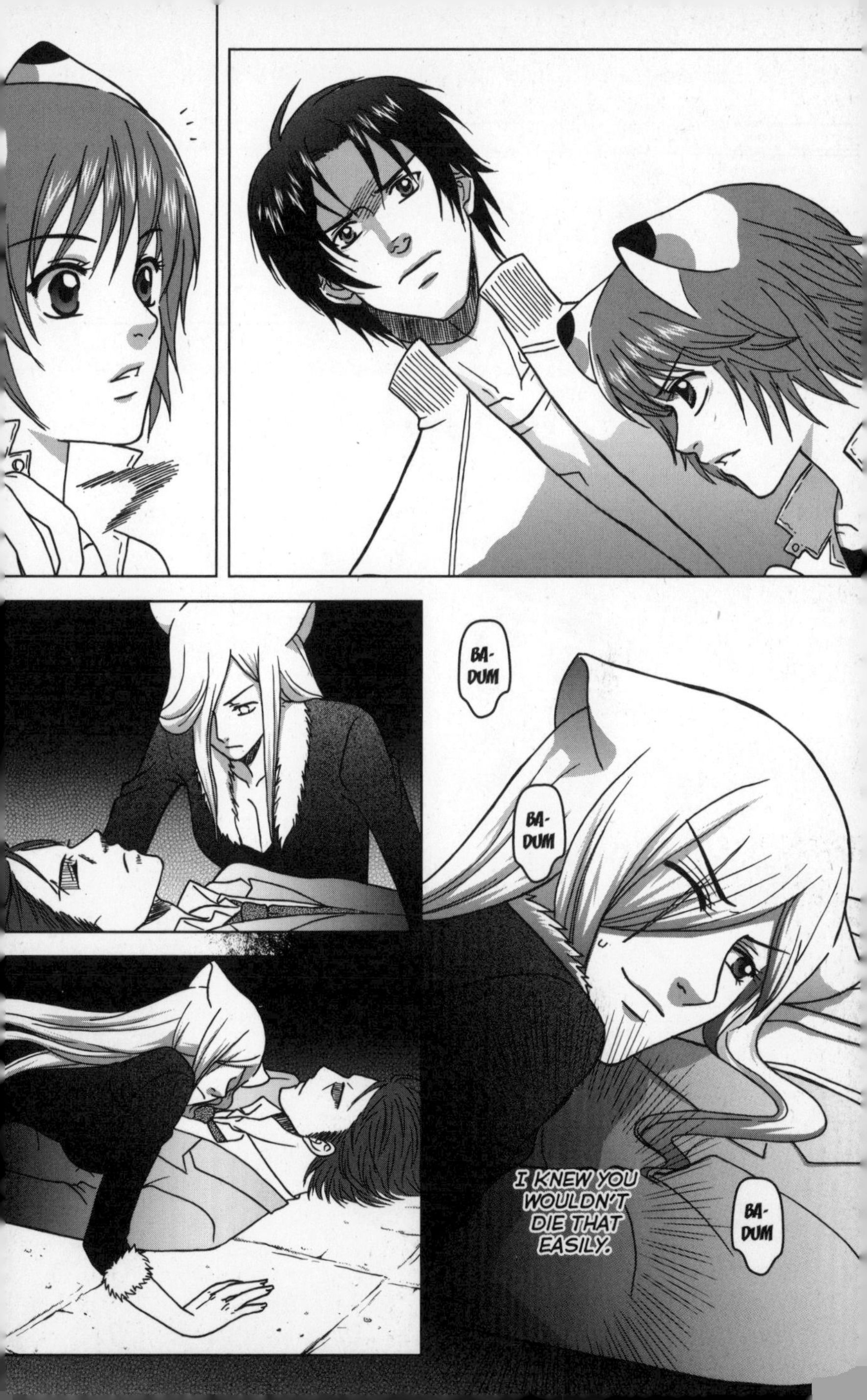
BA-DUM
BA-DUM
I KNEW YOU WOULDN'T DIE THAT EASILY.
BA-DUM

SHAAAAAA...

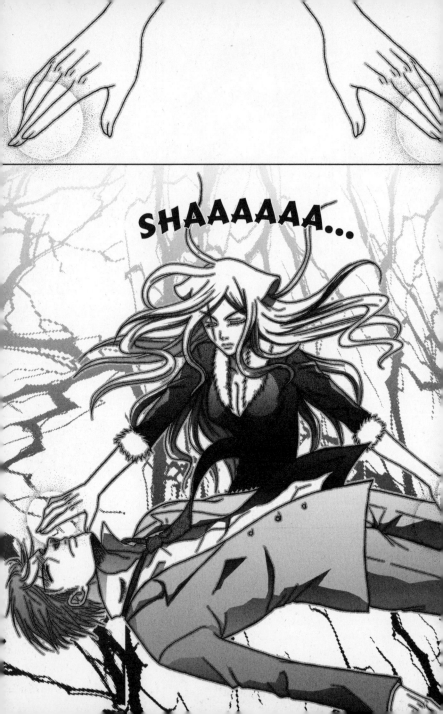

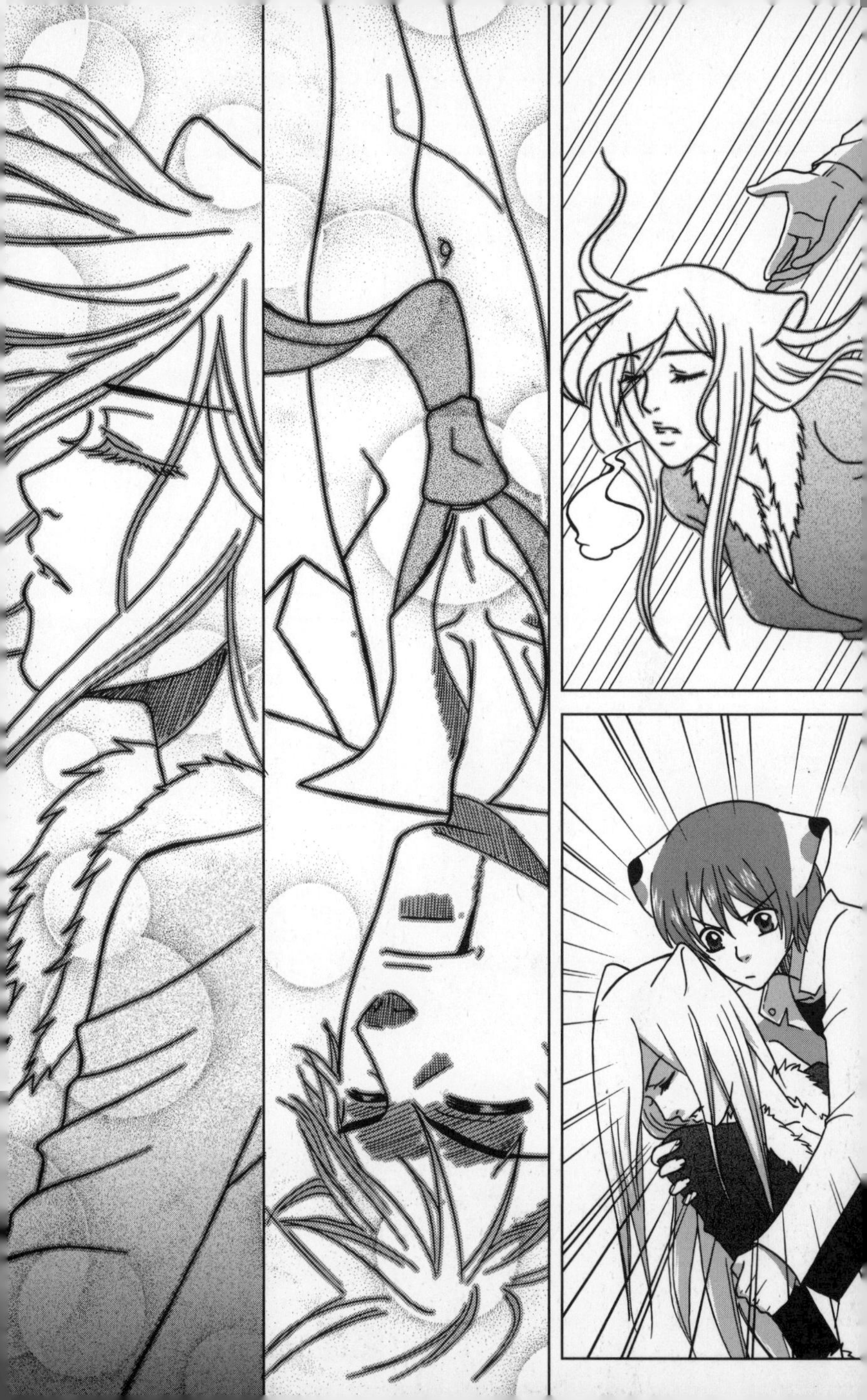

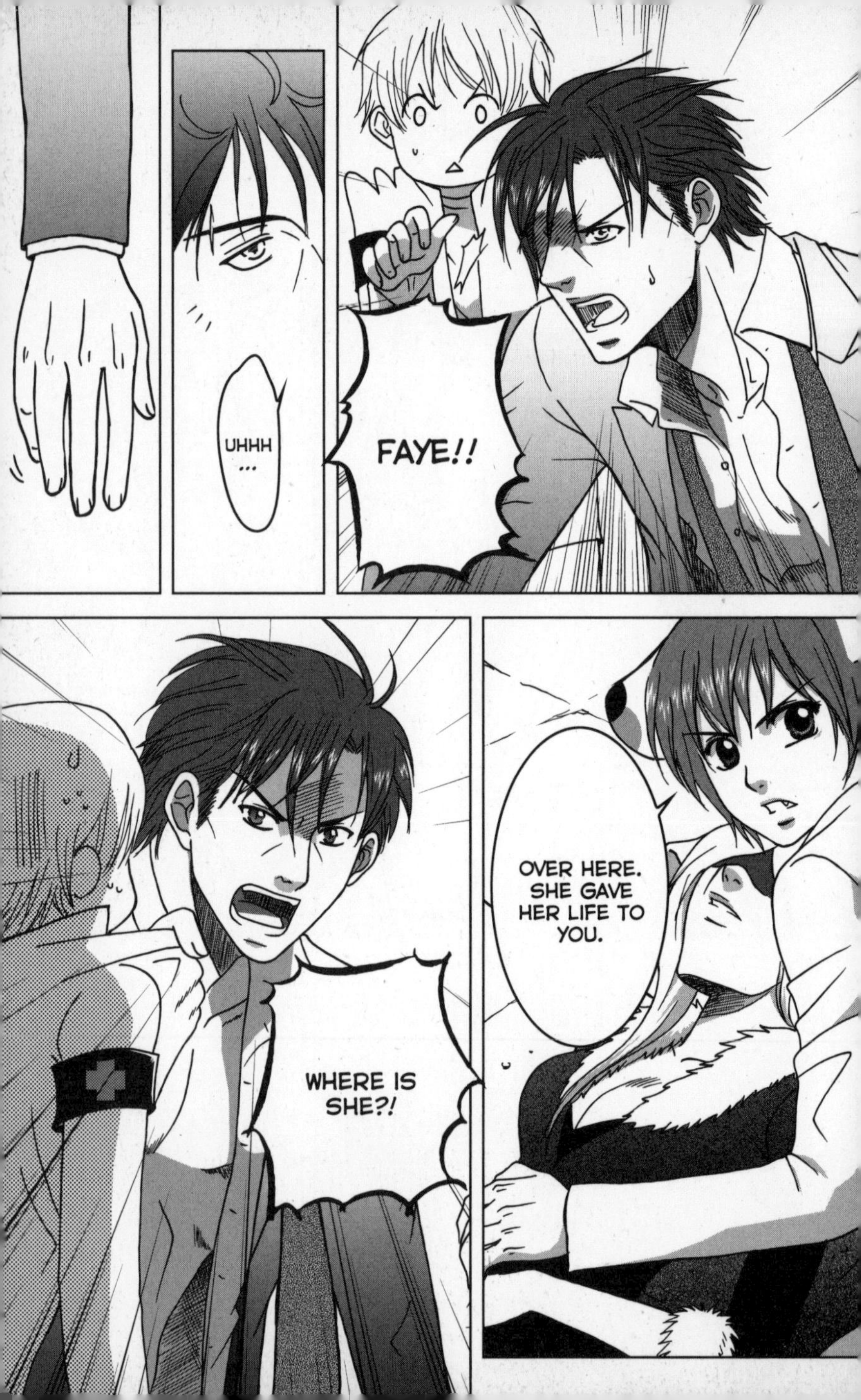
UHHH ...
FAYE!!
WHERE IS SHE?!
OVER HERE. SHE GAVE HER LIFE TO YOU.

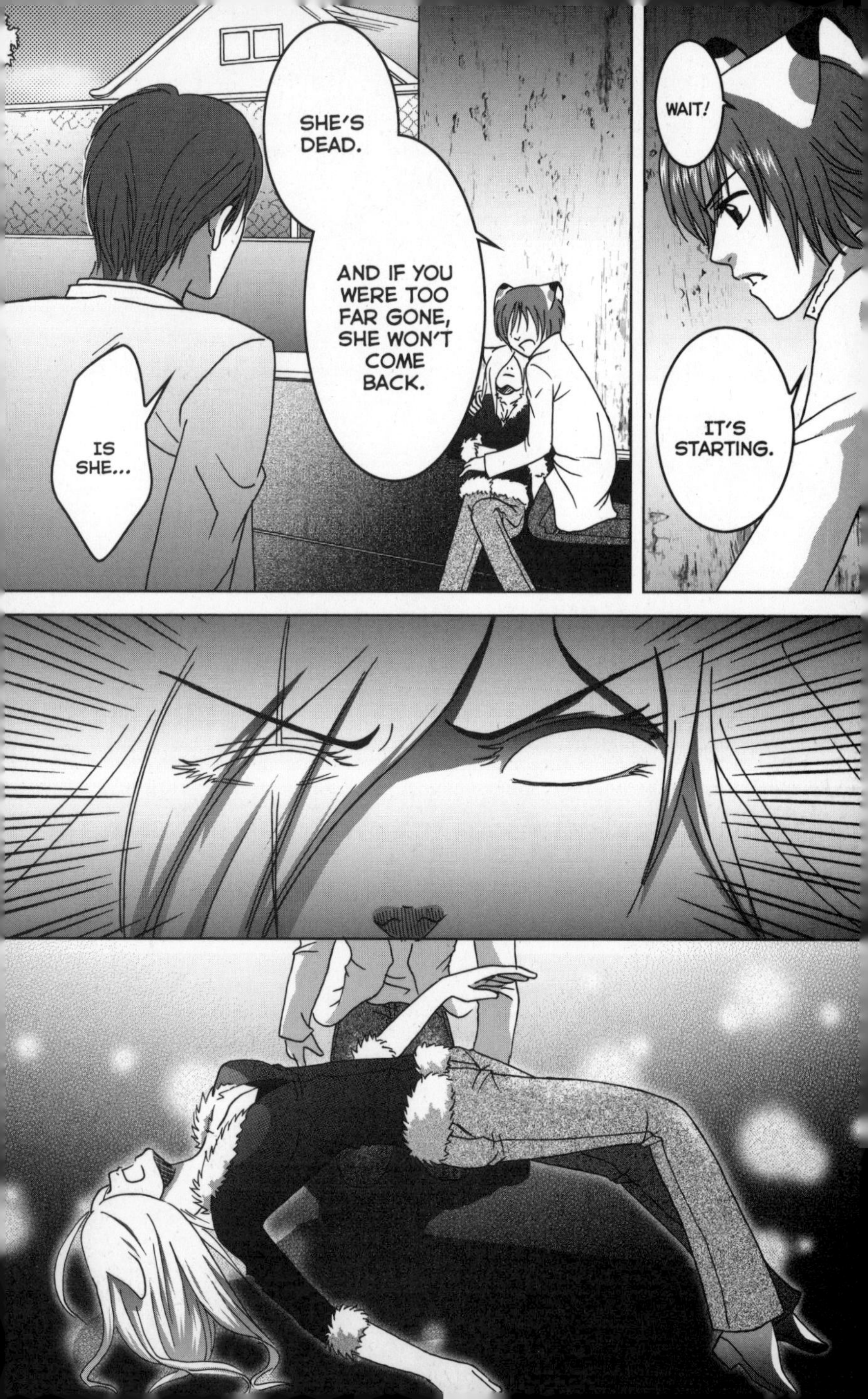
IS SHE...
SHE'S DEAD.
AND IF YOU WERE TOO FAR GONE, SHE WON'T COME BACK.
WAIT!
IT'S STARTING.

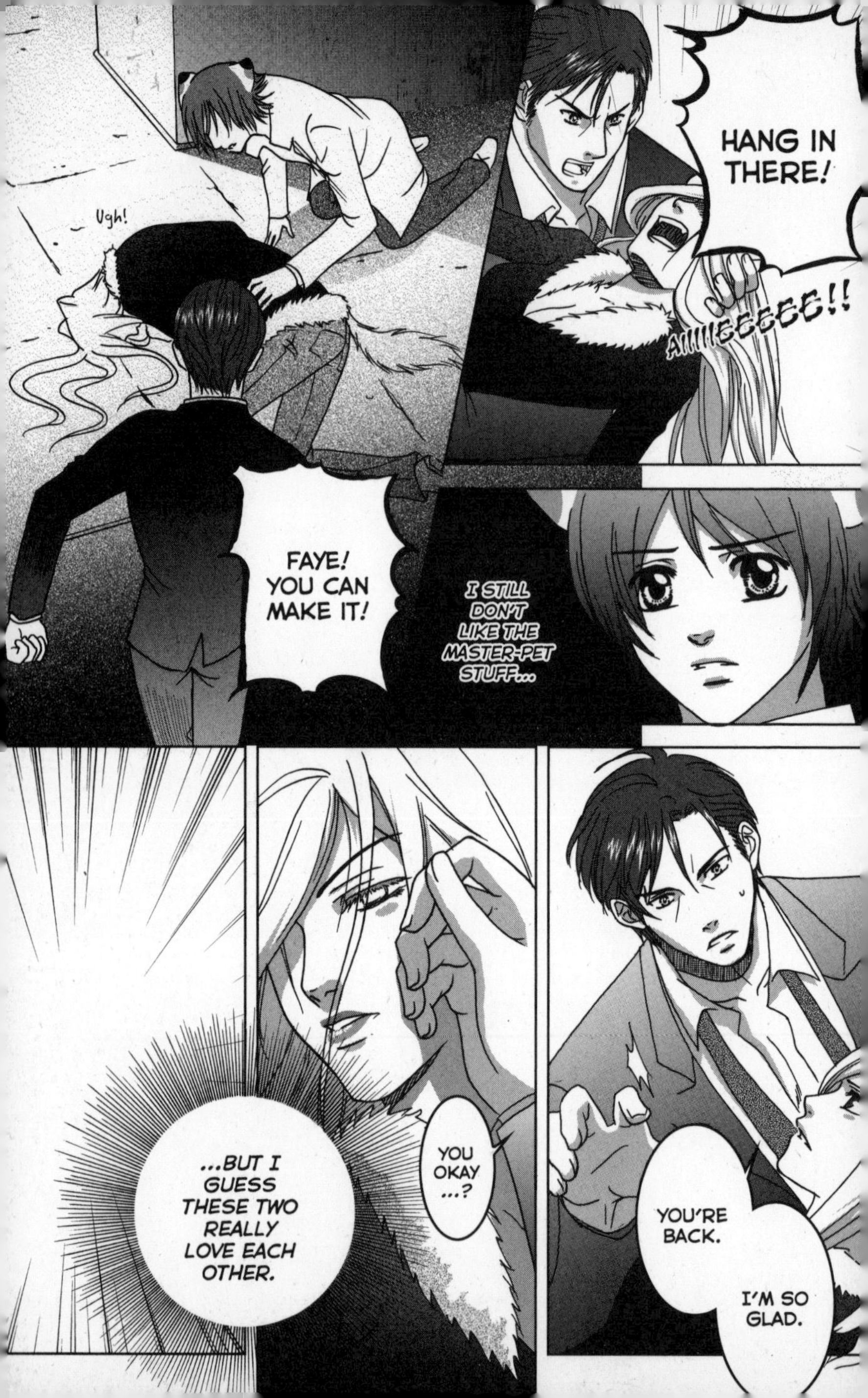
Ugh!
FAYE! YOU CAN MAKE IT!
HANG IN THERE!
AIIIIEEEEEE!!
I STILL DON'T LIKE THE MASTER-PET STUFF...
...BUT I GUESS THESE TWO REALLY LOVE EACH OTHER.
YOU OKAY ...?
YOU'RE BACK.
I'M SO GLAD.

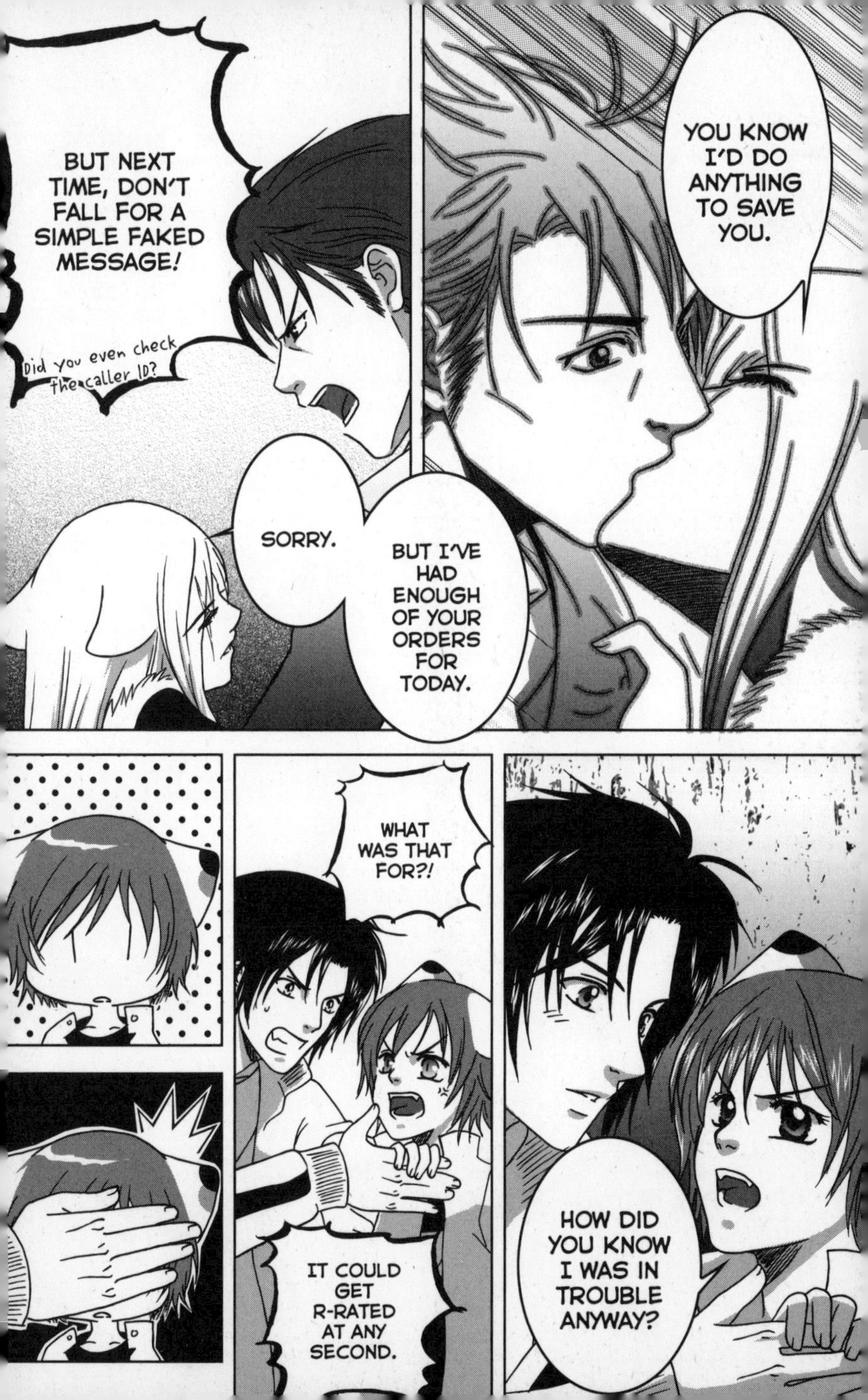
BUT NEXT TIME, DON'T FALL FOR A SIMPLE FAKED MESSAGE!
Did you even check the caller ID?
SORRY.
BUT I'VE HAD ENOUGH OF YOUR ORDERS FOR TODAY.
YOU KNOW I'D DO ANYTHING TO SAVE YOU.
WHAT WAS THAT FOR?!
IT COULD GET R-RATED AT ANY SECOND.
HOW DID YOU KNOW I WAS IN TROUBLE ANYWAY?

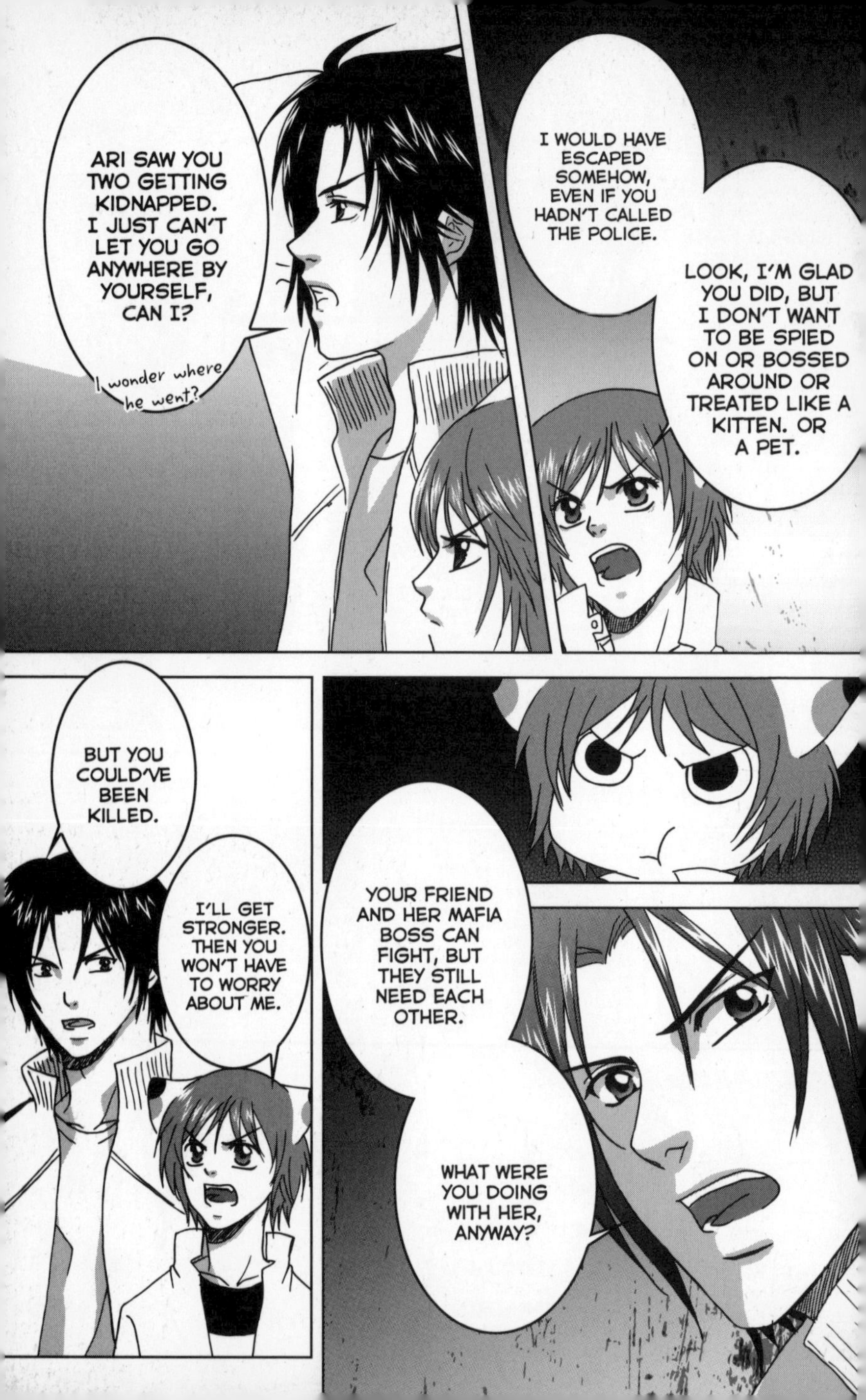
ARI SAW YOU TWO GETTING KIDNAPPED. I JUST CAN'T LET YOU GO ANYWHERE BY YOURSELF, CAN I?
I wonder where he went?
I WOULD HAVE ESCAPED SOMEHOW, EVEN IF YOU HADN'T CALLED THE POLICE.
LOOK, I'M GLAD YOU DID, BUT I DON'T WANT TO BE SPIED ON OR BOSSED AROUND OR TREATED LIKE A KITTEN. OR A PET.
BUT YOU COULD'VE BEEN KILLED.
I'LL GET STRONGER. THEN YOU WON'T HAVE TO WORRY ABOUT ME.
YOUR FRIEND AND HER MAFIA BOSS CAN FIGHT, BUT THEY STILL NEED EACH OTHER.
WHAT WERE YOU DOING WITH HER, ANYWAY?

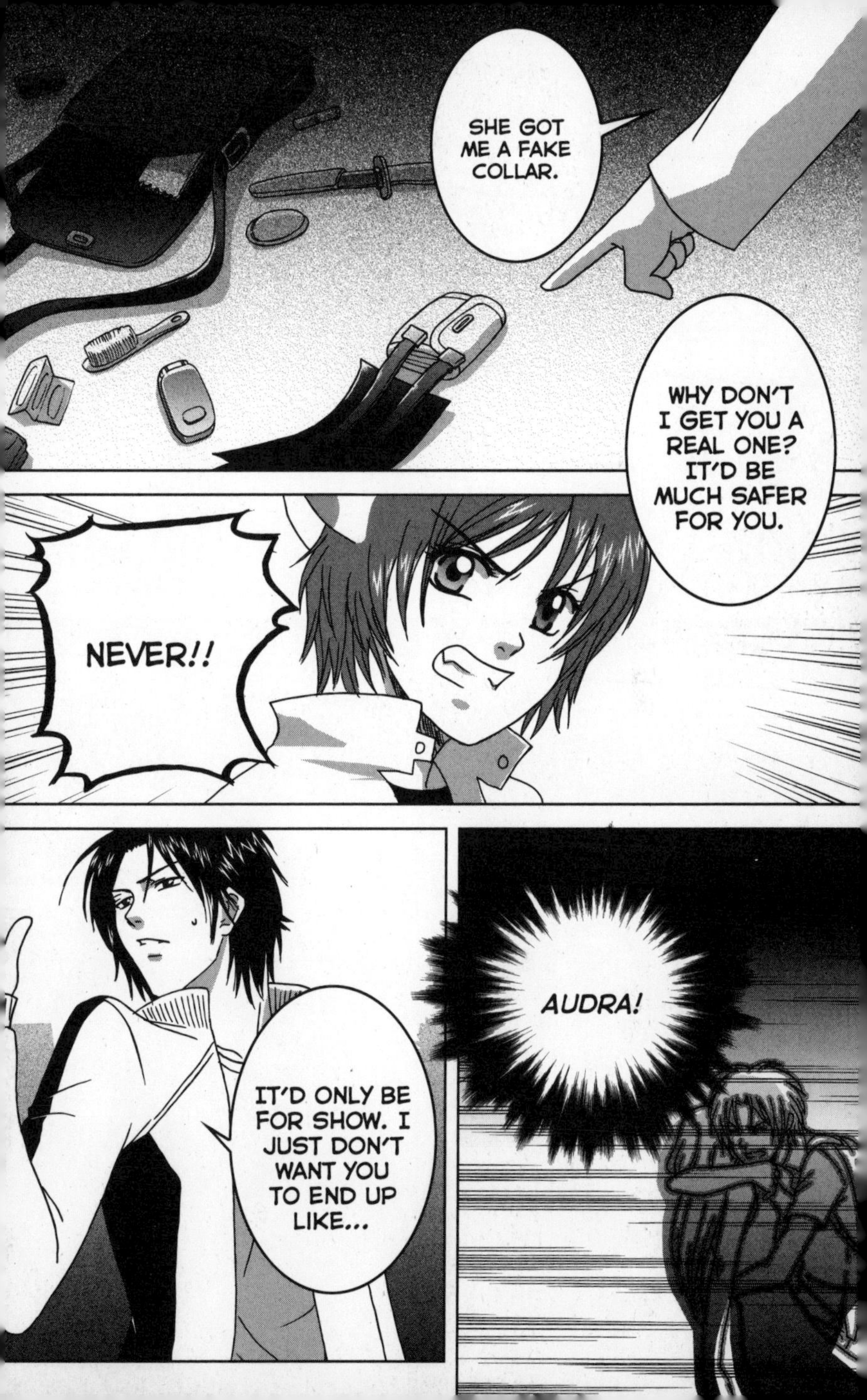
SHE GOT ME A FAKE COLLAR.
WHY DON'T I GET YOU A REAL ONE? IT'D BE MUCH SAFER FOR YOU.
NEVER!!
IT'D ONLY BE FOR SHOW. I JUST DON'T WANT YOU TO END UP LIKE...
AUDRA!

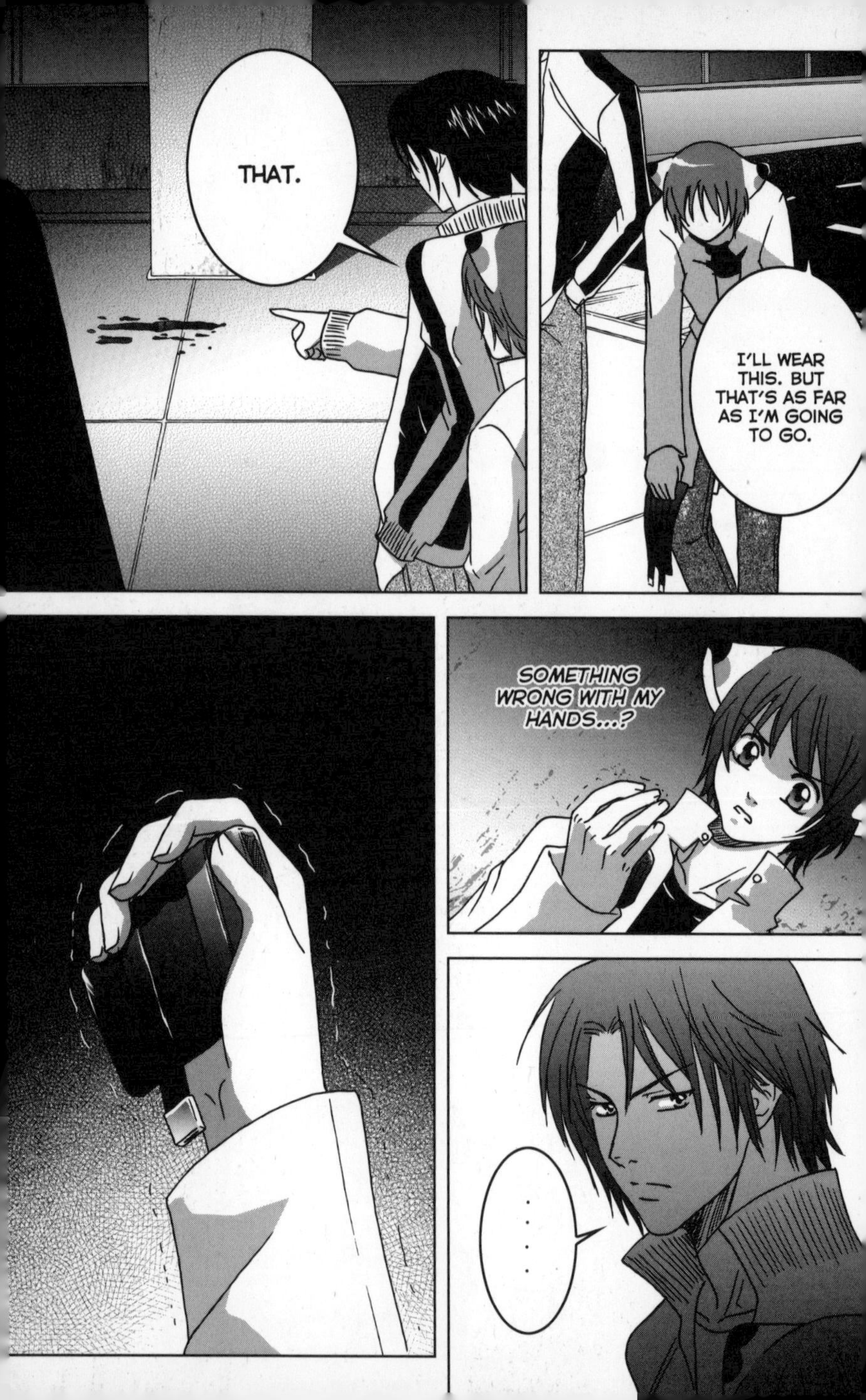
THAT.
I'LL WEAR THIS. BUT THAT'S AS FAR AS I'M GOING TO GO.
SOMETHING WRONG WITH MY HANDS...?
. . . .

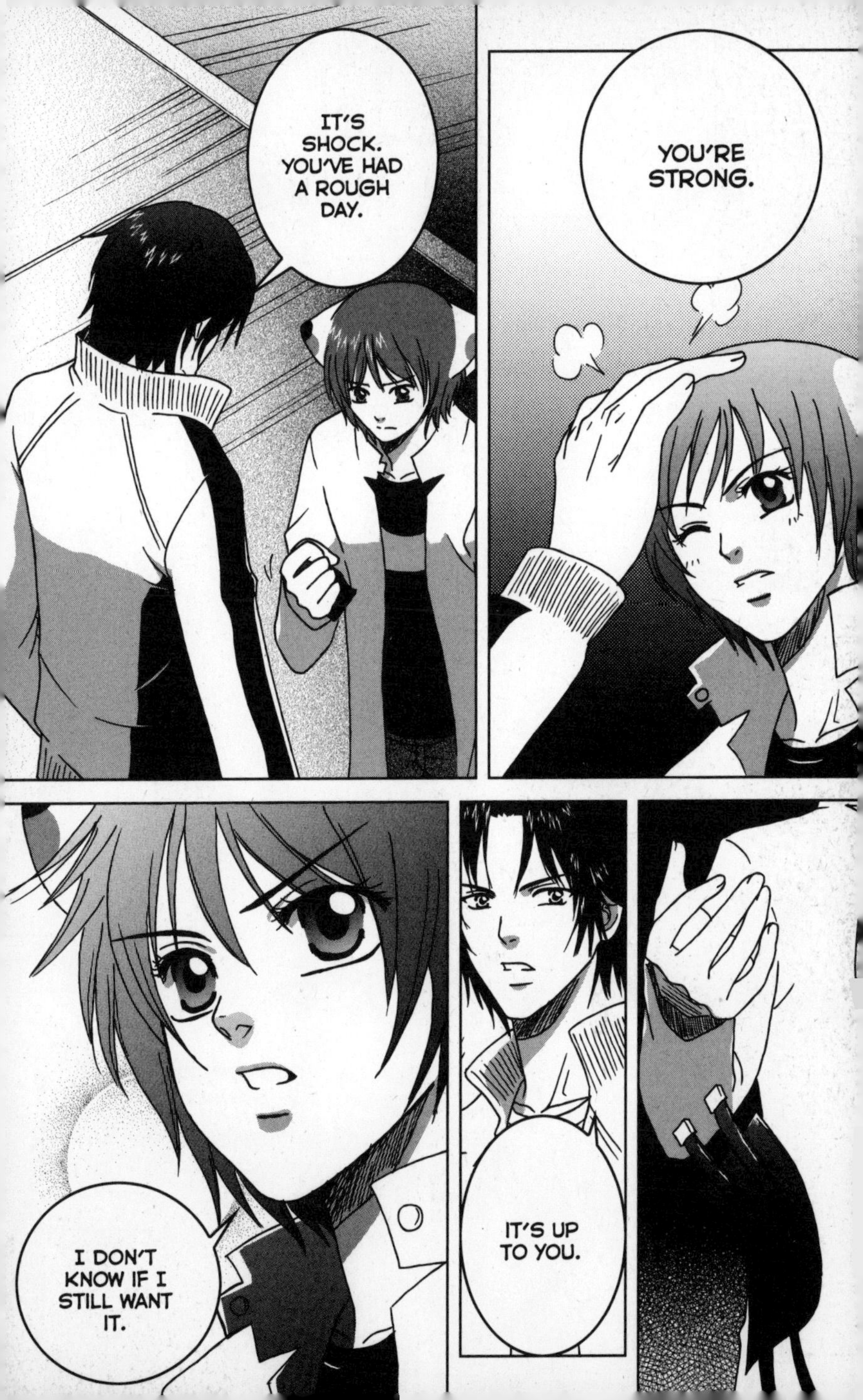
IT'S SHOCK. YOU'VE HAD A ROUGH DAY.
YOU'RE STRONG.
I DON'T KNOW IF I STILL WANT IT.
IT'S UP TO YOU.

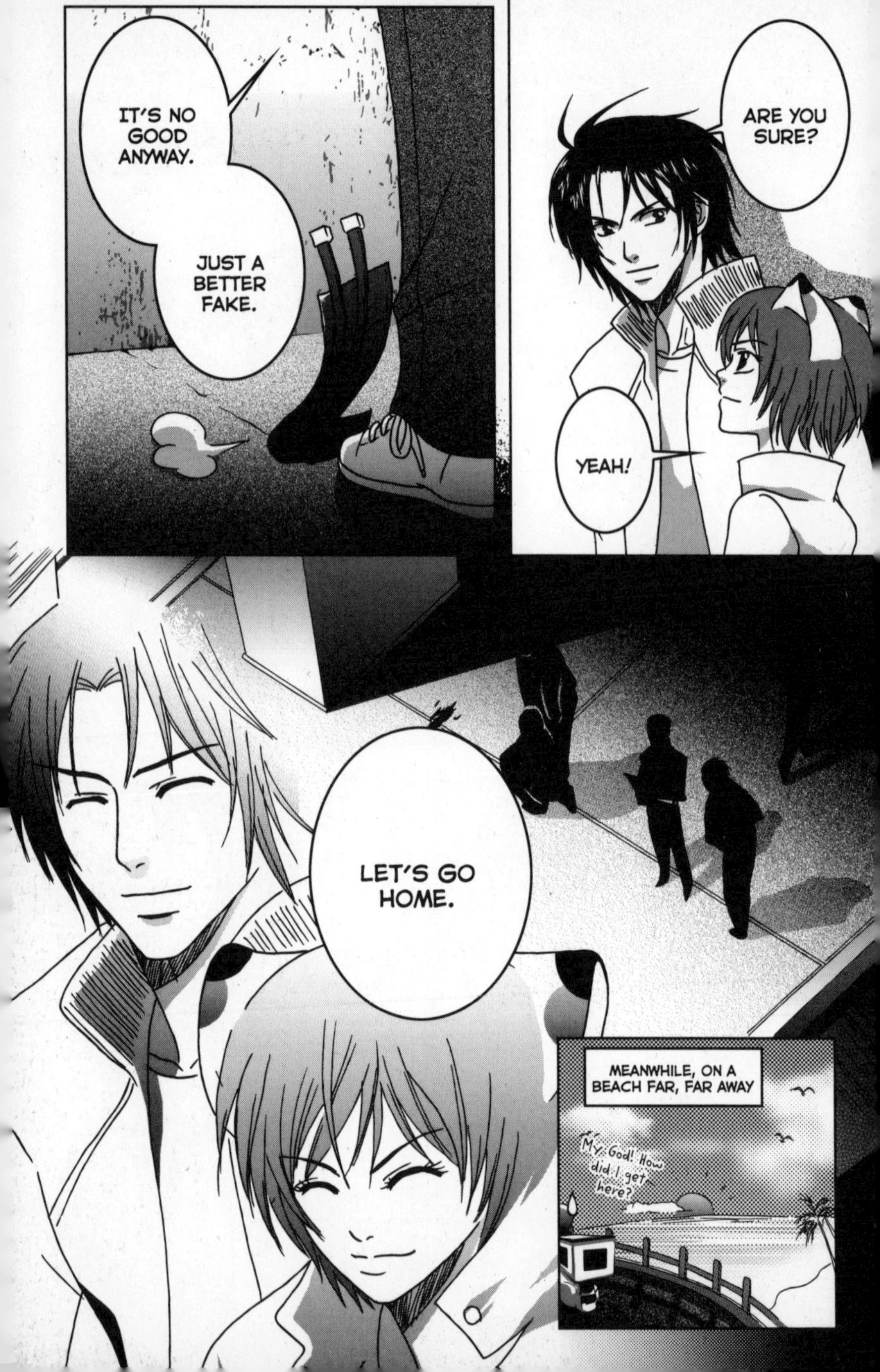
IT'S NO GOOD ANYWAY.
JUST A BETTER FAKE.
ARE YOU SURE?
YEAH!
LET'S GO HOME.
MEANWHILE, ON A BEACH FAR, FAR AWAY
My God! How did I get here?

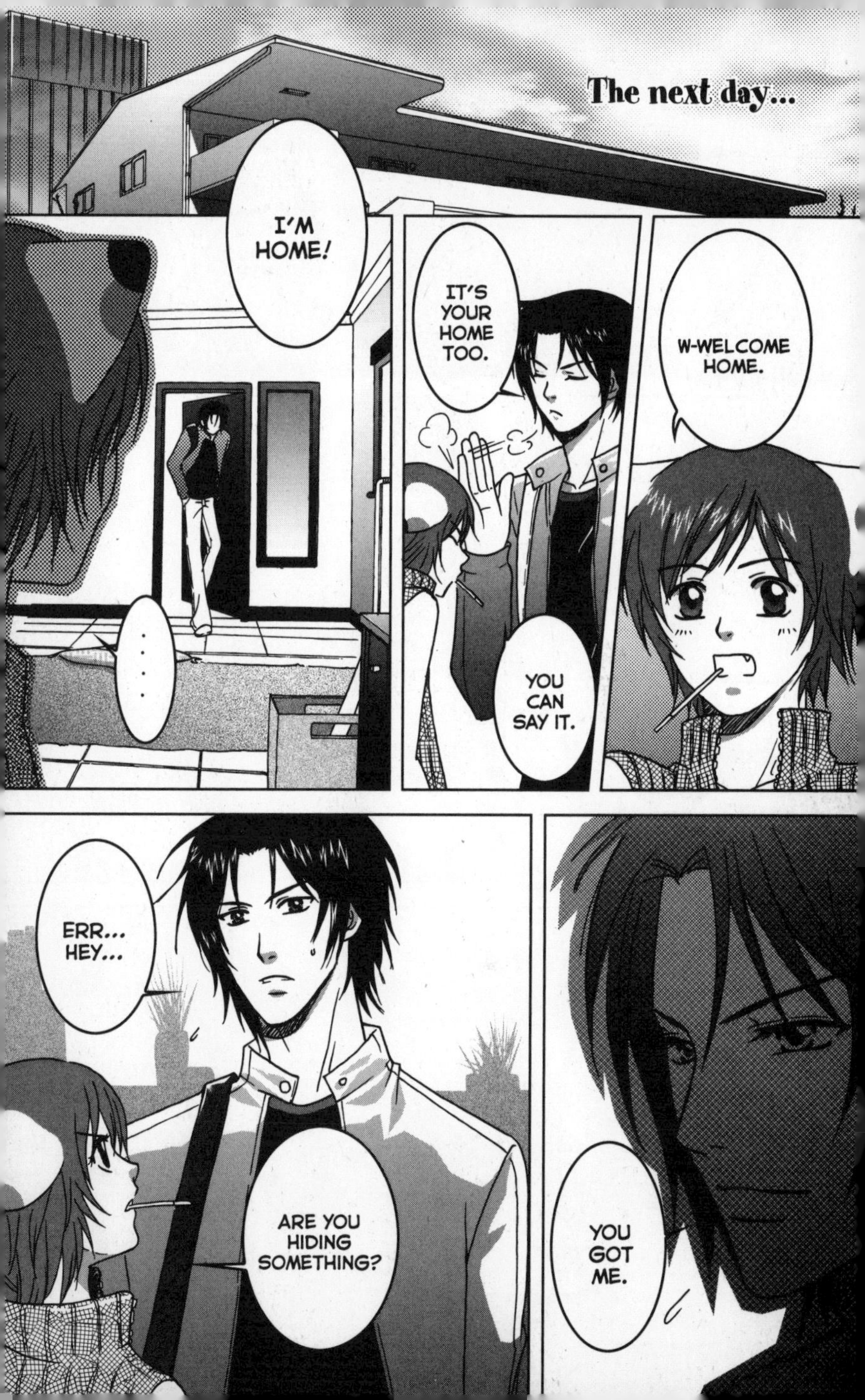
The next day...
I'M HOME!
. . . .
IT'S YOUR HOME TOO.
YOU CAN SAY IT.
W-WELCOME HOME.
ERR... HEY...
ARE YOU HIDING SOMETHING?
YOU GOT ME.

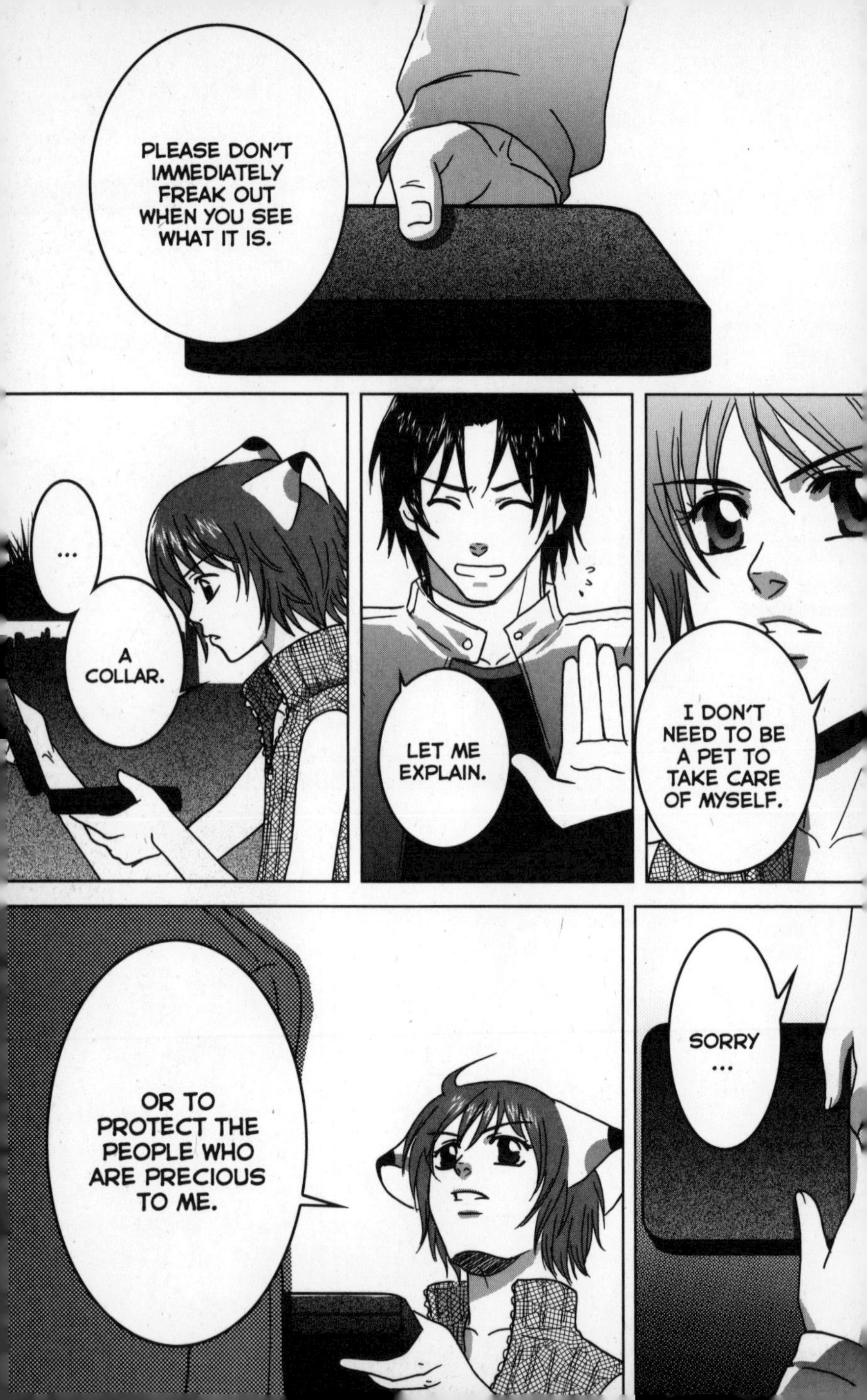
PLEASE DON'T IMMEDIATELY FREAK OUT WHEN YOU SEE WHAT IT IS.
...
A COLLAR.
LET ME EXPLAIN.
I DON'T NEED TO BE A PET TO TAKE CARE OF MYSELF.
OR TO PROTECT THE PEOPLE WHO ARE PRECIOUS TO ME.
SORRY ...

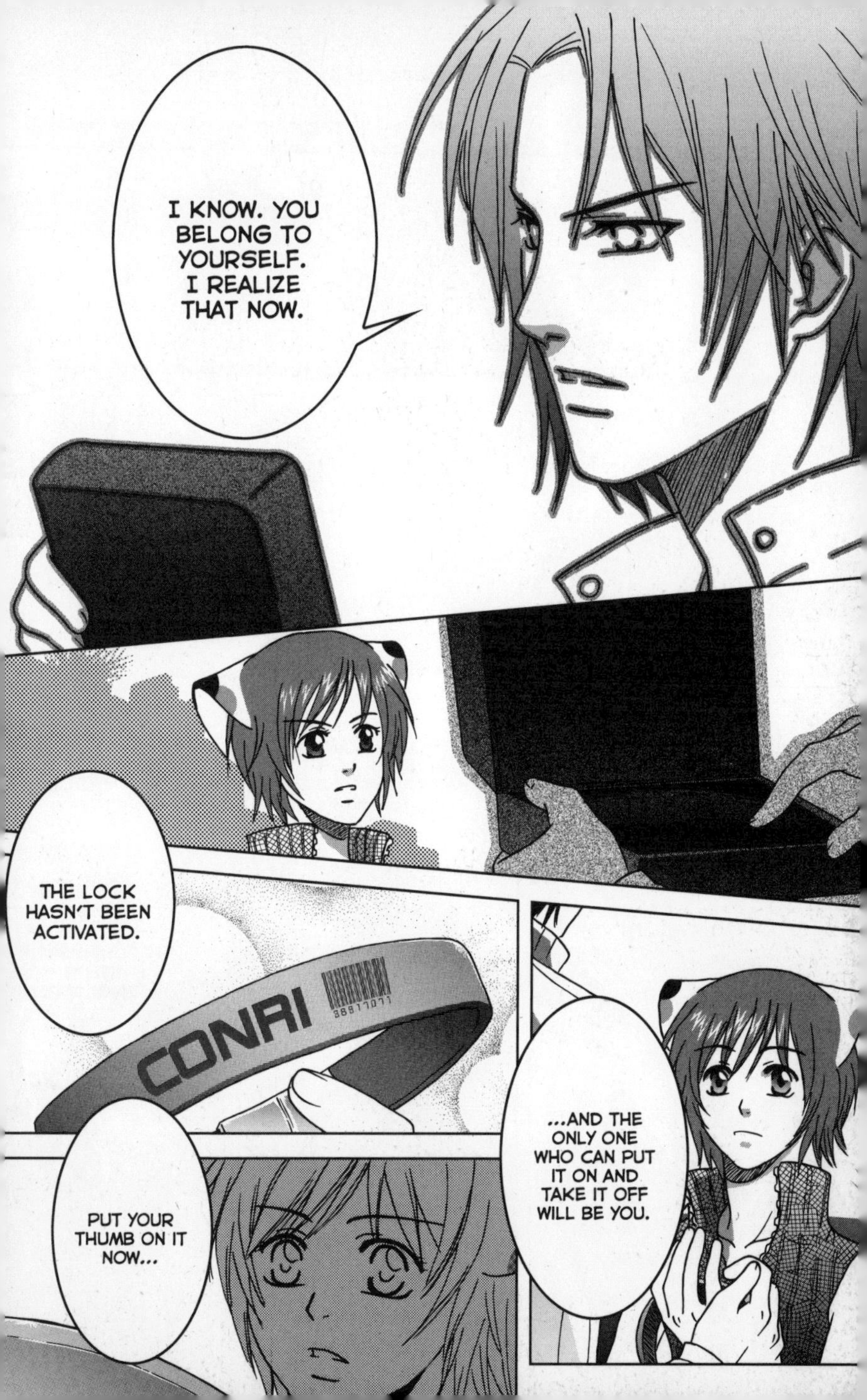
I KNOW. YOU BELONG TO YOURSELF. I REALIZE THAT NOW.
THE LOCK HASN'T BEEN ACTIVATED.
CONRI
PUT YOUR THUMB ON IT NOW...
...AND THE ONLY ONE WHO CAN PUT IT ON AND TAKE IT OFF WILL BE YOU.

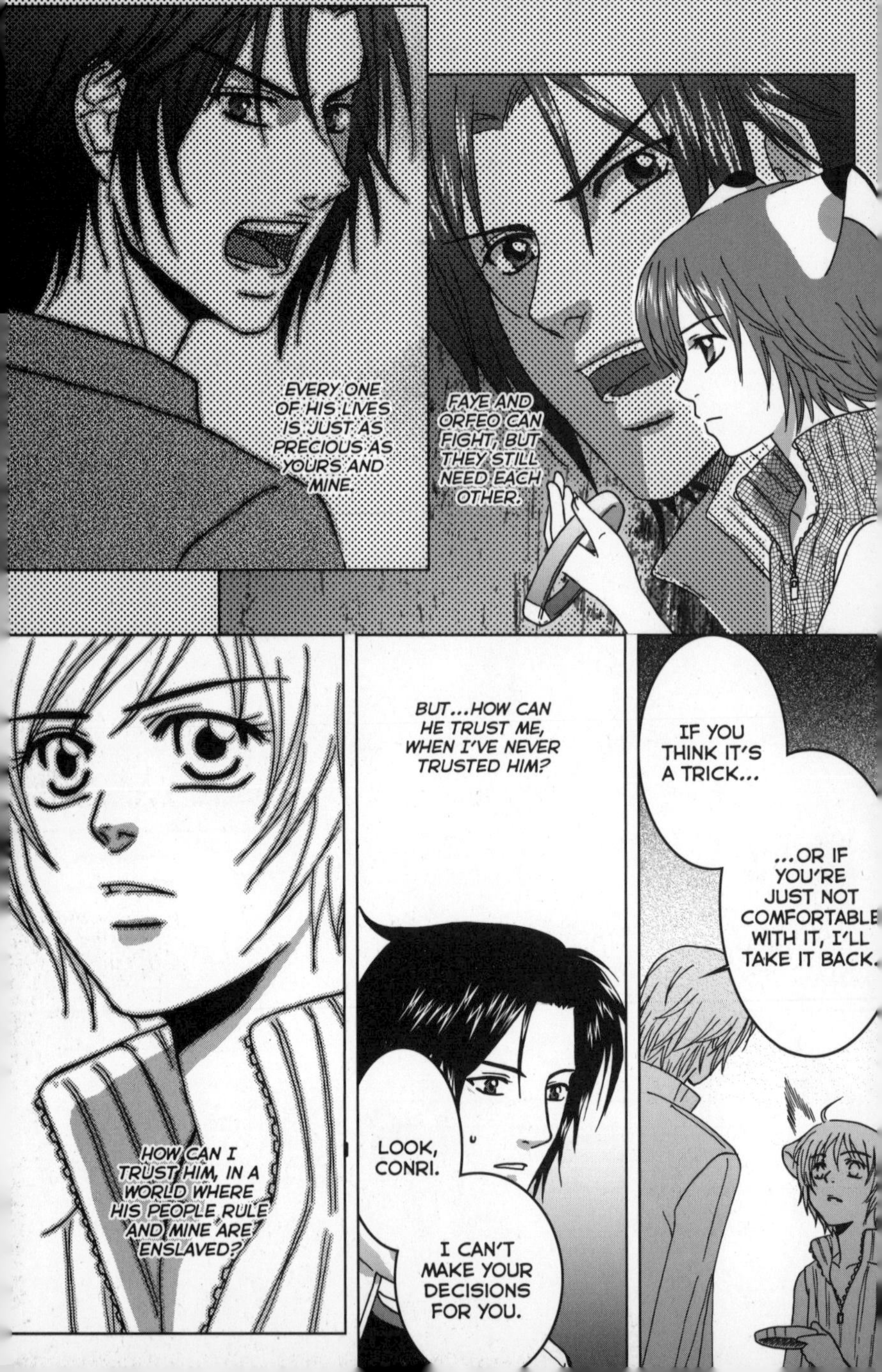
EVERY ONE OF HIS LIVES IS JUST AS PRECIOUS AS YOURS AND MINE.
FAYE AND ORFEO CAN FIGHT, BUT THEY STILL NEED EACH OTHER.
HOW CAN I TRUST HIM, IN A WORLD WHERE HIS PEOPLE RULE AND MINE ARE ENSLAVED?
BUT...HOW CAN HE TRUST ME, WHEN I'VE NEVER TRUSTED HIM?
LOOK, CONRI.
I CAN'T MAKE YOUR DECISIONS FOR YOU.
IF YOU THINK IT'S A TRICK...
...OR IF YOU'RE JUST NOT COMFORTABLE WITH IT, I'LL TAKE IT BACK.

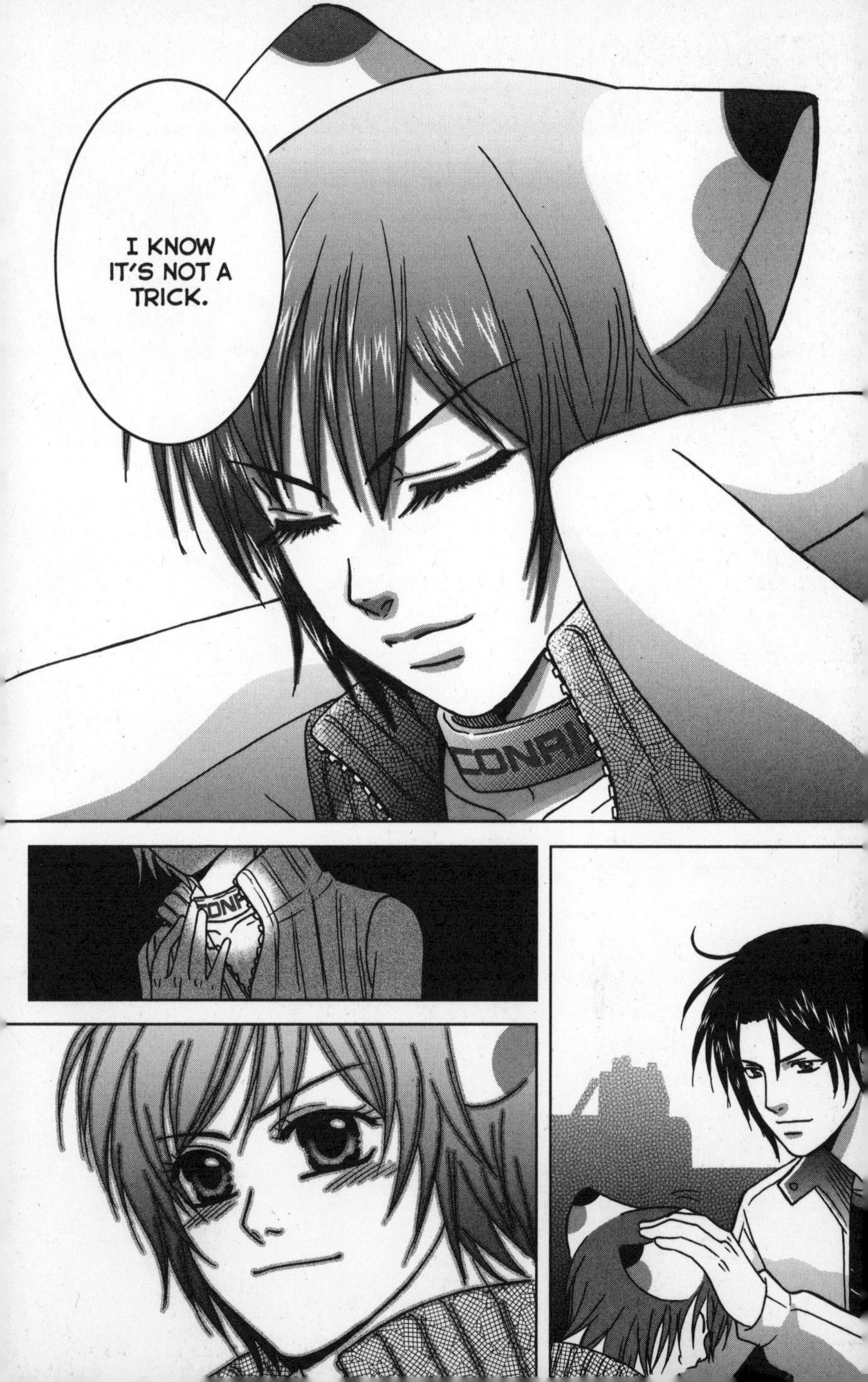
I KNOW IT'S NOT A TRICK.
CONAI
CONAI

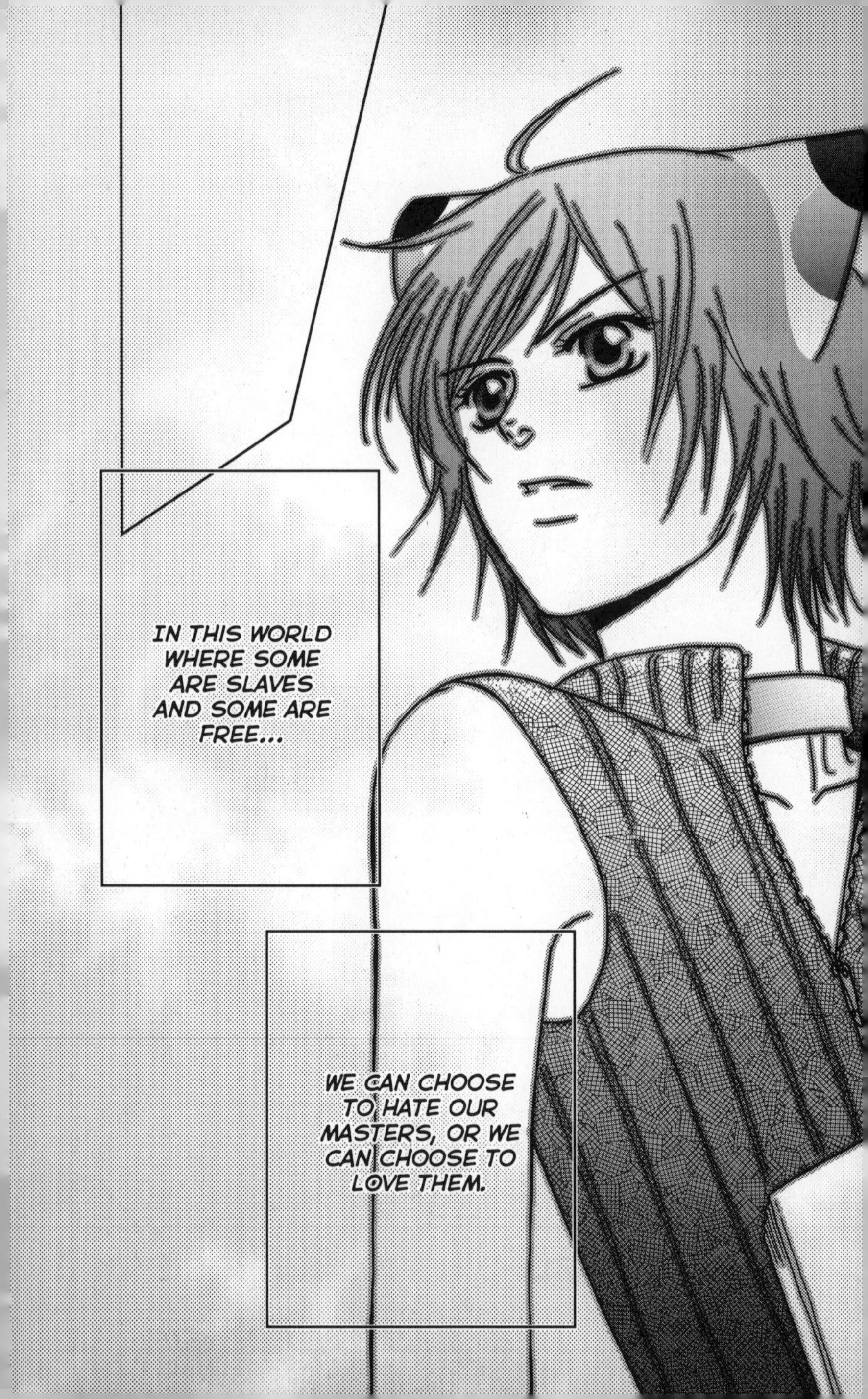
IN THIS WORLD WHERE SOME ARE SLAVES AND SOME ARE FREE...
WE CAN CHOOSE TO HATE OUR MASTERS, OR WE CAN CHOOSE TO LOVE THEM.

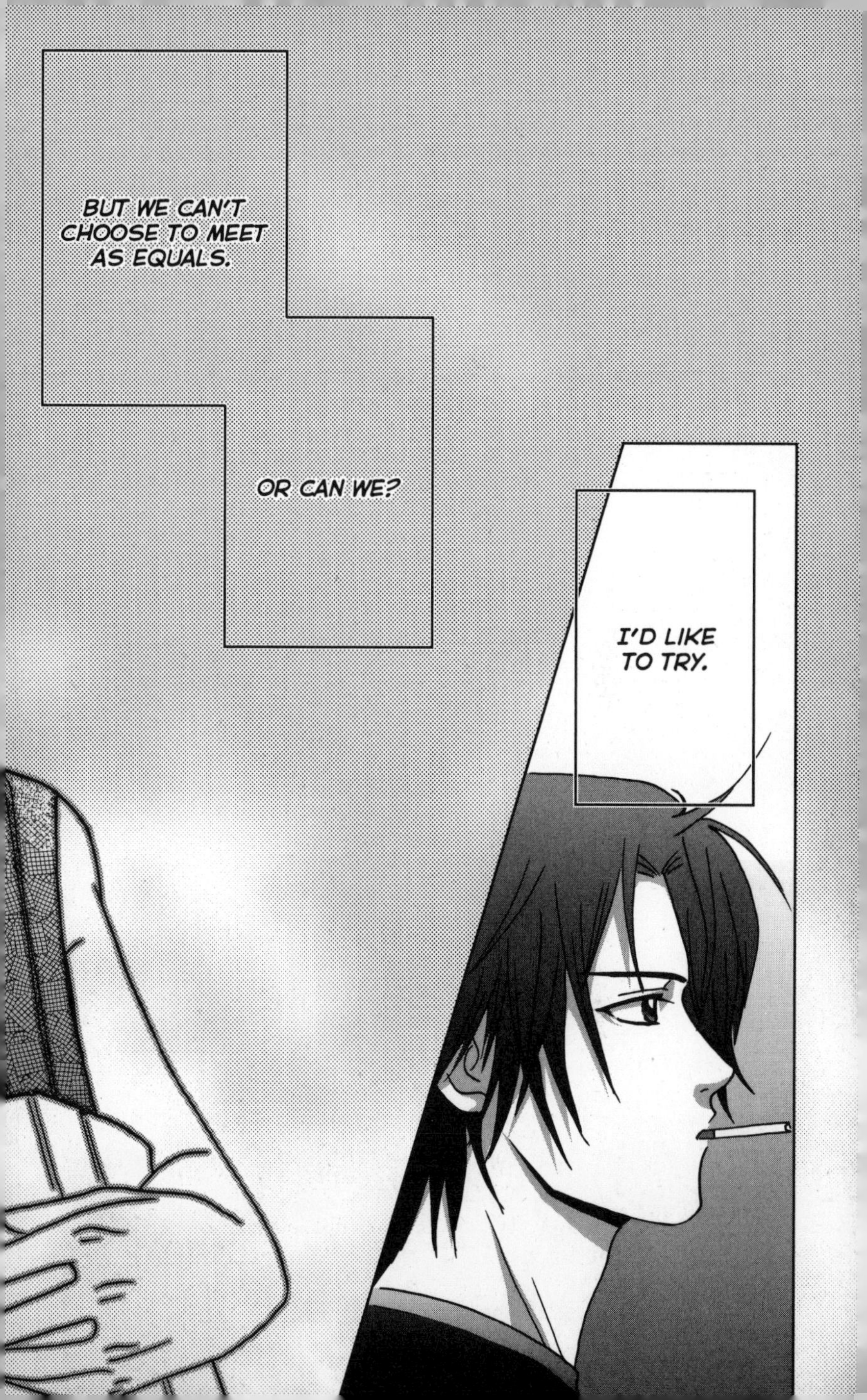
BUT WE CAN'T CHOOSE TO MEET AS EQUALS.
OR CAN WE?
I'D LIKE TO TRY.

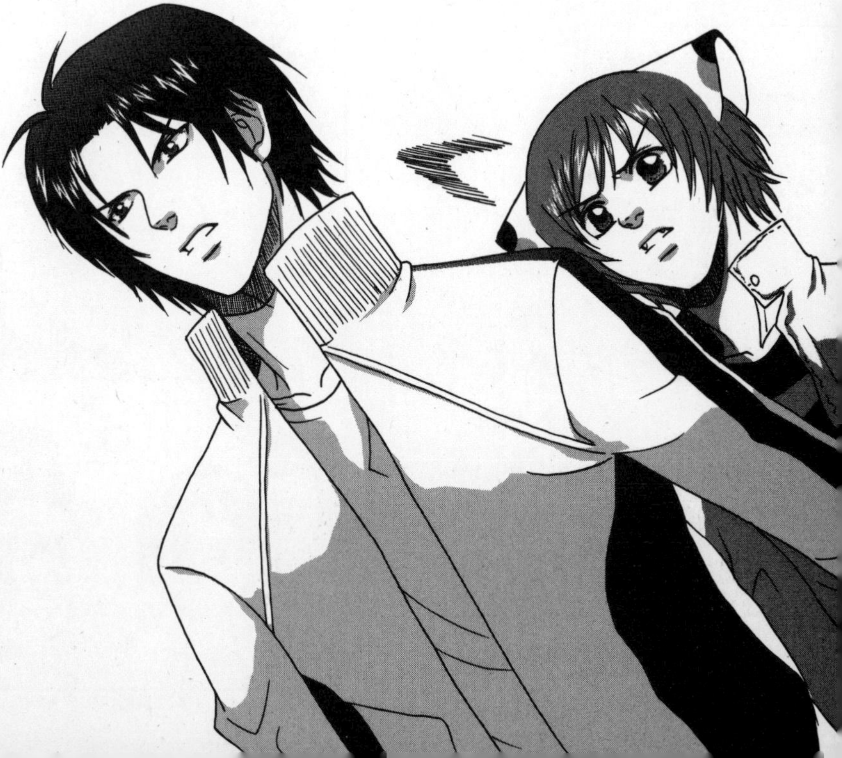

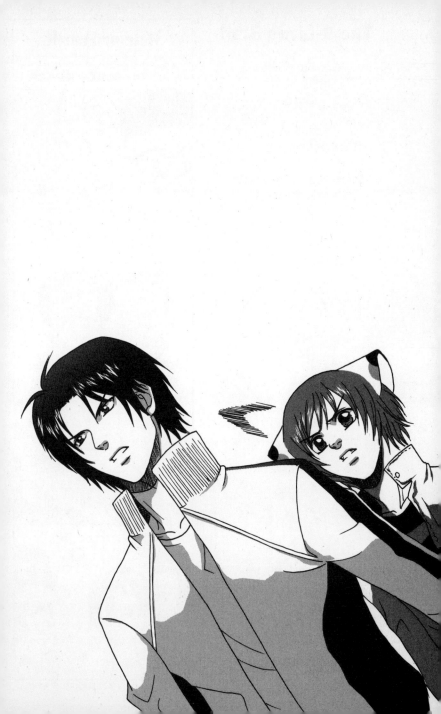

The 9-Lives Staff

Original Creator
and Illustrator:
Bayou

Scriptwriter:
Rachel Manija Brown

Background Assistants:
Wells (Pencils)
Y2 (Inks)

Tone Assistant:
Zelig Kay Alson

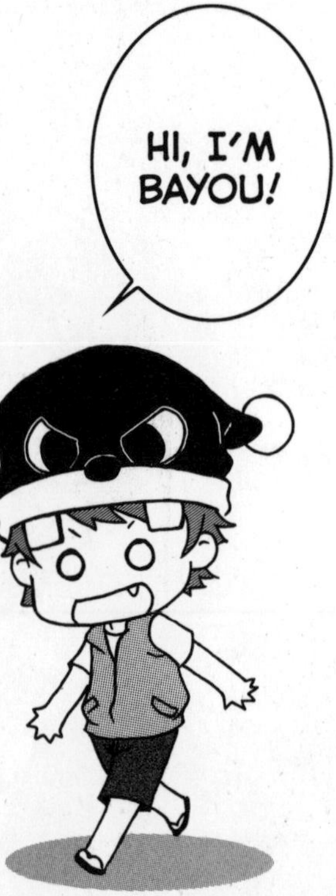
HI, I'M BAYOU!

Male or Female

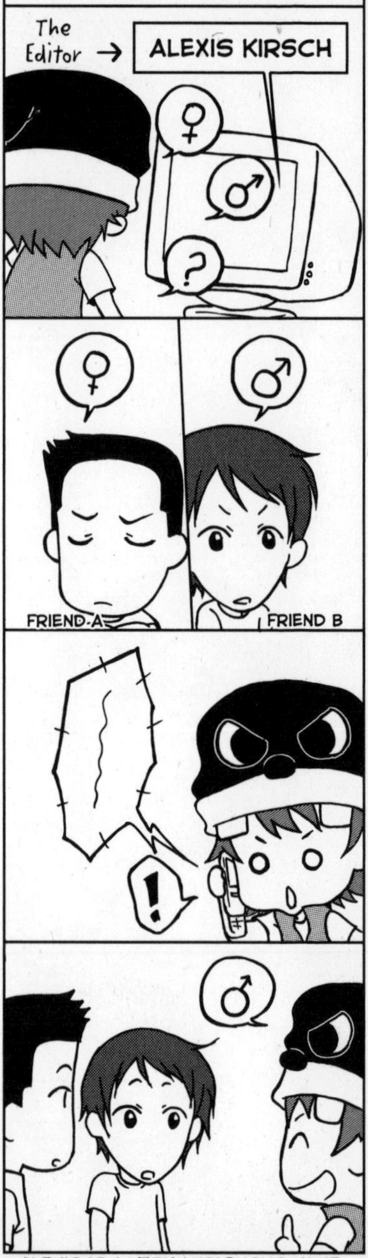
The Editor →
ALEXIS KIRSCH
♀
♂
?
♀
♂
FRIEND A
FRIEND B
!
♂

ALEXIS IS A VERY AMBIGUOUS NAME...

Cats Ate Our Homework

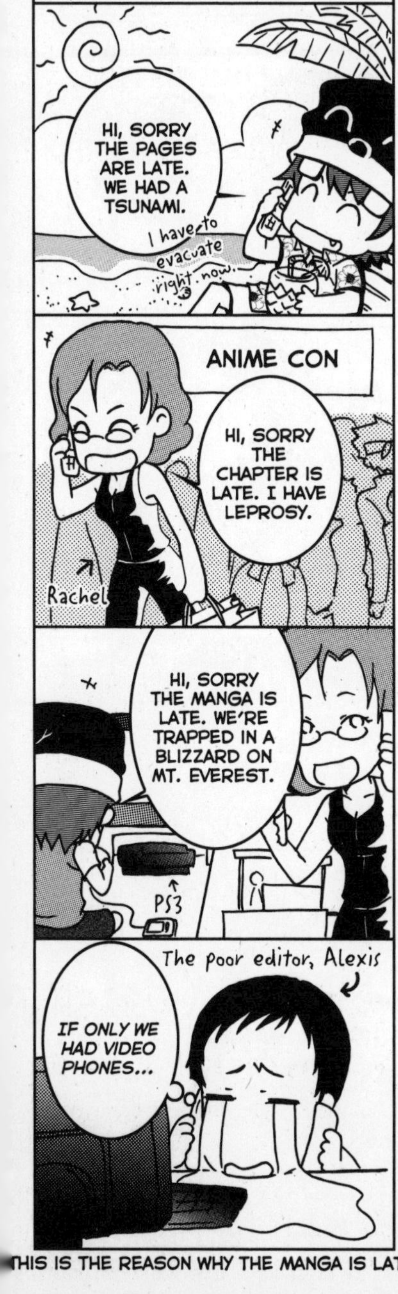
HI, SORRY THE PAGES ARE LATE. WE HAD A TSUNAMI.
I have to evacuate right now.
ANIME CON
HI, SORRY THE CHAPTER IS LATE. I HAVE LEPROSY.
Rachel
HI, SORRY THE MANGA IS LATE. WE'RE TRAPPED IN A BLIZZARD ON MT. EVEREST.
PS3
The poor editor, Alexis
IF ONLY WE HAD VIDEO PHONES...

THIS IS THE REASON WHY THE MANGA IS LATE.

Free Manga

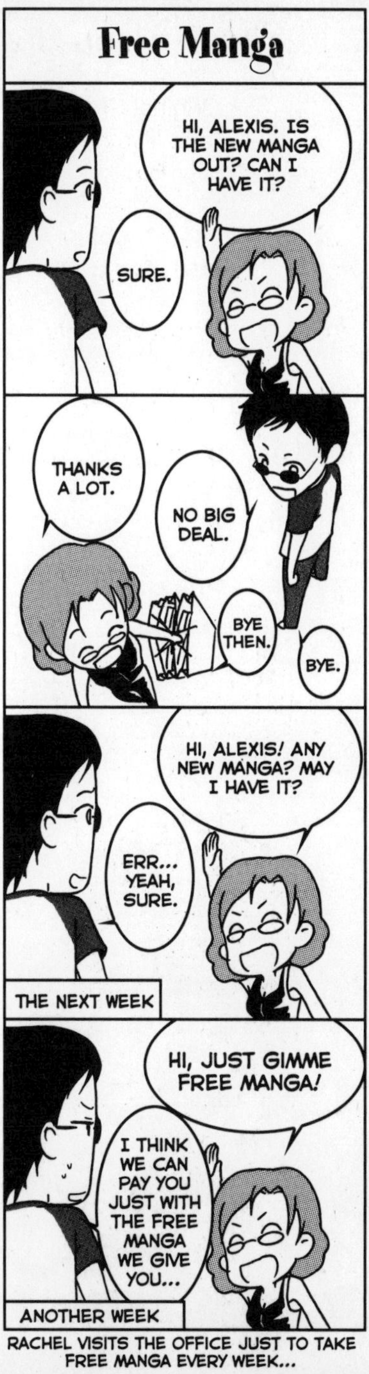
HI, ALEXIS. IS THE NEW MANGA OUT? CAN I HAVE IT?
SURE.
THANKS A LOT.
NO BIG DEAL.
BYE THEN.
BYE.
THE NEXT WEEK
HI, ALEXIS! ANY NEW MANGA? MAY I HAVE IT?
ERR... YEAH, SURE.
ANOTHER WEEK
HI, JUST GIMME FREE MANGA!
I THINK WE CAN PAY YOU JUST WITH THE FREE MANGA WE GIVE YOU...

RACHEL VISITS THE OFFICE JUST TO TAKE FREE MANGA EVERY WEEK...

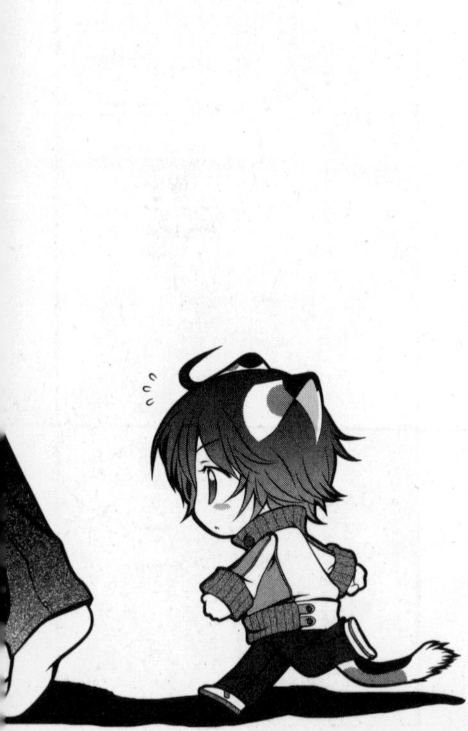

Durian

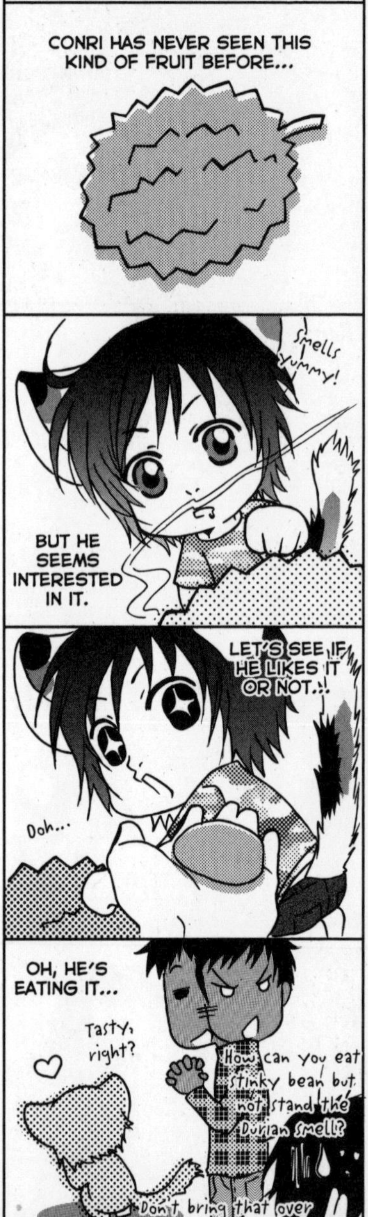
CONRI HAS NEVER SEEN THIS KIND OF FRUIT BEFORE...
Smells yummy!
BUT HE SEEMS INTERESTED IN IT.
LET'S SEE IF HE LIKES IT OR NOT..!
Ooh...
OH, HE'S EATING IT...
Tasty, right?
How can you eat stinky bean but not stand the Durian smell?
Don't bring that over while I'm here..!

SEEMS LIKE EVERYBODY HAS THEIR OWN TASTES

Having Fun

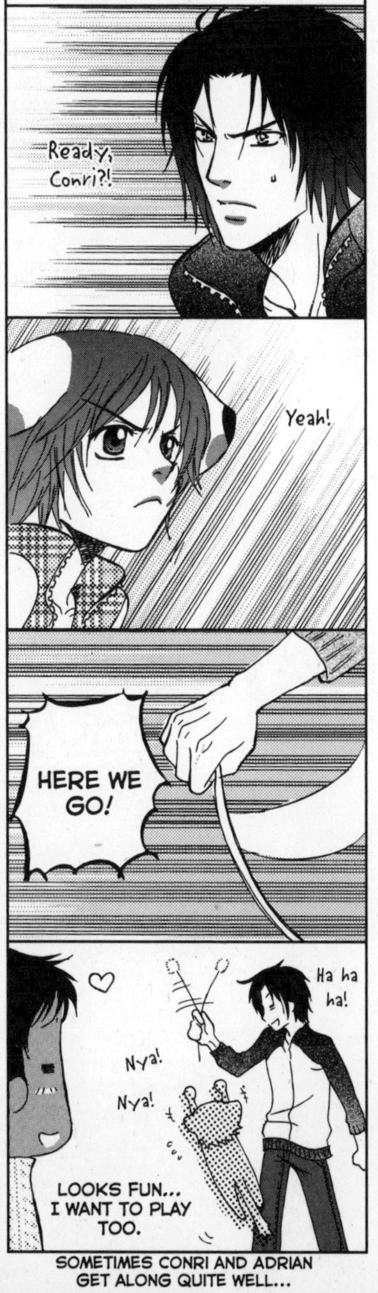
Ready, Conri?!
Yeah!
HERE WE GO!
Ha ha ha!
Nya!
Nya!
LOOKS FUN... I WANT TO PLAY TOO.

SOMETIMES CONRI AND ADRIAN GET ALONG QUITE WELL...

Recipe

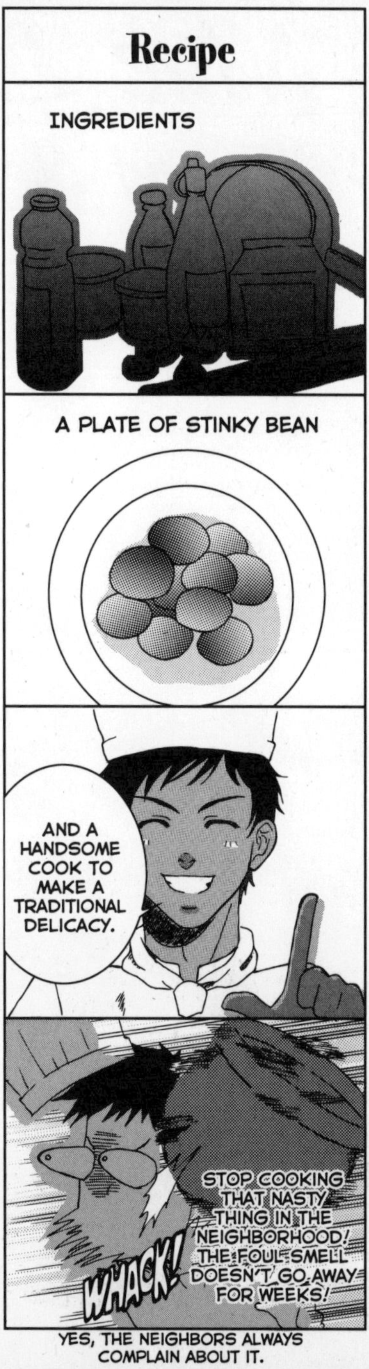
INGREDIENTS
A PLATE OF STINKY BEAN
AND A HANDSOME COOK TO MAKE A TRADITIONAL DELICACY.
WHACK!
STOP COOKING THAT NASTY THING IN THE NEIGHBORHOOD! THE FOUL SMELL DOESN'T GO AWAY FOR WEEKS!

YES, THE NEIGHBORS ALWAYS COMPLAIN ABOUT IT.

Nine Lives Fanart Section

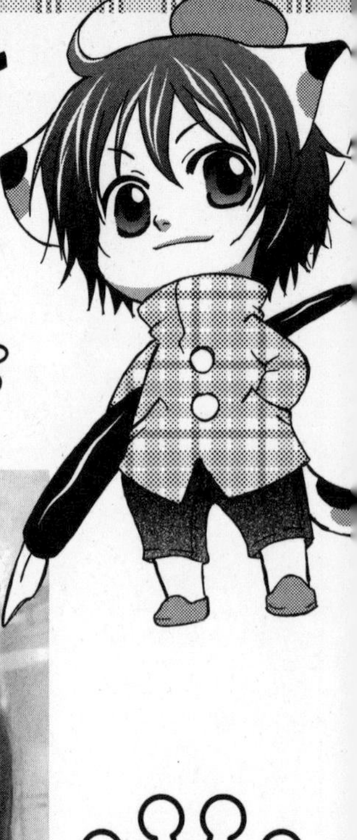

A WHILE AGO, BAYOU HELD A 9-LIVES FAN ART CONTEST ON HER BLOG. THE RESPONSE WAS QUITE IMPRESSIVE AND THE CONTESTANTS DID THEIR BEST TO DRAW THE 9-LIVES CHARACTERS! HERE ARE THE WINNERS!

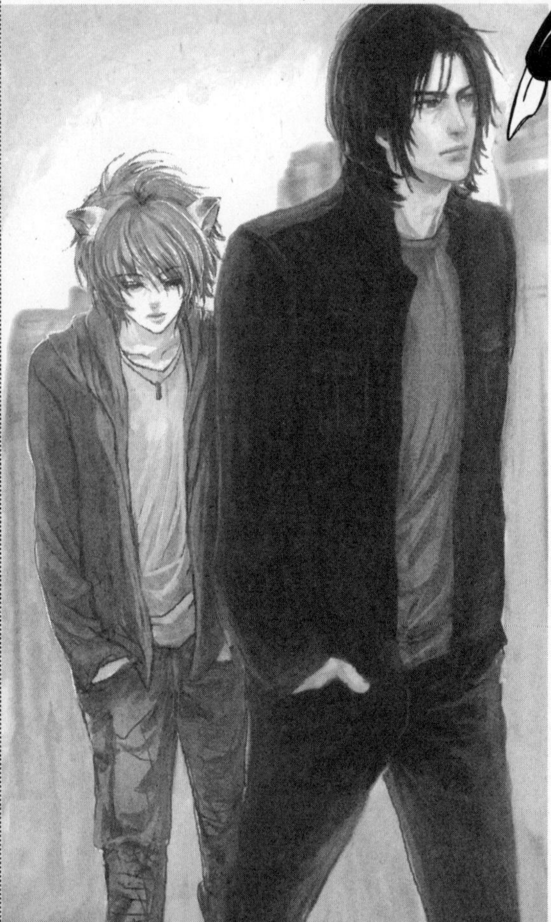

First Place

I Will Follow

By Qkie.

Special note:
I can't believe how handsome Adrian looks in this picture! It gave me such a warm feeling.

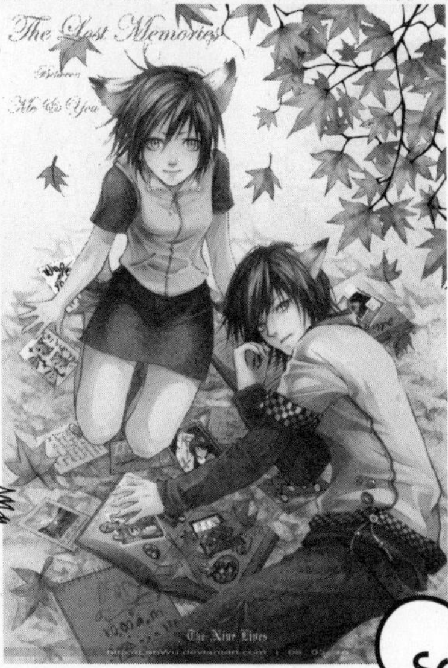
The Lost Memories
Between
Me & You

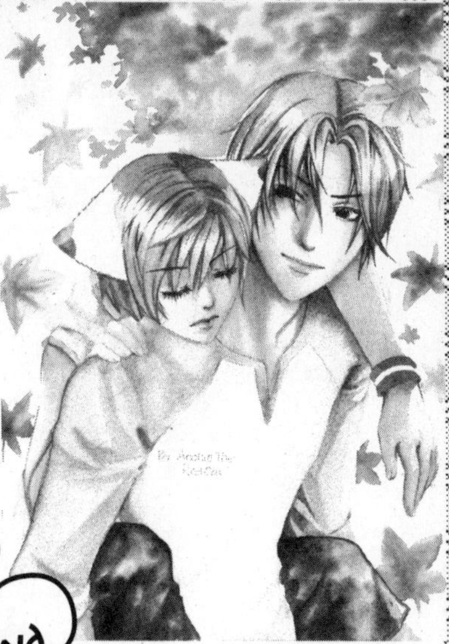

The Lost Memories
By LanWu

Second
Place

Piggyback
By Archie

This entry was used as inspiration for the cover!
↓
Little Bride
By DarkMello

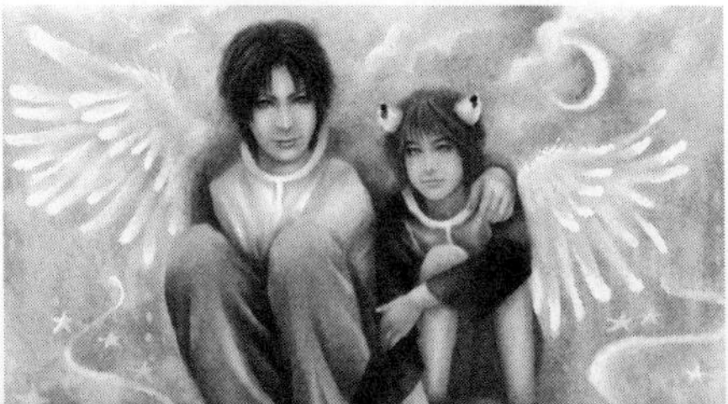

Afternoon
By Lan Lan

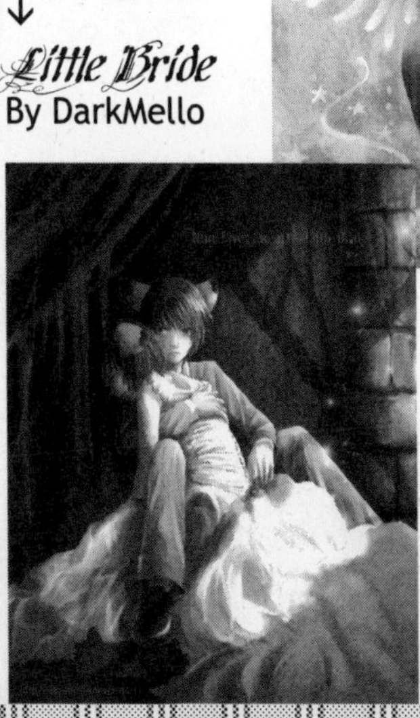

To Be By Your Side
By Aullya

Third
Place

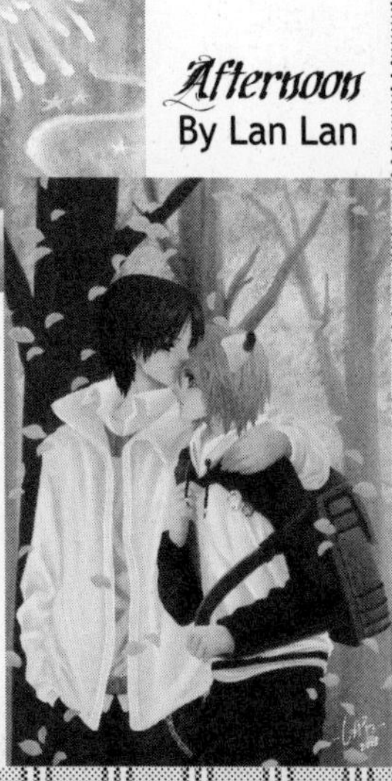

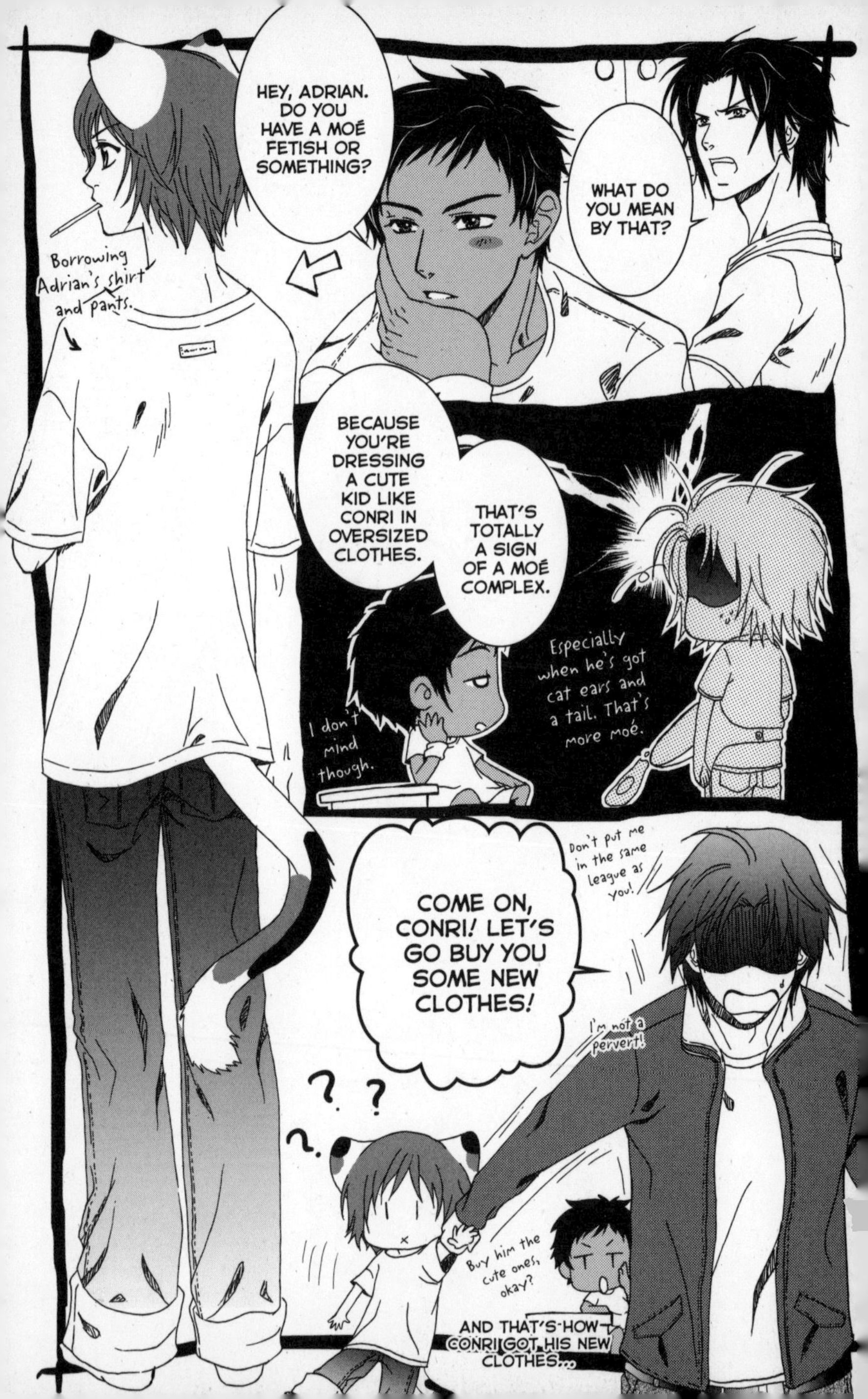
HEY, ADRIAN. DO YOU HAVE A MOÉ FETISH OR SOMETHING?
Borrowing Adrian's shirt and pants.
WHAT DO YOU MEAN BY THAT?
BECAUSE YOU'RE DRESSING A CUTE KID LIKE CONRI IN OVERSIZED CLOTHES.
THAT'S TOTALLY A SIGN OF A MOÉ COMPLEX.
I don't mind though.
Especially when he's got cat ears and a tail. That's more moé.
COME ON, CONRI! LET'S GO BUY YOU SOME NEW CLOTHES!
Don't put me in the same league as you!
I'm not a pervert!
Buy him the cute ones, okay?
AND THAT'S HOW CONRI GOT HIS NEW CLOTHES...

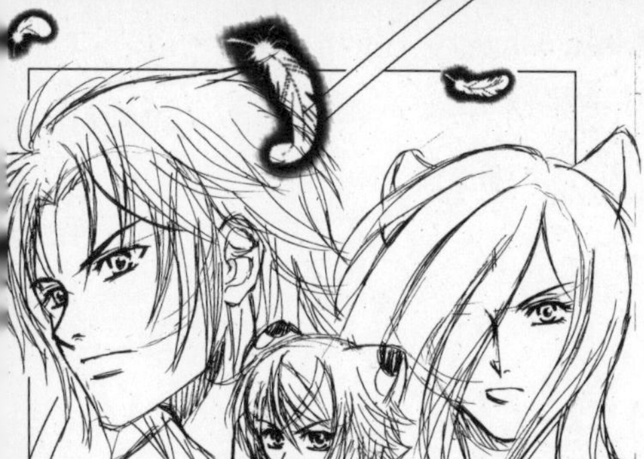

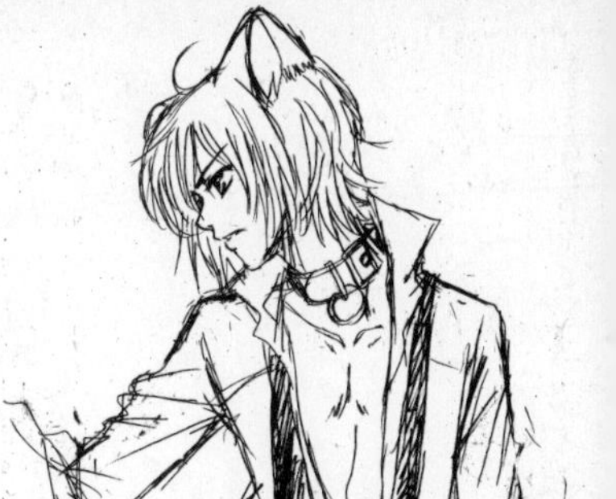

Rejected cover sketches.

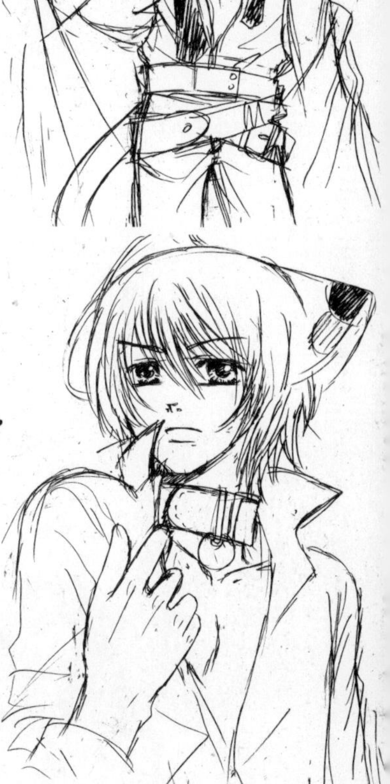

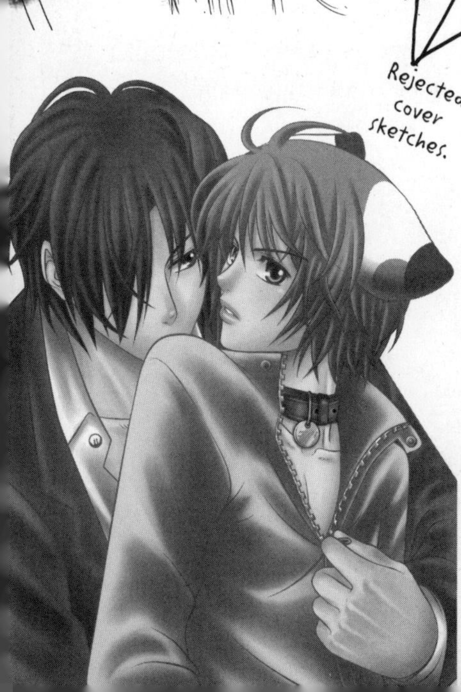

This one was approved before I was told to change it at the last minute... TT^TT

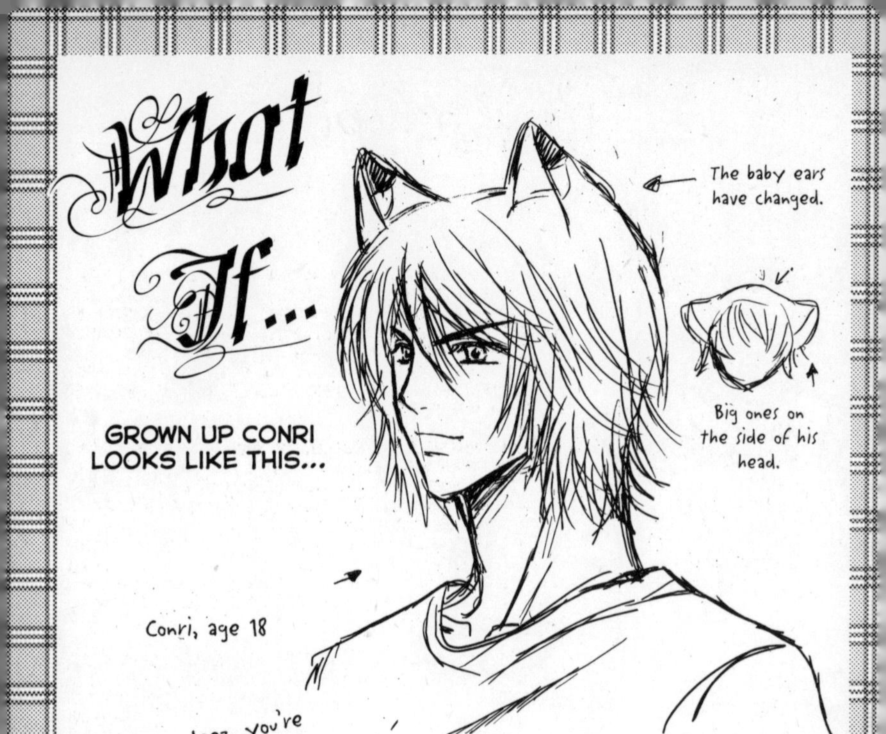
What If...
GROWN UP CONRI LOOKS LIKE THIS...
The baby ears have changed.
Big ones on the side of his head.
Conri, age 18
Jeez, you're not even cute anymore.
184cm
195 cm
Still likes Bocky.
He He He
Former kitten.
26
18

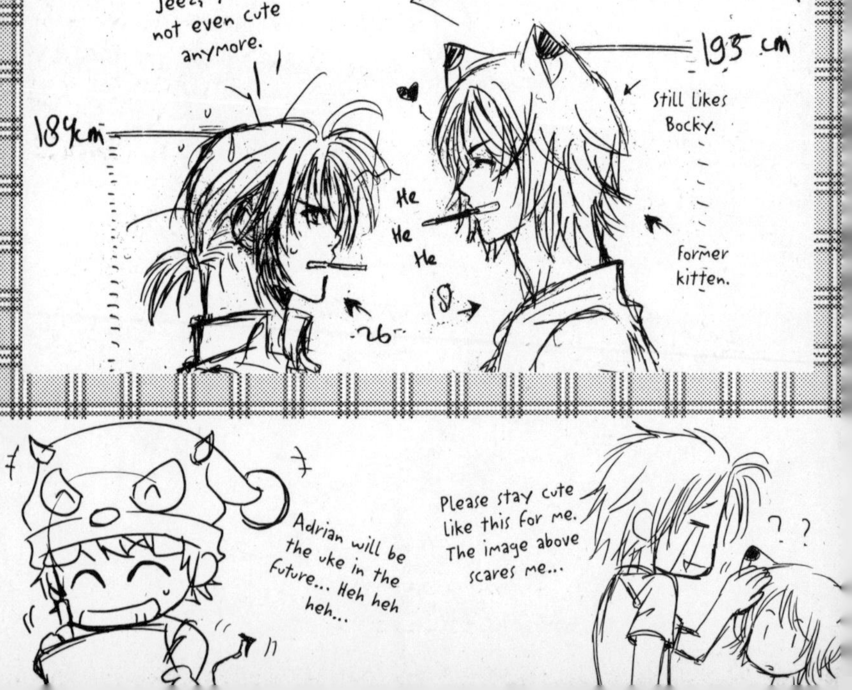
Adrian will be the uke in the future... Heh heh heh...
Please stay cute like this for me. The image above scares me...
? ?

Postscript

BAYOU SAYS : IT TOOK ME OVER A YEAR AND A HALF TO FINISH THIS BOOK BECAUSE I HAD TO ALSO JUGGLE A FULLTIME JOB WHILE DRAWING THE MANGA. I'M VERY GRATEFUL TO MY EDITOR WHO WAS EXTREMELY PATIENT IN TAKING CARE OF ME, WITH ALL MY LATENESS AND ALL... ^^
I ALSO WANT TO THANK RACHEL FOR ASSISTING ME IN MAKING THE SCRIPT AND FILLING IN THE MISSING PIECES OF THE STORY.

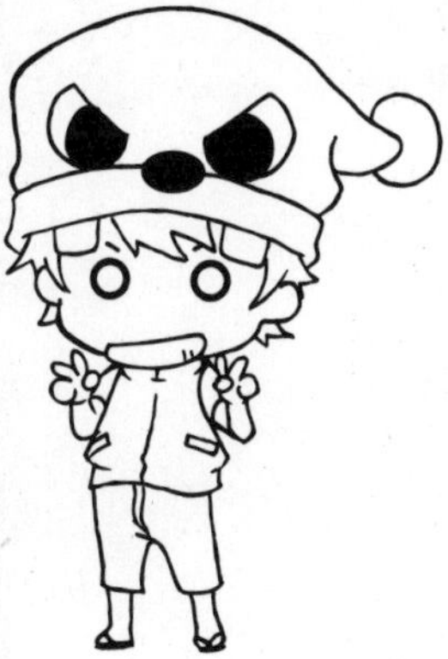

SPECIAL THANKS TO WELLS, Y2, AND ZELIG, MY LOYAL ASSISTANTS WHO HELPED ME A LOT WITH DETAILED BACKGROUNDS AND GREAT TONES. ALSO, TO MY OLD MAN AND MY CUTE LITTLE SIS, SARI, WHO ALWAYS LOVES ME UNCONDITIONALLY. TO MIKU TOO, BECAUSE SHE ALWAYS WILLINGLY LISTENS TO MY RANTS WITHOUT GETTING BORED. AND TO ALL MY FRIENDS WHO ARE ALWAYS BY MY SIDE IN GOOD TIMES AND BAD. (I DON'T HAVE TO MENTION YOU ONE BY ONE, YOU KNOW WHO YOU ARE!)

AND FINALLY, *THANKS TO ALL OF YOU* WHO SUPPORTED ME JUST BY ENJOYING THIS MANGA.

BAYOU
JUNE, 2008
BANDUNG, INDONESIA

: RACHEL SAYS

I HAD A LOT OF FUN WORKING ON *THE 9-LIVES* WITH BAYOU AND ALEXIS. I'M HAPPY THAT I LIVE IN A TIME WHEN AN ARTIST/CREATOR IN INDONESIA CAN JOIN FORCES WITH A HOLLYWOOD WRITER TO CREATE A STORY IN A JAPANESE STYLE IN ENGLISH, ABOUT COLLARED CAT-BOYS, GANGSTERS NAMED NUNZIO, AND THE MEANING OF TRUST, FREEDOM, AND LOVE.

SPECIAL THANKS TO BAYOU FOR PUTTING UP WITH MY MILLIONS OF QUERIES AND QUIBBLES, ALEXIS FOR DOING THE SAME AND ALSO SUPPORTING MY MANGA ADDICTION, AND MY CATS NUALA AND RIPLEY FOR THE INSPIRATION.

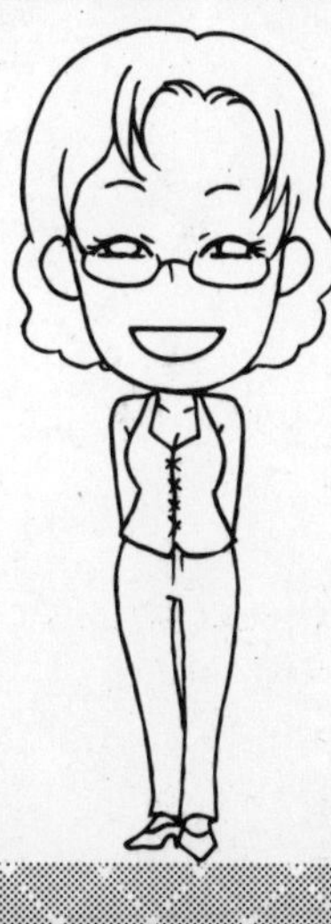

RACHEL MANIJA BROWN
JULY, 2008
LOS ANGELES, CALIFORNIA

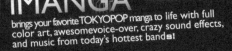

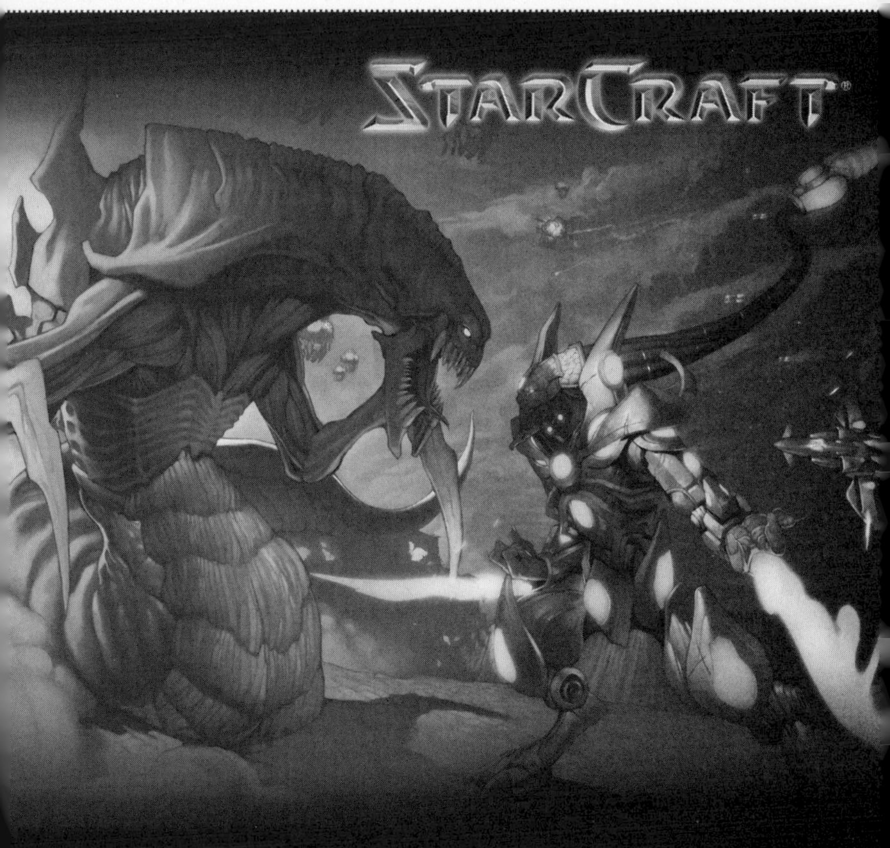
StarCraft®

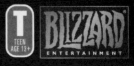

GAKUEN ALICE VOLUME FOUR

Mikan's daring rescue of Natsume has earned her an upgrade to One-star rank!

Mikan's upgrade to One-star rank has come just in time for the School Festival, and it's even more spectacular than Mikan ever dreamed. But what will happen when Mikan and Natsume get locked in the haunted house together?!

The hit series that inspired the anime CONTINUES!

Win free *Gakuen Alice* stuff at www.TOKYOPOP.com/ AliceAcademy

FANTASY

T TEEN AGE 13+